D1565178

# APPROACHES TO
# SOCIAL ARCHAEOLOGY

# APPROACHES TO
# SOCIAL ARCHAEOLOGY

COLIN RENFREW

HARVARD UNIVERSITY PRESS

Cambridge, Massachusetts

1984

Library of Congress Cataloging in Publication Data
Renfrew, Colin, 1937–
    Approaches to social archaeology
    Bibliography: p.
    Includes index
    1. Social archaeology—Addresses, essays, lectures.
2. Anthropology, Prehistoric—Addresses, essays,
lectures.  3. Man, Prehistoric—Addresses, essays,
lectures.
I. Title
CC72.4.R46    1984      306'.093      83-22548
ISBN 0-674-04165-8

# CONTENTS

# ACKNOWLEDGEMENTS

\*

I am grateful to Mr Archie Turnbull, Secretary to the Edinburgh University Press, for the invitation to publish this collection of essays, and to Mrs Patricia Williams of Harvard University Press for her encouragement. I am particularly grateful to the co-authors of chapters 3 and 11, Mr Eric V. Level and Professor Kenneth L. Cooke, who have generously allowed me to reprint these papers here. I am grateful also to Academic Press (Mr William Woodcock), Duckworth (Mr Colin Haycraft), Methuen (Miss Anna Fedden) and the University of New Mexico Press for permission to reprint material here that was originally published by them, and to Professors S. J. de Laet and Jeremy Sabloff for assistance in this respect.

The papers collected here were published first in the volumes listed below: Chapter 2; Space, Time and Polity, from M. Rowlands and J. Friedman, eds., *The Evolution of Social Systems*, London, Duckworth, 1974, 89–114. Chapter 3; Exploring dominance: predicting polities from centres, with E. V. Level, from C. Renfrew and K. L. Cooke, eds., *Transformations, Mathematical Approaches to Culture Change*, New York, Academic Press, 1979, 145–68. Chapter 4; Trade as action at a distance, from J. A. Sabloff and C. C. Lamberg-Karlovsky, eds., *Ancient Civilisation and Trade*, Albuquerque, University of New Mexico Press, for School of American Research, 1975, 3–59. Chapter 5; Alternative models for exchange and spatial distribution, from T. Earle and J. Ericson, eds., *Exchange Systems in Prehistory*, New York, Academic Press, 1977, 71–90. Chapter 6; Megaliths, territories and populations, from S. J. de Laet, ed., *Acculturation and Continuity in Atlantic Europe*, Dissertationes Archaeologicae Gandenses xvi, 1976, 298–320. Chapter 7; Islands out of time, from R. Sutcliffe, ed., *Chronicle; Essays from Ten Years of Television Archaeology*, London, bbc, 1978, 113–26.

## Acknowledgements

Chapter 8; Monuments, mobilisation and social organisation in neolithic Wessex, from C. Renfrew, ed., *The Explanation of Culture Change: Models in Prehistory*, London, Duckworth, 1973, 539–58. Chapter 9; Culture systems and the multiplier effect, from *The Emergence of Civilisation, the Cyclades and the Aegean in the Third Millennium BC*, London, Methuen, 1972, 19–44. Chapter 10; The multiplier effect in action, from *The Emergence of Civilisation*, London, Methuen, 1972, 479–504. Chapter 11; An experiment on the simulation of culture changes, with K. L. Cooke, from C. Renfrew and K. L. Cooke, eds., *Mathematical Approaches to Culture Change*, New York, Academic Press, 1979, 327–48. Chapter 12; The simulator as demiurge, from J. A. Sabloff, ed., *Simulations in Archaeology*, Albuquerque, University of New Mexico Press for School of American Research, 1981, 285–306. Chapter 13; Systems collapse as social transformation, from C. Renfrew and K. L. Cooke, eds., *Transformations, Mathematical Approaches to Culture Change*, New York, Academic Press, 1979, 481–506. Chapter 14; The anatomy of innovation, from D. Green, C. Haselgrove and M. Spriggs, eds., *Social Organisation and Settlement*, British Archaeological Reports International Series 47(i), Oxford, 1978, 89–117.

# INTRODUCTION

*

# 1

## SOCIAL ARCHAEOLOGY, SOCIETAL CHANGE AND GENERALISATION

*

In studying the human past it is not enough simply to reconstruct what happened. Reconstruction is indeed one of the legitimate concerns of the historian and archaeologists, and a necessary preliminary to further analysis. But we need to know more. We need to understand in some sense *how* it happened. We have to discern some pattern, to identify some simplifying principles. We have to decide what is significant for us, working either in the absence of written record or testimony to guide us, or coping with the complication of narrative and commentaries whose intentions may be very different from our own. Increasingly we are coming to appreciate that a social approach is a particularly rewarding one.

The past twenty years have seen a fundamental change in the objectives, the methods and in particular the aspirations of the archaeologist. Nowhere is this clearer than in the approach to the study of what has been termed 'social archaeology' (Renfrew 1973, cf. Redman *et al.* 1978), that is the reconstruction of past social systems and relations. The pessimism about this undertaking which overcame earlier writers on contemplating the scanty remains of the prehistoric past can be gauged by looking at almost any archaeological textbook written before the year 1968, and indeed most of those that have been produced subsequently. The difficulties inherent in the study of prehistoric institutions and social relations were not until then systematically examined. They were often simply asserted, and they were asserted with an emphasis which seemed to preclude any so apparently fruitless an undertaking.

It was not until the revolution in archaeological thought of the later 1960s and early 1970s that an alternative view emerged. The great contribution made by the New Archaeology of that time was the clearer realisation that we have no direct knowledge of anything

3

at all from the remote past. All that we do know has to be wrested from the relics of that past by a process of inference. Sometimes the inference may seem to us an easy one – identify the animal bones in that refuse tip, for instance, and you may gain some insight into the protein component of the prehistoric diet of those who made it. Sometimes it is much less evident – does the great quantity of artefacts found associated with the skeleton in a particularly 'rich' burial indicate that the deceased was a man of wealth, or of social prominence, or perhaps a sacrificial victim interred with particular ceremony? These are issues which the archaeologist now feels entitled to raise. Moreover, they no longer seem idle questions to which one observer might volunteer an answer of one kind, and another a completely different interpretation of equal validity. Snap answers are not often sound ones. Archaeologists now realise that such matters require sustained and systematic examination, and that the individual case must be set in a wider and more coherent context. In short, what is needed is the development of a body of coherent interpretive argument which it may not be too pretentious to dignify with the title of archaeological theory.

This book represents a personal attempt to work towards that goal in the field of social archaeology. The papers presented here, all of them written within the last dozen years, tackle a series of issues which are basic to our understanding of early human social institutions, and of the changes taking place within them. Already it is possible to recognise some of the approaches advocated here as rather simple ones, and to suggest how they might be made more effective or more flexible.

Social archaeology, seen as based upon a body of explicit interpretive theory, is a new subject. Increasingly we are coming to realise that it is not simply a prehistoric counterpart to social anthropology. The preoccupations of the social anthropologist have so far only rarely been directly relevant to the work of the archaeologist, and attempts towards the direct incorporation into archaeological thinking of the assumptions and procedures of the social anthropologist have in the main been fairly disastrous. Much more work is needed upon the philosophical assumptions which underlie both these disciplines before the interface between them can be crossed other than with caution and with keen self-awareness. In the papers which follow, some of the important questions are raised, and several methods are suggested which allow us to make inferences of a social nature from the archaeological data.

Although the title of this volume, *Approaches to Social Archae-*

*ology* reflects accurately both the tentative nature of these exercises and their diversity, it does not sufficiently indicate that their concern is as much to understand *change* as to clarify static social and other structures. A more accurate title, if a cumbersome one, would have been *Approaches to Social Archaeology and Long-Term Societal Change*. Parts IV and V here focus upon the twin themes of continuous and discontinuous change in human societies.

Usually in writing an article, my starting point has been a specific problem arising within the geographical area and the time range of my work at that time. In many cases the problem in question has proved, at least in part, to be simply a variant of one very general question which recurs again and again in different parts of the world over the past century of archaeological research (Adams 1968, 1978): how do we find some alternative explanation for the various developments in Europe (or in the other areas under consideration) which we may put in place of the 'diffusionist' accounts so widely offered until the last decade? Thus the papers which here form Part III were prompted by the need to 'explain' the impressive prehistoric sites and monuments of Britain and north-western Europe in terms other than 'the irradiation of European barbarism by Oriental civilisation' (Childe 1958, 70). The diffusionist model of culture change held that most of the significant developments in the area under study came about as the result of earlier innovations occurring in an area of supposedly 'higher' cultural attainment situated some distance away. In the European case this irradiating centre was of course thought to be located in the east Mediterranean, in the lands of Egypt and Western Asia. In the 1960s a growing scepticism about the standard explanations on offer (and some of the evidence upon which they were based), together with the development and in particular the calibration of radiocarbon dating, allowed us to see that this was not an adequate picture for Britain (Renfrew 1968), nor for Europe as a whole (Renfrew 1970). Explanations of a completely different kind were needed, rooted rather in the economic and social conditions of the societies of that time.

The solutions which emerge are, however, emphatically *not* specific to the single instance in relation to which they were initially conceived. These papers address *general* issues arising in the examination of the social organisation of past societies and of the changes taking place within them. How general in their application are the insights arising from them remains to be judged. Already some of them must be read in the light of commentaries upon them and of further work undertaken since they were written. They share a conviction that the field of social archaeology is as yet relatively underdeveloped, and that this situation has to be rectified if we are to achieve any adequate understanding of change. They carry with them also the view that as research workers we are in the business of making *generalisations*. Quite what form our generalisations should take is something which is still a matter for discussion and debate within archaeology, and this question is further discussed below.

## The Possibility of a Social Archaeology

In the year 1955, M. A. Smith wrote an article entitled 'The limitations of inference in archaeology' (Smith 1955) in which she gave eloquent expression to the pessimism then prevailing about the possibility of what was later to be termed 'social archaeology'. Although the passage has often been cited, indeed it was used as an epigraph by Lewis Binford in the seminal work of the New Archaeology, published in 1968 (Binford and Binford 1968, v), and is found again here in the papers which follow, it is worth quoting at this point at greater length:

> Since historical events and the essential social divisions of prehistoric peoples don't find an adequate expression in material remains, it cannot be right to try to arrive at a knowledge of them in archaeological interpretation. A recognition that archaeological evidence, when it is confined to material remains, demonstrably supports only a limited range of conclusions about human activity, is incompatible with too ambitious a programme for archaeology. It is incompatible, as I see it, with an attempt to 're-create the past' in any real sense, or with a claim to recognise prehistoric societies from their surviving relics, so that the subject could be compared either to history or to social anthropology. Moreover, if it appears that archaeologists do make such a claim, or are engaged in such an attempt, it may seem to an outsider, conscious of the weak logic this involves, that the subject has no sound intellectual basis at all.

She was not alone in that assessment. To the modern eye it seems that most archaeological writers in the 1950s were unduly nervous, unduly timid in their approaches to this problem.

Even when we turn to the most coherent work on this subject by no less a thinker than Gordon Childe, expressed in his *Social Evolution* (1951, 55), we read:

> Examples already given show that in certain circumstances and always with reserve, archaeology can provide some indications

as to the form of government and of the family, the recognition of rank, the distribution of the social product, and the practice of war. It is never likely to be able to tell us anything about the administration of justice, the penalties used to enforce it, nor the content of any laws, the way in which descent rather than inheritance of property is determined, the effective limitations on the powers of chiefs, or even of the extent of their authority. The content of religious belief and the nature of the prestige conferred by rank are irretrievably lost. Worst of all, negative evidence is worthless; rich graves or palaces may be evidence for the existence of chiefs, but the absence of the evidence cannot be taken as proof that they did not exist. And much of the available evidence is often ambiguous. As to 'government', without inscribed documents we can form no idea at all of the extent of the political units, save very tentatively in two most exceptional cases.

Childe here lists a series of difficult problems, and his negative judgement may well ultimately prove in many cases amply justified. But it is the declamatory style of this litany of limitations which so offends the modern ear, the willingness to accept as axiomatic those difficulties whose evaluation should instead be the basis for detailed study. To take one example, the problem to which he refers of the definition of the extent of political units forms the subject matter for the first two papers in the present book. And they only examine *one* possible approach to the problem, which is seen very much in spatial terms, without giving any detailed considerations to the distribution of distinctive artefacts such as might also indicate the exercise of power or the extent of allegiance. In those two chapters I do not claim to have solved the problem, even from the single standpoint employed in the detailed discussion. But I would certainly assert that these two papers refute rather conclusively Childe's hasty and dogmatic evaluation that 'we can form no idea at all of the extent of the political units'. The important work now being undertaken in the Maya Lowlands (Marcus 1976, Freidel 1983) offers a still more conclusive refutation. Here the symbol systems employed by the Maya have been used to excellent effect to give insights into what Marcus has aptly termed (Marcus 1974) 'the iconography of power'. And although we should perhaps allow that the Maya stelai have the status of 'inscribed documents', there are in many societies explicit symbol systems, some of them used to reflect and indeed maintain the exercise of power, which do not reach that level of complexity nor fulfil the other criteria of systems of writing.

7

*Introduction*

It is worth looking more closely at Childe's approach in his *Social Evolution*, for it represents the most ambitious attempt up to that time to tackle the problems of what we would today call social archaeology. He considered each of four societies under the rubric 'culture sequences in barbarism', taking in turn temperate Europe, the early Aegean, the Nile valley and Mesopotamia, and comparing the sequence of development in each. For each instance the evidence was reviewed under twelve headings: rural economy, specialisation of labour, means of transport, volume and extent of trade, warfare, population, form of the family unit, descent, ownership by individuals, existence of chiefs and administration, slavery, and art. But despite the perceptiveness, and in some respects the pioneering nature of Childe's discussion, it differs in one significant respect from the literature on social archaeology which has built up over the past decade. Nowhere does Childe pause at one of these twelve categories of evidence and set out to analyse in detail the processes of inference by which he would hope to reach conclusions about the existence and nature of the social relations under study under that heading. Relevant evidence is certainly adduced in each case with the wide-ranging scholarship for which Childe was justly famed, but in most cases the facts are left almost to speak for themselves, or are elucidated in discussions usually within a single sentence, and rarely of more than a paragraph.

Today, while admiring the scope of Childe's survey and the justness of the examples which he chose, we see more clearly that this level of analysis was simply not appropriate to the task. The interpretative problems for each of the categories which he chose each require a monograph-length consideration in their own right. Some of them have indeed already been accorded such treatment: the study of population and population density from archaeological evidence, for instance, (Spooner 1972, Hassan 1981), and already those substantial discussions today themselves seem sketchy and inadequate. These works will soon have to be revised to take into account the numerous lessons being learnt in different parts of the world from the practice in the field of intensive survey. To take another example, the inferences from burial, which Childe generally dealt with in a few paragraphs in his discussion of descent and of the existence of chiefs, have now been treated systematically in several monographs and dissertations (Brown 1971; Chapman, Kinnes and Randsborg 1981; Shennan 1975; O'Shea 1978; Buikstra 1976), and the basic principles of interpretation, the necessary theory, are still only gradually beginning to emerge.

8

We now find ourselves as archaeologists embarked upon a vast new enterprise, where each avenue of inference requires systematic consideration, and the development of what Binford and others have termed 'middle range theory' (e.g. Binford 1977, 7) so that sound principles of archaeological inference can be established. We can now see very clearly that what seemed to Childe, and certainly to his contemporaries, as an exercise in interpretation and speculation that pushed at the very frontiers of what was known or indeed knowable about the prehistoric past, was in reality little more than a selective listing of a number of essentially unexplored problem areas. The pessimism which Childe to some extent expressed, and to which others such as M. A. Smith gave utterance more emphatically, sprang from a reluctance to initiate the thorough and sometimes laborious explorations of theory and of methodology which now seem necessary. Without such an exploration there was, indeed, little that could be said beyond the concise judgements offered by Childe or the negative pronouncements of Smith. In short, what to Childe seemed a listing of conclusions, offered at the very limits of archaeological inference, seems to us today, on the contrary, an inventory of potential fields of archaeological inquiry, ripe for investigation.

## Formulating the Questions

It is up to us to formulate the questions, and to define this field of inquiry. Indeed in some ways this rather simple-seeming task is the most difficult and decisive in the whole enterprise of research. For very often the form of the question determines the form of the answer. It is inherent in the undertaking of research that we do not know the answer before the data reveal it to us, yet we cannot learn more from it than the confinements of the question allow.

In my view the still rather inadequate condition of the field of social archaeology today springs mainly from the reluctance of archaeologists to sit down and decide precisely what it is that they want to learn. As I suggested above, many have assumed that a fully-fledged social archaeology, when it develops, will look rather like the discipline of social anthropology and will proceed to partition the subject under the same headings.

The questions arrived at in this way naturally reflect the preoccupations and concerns of the social anthropologist, very often focusing first on matters of kinship and kinship terminology, and proceeding to other topics whose investigation would be very difficult or indeed impossible without a good knowledge of the language,

9

and in particular the vocabulary, of the group under study.

The concerns of the archaeologist overlap with these, but they are not the same. In the first place, there are many things which the archaeologist seeks to learn which the social anthropologist would usually regard as obvious, since they are already known to anyone who has lived within the society in question, as a social anthropologist will have done. Thus the size of the social unit, its political organisation, its relations with its neighbours, and the range of roles and statuses held within it will usually be rather obvious background information to the anthropological fieldworker: to the archaeologist these can be matters of urgent concern, whose elucidation requires much patient research and analysis.

In the second place, the archaeologist is concerned with material culture: with artefacts and buildings and all those human products whose preserved remains constitute the archaeological record. In recent years, the social anthropologist has been less concerned with these material things, as ethnography has slipped from its former central position in the discipline. This is, of course, why archaeologists are increasingly undertaking their own fieldwork among living societies, seeking by this research in ethnoarchaeology to understand better the role of material culture in living societies as well as in past ones.

The papers which follow have been divided into five Parts, each taking a single more-or-less coherent approach to the problems of social archaeology. There are, of course, many more lines of investigation which could have been pursued, indeed which have been traced by other writers. It is worth considering these five approaches briefly in turn here, not because together they form an integral whole, but as an illustration of the way different preoccupations lead to very different outcomes.

*I. Societies and space* (The landscape of power). One approach to the investigation of early societies is to examine them in *spatial* terms, indeed in territorial terms. The papers forming Part I adopt a spatial approach, and develop a methodology for breaking down the social landscape into a number of discrete units. Each of these occupies a definite territory on the map.

It should be noted that the question: 'How shall we divide this landscape up into social units?' carries with it the assumption that such a division is possible and useful. In many ways the fact that we can usually make this assumption is very remarkable in itself, and is certainly more interesting than the details of the specific methods which have been used to work out the implications in detail. It is of course a perfectly reasonable assumption in the light of our experience of the modern world, where each of us belongs to a nation state, and inside that nation state to a whole hierarchy of smaller and less inclusive organisational territories. The assumption does, however, have the effect of predetermining to some extent the shape of the answer.

This special approach, where the size and position of settlements is analysed within a spatial framework only uses one aspect of the available information: it has its limitations. But this is in part its interest: it is using data relating solely to location and scale. From these data alone it is possible, albeit in a rather simplistic way, to begin to investigate questions of dominance, and hence of power.

*II. Network and flow* (Trade and interaction). It is possible to contrast the foregoing partitioning into separate and distinct entities with a view where human individuals are all part of a wide-reaching network of interactions. From this standpoint it may not be helpful to break the world down into individual units, but rather to stress the great variety in the range and nature of interaction occurring between individuals. Such an approach has recently become popular in archaeology, where the notion of a network of interactions, for instance in northern Europe around 2000 BC, has been influential in the consideration of the beaker phenomenon (Shennan 1982). The same ideas enjoy a much wider currency beyond the European case (e.g. Braun and Plog 1982). They indicate for us that in order to gain a clearer understanding of human societies in terms of patterns of interaction, it will be necessary to think more creatively about networks, information flow and the mechanisms of communication. It is of course a truism of modern economics that significant interactions extend far beyond the territorial limits of the political units involved. But the full range of such interactions at the symbolic as well as the material level has yet to be explored. Indeed, the interactions between the units, when the latter can be defined, are sometimes as significant to their continuing development as those within them (see Renfrew and Cherry, in press).

*III. Authority* (Monuments, and the structure of pre-urban societies). Neither of the foregoing themes focuses specifically upon the exercise of authority within societies, or the forms of organisation which they sustain. The spatial approach, with its emphasis upon dominance, does of course lead towards the investigation of power relations, particularly from a spatial or territorial viewpoint. And the interaction approach certainly leads to a consideration of asymmetric relationships, such as those between persons of high and of

11

low status. Neither, however, as they are treated here has much to say about interpersonal relationships.

The monumental constructions, which are the main focus of Part III offer one specific line of inquiry, leading to some considerations of the nature of authority in the societies which created them. In some cases a rather egalitarian social structure may be suggested, in others a very strong group solidarity capable of mobilising large task-forces of manpower for building works. In other instances the high status and prestige of single individuals, and the exercise by them of coercive power may sometimes be inferred.

The discussion here focuses upon the monuments themselves as potential sources of information. Other approaches, perhaps in terms of artefacts and their differential distributions, for instance within cemeteries, can be profitably followed.

One solution is offered here in terms of the rather simplistic concept of 'chiefdom'. Elsewhere many writers have tackled the same problem in terms of the equally stereotyped notion of the 'state'. Once again the answers are limited in their scope by the questions and by the categories which these questions themselves anticipate. It will need a radically fresh analysis of social formations to allow us to transcend these existing categories or others like them.

*IV. The dynamics of continuous growth* (Systems thinking). In seeking to understand change, one fundamental question which we have to ask is how do societies grow? How do they change both in scale and in internal structure? Often in the past, as mentioned above, such changes have been assumed automatically to be the product of significant outside influences, so that the original inception of the change is consequently relegated to some outside area beyond the immediate field of study.

One of the most influential approaches to the questions and problems of change has been in terms of systems thinking. This entails the adoption of concepts and of a vocabulary which permit the analysis of a very complex situation into a number of identifiable components. Their own functioning can be considered in turn, and the effects of their mutual interactions taken into account. At one level, such an approach may seem like little more than the translation of a description using one set of terms into a different vocabulary, using other terms to no greater benefit. But in fact the approach has several advantages. In the first place it allows one to overcome the apparent paradox that a society can be very stable, over a long period of decades and of centuries, while the individual people constituting that society are certainly not personally stable, each person enjoying a lifespan much shorter than the period of stability. The notion of dynamic equilibrium is, I would argue, a very important one. The systems approach allows one to overcome the old analogy of the birth and death of civilisations, for instance, by breaking down the analysis into several levels simultaneously. It is only one approach, and may not be a convenient form of description for all research purposes. I would argue, nonetheless, that it represents archaeology's first coherent effort to find a terminology appropriate to the discussion of change, in all its multivariate complexity.

*V. Discontinuity and long-term change.* In order to understand sudden or discontinuous change, a rather different approach is needed. The systems approach discussed above will more often yield an output in terms of continuous and steady change and development. But in human societies as in nature, change is sometimes sudden. How can we understand a sudden, discontinuous change? This is an old question, and one which has nearly always in the past led to an analysis in terms of sudden and discontinuous causes. It is now possible to see that the connection is not a necessary one, and that a discontinuous change can be the consequence of the action of continuous causal variables. This is a simple yet important notion whose implications have not yet been adequately explored.

The approach outlined in Part v has its limitations: its contribution is to make intelligible this particular feature of discontinuity. It does not set out for us why any change should happen at all, be it sudden or gradual. That must come from the archaeologists own model.

Each of these approaches is a different one, with its own concerns and perspectives. Many others could have been followed instead. The specific structures of society have been very little considered in any of these cases, and many aspects of social organisation have not been addressed. For instance, the issue of the organisation of production, and notably of craft specialist production (see Evans 1978) is a whole neglected field, of as much interest as are the mechanisms of trade and exchange by which the products of production are distributed. Furthermore, there is little consideration here of questions of rank or status, and this omission perhaps creates the outstanding lacuna in a book purporting to deal with the social aspects of human communities. Subsistence too is here virtually ignored, although one of the most interesting approaches to social change is in terms of the intensification of production (see Renfrew 1982a). Nor is population density accorded the causal significance which a more balanced treatment might suggest.

These are omissions, but not necessarily defects. The approaches here offer no claim to completeness. They are attempts to develop coherent procedures for the investigation of early societies. What each of them seeks to attain is a perspective allowing for the development of some theoretical concepts which may be of general application.

## *On Generalisation*

Each of the papers offered here touches, whether explicitly or implicitly, upon the question of generalisation. How far is it legitimate to generalise about human societies? To what extent must historical explanation be restricted to the consideration of the specific case in point: how far can it proceed by more general statements? These are matters of endless debate, where little agreement has yet been reached.

No apology is needed, however, for bringing to the fore once again these issues which, to every historian and social scientist, are familiar to the point of repetition. For archaeology has over the past fifteen years been much preoccupied with them. They have been debated at length, and certain misconceptions have become very much clearer.

In the first place, in order to explain it is necessary to have some conception of what form an acceptable explanation would take. Without going over yet again much familiar ground (e.g Renfrew 1982b), it seems very widely agreed that most explanations can be divided into a more specific or particular component on the one hand, which rehearses the specific data bearing on the case in question, and a much more general assertion on the other. This general assertion will of course be relevant to the case in question, relating the explanatory data in question to those actual circumstances which it is desired to explain. I have been careful so far not to claim too much for this 'general assertion', and of course many philosophers have asked for more, suggesting that it should take the form of a universal law (e.g. Hempel and Oppenheim 1948). This point can be dealt with later, but at the moment it is sufficient to seek the common ground between the advocates of scientific explanation (who tend to favour laws), and those preferring more traditional historical explanations (who in general do not). Among the latter was R. G. Collingwood. Yet even he felt constrained to point out that explanation also involves more general principles. He wrote (Collingwood 1939, 140):

> If you want to know why a certain kind of thing happened in a certain kind of case, you must begin by asking, 'What did you expect?' You must consider what the normal development is in cases of that kind.

This notion of 'normal development' does surely imply some kind of general exemplar, some guiding principles by which the appropriate expectation might be formed. Here then is the common ground: the 'general assertion' which advocates of scientific explanation and, it would seem, of historical explanation, would both see as a necessary component.

It is when we consider the precise form which this general assertion should take that differences emerge. From the very early days of the New Archaeology (as it then was) there was a much sharper awareness than hitherto of the need to make such general assertions explicit. Indeed, one of the principal thrusts of processual archaeology was towards generalisation, and this remains the case today. An explicit generalisation can then be compared with the evidence in a particular case – to be 'tested', in the terminology of Sir Karl Popper (1959) – and hence discarded if found to be inappropriate in the light of fresh data. It is of course this possibility of refutation which, in Popper's view distinguishes scientific statements from those of other kinds whose truth or validity is not open to examination in this way.

It is a significant observation that most of the leading processual archaeologists of this time, such as L. R. Binford or K. V. Flannery were in general rather cautious about the precise *form* which these general assertions would take. Binford has made occasional reference in his writings to 'laws of cultural development' (e.g. Binford 1968, 9), but nowhere I think has he asserted that universal laws are a *sine qua non* for meaningful explanation. Flannery has used a number of explanatory generalisations, including some couched in systems terminology (e.g. Flannery 1968), but without any prescriptive statements about the form which explanations should take. I have myself, while aspiring to statements of high generality, likewise never advocated the use of general laws in relation to the archaeological record, mainly because I have never been able to discern any. (Honourable exception must be made here for the 'Law of monotonic decrement' set out in chapter 5 which was initially formulated as a *jeu d'esprit* for a session at the Society for American Archaeology: I do not claim any overwhelming metho-

15

dological significance for it.)

It was therefore a significant, and in retrospect unfortunate step when Fritz and Plog (1970) adopted in its entirety the argument of Hempel and Oppenheim (1948) that all valid explanations consist of a general and universal law, in addition to the statement of antecedent circumstances, about which nobody disagrees. The same position was taken by Watson, Le Blanc and Redman (1971) in their book *Explanation in Archaeology*. Since I was, I believe, one of the first to deplore this application to archaeology of the Hempel–Oppenheim model for scientific explanation, it may be appropriate to quote here what I then said (Renfrew 1973b, 1929):

> Very properly they insist upon testability as a criterion of meaning. Unfortunately they proceed to adopt a very restrict-ive notion of science, adopted from Carl Hempel – 'A scientist explains a particular event by subsuming its description under the appropriate confirmed general law.' In doing so they ter-minate the debate on the nature of explanation before it has even begun, without any mention of the work of such philo-sophers of science as Sir Karl Popper or Richard Bevan Braith-waite or any discussion of the objections which have been raised against Hempel's views . . .
>
> Despite the spirited advocacy of Fritz and Plog (1970), I believe this prescriptive, legalistic approach, that scientific ex-planation must always take the form of general laws to be wrong, and its advocacy in so central a position in a book such as this to be harmful. The advocates of Law and Order in archaeology, by setting an impossible goal, may confuse rather than clarify the question of what constitutes a satisfactory, valid and scientific explanation in archaeology . . .
>
> I would argue that what does or should make scientific archaeology scientific is not the precise logical form of the explanations which it adopts but the open and repeatable pro-cedures used for testing them, and the systematic research methods with the aid of which they are formulated. By prema-turely selecting one specific form of explanation taken from the physical sciences (for the life sciences, for example, do not function in as neat a hypothetico-deductive framework as Hempel might wish) it becomes more difficult to make formu-lations derived from archaeology itself, and in a form conveni-ent to it. The key to archaeological explanation is the investi-gation of culture process, and general laws provide only one of the conceptual tools. The authors themselves devoted an entire

16

chapter to the systems theory approach without acknowledging that the logical structure of a systems model applied to some part of the archaeological record which is to be explained, differs fundamentally from that of a hypothetico-deductive explanation. Yet they rightly stress the importance of the systems approach as a valuable weapon in the conceptual armoury of the scientific archaeologist.

Already in the archaeological literature one sees the dangers of adopting a rigid Law and Order approach too readily. All too often, when important but specific problems are being investigated, the researcher seems constrained to formulate hypotheses in needlessly general terms – often indeed in such a form that his project could not hope to test it effectively. Too rigid a theoretical framework can make for bad research, so that the worker is unduly concerned with the form of the explanations rather than with their content. The real advances in archaeological theory will come – and are coming – from a closer examination of human behaviour and of consequent artefact variability under different conditions. The authors discuss many of the relevant fields illuminatingly: ecology, trade and interaction spheres, and patterns of settlement, to which socio-political organisation and cognitive/symbolic systems should certainly be added. To relate these effectively together, as we must aspire to do, is a task too complex and too ambitious to be undertaken with the simplistic formulation offered by Hempel.

The development of archaeology over the decade and more since I wrote those words has confirmed my gloomiest forebodings. On the one hand the Fritz and Plog formulation has been seized on by commentators deliberately espousing what they see as an 'anti-positivist' point of view, allowing them so far to misrepresent processual archaeology as to suggest that its procedures are accurately reflected in the book by Watson, LeBlanc and Redman criticised above (e.g. Hodder 1982, 2). So in the first place the opponents of scientific methodology in archaeology have been given a ready-made straw man at whom to fire off their post-positivist (and even post-structuralist) salvoes.

What is perhaps worse, those who do genuinely seek to define a methodology for archaeology inspired by the same rigour which is often applied in the sciences, have allowed themselves to become involved in the wrong arguments. Thus Salmon (1982) is able to devote much of her discussion to the Hempelian model of explanation before going on to develop her favoured alternative, the Statistical-Relevance model. This is not the place for a detailed criticism of s-r, other than to say that in its own way it presents as many difficulties for archaeology as its Hempelian forerunner. The philosophers of science are allowing themselves, it seems to me, to become involved in a series of debates which, although they purport to be about the nature of explanation in archaeology, in reality sometimes bear little specific relation to the subject matter of archaeology as such. One sometimes almost feels that they are, in fact, earning a precarious living taking in each other's washing.

These points are pertinent to most of the papers which follow, because I feel that the nature of explanation in archaeology remains a field which has not yet received very satisfactory treatment by anyone, although Mellor (1973) has made some relevant points and the recent work of Salmon (1982) usefully covers much of the ground. It is clear to me – although this point might be disputed, for example, by Trigger (1978) – that we are indeed in the business of making generalisations. But these are not universal generalisations, valid for all time and space: they are not general laws. In the first place, they are of course restricted to human behaviour, and perhaps in some cases to human behaviour at certain stages in the development of the species rather than at others. The behaviour in question is also variable in relation to certain social conditions. For instance, we might be able to make generalisations about human behaviour in band societies which would not be true of those living in state organisations, and vice versa. Moreover, the sort of explanations which might apply to one class of state societies might not be applicable to another. These are matters for empirical investigation as well as for theory building.

Clearly we are able to make some generalisations. For if each statement that we made was really only applicable to a single society, there would be little to be learned from any comparison between societies. Such a position is indeed logically possible, but it runs counter to the experience that in certain circumstances we can make wider assertions.

It is in this area of discussion that the interest of the papers which follow most lies. In each an attempt is being made to generalise, without any claim that what is being asserted is *universally* valid. It would be possible to find, and if not to find to invent, alternative cases for each of the examples given. There are no universal laws here – even the 'law of monotonic decrement' (Chapter 5) has the proviso 'in the absence of highly organised directional exchange'.

But there do exist simplifying assumptions and abstract formulations of considerable generality. In precisely what conditions these generalisations do hold and in which they do not is a matter which has to be investigated further.

The papers which follow are all working papers, and none claims to make final or definitive statements. They naturally focus upon the problems of the archaeology of the past decade. In some instances their attempts to reach towards generalisation already look rather simple, simplistic even, in the light of further work which has proceeded in the same direction. But that is how it should be, and those papers which have stimulated the most further work are inevitably precisely the ones which require re-evaluation in the light of it. In the introductory section to each Part, I have attempted to review some of the ideas and the contributions produced in recent years which have added to the effectiveness of the approach in question.

It is too early, at the moment, to write a satisfactory manual of social archaeology. Nor can we yet expect any treatment of change in early societies which is generally satisfactory in most of its aspects. The subject is still at an exploratory stage, and the most which we can hope for is a number of insights, some of which may prove helpful in the construction of a coherent methodology for the study of the social organisation of early societies, and in the development of a relevant body of archaeological theory.

It is my hope that some of these papers do raise some of the relevant issues, and do develop approaches which may be found fruitful in the light of further work. In particular, the lessons they offer, whether intentionally or not, may bring us a little closer to some resolution of what I see as an enduring central problem for archaeology, as it is for the social sciences in general and indeed for the study of history: What are the appropriate forms for the generalising assertions which we can properly hope to make about human societies and their past?

### Bibliography

Adams, W. Y. ( 1968) Invasion, diffusion, evolution? *Antiquity*, 42, 194–213.

Adams, W. Y., D. P. van Gerven and R. S. Levy ( 1978) The retreat from migrationism, *Annual Review of Anthropology*, 7, 483–532.

Binford, L. R. ( 1968) Archaeological perspectives, in L. R. and S. R. Binford, eds., *New Perspectives in Archaeology*, Chicago, Aldine, 5–32.

Binford, L. R. and S. R. Binford, eds. ( 1968) *New Perspectives in*

*Archaeology*, Chicago, Aldine.

Binford, L. R., ed. (1977) *For Theory Building in Archaeology*, New York, Academic Press.

Braun, D. P. and S. Plog (1982) Evolution of 'tribal' social networks: theory and prehistoric North American evidence, *American Antiquity*, 47, 504–25.

Brown, J. A., ed. (1971) *Approaches to the Social Dimensions of Mortuary Practices*, (Memoirs of the Society for American Archaeology 25).

Buikstra, J. E. (1976) *Hopewell in the Lower Illinois Valley: a Regional Approach to the Study of Human Biological Variability and Prehistoric Behavior*, (Northwestern University Archaeological Program Scientific Papers No. 2).

Chapman, R., I. Kinnes and K. Randsborg, eds. (1981) *The Archaeology of Death*, Cambridge, University Press.

Childe, V. G. (1951) *Social Evolution*, London, Watts.

Childe, V. G. (1958) Retrospect, *Antiquity*, 32, 69–74.

Collingwood, R. G. (1939) *An Autobiography*, Oxford, Clarendon Press.

Evans, R. K. (1978) Early craft specialisation, an example from the Balkan chalcolithic, in C. L. Redman, *et al.*, eds., *Social Archaeology, Beyond Subsistence and Dating*, New York, Academic Press, 113–130.

Flannery, K. V. (1968) Archaeological systems theory and early Mesoamerica, in B. J. Meggers, ed., *Anthropological Archaeology in the Americas*, Washington D. C., Anthropological Society of Washington, 67–87.

Freidel, D. A. (1983) Political systems in Lowland Yucatan: dynamics and structure in Maya settlement, in E. Z. Vogt and R. M. Leventhal, eds., *Prehistoric Settlement Patterns: Essays in Honor of Gordon R. Willey*, Albuquerque, University of New Mexico Press, 375–86.

Fritz, J. M. and F. T. Plog (1970) The nature of archaeological explanation, *American Antiquity*, 35, 405–12.

Hassan, F. A. (1981) *Demographic Archaeology*, New York, Academic Press.

Hempel, C. G. and P. Oppenheim (1948) Studies in the logic of explanation, *Philosophy of Science*, 5, 135–75.

Hodder, I. (1982) Theoretical archaeology: a reactionary view, in I. Hodder, ed., *Symbolic and Structural Archaeology*, Cambridge, University Press, 1–16.

Marcus, J. (1974) The iconography of power among the Classic Maya, *World Archaeology*, 6, 83–94.

Marcus, J., (1976) *Emblem and State in the Classic Maya Lowlands: an Epigraphic Approach to Territorial Organization*, Dumbarton Oaks, Trustees for Harvard University.

Mellor, D. H. (1973) Do cultures exist?, in C. Renfrew, ed., *The Explanation of Culture Change*, London, Duckworth, 59–72.

O'Shea, J. (1978) Mortuary variability: an archaeological investigation with case studies from the nineteenth century Central Plains of North America and the early bronze age of southern Hungary, Ph.D. dissertation, University of Cambridge.

Popper, K. R. (1959) *The Logic of Scientific Discovery*, London, Hutchinson.

Redman, C. L., M. J. Berman, E. V. Curtin, W. T. Langhorne, N. M. Versaggi and J. C. Wanser (1978) *Social Archaeology, Beyond Subsistence and Dating*, New York, Academic Press.

Renfrew, C. (1968) Wessex without Mycenae, *Annual of the British School of Archaeology at Athens*, 63, 277–85.

Renfrew, C. (1970) New configurations in Old World archaeology, *World Archaeology*, 2, 199–211.

Renfrew, C. (1973a) *Social Archaeology, an Inaugural Lecture*, Southampton, University of Southampton.

Renfrew, C. (1973b) Review of *Explanation in Archaeology, an Explicitly Scientific Approach*, by P. J. Watson, S. A. LeBlanc and C. L. Redman, *American Anthropologist*, 73, 1928–30.

Renfrew, C. (1982a) Polity and power: interaction, intensification and exploitation, in C. Renfrew and J. M. Wagstaff, eds., *An Island Polity: the Archaeology of Exploitation in Melos*, Cambridge, University Press, 264–90.

Renfrew, C. (1982b) Explanation revisited, in C. Renfrew, M. J. Rowlands and B. A. Segraves, eds., *Theory and Explanation in Archaeology*, New York, Academic Press, 5–24.

Renfrew, C. and J. F. Cherry, eds., in press, *Peer Polity Interaction and the Development of Sociopolitical Complexity*, Cambridge, University Press.

Salmon, M. (1982) *Philosophy and Archaeology*, New York, Academic Press.

Shennan, S. (1975) The social organisation at Branc, *Antiquity*, 49, 279–88.

Shennan, S. J (1982) Ideology, change and the European early bronze age, in I. Hodder, ed., *Symbolic and Structural Archaeology*, Cambridge, University Press, 155–61.

Smith, M. A. (1955) The limitations of inference in archaeology, *Archaeological Newsletter*, 6, 3–7.

Spooner, B., ed. (1972) *Population Growth: Anthropological Implications*, Cambridge, Mass., MIT Press.

Trigger, B. (1978) *Time and Traditions*, Edinburgh, University Press.

Watson, P. J., S. A. LeBlanc and C. L. Redman (1971) *Explanation in Archaeology, an Explicitly Scientific Approach*, New York, Columbia University Press.

# I

## SOCIETIES IN SPACE:
## THE LANDSCAPE
## OF POWER

*

Power – the ability to exercise control or command over others – is one of the most fundamental social realities. The various devices used either to restrict power or to institutionalise and perpetuate it are among the most characteristic features of human societies. This is an obvious area of interest for the social archaeologist.

Power as such is not often directly reflected in the archaeological record. Wealth finds more obvious expression, for instance in the discovery of accumulations of special, and by inference valuable, objects. Status is often reflected and maintained by the use of conspicuous symbols. Power, on the other hand, must be exercised to be visible: perhaps the most obvious expression of the sustained exercise of power is seen in the orderly structures of organisation. These abstract points merit more careful consideration than they have so far received from the archaeologist. For the reasons discussed in Chapter 1 there is at present little literature in the field of social anthropology on the material correlates of power such as might be useful to the archaeologist.

The archaeological record does contain vast amounts of data which are of potential value in understanding and reconstructing the exercise of power in past societies (see Trigger 1974). The most obvious indicators are symbolic: the use of symbols as 'instruments of domination' (Bourdieu 1977) is widespread. It has already been utilised by archaeologists concerned with systems of dominance, and Marcus (1974) has written in this context of 'the iconography of power', although, as indicated above, this is not easily distinguished from the iconography of status. Such an approach is only workable in practice, however, in cases where such a symbolic system is sufficiently well developed and explicit as to be potentially intelligible to the modern observer. In general highly specialised symbolic systems are seen only in well-established state societies, and the iconography of power in less centralised communities is not so readily analysed.

The approach followed here is a very much more general one,

24

resting upon the sound principle that, whatever the limitations of the archaeological record, most archaeological finds have a precise provenance in space. We know where they were found. It is a central idea of the two papers which follow that power has spatial correlates. For it is the essence of power relationships that they are asymmetrical: when all relationships are symmetrical, we are dealing instead with an egalitarian society characterised by what Durkheim called 'mechanical solidarity'. Symmetry and asymmetries associated with power can be understood, at least in part, in spatial terms.

There are other reasons than this for considering the spatial behaviour of societies. Indeed the archaeologist's first problem – and one which rarely delays the social anthropologist for long – is to define what he means, in a particular case, by a society. What is the *unit* of study? Such a question is by no means easy to answer, and the decision on the scale of the unit under consideration is one of the most crucial to the whole outcome of the research.

This matter of scale and the selection of the social groups with which the archaeologist deals has proved one of the most difficult problems in the practice of archaeology. In the first of the papers which follow it is argued that the decision made by Gordon Childe to define the archaeological 'culture' as the appropriate unit for the discussion of social questions was largely responsible for the subsequent disappearance of effective discussion of social questions for more than four decades. The same accusation can be levelled at the taxonomic systems developed in the same period in the United States. The basic misconceptions were to confuse questions of social organisation with those about ethnicity (for Childe and his contemporaries interpreted the term 'culture' in an ethnic sense), and to assume that arbitrarily defined taxonomic units (i.e. 'cultures') had clear ethnic correlates. As I seek to show below, both of these are errors of method. Different societies formulate their ethnic concepts in different ways and at different scales. The feeling of belonging to a definite group, of being one of a specific 'people' is indeed a widespread one in human societies, but it is too complicated a matter for ready assumptions.

The exercise of power in society implies asymmetry, then, and it is, moreover, the kind of asymmetry which results principally from centrality. Power is often, although not inevitably, concentrated into the hands of a restricted group of people, the investigation of the archaeological indications of such *central persons* is one of the most fruitful avenues for the elucidation of past power relationships.

One approach to this problem, and it is the one carried forward by a specific example in Chapter 3, is to assume a correlation between *central persons* and *central places*. The study of the location and exercise of central functions, and especially those of government, can then offer one of the most useful sources of information not only about the organisation of society but about the exercise of power in it, and about the scale of the units with which we are dealing.

At first sight this may seem a geographical question, as indeed in a sense it is. But the main thrust of geographical analysis has been in a different direction, resting upon the assumptions of Central Place Theory, about which there is a vast literature. Most investigations operating within a Central Place Theory framework have operated *within* a single known political unit, usually a modern nation state, and have centered upon economic relations. This was the starting point for Christaller himself (1966), who was studying distributional relationships within south Germany, and it has been the perspective of many of his most interesting followers (e.g. Skinner 1964). It begins by assuming things which the archaeologist needs to discover.

Other workers, in the field of urban geography, on the other hand, have often ignored political boundaries altogether or alternatively have considered the frequency distribution of cities of varying size within the given political units, without taking locational factors into account at all. Work of this kind on primate cities (Jefferson 1939; Berry 1961) has nonetheless proved very stimulating to archaeologists and anthropologists (e.g. Smith 1976) and develops ideas more promising for archaeology than those of the sometimes rather mechanistic classical Central Place Theory approach.

Rather curiously, the political geographers themselves have not in general shown the quantitative sophistication of their economic colleagues, despite the useful programmatic statements made, for example by Hartshorne (1950), Jones (1954), Pounds and Ball (1964) and Cohen and Rosenthal (1971), and perhaps most usefully from the anthropological viewpoint, by Soja (1971).

The archaeological problem, at least in the first instance, is to find a means of reconstructing the political organisation, and in particular of deciding which were the dominant centres (see Marcus 1973; Hammond 1974). Often this has been attempted by applying a straightforward Central Place Theory approach, preparing a frequency histogram for sites in terms of their size and looking for 'natural breaks' in the distribution, on the assumption that the sites may be divided into first, second and third order centres in terms of absolute size (e.g. Johnson 1972, for a pioneering application of Central Place Theory to archaeology). But in a large area it is perfectly possible that centres will actually be much smaller in absolute size than others. They may even be smaller than some of the 'second order' centres of the largest units. This seemingly technical point is significant: it means that a simple frequency distribution approach is not adequate.

It is necessary instead to return to the crucial ideas of power and of *dominance* and to develop an approach which will make clear which centres are dominant and which are subordinate, while allowing for some differences in scale among the territorial units. This idea runs counter to the inverse square law interaction model used by some workers. It has not so far been developed by the political geographers, although it has been illuminatingly discussed by Stinchcombe (1968, 217–31). Some of the most interesting recent archaeological articles dealing with the exercise of power in space (e.g. Steponaitis 1978, Alden 1979) have managed to avoid the pitfalls of too close an adherence to traditional Central Place Theory, but not to the point of rejecting the inverse power or 'gravity' model (cf. Renfrew 1981, 269), as advocated here.

In Chapter 3 a different approach is set out, which avoids this difficulty, although it has to make its own simplifying assumptions. In particular it does assume that the power centre or capital of a given polity will always be the largest centre within it. As indicated in Chapter 3, this is not the case for modern federal states, where Washington D.C. is smaller than New York, for instance. This point has been well brought out by Blanton (1976) with his discussion of the 'disembedded capital'. He rightly indicates that, in addition to the case of federal capital centres, there are other instances where the seat of power within a territory may not in fact be its largest centre. The 'roving palace', a term he aptly applies to the mobile courts of early mediaeval Europe, is one such, and the 'temporary capital', where a new city is built on the accession of a new ruler to the throne, is another (see Willey 1979). These cases do offer difficulties to the model presented here.

The papers which follow, however, are intended as exploratory rather than definitive. They do develop an approach to the archaeological investigation of social organisation in terms of power and of dominance. The first of them offers a very general discussion which leads to the specific procedures, applied in a series of computer-based applications, set out in the second. The underlying concepts seem to apply to all scales of human societies: the notion of 'polity' as used here does not imply that we are dealing only with urban communities or state societies. Evidently the specific model advanced here has a number of limitations. But I would claim that these papers are a deliberate step towards the development of methods which allow some aspects of the social organisation of hierarchically structured societies to be investigated systematically.

## Bibliography

Alden, J.R. (1979) A reconstruction of Toltec period political units in the Valley of Mexico, in C. Renfrew and K.L. Cooke, eds., *Transformations, Mathematical Approaches to Culture Change*, New York, Academic Press, 169–200.

Berry, B. (1961) City size distribution and economic development, *Economic Development and Culture Change* 9, 573–88.

Blanton, R.E. (1976) Anthropological studies of cities, *Annual Review of Anthropology*, 5, 249–64.

Bourdieu, F. (1977) Symbolic power, *Annales*, 32, 405–11.

Christaller W. (1966) *Central Places in Southern Germany*, translated by D.W. Baskin, Englewood Cliffs, Prentice-Hall. (First German edition, 1933).

Cohen, S.B. and L.D. Rosenthal (1971) A geographical model of political systems analyses, *Geographical Review*, 61, 5–31.

Hammond, N. (1974) The distribution of Late Classic Maya major ceremonial centres in the Central Area, in N. Hammond, ed., *Mesoamerican Archaeology, New Approaches*, London, Duckworth, 313–34.

Hartshorne, R. (1950) The functional approach to political geography, *Annals of the Association of American Geographers*, 40, 95–130.

Jefferson, M. (1939) The law of the primate city, *Geographical Review*, 29, 226–32.

Jones, S.B. (1954) A unified field theory of political geography, *Annals of the Association of American Geographers*, 44, 111–23.

Johnson, G.A. (1972) A test of the utility of Central Place Theory in archaeology, in P.J. Ucko, R. Tringham and G.W. Dimbleby, eds., *Man, Settlement and Urbanism*, London, Duckworth.

Marcus, J. (1974) The iconography of power among the Classic Maya, *World Archaeology*, 6, 83–94.

Pounds, N.J.G. and S.S. Ball (1964) Core areas and the development of the European state system, *Annals of the Association of American Geographers*, 54, 24–40.

Renfrew, C. (1981) Space, time and man, *Transactions of the Institute of British Geographers*, 6, 257–78.

Skinner, G.W. (1964) Marketing and social structure in rural China, *Journal of Asian Studies*, 24, 3–43.

Smith, C.A., ed. (1976) *Regional Analysis*, New York, Academic Press.

Soja, E.W. (1971) *The Political Organisation of Space* (Association of American Geographers, Commission of College Geography, Resource Paper No. 8).

Steponaitis, V.P. (1978) Location theory and complex chiefdoms, a
    Mississippian example, in B.D. Smith, ed., *Mississippian
    Settlement Patterns*, New York, Academic Press, 417–53.
Stinchcombe, A.L. (1968) *Constructing Social Theories*, New York,
    Harcourt Brace.
Trigger, B. (1974) The archaeology of government, *World
    Archaeology*, 6, 95–106.
Willey, G.R. (1979) The concept of the 'disembedded capital' in
    comparative perspective, *Journal of Anthropological Research*,
    35, 123–137.

# 2

## SPACE, TIME
## AND POLITY

*

How can the archaeologist reconstruct the social organisation of prehistoric communities? Can we hope to trace the evolution of societies from the palaeolithic hunting group to the modern state from archaeological data by the use of logically tenable procedures of reasoning, or must any statement about the social organisation of an early society be based upon a facile and ultimately untenable 'analogy' with some entirely unrelated modern community? In this article I hope to approach this problem in terms of spatial organisation – not because the notion of 'territoriality' has recently been fashionable in anthropology, but because the insights of the modern human geographer into spatial organisation offer many potential applications to archaeology which we are only just beginning to explore. In general the geographer, with a frequently simplified model of modern economising man blindly obeying a Law of Least Effort or a Principle of Least Action, is no more concerned with the social organisation of non-market societies than is the structural anthropologist with a Christaller hexagonal lattice. Yet, as I hope to show, the evolution of human society can profitably be considered in terms of spatial patterning. To do so, however, inevitably implies for the archaeologist the final abandonment of the simple notion of 'culture' with its counterpart of 'people' as a fundamental unit of discussion, for these impose upon the data, and hence upon our vision of the past, categories of thought which seem today of doubtful value or validity, obscuring just those questions which we may hope to answer. A further factor contributing to the failure of archaeology to arrive at a coherent view of the development of social organisation may be the sometimes uncritical use of ready-made anthropological concepts which are validated by reference to data different from those of archaeology. It is our task to formulate

30

concepts and ideas which can operate upon archaeological data, but which do at the same time have real meaning and interest when applied to living societies.

## *Social Anthropology and Social Archaeology:*
## *a Distinction*

The prospect of reconstructing prehistoric social organisation has been regarded by some anthropologists with pessimism (Leach 1973). Given the limited range of ethnographic reporting before the accounts of Cook and Forster, the view that 'The belief that something significant about the sociology of a remotely antique human society can be inferred from a study of its material residues is similar to supposing that if we had a random selection of the utterances of unknown meaning from some dozens of unknown and now disused languages we could use this evidence to validate useful general propositions about the nature of human language' (Leach 1974) effectively abandons the hope of studying non-literate societies prior to about 1700 A D.

In order to counter this claim, it is necessary to bring out the rather special interpretation of social organisation which underlies it. Leach is so mesmerised by the variety in human communities, by the intriguing uniqueness of each, that no suspicion of discernible order or pattern emerges: 'in archaeology the accumulation of more and more evidence increases our information about historical arte-facts; it does not increase the probability of our sociological guess-work, since the whole range of contemporary ethnographic variety still needs to be taken into account for each new sample of evidence' (Leach 1974). The image which this statement conjures up of social anthropology as a disordered thesaurus of anecdotal observations, entirely lacking in structure, may not be what Leach intends. The dissociation between 'material residues' and 'sociology' does establish, however, a curious polarisation between mind and matter which the best of recent anthroplogical work, including Leach's own earlier writings, has managed to avoid.

The crux of the matter may well indeed be language, as Leach's analogy perhaps betrays. For the social anthropologist invariably proceeds by learning the language of the community which he is studying, seeking to perceive the world as his informants perceived it, working towards a shared perception, a shared cognition, which he can then interpret. From this cognised model which he forms of the society (and the world) as its members see it, he proceeds to an analysis of the society as it operates 'in reality', that is to say from the standpoint of the modern anthroplogical observer. The focus of study shifts as follows:

| Direct testimony and observation | → | Cognitive model | → | Operational perspective |

Whether dealing with kinship, myth or religion, the social anthropologist has traditionally worked in this way, the functionalist school focusing upon the relation between the cognitive and operational aspects within specific societies, the structuralists comparing the cognitive perceptions in different societies. To the outsider it often seems that the social anthropologist is more concerned with what people think than with what they actually do, which perhaps partly explains the comparative neglect into which ethnography has fallen.

The prehistoric archaeologist has no access to direct verbal testimony, and testimony of of any kind – in the form of visual representation of the world or other explicit symbols – forms only a small part of his material of study. His progression must therefore be from the data – the artefacts and associated materials in their contexts – as relics of past actions, towards a knowledge of these actions (whether individually or in aggregate) and hence of the operation of certain aspects of the society. In certain cases it may be legitimate to infer or propose aspects of the world picture, the working of the society as recognised by that society, from such operational data:

| Sites, artefacts and associated data | → | Operational features | → | Cognised aspects |

I suggest that it is a failure adequately to distinguish these very different procedures, to distinguish between the actions of a society as interpreted by its members and as analysed by the modern anthropologist, which has recently darkened counsel. The distinction has been made to very good effect in practice by Rappaport (1969). And it is, of course, precisely that which some anthropologists seek to convey by those infelicitous and synthetic terms 'emic' (i.e. cognitive) and 'etic' (i.e. operational) (Harris 1968a). Harris's words indeed offer the archaeologist comfort and encouragement: 'You are relatively free from the mystifications which arise from the emic approach . . . Your operationally defined categories and processes are superior to the unoperational definitions and categories of much of contemporary cultural anthroplogy . . . Archaeologists, shrive yourselves of the notion that the units which you seek to reconstruct must match the units in social organisation which contemporary ethnographers have attempted to tell you exist' (Harris 1968b).

But what then are the effective units of social organisation, these 'operationally defined categories of the archaeologist?' Elman Service, after offering us a hierarchy of band, tribe, chiefdom and state, increasingly used by the archaeologist, dramatically lost his nerve, suggesting instead 'Three aboriginal types which might represent evolutionary stages: (1) the Egalitarian Society out of which grew (2) the Hierarchical Society, which was replaced in only a few instances in the world by the Empire-State that was the basis of the next stage (3) the Archaic Civilisation or Classical Empire' (Service 1971). This offers an alternative so imprecisely formulated that even the initial capitals can do little to recommend it. Are the other existing archaeological categories and procedures for dealing with social organisation as 'superior' as Harris flatteringly suggests?

## The Archaeological Conundrum: What Is a Social Group?

For fifty years archaeologists have imagined that they knew the answer to this question. In Europe it was most clearly expressed by Gordon Childe, who introduced the concept of a culture as entity with extension in space and time (Childe 1929). He wrote:

> We find certain types of remains – pots, implements, ornaments, burial sites, house forms – constantly recurring together. Such a complex of regularly associated traits we shall term a 'cultural group' or just a 'culture'. We assume that such a complex is the material expression of what today would be called a people.
>
> The same complex may be found with relatively negligible diminutions over a wide area. In such cases of the total and bodily transferance of a complete culture from one place to another we think ourselves justified in assuming a 'movement of people'.

Precisely this view, which has been stigmatised in recent years as the 'normative approach' (Binford 1962) has been lucidly reasserted recently by Rouse (1972, 62): 'Prehistorians start with the archaeological facts and from them synthesise a picture of ethnic groups and their distribution, nature and development, using an inductive strategy . . . [There are] four questions that the prehistorian attempts to answer by means of his research: (1) Who produced the archaeological remains under study, that is to which ethnic groups did the producers belong? (2) Where and when did each group live? (3) What was each group like in its culture, morphology, social structure, or language, as the case may be? (4) How and why did each group become that way?'

On this view the archaeologist makes two important implicit assertions, neither of which is explicitly questioned. First that the archaeological record contains homogeneous assemblages of objects (i.e. cultures) which may be distinguished as entities from other assemblages; second that these homogeneous distributions are the material expression of a social reality, the ethnic group. This term, 'ethnic group', is rarely defined with precision, but does not necessarily have racial implications. Rouse (1972, 6) uses the term 'in a general sense to refer collectively' to four different kinds of groups: cultural, morphological (i.e., racial), social, and linguistic: 'A "people" and its culture are but sides of the same coin, the term "people" referring to the individuals who compose the group, and the term "culture" to the activities that distinguish the group.'

Already in 1958, Willey and Phillips (1958) recognised the difficulties in such a view, and admitted that 'phase' (which in their special terminology is analogous to Childe's term 'culture' with its specific and often restricted spatial distribution) cannot be directly equated with 'society'. In their words:

> The equivalent of phase, then, ought to be 'society', and in a good many cases it probably is . . . Unfortunately in practice it does not work. We have no means of knowing whether the components we group together into a phase are the same communities an ethnographer . . . would group into a society. We cannot be sure that the individual members of these communities would recognise themselves as belonging to the same 'people' . . . In sum, it looks as though the present chances are against archaeological phases having much if any social reality, but this does not prevent us from maintaining that they can and that in the meantime we may act as if they did have.

The normative approach has been criticised to good effect by Binford (1962) on the appropriate ground that 'change in the total cultural system must be viewed in an adaptive context, both social and environmental, not whimsically viewed as the result of 'influences', 'stimuli', or even 'migrations' between and among geographically defined units'. In a subsequent article, Binford (1965) carries the discussion much further, suggesting that 'culture be viewed as a system composed of subsystems', advocating the separate study of the subsystems within specific culture systems, so as to avoid the holistic simplicities of the normative approach. A distinction is made between adaptive areas – within which similar techniques for exploiting the environment are used, whatever the stylistic variation – and interaction spheres, large areas within which social interactions occur. The problem of identifying the geographical extent of the specific culture systems to be studied is not considered – indeed the article does not rule out the possibility that this decision might be an arbitrary one. In any case the question of recognising social units is not specifically considered.

Ironically too it is a problem which the increasing taxonomic sophistication of the archaeologist has obscured rather than clarified. For in practice, in specific cases, it has often been difficult to define the boundaries or extent of particular archaeological cultures, and this might have led to doubts about the validity of the concept itself. But instead a willingness to consider at once the differing distributions of the various artefacts which go together to make up the 'recurring assemblage' which defines the 'culture', – a polythetic approach, in other words – serves to overcome the difficulty. David Clarke (1968) discussed the problem in some detail, and finally established a hierarchy of attribute, artefact, assemblage, culture, culture-group and technocomplex. Ultimately however, and with some sophistication, culture as an entity (as defined and established by the archaeologist) is equated by Clarke with social groups as formulated by the ethnographer:

> An archaeological cultural assemblage is not identical in space or time distribution with a tribal group, a language, or a subrace and these sets themselves share different boundaries. Nevertheless, archaeological culture is most likely to have been the product of a group of people with a largely homogeneous tribal organisation, language system and breeding population – whether the people themselves recognised the set or not. The archaeological culture maps a real entity that really existed, marking real interconnection – that this entity is not identical to historical, political, linguistic or racial entities does not make it the less real or important. The archaeological entities reflect realities as important as those recognised by the traditional classifications of other disciplines; the entities in all these fields are equally real, equally arbitrary and simply different.

I suggest that the only solution is the total abandonment of the notion of the culture (and the 'phase' of the Midwestern taxonomic system) as recognisable archaeological units. For very often, while imagining that we are allowing real patterns to emerge from the

35

archaeological data – patterns which must, it is thought, betoken some social reality – we are instead imposing taxonomic categories upon the data which are purely constructs of our own devising. Of course we are at liberty to classify the material remains of the past in any way we choose, but the inference should be avoided that such arbitrary categories mean anything in terms of 'peoples' or 'societies', if these themselves are conceived as more than the arbitrary creations of the modern archaeologist.

For it is easy to show how spatial distributions, equivalent to the traditional cultural entities, can be generated by the archaeologist out of a continuum of change. If uniformities and similarities in artefact assemblage are viewed as the result of interactions between individuals, and if such interactions decrease in intensity uniformly with distance, each point will be most like its close neighbours. Consider the point P lying in a uniform plain, with its neighbours fairly regularly spaced around it. Similarity in terms of trait $C$ decreases with distance from P. At the same time the variables $A$ and $B$ vary uniformly across the plain with distance along the axes $x$ and $y$. If the excavator first digs at P and recovers its assemblage, he will subsequently learn that adjacent points have a broadly similar assemblage, which he will call 'the P culture'. Gradually its boundaries will be set up by further research, with the criterion that only those assemblages which attain a given threshold level of similarity with the finds from P qualify for inclusion. So a 'culture' is born, centring on P, the type site, whose bounds are entirely arbitrary, depending solely on the threshold level of similarity and the initial, fortuitous choice of P as the point of reference.

If the plain is not homogeneous, but there are in fact barriers to interaction, for instance mountains or water, the rate of change of similarity with distance will be modified, so that similarity clines will emerge. To the archaeologist the real (that is, taxonomically real) entities so observed will serve to confirm his definition of 'culture' and its equation with 'people' or 'society'. Of course it does not follow, simply because archaeologists can create arbitrary taxonomic units, that less arbitrary units may not be found. But if the question is firmly posed, it is clear that such entities could only maintain their unity or homogeneity through the persistence of interactions operating preferentially among their members. These interactions would not in general be operating with comparable intensity between one entity and its neighbour. Some of the archaeological units termed 'culture' are so large in extent that this intense sharing is questionable. One would wish to be assured that the

36

differences observed between the archaeological remains found at points P and Q are more than the result simply of diminished interaction resulting from distance or limited accessibility. Ian Hodder at Cambridge has been the first, I believe, to study archaeological distributions from this standpoint (Hodder and Orton 1976), and his approach is clearly a very fruitful one.

The archaeologist's interest clearly is not – or at least should not be – limited simply to the attenuating effects of distance upon human interactions. In attempting to say something more about human society, his interest must centre upon specially patterned interactions which are indicative of organisation, or the membership of some society or group.

Seen in this rather sceptical perspective, the notion of social group is seen urgently to require definition: it cannot be allowed to emerge from the archaeological data as an uncritical distribution of similar artefacts. And the idea of 'people' as deriving from social group begins to look a very doubtful one. One might well enquire, indeed, whether the notion of 'people' in the sense of a large group of broadly similar and related individuals and greater in size than individual community groups, is not itself dependent upon the existence in the world of large political units. The notion of 'one people', familiar from the modern nation state, can perhaps be traced back to the Romans, but it may not be necessary to take it very much further. Both Binford (1972) and Isaac (1972) have asked at what point in human development did 'ethnicity' come into the world. And very possibly social groups beyond the band level, with special interactions within them, may have developed during the palaeolithic. But to take this further, to suggest widespread, homogenous units of distinct and distinguishable 'peoples' prior to the emergence of very large political units or 'empires' may not be warranted. What is a people if it is not a political unit? The anthropologists who speak of 'tribes' may have the answer, but the archaeologist will ask what is the essential unitary nature of the tribe, if it is not a political unit (Fried 1968). The observed 'culture' defined by the archaeologist may arise from special interactions at the time in question due to social affiliation. It may even be observable as a result of past interactions within the area, even though that social affiliation has now broken down – this is what some writers mean by 'tradition'. But often it is no more than a reflection of diminishing interaction with distance.

The moral to be drawn from this discussion is not necessarily a pessimistic one, even if the taxonomic manipulation of artefact distributions can no longer be expected automatically to yield social or ethnic information. It is rather that to produce social answers we must formulate social questions. When we go ahead and do so the problem emerges in a very different light. We have to ask ourselves what we mean by social organisation – or rather what we choose to mean by it, since the discussion in the first section indicated that our choice may be something very different from that of the social anthroplogist, and it is at this point in the discussion that the possibility arises of breaking new ground, with the realisation that the traditional archaeological notion of social organisation may be as invalid as the traditional anthropological one is inappropriate.

The archaeologist may well be concerned to establish many things about early societies which the anthropologist will take entirely for granted. And the first of these could be, indeed should be, to identify units of analysis. The social anthropologist can avoid this problem on arrival to conduct his fieldwork by (a) asking 'Who are you? To what group do you belong?', and (b) requesting 'Take me to your leader'. Few anthropologists or archaeologists have recognised the fundamental nature of the assumptions which these procedures entail.

Is there in fact any area of administrative or 'ethnic' unity, beyond that of the individual settlement unit? What is its size? Does it occupy a specific territory? With boundaries? Is the community sedentary – over one year, over many years? Can it be subdivided into smaller social units? Is settlement dispersed or aggregated? What hierarchies of power, of prestige and of wealth exist within it? Is the administration – political, religious or economic – centralised at all? Do these functions overlap in a single place or person? What investment of labour and produce is devoted to the organisational and religious centres? By what means are status, power, wealth and sanctity expressed or symbolised? What degree of specialisation is there in these fields, as well as in agriculture and technology? What other kinds of interaction take place within it? Is the group affiliated with neighbouring groups by joint membership of any kind of association? Is it related to neighbouring groups by any position of dominance? What interactions take place with neighbouring groups outside the territory?

These indicate the kind of question which the archaeologist will wish to ask – and of course many of the answers would be self-evident to the field worker in a living society. In framing them it was no longer possible to avoid the idea of the group as in some sense an entity – the term is meaningless otherwise. This implies the assumption that, at least among living communities, societies or groups can be recognised that are not merely the product of interactions varying in intensity with distance yet otherwise unstructured. Because human beings are acutely aware of many social relationships I suggest that they will be explicitly aware of membership of such groups – these are therefore cognised entities, and in any given case a specific individual is either a member of a group or he is not. Clearly an individual can belong to several groups, but not without being aware of it. The kind of social group we are speaking of here is relevant to the notion of identity, to the 'Who are you?' question. So that operative groups, visible to the modern observer but not to the participant (e.g., 'middle income group', or group sharing a specific blood type) are not relevant. But for once we are not defeated by the evanescent, irrecoverable nature of past cognitive categories. For *it is precisely the recognition of the group that governs group behaviour.* When we are dealing with social groups their cognitive existence, recognised by those included and those excluded, reinforces their operational existence or may indeed create it. And the distinctive group behaviour – the differential nature of interactions with members of the group in distinction to those outside it – reinforces its cognitive recognition. It is this feedback mechanism that gives social groups their distinctiveness – for the group does not count as such if you cannot recognise it. (Even secret societies are no exception – considerable care is taken that their members should be mutually recognisable.) This being so, we ought to be able to see them, in favourable cases, in the archaeological record.

## Social Organisation and Social Groups

In what I have written so far there has perhaps been a preoccupation with the definition and reality of entities of supposed 'social groups'. The social anthropologist will remark that there is more to social anthropology than this, and may find the foregoing critique of the entities traditionally used by the archaeologist altogether unsurprising. Indeed it could be argued that many of the social aspects studied by the anthropologist could function without the recognition of groups at all.

The whole web of kinship relations, for instance, is often studied in terms of *rules* of behaviour operating within the specific area under discussion. There is no reason here why its bounds need be defined. We can envisage a network of local kin relationships extending indefinitely in all directions, accompanied by a gradual and fairly continuous change with distance in the rules of exchange. We could then contrast the practices in operation at points A and B without any need to consider the definition of entities.

This brings us right back to a fundamental question which should perhaps have been posed earlier: just what do we mean by 'social organisation' in the context of a study of its evolution? Clearly the term entails consideration of the whole field of human interactions – of languages and symbolic systems, of kinship, or resource allocation between individuals, of government and war, and of other forms of exchange. In each of these fields, entities or groups may be defined: language groups, kin groups, economic units, polities, sodalities, etc. Or in each of them the discussion may well proceed without any definition of such entities.

I would suggest that, in studying the evolution of social organisation, what we are in the broadest sense concerned with is the emergence of inhomogeneity. It is true that in the case of the hypothetical network mentioned above, there can be complete continuity, with one individual acting much like another, and we may nonetheless be concerned with the rules of behaviour, that is to say, with the social organisation of the system. But in a certain sense, however elaborate the rules of interaction may be, the lack of specialisation and differentiation of this network would lead us to regard it as existing at a low level of organisation. When we think of higher levels of organisation we are certainly thinking in terms of *differential interactions* among the individuals participating in the organisation. Of course these interactions can be of many different kinds, so that two individuals may interact strongly in one subsystem of society, as it were, and hardly at all in another. It is precisely when a number of individuals do interact fairly strongly in a number of different ways, and less strongly with others outside that number, that we can begin to speak in terms of a social group. I would suggest that it is difficult to imagine a social hierarchy of any kind without the effective fulfilment of this condition.

It remains to ask just what kind of group the archaeologist is likely to be interested in. And here the material nature of the archaeologist's finds does impose some restrictions. For we can only legitimately speak, as archaeologists, of activities which leave at least some discernible trace in the material record. Prehistoric linguistic groups, for instance, cannot be recovered archaeologically unless there is some kind of correlation between language and the material world. One aspect of organisation which is very pertinent here is administration: it implies both government (with the exercise of power) and resource allocation. Both imply some partition of the world into persons and resources governed or allocated, and those which fall out of the control of the administration, and hence by their very nature some kind of delineation of an entity, the polity.

An increasing number of archaeologists have come to rely on the 'neoevolutionary' classification of social organisation in order to consider human societies. The hierarchy of band, tribe, chiefdom and state (Service 1962) has recommended itself to many workers concerned to make generalisations of some kind about culture change, or to fit specific societies under study into some more general perspective. The notion of chiefdom in particular has helped to fill the gap in the workings of earlier anthropologists between the tribe and the state.

These classificatory terms have been criticised by some, either because they are not observable from the archaeological record (e.g. Leach 1973) or because they have no real existence (Fried 1968) or again because the hierarchy is thought to imply some evolutionary necessity (Tringham 1974), an implication which those who have used these terms would reject. Like the terms in any classificatory scheme they are constructs which are justified if found useful in practice. And their application to the prehistoric past is greatly strengthened by the effectiveness with which they have been applied to living societies. Certainly they appear less regularly sequential than classifications with a strong chronological component such as Palaeolithic, Neolithic, Bronze Age, etc, or Formative, Classic, Florescent, Decadent, etc. They certainly supersede the older social categories of savagery, barbarism and civilisation, which later took on both chronological and economic/technological overtones in a confusing way. Childe sometimes used barbarism as the equivalent of Neolithic-to-Bronze Age where today we find it convenient to speak of hunter/gatherer bands and agricultural tribes.

The real operational difficulty of recognising these forms of society in many cases should not be underestimated, however – which is not the same as Leach's assertion that to do so is logically not possible. And it should not be overlooked that increasingly they are being distinguished in terms of settlement pattern. For the sake of argument, and to stimulate discussion, I would like to suggest here that tighter and more effective definitions can be obtained by replacing the band/tribe/chiefdom/state hierarchy *in toto* with a classification based on the spatial arrangement of society.

The term band, for instance, is recognisable by its small size – normally less than 100 persons – and by the impermanence of its place of residence. (For some reason no one calls a sedentary village of the same number of persons, living in complete isolation, a band – it is automatically considered 'tribal', generally without the application of any positive criteria to justify that term.)

And at the other end of the spectrum the term state has always proved almost impossible to define – just as difficult indeed as 'city' and 'civilisation', with which it generally overlaps. At a recent conference in Santa Fe it proved very difficult to hit on any criteria which can be recognised archaeologically, since the one clear criterion proposed by Service is not a practicable one, 'the presence of that special form of control, the consistent threat of force by a body of persons legitimately constituted to use it' (Service 1962, 171). Instead both Wright (1978) and Johnson (1975) suggested that the most characteristic feature was a three-tier hierarchy of control, which is best seen archaeologically in the trimodal settlement size distribution of city, town and village.

Turning now to chiefdoms, I suggest that their most distinctive feature in the archaeological records is the presence of central places. For the central person who is the permanent chief is generally situated at a central place, even if this may be a periodic one, either in the sense of rotating (i.e., changing regularly in location) or in the sense of operating only for part of the year. Most of the Polynesian chiefdoms were of the latter kind. But the central place was usually dignified by special buildings pertaining to the chief, and sometimes by monumental ones relating to ceremonies of life or death. As Service remarks, chiefdoms are distinguished from tribal societies 'by the presence of centres which co-ordinate economic, social and religious activities' (Service 1962, 173).

One cannot go so far as to assert that those societies which are not organised as chiefdoms or states, or with comparable complexity, entirely lack central places. But it is difficult to point to permanent central places with a permanent population which do not, in fact, exercise a central administrative authority over the territory which they serve.

As for the tribe, the concept remains archaeologically undefined. Steward (1955) has stigmatised 'tribal society' as an 'ill-defined catchall', and Service's definition is perhaps the least satisfactory of any in his hierarchy. It gives little clue as to how the limits of the tribe in space might be ascertained: 'Pan-tribal sodalities make a tribe a tribe, for if they did not exist then there is nothing but a series

42

of bands, more affluent than hunters and gatherers, but still bands, with only intermarriage between certain ones providing any unity' (Service 1962, 115). Nowhere do we find a clear picture of the nature of those interactions, taking place within the tribe but not across its boundaries, which work to maintain and enhance its unity and homogeneity. Until we have some inkling of what we are searching for in the archaeological record we shall not find it, for, as I have indicated above, the simple fall-off in interaction with distance is sufficient to allow the generation of 'cultures' by the archaeological taxonomist which need have no cognitive meaning.

Fried's criticisms of the concept of tribe have not been adequately answered, and his suggestion that 'most tribes seem to be secondary phenomena . . . the product of processes stimulated by the appearances of relatively highly organised societies amidst other societies which are organised much more simply' (Fried 1968, 15) is paralleled by the suggestion above that the notion of 'a people' is largely the product of modern (or early imperial) nationalist thought.

Goody's discussion in *The Social Organisation of the LoWiili* (Goody 1967) is particularly useful here, for he makes it clear that the recognition of tribal entities among the Dagari-speaking peoples is largely the act of outside observers taking relative terms as fixed, tribal designations: the diffuseness of the political organisation gives rise to the lack of distinct tribal nomenclature. Such designations as exist, however, arise not primarily from a consciousness of unity, which would surely lead to a recognised name within the tribe itself, but 'from a consciousness of the differences between their own institutions and those of neighbouring peoples' (Goody 1967, 113). Goody shows clearly (chapter 5) that the basic territorial division of the land in the region is the 'parish', the ritual area associated with a particular earth shrine. The inhabitants of this area may be described as a political group, and it is clear that in any discussion of social organisation the 'parish' must be a fundamental unit of discussion, although the members of several parishes can meet at a market for purposes of exchange. The case of the LoWiili is a particularly interesting one for the archaeologist, illustrating as it does the diffuse nature of a supposed social grouping above that of the operative and cognised territorial units. The 'tribe' is a dangerous concept for the archaeologist.

This critique is not offered in a negative sense however, since the 'evolutionary' hierarchy at least gives us something to compensate for the failure of archaeology to talk about social organisation at all until very recently. A discussion in spatial terms is operationally more convenient and perhaps no less apposite for social description. For is not the most important feature of a chiefdom the existence of a central person, resident at a central place, whether this be periodic or permanent? And is not the distinguishing feature of the state generally accepted as the existence of a permanent hierarchical structure of administration and authority – a structure generally reflected in a hierarchy of central places, so that between the major centre (or state capital) and the minor residence unit (or village) there is at least one intermediate settlement and administrative unit, the regional centre?

## Polity and Space

The spatial structure of society has never been adequately explored. Locational analysts have developed sophisticated techniques in modern geography for investigating settlement distributions, but their implications in terms of social organisation have not been investigated. Anthropologists have written of territoriality, but focused upon the behavioural analogy between non-human primate behaviour and the most closely analogous human societies, generally choosing nonsedentary societies. And thinkers such as Eliade (1965) have commented on the symbolic aspects of space without, however, using it in the study of society as a whole.

I suggest that there is a whole range of generalisations to be made, many of them exceedingly obvious (and no doubt formulated in isolation often enough) which together might lay the foundations for a general study of human social organisation in a manner that is operationally explicit, so that it can, in favourable cases, be applied to past societies as well as to living ones. Some of these possibilities have been indicated in a number of useful articles by Trigger (1972 and 1974).

The presentation offered here, like the whole of this paper, is provisional. But I hope it may serve as a basis for discussion.

(1) *The basic social group is defined by the habitual association of persons within a territory*. These are the persons who live together throughout the year, what Murdock terms the community, 'the maximal group of persons who normally reside together in face-to-face association' (Murdock 1949). Among hunters this may be a group of families who normally camp together, i.e., a 'band'. Among sedentary communities with fairly aggregate settlement it will be a village, or in some areas such as south Italy without villages, a town. With a dispersed settlement pattern it may even be a household. It is often possible to subdivide the group into families

44

or households, but these live at the same location: if they split up for part of the year the smaller units so formed would be regarded as the basic social group.

This definition implies two statements about human behaviour. First that there are such habitual associations. And second that human behaviour is territorially organised. This operational assertion carries with it cognitive implications: 'L'installation dans un territoire équivaut à la fondation d'un monde' (Eliade 1965, 43).

Perhaps the most fundamental assumption of all, however, is that the individual can belong to only one such basic social group at a time, whatever his affiliations to groups of other kinds.

(2) *Human social organisation is segmentary in nature: human spatial organisation is therefore cellular and modular.* This is to say that the basic social group, with its territory, is repeated in space, so that a simple cellular pattern is generated. The boundaries of the units need not, however, be particularly well defined: the territory may rather consist of a 'core area' with a 'development of a territorial gradient from the 'core' to the 'periphery' of their home range' (Flannery 1972a). What is being asserted here, however, is that the essential unit, the basic group, whatever its precise nature, is repeated spatially. There is, of course, no *a priori* reason why this should be so – an entire range of different kinds of such basic groups could live in juxtaposition, each quite unlike the others in its scale or internal structure. But this is not the way it works in practice. The adjacent units do have comparable organisation and also comparable size – which is the implication of the term modular.

This modular feature of the segments, that in a given region the territories are of approximately the same size is a feature not generally discussed, but appears in fact to be one of the most fundamental features of human social and spatial organisation. It has been demonstrated for the Australian Aborigines by Birdsell (1973) who has shown that the modular size of 'hordes' in Australia correlated with rainfall in a regular way.

Binford (personal communication) is at present working on more general regularities in the territorial group sizes of hunters and gatherers. But clearly the concept bears investigation in more general terms, since a modular arrangement is evident among sedentary village societies likewise, and the idea is inherent in most Central Place studies, although rarely brought out explicitly.

Archaeologically the important aspect of this observation is that it can in fact be investigated. Studies of settlement spacing of basic groups have in fact been undertaken (e.g. MacNeish 1964), although clearly there is a risk of error when the settlements considered are not precisely contemporary (cf. Ellison and Harriss 1972).

Birdsell's work promotes the thought that we may be dealing not primarily with a territorial module but a population one – that is to say that it is the size of population of the groups which remains stable rather than the area they occupy. The two will be the same only when ecological conditions are constant. There may be underlying social reasons for such modular size, that is to say thresholds beyond which the group population cannot grow without a change in the nature and structure of the group (cf. Forge 1972).

Alternatively there may be mechanisms which tend to keep the territories and population sizes of groups in a given region at about the same size one-to-another, without discriminating in favour of a particular size range. Rowlands (1972) has discussed the relation between territoriality and defence, and one can envisage factors which might work toward parity among the social units (and hence for a *local* modular size).

Archaeologically this pattern is a very frequently recurring one, discernible in almost every case where there are sedentary communities. When the settlement is aggregated into villages, their spacing and placing can be viewed in these terms. Such a patterning may certainly be discerned, for example, over much of prehistoric Europe. The notion of modular organisation, for what has been termed the Early State Module (esm) has been discussed further in a recent paper (Renfrew 1975; see pp.94–101 below).

(3) *Basic social groups do not exist in isolation, but affiliate into larger groups, meeting together at periodic intervals.* The affiliated groups are generally adjacent to each other, so that their territories, taken together, may be regarded as forming a larger, continuous and uninterrupted territory.

Among hunting groups the meeting place itself may vary from time to time (Birdsell 1973). Among sedentary communities the place of meeting may move in rotation (cf. the Kyaka). Often it is a permanent meeting place, however – that is to say the meeting always takes place at the same location, and it must then rank as a central place. (If the meeting takes place only on specific occasions through the year it can be regarded as a periodic central place.) Moreover it is a feature of many societies that they express the uniqueness of this location by symbolic means, sometimes by monumental construction, since the location may have a religious significance as well as expressing the affiliation of groups itself. Once

46

again the observed operational reality has further cognitive over-tones: 'Notre monde se situe toujours autour d'un centre' (Eliade 1965).

This is precisely the situation described in detail for the LoWiili by Goody (1967, chapter 5 and fig.6), where the Earth Shrine is the focal point of the polity, and the principal feature of its territory. In archaeologically favourable cases these constructions are of a durable nature – in the Tuamotu islands of Polynesia the *marae* is the focal point of the lineage territory (Ottino 1967), and archaeological research has produced patterns in location (Garanger 1966) which even without the ethnographic observations available would have been suggestive of a cellular and modular territorial arrangement and social partitioning (see pp.178–80 below).

Analogous spatial patterning has been noted among the collective tombs of Neolithic northern Europe (see chapter 8 of this book), and a segmentary social grouping suggested in consequence. The monuments are there viewed as the traditional ceremonial focal point in a territory where household location is either dispersed or shifting every few years. The modular aspect of the patterning is reflected in the approximately equal size of territories, or more often in the approximately equal area of arable land within each, suggesting approximate equality of population. In some cases, as Fleming has pointed out (Fleming 1972) the interior division of the tombs is itself cellular, reflecting perhaps the division of the territory into several households, or other sub-division, each of which would have access to one part of the tomb.

(4) *Human society is hierarchical in nature: human spatial organisation is therefore stratified*. This generalisation effectively follows from the cellular pattern discussed above. Once the cells are contiguous, sharing common boundaries, they can no longer all expand territorially simply by increasing in size. It would, of course, be possible for some to expand at the expense of others, so that there would be fewer, larger cells, each organised just as before. And no doubt examples can be found of such aggrandisement without further organisation or complexity.

Instead, however development occurs by the union of a number of basic cells or segments into the kind of affiliation indicated above with the emergence of a new and (in the sense of our stratification) higher organisation to deal with the consequences of union, *while retaining elements of the former cellular pattern*. These observations hold whether the union occurs by direct conquest, in which case the conqueror takes over the central administrative functions of the

47

conquered group, or by peaceful assimilation or symbiosis. In each case the union of a number of cells into a higher order cell implies the emergence of a higher order centre, but the lower order centres normally survive.

And growth continues in this way in stratified order, the cellular units at each level of organisation together forming the sub-units for the next with the emergence of a higher order centre, usually located at the traditional centre of one of the constituent subunits.

Already this process is seen in operation in embryo among the Tiv (Bohannan 1954), an example worth citing because it has been described in explicitly spatial terms. Evidently the process of urbanisation, although it is conventionally considered primarily in terms of the urban centre itself, can perhaps be seen as appropriately of territorial amalgamation of this kind, although the importance of increasing population density should not be overlooked in any discussion of territorial size.

(5) *The effective polity, the highest order social unit, may be identified by the scale and distribution of central places.* In the stratified ordering of cellular territories, the individual person has allegiance at a number of levels – to the basic group (the community), to the logical region focused on its main town, and to the higher order realm comprised of several regions, focused upon its capital. He is a member of each, but he is a *citizen* of the highest order polity. For it is the central organisation of this polity, usually its central person, who wields supreme power. This is the highest level of society, in M.A. Smith's words: 'A group of people ackowledging a single system of law, and in some degree organised to resist attack from other such societies' (Smith 1955). This is the highest social unit effective in political terms, which means in military terms.

Now in order to recognise such a unit archaeologically, one approach is certainly to study the symbolism which the central authority employs to express its power. For instance the extent of the Roman Empire, if it were not known to archaeologists, could be established by plotting the distribution of monumental Imperial inscriptions. This is certainly more effective than trying to follow boundaries (which may not always be delineated by a Hadrian's Wall) or attempting to follow artefact uniformities. For we saw in the last section how archaeologists can create 'cultures' where no social group need have existed. And equally the boundaries of existing social groups may be blurred by interactionsacross them.

A feasible alternative is to study the hierarchy of central places, establishing first the approximate size of the highest order centres.

48

Assuming these can safely be identified as such (and here the symbolic evidence may be required as corroboration) their distribution marks the centres of the highest order cellular territories, that is of the polities. And some attempt can be made at reconstructing the subsidiary cells of this stratified arrangement.

Precisely such a study has been undertaken by Johnson in Mesopotamia, with this underlying implication that spatial organisation is the counterpart of social organisation. Spatial hierarchy has been examined in Britain by Hodder and Hassall (1971), although the social implications were less obvious since the centre of the polity was by then outside the British Isles, in Rome. It was clearly brought out in the Tehuacan valley by MacNeish in a pioneering study (MacNeish 1964), and in the Maya lowlands by Flannery, Hammond and Marcus (1972b, 1972 and 1973). The existence of a social hierarchy in Neolithic south Britain has been postulated on the basis of a hierarchy of places (see p.236 below).

The modular arrangement is apparently reproduced at each level in the hierarchy, including the highest, so that for each polity, with its centre (or 'capital'), there will be an analogous one with a contiguous territorial boundary, until the polity is so large that it occupies all the available land of the land mass (i.e. continent) or island group where it is situated.

In asserting the widespread nature of the modular arrangement it is not of course claimed that all the neighbours of a polity need be unified into territories of a comparably higher order – this would be to assert the worldwide nature of a specific social organisation at a given time. But this is, nonetheless, a general tendency over fairly large regions.

The social and political aspects of spatial hierarchy are frequently overlooked by geographers, but it does seem broadly true that the polities of the world each boast a capital city, and that within broad regions these capitals could be recognised by their size and relation to subsidiary centres, as well as by the attendant symbolism, without prior information about national boundaries. (Artificial capitals such as Canberra or Washington D.C. clearly present a specific problem, foreshadowed by the summer palaces of early emperors, but again it is a problem which a consideration of symbolism would help to solve.)

(6) *Special interactions between polities undoubtedly take place, creating uniformities in artefact distribution, and require closer study: such uniformities in themselves do not document societies or 'peoples'.* This is a re-statement of the critique of the normative

approach discussed above. Generalisation 3 (above) contains the germ of an idea, however, that the highest units of the social hierarchy (i.e., the polities) sometimes enter some kind of affiliation without losing any element of their autonomy. This may have been the case in the early Greek city leagues, (Fustel de Coulanges 1873) and at a lower level may be true of tribes which are recognised as such without sharing any central tribal organisation whatever.

Clearly the tribe still presents a problem, which the archaeologist alone cannot be expected to solve if the anthropologist remains in doubt about precisely what a tribe is. I suggest, however, that the concrete approach outlined here, of considering first effective polities and territories, together with their hierarchical arrangement socially and spatially, may be useful, since it is an approach which has meaning both for the archaeologist and the anthropologist. This will leave for further examination the nature of the 'tribal' links across and between polities and territories – the sodalities and other affiliations and the linguistic affinities. It may be that in some cases the symbolism used to express such affiliations may offer the hope of archaeological interpretation.

The procedure adopted here has been to risk certain generalisations about the spatial behaviour of social groups – that is to say as groups recognised as such by their participant members, and recognised as operational by external observers. The consideration has been limited to groups whose members are spatially contiguous, so that the group can be delimited spatially. Clearly other kinds of group could be considered, but they are less easy to approach archaeologically, and in any case it is suggested that polities are indeed bounded units of this kind. If these generalisations can be accepted as holding – broad as they are – for human societies as a whole, then they do offer the possibility for the archaeologist of proceeding from observations of spatial organisation to conclusions about social organisation.

No doubt these specific formulations can be questioned on a number of grounds. But unless some such formulations as these can be made, I see little hope of using archaeological data to suggest conclusions which would interest the anthropologist. Of course it may be argued that the kind of conclusions suggested here are altogether unremarkable, and the generalisations attempted above highly banal. Nonetheless, if they are accepted, they can lead to a clear and simple picture of the growth of some aspects of social organisation, a picture which so far has been outlined only in a few specific areas of study, especially Mesoamerica and Mesopotamia.

Nor should the practical difficulties be overlooked that are inherent in the eliciting of spatial patterning from archaeological data. Incomplete survey evidence, and the difficulties of setting up a chronology sufficiently exact to identify settlements occupied contemporaneously present real problems. And some of the necessary procedures have hardly yet been worked out: there is so far no general treatment of the problems involved in the ordering of places into a hierarchy from archaeological evidence. This may be effected by a consideration of size (Johnson 1972), of labour invested in their construction, of functional aspects such as defences (e.g. Romano-British walled towns; Hodder and Hassall 1972), of monumental ceremonial centres (e.g. Maya centres; Marcus 1973), of the finding of artefacts interpreted as symbolically relevant (e.g. clay nails in Mesopotamia; Wright 1972), and no doubt in other ways.                                                                [1974]

## Bibliography

Binford, L. R. (1962) Archaeology as anthropology, *American Antiquity*, 28, 217–25.
— (1965) Archaeological systematics and the study of culture process, *American Antiquity*, 31, 203–10.
— (1972) Paradigms and the current state of Palaeolithic research, in D. L. Clarke, ed., *Models in Archaeology*, London.
Birdsell, J. R. (1973) A basic demographic unit, *Current Anthropology*, 14, 337–56.
Bohannan, P. (1954) The migration and expansion of the Tiv, *Africa*, II, 4, Fig. 1.
Childe, V. G. (1929) *The Danube in Prehistory*, Oxford, v–vi.
Clarke, D. L. (1968) *Analytical Archaeology*, London, 358–65.
— ed. (1972) *Models in Archaeology*, London.
Eliade, M. (1965) *Le sacré et le profane*, Paris.
Ellison, A. and J. Harriss (1972) Settlement and land use in the prehistory and early history of southern England, in Clarke, ed. (1972).
Flannery, K. (1972a) The origins of the village as a settlement type in Mesoamerica and the Near East, in Ucko, Tringham and Dimbleby, eds. (1972) 28.
— (1972b) The cultural evolution of civilisations, *Annual Review of Ecology and Systematics*, 3, 399.
Fleming, A. (1972) Vision and design, approaches to ceremonial monument typology, *Man.*, 7, 57–72.
Forge, A. (1972) Normative factors in the settlement size of neolithic cultivators, in Ucko, Tringham and Dimbleby, eds. (1972).
Fried, M. (1968) On the concept of 'Tribe' and 'Tribal Society', in J. Helm, ed., *Essays on the Problem of the Tribe*, American Ethnological Society.
Fustel de Coulanges, N. D. (1873) *The Ancient City*, London.
Garanger, J. (1966) Recherches archeologiques a Rangiroa, *Journal de la Société des Océanistes*, 22, Fig. 1.

Goody, J. (1967) *The Social Organisation of the LoWiili*, Oxford.
Hammond, N. D. C. (1972) Locational models and the site of Lubaantun, in Clarke, ed. (1972).
Harris, M. (1968a) *The Rise of Anthropological Theory*, 571 ff.
— (1968b) Comments, in L. R. and S. R. Binford, eds., *New Perspectives in Archaeology*, Chicago, 360–1.
Hodder, I. and Hassall, M. (1971) The non-random spacing of Romano-British walled towns, *Man*, 6.
Hodder, I. R. and C. Orton (1976) *Spatial Analysis in Archaeology*, Cambridge.
Isaac, G. Ll. (1972) Early phases of human behaviour, in Clarke, ed. (1972).
Johnson, G. (1972) A test of central place theory in archaeology, in Ucko, Tringham and Dimbleby, eds. (1972).
— (1975) Locational analysis and the investigation of Uruk local exchange systems, in J. A. Sabloff and C. Lamberg-Karlovsky, eds., *Ancient Civilisation and Trade*, Albuquerque, 285–340.
Leach, E. R. (1973) Concluding address, in C. Renfrew, ed., *The Explanation of Culture Change: Models in Prehistory*, London.
— (1974) Reply to Dr Mellor, *Cambridge Opinion*, 95, February 1974, 73.
MacNeish, R. S. (1964) Ancient Mesoamerican civilisation, *Science*, 143, 531–7.
Marcus, J. (1973) Territorial organisation of the Lowland Classic Maya, *Science*, 180, 911–16.
Murdock, C. P. (1949) *Social Structure*, New York, 79.
Ottino, P. (1967) Early Ati of the Western Tuamotus, in G. A. Highland *et al.*, eds., *Polynesian Culture History*, Honolulu, 451–82.
Rappaport, R. A. (1969) Sanctity and adaptation, paper presented at the Wenner-Gren Symposium no. 44, *The Moral and Aesthetic Structure of Human Adaptation*.
Renfrew, C. (1973a) Monuments, mobilisation and social organisation in neolithic Wessex, in C. Renfrew, ed., *The Explanation of Culture Change. Models in Prehistory*, London, 543.
— (1973b) *Before Civilisation*, London, figs 29 and 30.
— (1975) Trade as action at a distance, in J. A. Sabloff and C. C. Lamberg-Karlovsky, eds., *Ancient Civilisation and Trade*, Albuquerque, 12.
Rouse, I. (1972) *A Systematic Approach to Prehistory*, New York, 62.
Rowlands, M. J. (1972) Defence – a factor in the organisation of settlements, in Ucko, Tringham and Dimbleby, eds. (1972).
Service, E. R. (1962) *Primitive Social Organisation*, New York.
— (1971) *Cultural Evolutionism*, New York, 157.
Smith, M. A. (1955) The limitations of inference in archaeology, *Archaeological Newsletter*, 6, 3–7.
Steward, J. H. (1955) *Theory of Culture Change*, Urbana, 44 and 55.
Trigger, B. (1972) Determinants of urban growth in pre-industrial societies, in Ucko, Tringham and Dimbleby, eds. (1972), 575–99.

Trigger, B. (1974) The archaeology of government, *World Archaeology*, 6, 95–100.

Tringham, R. (1974) Comments on Prof. Renfrew's paper, in C. B. Moore, ed., *Reconstructing Complex Societies*, 88.

Ucko, P. J., R. Tringham and G. W. Dimbleby, eds (1972) *Man, Settlement and Urbanism*, London.

Willey, G. R. and P. Phillips (1958) *Method and Theory in American Archaeology*, Chicago, 49.

Wright, H. T. (1972) A consideration of interregional exchange in Greater Mesopotamia: 4000–3000 BC, in E. N. Wilmsen, ed., *Social Exchange and Interaction*, Ann Arbor.

Wright, H. T. (1978) Towards an explanation of the origin of the state, in R. Cohen and E. R. Service, eds., *Origins of the State*, Philadelphia, 49–68.

# EXPLORING DOMINANCE:
# PREDICTING POLITIES
# FROM CENTRES

## ( WITH ERIC V. LEVEL )

*

Sociopolitical organisation is not the same as economic organisation, and social space differs from the spatial ordering of markets
and other spatial features of market economy. This chapter starts
with a specific underlying problem in archaeology: the reconstruction or prediction (retrodiction) of sociopolitical organisation from
archaeological data. How can we use settlement remains, as documented archaeologically, to formulate the social and political configurations which helped to generate them, and were influenced by
them?

The investigation hints at regularities in the spatial patterning of
society which remain to be explored, and in particular in the absolute size of the political territory which an autonomous centre of a
given population size can expect to exploit. Such cross-cultural
regularities, if documented, would have a significance well beyond
the confines of archaeology.

The general background to the problem has been treated in the
previous paper (chapter 2) and six axioms developed:

1) The human social group is defined by the habitual association
of persons within a territory.

2) Human social organisation is segmentary in nature: human
spatial organisation is therefore cellular and modular.

3) Basic social groups do not exist in isolation, but affiliate
together into larger groups, meeting together at periodic intervals.

4) Human society is often hierarchical in nature: human spatial
organisation is therefore stratified.

5) The effective polity, the highest order social unit, may be
identified by the scale and distribution of central places.

6) Special interactions between polities undoubtedly take place,
creating uniformities in artefact distribution: such uniformities in

themselves do not document societies or peoples.

Our aim in undertaking the work discussed here was to investigate the fifth of these in particular.

It should be stated clearly that our outlook owes little to classical central place theory of the geographers (Christaller 1933, Lösch 1954). It is an alternative approach to the question of human spatial organisation, making none of the assumptions about 'economic man' and his behaviour (many of them no doubt entirely valid) underlying central place theory. It has much more in common with the perspective of Soja (1971).

The following assumptions are made:

1) Polities have continuous territorial jurisdiction over their domains, without intervening parcels of land.

2) A piece of land is normally under the jurisdiction of a single autonomous authority (and, where appropriate, its deputies within a hierarchical structure). This does not necessarily exclude areas of no-man's land, where territorial authority is not exercised.

3) 'Capitals,' the autonomous administrative centres of independent sociopolitical polities, are in general the largest settlement or administrative sites within the territories of their polities. (Cases in which the 'capital,' the seat of administration of the polity, is not the largest settlement or administrative centre, often reflect clearly identifiable special factors: most of them are artificial creations, summer palaces, or federal capitals reflecting the rather sophisticated device of a voluntary association of states.)

4) There is some positive correlation between the size of the autonomous 'capital' centre (whether measured by area or by population) and the territorial area of the polity over which it has control.

We make no initial assumption about the precise relationship indicated in assumption 4 (or 'hypothesis' 4). It should be particularly noted that we do *not* assume that settlements above a given arbitrary size all rank as autonomous centres whereas those below do not. In this respect our analysis differs fundamentally from that of most archaeologists using central place considerations, including Johnson (1972 and 1975). Likewise the writings of Berry (1961) and Crumley (1976) concerning the primate city, although of very real interest and relevance, do not focus upon precisely the problem we consider.

Our investigation is limited at present to sedentary societies: the formulation, as stated here, is not applicable to nomadic or other mobile groups.

The model is applied in the first instance at a given time: it is static. But when successive time points in a settlement system are considered, and changing political configurations and boundaries predicted, it becomes dynamic. Indeed the model could be linked with some procedure to predict the growth of centres (not attempted here) to foretell changing political boundaries and the conflicts that accompany them.

## Problems in Reconstructing the Territories of Polities

Consider the landscape of autonomous polities, each with at least one permanent settlement within its territorial boundary. The existence of some measure of territoriality is assumed, although the boundaries could well be 'fuzzy' (for fuzzy sets cf. Zadeh 1965) with overlapping at territorial extremes (cf. Soja 1971, fig. 8). These polities may range from relatively simple acephalous societies whose principal settlement is a single village to highly complex nation states with populations measured in millions.

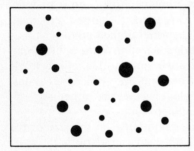

*Figure* 1. A settlement distribution. The size of settlement is proportional to the area of the dot.

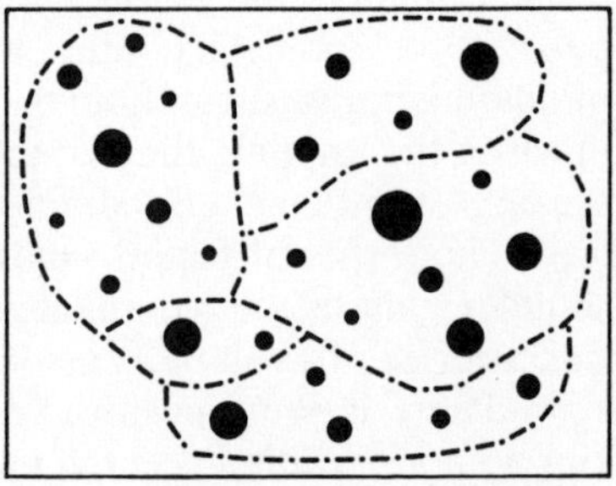

*Figure* 2. Political divisions associated with the settlement distribution of figure 1. Territorial boundaries are indicated by the broken lines.

We imagine a settlement distribution (figure 1) in which there are several settlements within the confines of each polity. In the archaeological case, let us suppose that no prior evidence remains for the political organisation or the arrangement of territories (figure 2). The problem is to reach some reconstruction of these.

If the archaeological sites were in contemporary use (and this is an important condition), a first approach might be to construct Thiessen polygons around each (figure 3). Each piece of land would then be allocated the jurisdiction of the settlement nearest to it. This ignores, rightly or wrongly, the size of the centres as well as any

hierachical arrangement among them. Several examples of such a
procedure may be found in the literature (e.g., Renfrew 1973, 133),
all assuming, explicitly or implicitly, the absence of hierarchy.

This procedure can be modified, for instance by means of weighted Thiessen polygons, so that the territorial area is dependent on
the size of the centre (cf. Hogg 1971).

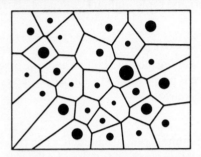

*Figure* 3. Unweighted Thiessen polygons giving a notional territorial
division for the settlement pattern of figure 1. The archaeologist will
often draw such a map as a provisional first attempt to reconstruct the
territorial divisions of figure 2 from settlement data.

So far, however, no account is taken of *dominance*. For only in
the most strictly acephalous societies are there no sites which are
subordinate to others in the political or administrative hierarchy.
But how are we to decide which sites dominate which? The opposite
extreme to that seen in figure 3 would be to assume that the largest
centre dominates all others, giving a single unified polity. The
solution offered by some workers (cf. Johnson 1975) is to take sizes
of centres in rank order, in the hope of finding some discrete
separation between large (viewed as dominant, independent capitals) and small (seen as subordinate, second- or third-order locations). But in many cases, as envisaged earlier, this just does not
work. To take an example from modern Europe, the population of
Belgrade, the capital of Yugoslavia, is less than that of the seventh
largest centre in the United Kingdom. Standard geographical extensions of the rank–size rule are not in practice appropriate. What
if there are no convenient breaks between first-and second-order
centres, nor any 'primate' capitals, larger by an order of magnitude
than their nearest rivals within the polity?

The answer lies in considering dominance within a spatial context, rather than in isolation in terms of size alone. It is necessary to
assert some relationship of size and distance, whereby the larger

dominates the smaller if the distance between them is sufficiently small, whereas the smaller retains autonomy if that distance is great. In effect we assume some law of monotonic decrement (cf. p.136 below) for political influence, and hence for the dominance of capital centres. We assert that some such relationship everywhere held until the development of near-instantaneous communication methods (radio) and rapid, militarily effective air transport.

## The XTENT Model

As a trial formulation, and nothing more is claimed here, we assume that the influence of a centre is proportional to a function of its size, and declines linearly with distance:

$$I = f(C) - k \cdot d \quad (I \geq 0) \tag{1}$$

where $I$ is a measure of the potential political influence of a centre at a location $x$, $C$ is a measure of the size of that centre, $d$ is the distance between $x$ and the centre, and $k$ is a constant.

Any location $x$ will fall within the territorial jurisdiction of the polity whose centre exercises the greatest influence at $x$. In particular, if the location $x$ is the location of a centre $C_2$, a neighbouring centre $C_1$ will dominate location $x$ and thus $C_2$ if $I_1 > I_2$ at location $x$; that is, if

$$f(C_1) - f(C_2) > k \cdot d_{1,2} \tag{2}$$

where $d_{1,2}$ is the distance between the two centres.

The position is seen in figure 4. The influence of each centre is indicated on the $y$ axis, and declines linearly with distance from the centre, reaching zero at the point where $f(C) = k \cdot d$. The second centre, $C_2$, by virtue of its position, is subordinate to $C_1$, while $C_3$, which is the same size as $C_2$, remains autonomous. The more distant centre $C_4$, although actually the smallest in size, likewise remains autonomous. There is an area of no-man's land between the territories of $C_4$ and $C_5$.

We have found it convenient to think of this as a 'tent pole' model, the dominance of a centre being comparable to a radially symmetrical bell-tent with the size of the centre governing the height of the central pole (figure 5). Those smaller settlements whose own tents can be pitched entirely within the bell-tent of their larger neighbour are dominated by that neighbour. Those whose central pole would protrude beyond the surface of the tent are the centres of autonomous polities.

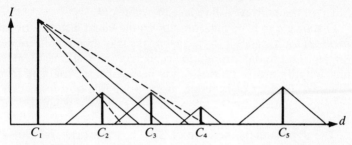

*Figure* 4. The XTENT model, with influence of centre as ordinate and distance as abscissa. Five centres are shown along a single line, the size of each indicated by a thick vertical line. The radius of domination for each is given by the intersection of the solid line with the $I = 0$ axis (the dashed line indicates the effect of varying the slope). Note how $C_2$ is entirely dominated by $C_1$ whereas $C_4$, although smaller in size, has its own independent territory.

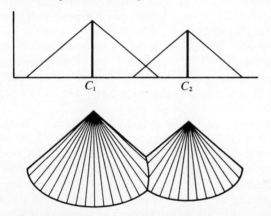

*Figure* 5. The XTENT model, with (*above*) distance along a single line joining two centres (as in figure 4) and (*below*) a three-dimensional sketch showing how the influence exerted by the two centres may be represented by two intersecting radially symmetrical bell-tents.

This formulation, which we claim as the simplest conceivable approach to the problem of dominance, without the prior assumption of specific hierarchical levels, allows us to work with a single variable, $k$, the slope of the fall-out of influence (i.e., of the tent).

It is a central tenet of our approach that the value of $k$ is not assumed, but is to be investigated empirically until general rules for its size can be formulated. It is at once inherently obvious that development in transport facilities, such as the introduction of the horse or the railway, will reduce the value of $k$.

Distance $d$ may be measured as simple linear distance, or *transformed* (for instance into travel time) to take account of varieties of terrain. Our initial formulation considers political control on land, and initially makes no distinction between terrestrial and marine distance. Further elaboration, using a suitable transformation for marine distance, would allow this over-simple assumption to be adjusted.

The approximate measure of 'size' is a practical archaeological problem to be approached empirically in each case. If figures were available for population, this might be the best measure. Alternatively, area of settlement may be used, although this presents several practical problems familiar to archaeologists. Other possibilities would be the number of coins issued by a mint (if a polity may contain more than one mint centre), the size of ceremonial monuments at the centre, or any other plausible construct from the archaeological data. Clearly the validity of each measure has to be critically evaluated for each case.

The other element of choice, in addition to the value of $k$, concerns the function $f(C)$. We have worked with the formulation $f(C) = C^{\alpha}$, experimenting with different values of the exponent $\alpha$, and measuring $C$ in terms of either population (known) or area (estimated).

The most convenient allocation of territories to centres develops naturally from this model. Centres or settlements that have been 'dominated' by others have no independent territory (at this level of analysis). Any location is assigned to the centre whose influence upon it, as defined earlier, is greatest. If this location is not dominated by any centre (i.e., the location does not lie under any tent), then it is left politically unassigned: the location is in 'no-man's land.'

Boundaries then occur in one of two ways. Either a boundary is a line of minimum influence between two centres, or else it is a line of division between 'no-man's land' and a region under domination by some centre. Thus the first type of boundary falls along the furrows created by the intersection of tents, whereas the latter type falls along the edges of tents where they meet the ground.

The model thus allows the creation of hypothetical political maps, using only the location and size of settlements (or other centres) as input information, and generating political divisions without any prior knowledge of them.

## The Computer Program and Display

The computer utilized was the PDP 11/45 of the Institute of Sound and Vibration Research at Southampton University (with interactive graphic facilities). This permitted both immediate interactive display and hard-copy graphic printout. The program, in FORTRAN, requires three data files for each case studied.

The first file, INPUT FILE (COORDS), lists the coordinates, in pairs, of all location (settlements, centres, monuments, or whatever) under consideration.

The second, MAP OUTLINE FILE, gives in coordinate form the map boundary data which it is desired the computer should display. For instance, the simplified map of Europe, seen in figure 9, is drawn by the computer from a file with coordinates for 283 points of coastline.

The third file, POP FILE, gives the measure for the size of different centres (which in the first case examined was the population, and in others area) in the same sequential order as their coordinates in INPUT FILE.

Using the data in the INPUT FILE and POP FILE, the program examines each centre, checking it for dominance by neighbouring centres. If a centre is not dominated, it will have a boundary surrounding its political territory. The program marks such a centre as autonomous, computes the boundary location, and draws it in.

If a centre is dominated, it will not have a political boundary of its own since our model permits only autonomous centres to have independent political territories. The program marks such a dominated centre as non-autonomous and omits it from any future calculations.

After all boundaries have been drawn, the autonomous centres are displayed with a given sign (in this case, a cross) and the dominated, subordinate centres falling within their territories by a square. Where appropriate the map outline is then automatically added from the MAP OUTLINE FILE.

A normalisation factor is used, by which the sizes of all locations are divided: in general it is the size of the largest centre in the series.

Various values of the exponent $\alpha$ were selected, in general between 1.0 and 0.125. A high value of $\alpha$ leads to the dominance of the entire area by the single largest centre; a low value of $\alpha$ tends toward local autonomy by levelling out the size differences.

During the course of the investigation the program was modified to give with each hard-copy map a value for the number of autonomous centres, for the average nearest neighbour distance between autonomous centres, and for the average maximum radius of centres (i.e., the arithmetic average taking in turn the maximum distance attained between the boundary of each polity and its centre).

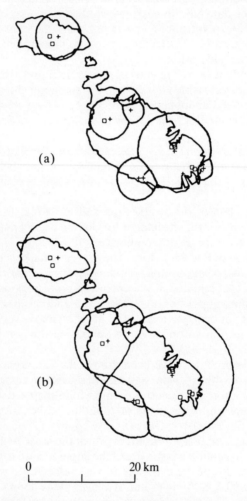

*Figure* 6. Computer graphic maps of territorial divisions in neolithic Malta. Temples are indicated by a cross when an autonomous centre, by a square when subordinate. The slope parameter varies: (a) 0.05 (b) 0.03 (c) 0.02 and (d) 0.01. The exponent is 0.5 throughout.

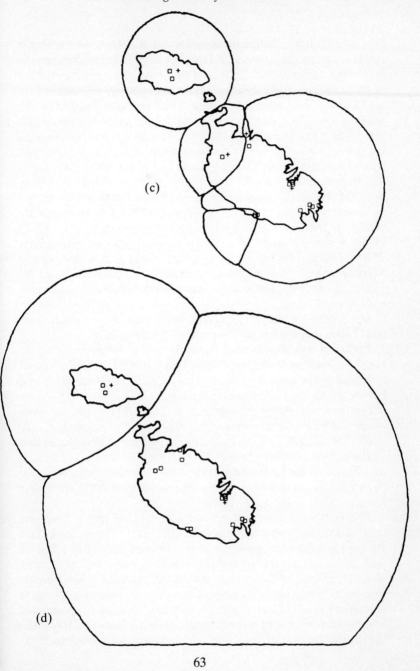

(c)

(d)

*Experiment 1: Malta*

One of our first experiments involved the distribution of neolithic temples on the island of Malta (Evans 1971), dated to the approximate time range 3500 to 2500 BC. Few prehistoric settlements have been found on Malta, but these impressive stone monuments are well known. The appropriate measure of size was taken to be the area enclosed by stones, for which $\frac{1}{2}l^2$ (with $l$ as the longest dimension) was taken as a convenient approximation. It had been suggested that groups of temples reflected some hierarchical organisation, with territorial division by chiefdoms (Renfrew 1973, 154), and it was hoped that the model would offer some insights in this direction. Of course the assumption should be explicitly stated that the area occupied by the temple buildings reflects in some measure the power, influence, and size of the parent community, and that its location lies within the residential territory of that community. These assumptions are certainly questionable in this case, and so must be any conclusions about prehistoric Malta derived from the model. As a simple test case for the method, however, the example is a convenient one.

The computer was given (*a*) coordinate pairs for the locations of the 17 sites in question, (*b*) an estimate for the area of each, and (*c*) 221 pairs of coordinates read manually to give a digitized coastline for the islands of Malta and Gozo. This last is for display purposes only and plays no part in the computations, which take place as if the locations were on an isotropic plain.

For the first run, the exponent $\alpha$ was set at 0.5 (i.e., the computer worked with the square root of the area actually occupied by each site). This area in each case was first normalized by dividing by that of the largest temple: in effect, for convenience we start by adjusting the size of the largest location to unity. The slope parameter was then allowed to vary in steps of 0.01 from 0.05 to 0.01 (see figures 6a–d).

The computer then printed out autonomous and subordinate centres and territorial boundaries in each case. The greatest (i.e., steepest) slope corresponding to the sharpest fall-off in influence with distance, naturally produced the largest number of autonomous locations and the smallest number of 'captures' by dominance. The relationship of the number of autonomous centres to the slope is seen in figure 7. The linear relationship in equation (1) postulated for distance means that boundaries, except where two territories touch, are circular in form. Outside the boundary the effect of the

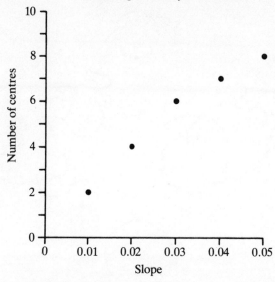

*Figure* 7. Relation between the number of autonomous centres and the slope parameter for the Maltese temples.

centre in question is zero. This differs from the Thiessen polygon approach, where the entire region is divided up, influence being inversely proportional to distance. With weighted Thiessen polygons an inverse square relationship can be used, which in formal properties is related to Reilly's gravitation relationship (Hodder and Orton 1976, 188).

Gradual reduction in slope produces the assimilation of progressively more locations into larger political units, and offers a fascinating caricature for the evolution of a hierarchical political system from an egalitarian one. It should be noted that the initial hypothesis is strongly supported by the persistent association of several small groups of sites, including the group of three on the northern island of Gozo, dominated by the great Ġgantija temple, the temples of Mgarr and Skorba in northwest Malta, and the grouping of the three Kordin temples in every case with the great centre at Tarxien. An interesting feature of the model then is that varying the slope changes certain aspects of organisation, while leaving others invariant.

As a second experiment, the slope parameter was now fixed at 0.05, using the same data set, and the exponent $\alpha$ varied, by a factor of 2 in each case, from 1 to 0.125 (figures 8a–d). An exponent of

65

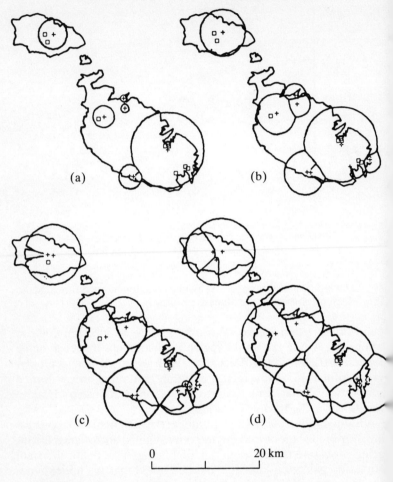

*Figure* 8. Territorial divisions in Malta with varying exponent $\alpha$:
(a) 1.0 (b) 0.5 (c) 0.25 (d) 0.125. The slope parameter is 0.05
throughout.

0.125 implies that the eighth root of area is being taken for the
magnitude of each site, the largest site (at Tarxien) being regarded
throughout as unit size. The territorial sizes of smaller sites therefore increase with decreasing exponent, and when $\alpha = 0.125$ there
are no fewer than 14 autonomous centres, since the eighth root of
each is itself close to unity and they become effectively of almost
equal size. But the map 'looks wrong' because of the distortions, so

that individual centres are no longer near the middle of their territories. Here perhaps the experiment suggests to us a criterion for
selecting an appropriate value of $\alpha$.

This and other experiments have shown, in a rather pragmatic
way, that an exponent of 1 allows the larger centres to dominate the
smaller to what seems an untoward extent, whereas an exponent of
less than 0.25 produces what look like territorial distortions. No
doubt both these statements require further substantiation. In most
subsequent work we have used an exponent of 0.5. This has the
consequence, when we use area as a measure of size for a centre,
that we are comparing linear measure for territory (radius) with
linear measure for centre (root area). The territorial area dominated by the site is thus proportional to the area actually occupied by
the site itself. Likewise, when we use population, we are thinking of
root population as proportional to radius of territory, and hence (by
squaring) population as proportional to territorial area.

*Experiment 2: Cities of Europe*
In order to test the model against a case in which real political
boundaries are accurately known, population sizes for the 117 cities
in Europe in the year 1960 whose population exceeded 500,000
(Showers 1973, 260–286) were listed, together with their coordin-
ates, and a digitized coastline for Europe. With an exponent of $\alpha = 1$, there were large areas of no-man's land between territories for all
values of the slope greater than 0.1, and once again an exponent of
$\alpha = 0.5$ was chosen as more appropriate. The resulting configurations for values of the slope parameter between 0.006 and 0.020
are seen in figures 9a to 9d. The relationship between slope and
number of autonomous centres is seen in table 1. Each centre of a
given population size has a maximum radius of influence, determined by the slope, although naturally when centres lie close together their common boundary falls within their theoretical radii of
influence. For a given slope, any city of population one million will
have the same radius of influence. Moreover, when the exponent
$\alpha = 0.5$, the radius of influence for a population of 10,000 will be
precisely one-tenth of that for population one million. These figures
are also seen in table 1. Note that the figures given in the first
column of tables 1 and 2 and on the abscissa of figures 7 and 10 are
convenient parameters which are inversely proportional to the
physical parameters listed in column 3 of the tables.

It should be noted that no distinction was made between distance
over sea or over land. Had maritime distance been seen as an

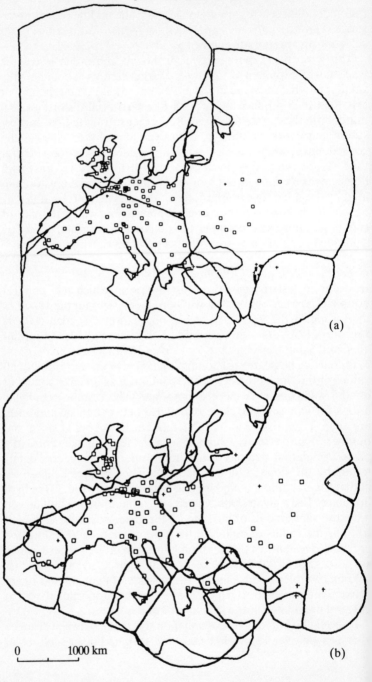

(a)

(b)

0    1000 km

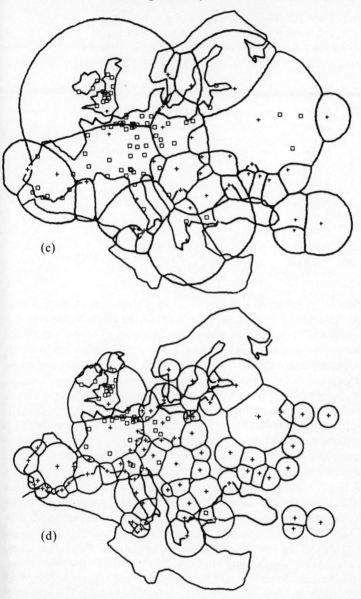

(c)

(d)

*Figure* 9. Computer graphic maps of European polities in AD 1960 as predicted by the XTENT model. The exponent $\alpha$ is 0.5 throughout. The slope parameter varies: (a) 0.006 (b) 0.010 (c) 0.014 and (d) 0.020.

*Table* 1. The effect of varying the slope on the number
of autonomous centres and on the radii of influence
for the cities of Europe in 1960 ($\alpha = 0.5$).

| | | Radius (km) | |
|---|---|---|---|
| Slope parameter | Number of autonomous centres | For 1,000,000 population | For 10,000 population |
| 0.006 | 9 | 1166 | 116.6 |
| 0.008 | 15 | 875 | 87.5 |
| 0.010 | 19 | 700 | 70.0 |
| 0.012 | 29 | 583 | 58.3 |
| 0.014 | 36 | 500 | 50.0 |
| 0.016 | 45 | 437 | 43.7 |
| 0.018 | 47 | 389 | 38.9 |
| 0.020 | 53 | 350 | 35.0 |
| 0.030 | 73 | 233 | 23.3 |
| 0.040 | 86 | 175 | 17.5 |

obstacle to effective domination, the jurisdiction of Paris would
have extended in each case to the coast of the English channel.

A second apparent distortion is the tendency toward autonomy of
a number of areas within the USSR. For instance, in the case in which
the slope parameter is 0.006, Tbilisi, Baku, and Yerevan emerge as
the capitals of autonomous provinces. But as so often in such cases,
the exceptions prove interesting in themselves: the computer is
mischievously predicting the autonomy of the Transcaucasian
People's Republics of Georgia, Azerbaijan, and Armenia. This
need not give comfort to separatist movements: it is a first instance
among many on these maps where we appear to see a configuration
appropriate to one time period appearing also at another.

Clearly the two maps approximating most closely to the actual
political reality are those for which the slope parameter is 0.014
(36 autonomous centres) and 0.010 (19 autonomous centres). The
relation between the slope parameter and number of centres is seen
in figure 10. In the latter case, London, Paris, Madrid, Lisbon,
Rome, Athens, Istanbul, Moscow, Stockholm, Berlin, Budapest,
Sofia, and Bucharest all acquit themselves appropriately (Istanbul
since Ankara, lying outside Europe, is not included). The odd-men
out, apart from the three Transcaucasian provincial centres, are
Leningrad – a city whose former capital status is notable – and
Odessa and Ufa in the USSR.

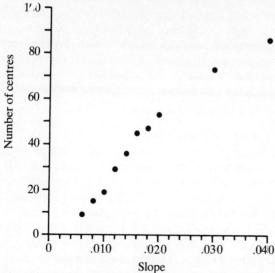

*Figure* 10. Relation between the number of autonomous centres and the slope parameter for the European cities.

In the case in which the slope parameter $\alpha$ is 0.014, Belgrade, Vienna, Oslo, Copenhagen, and Warsaw are now among the territorial capitals, while Syracuse and Palermo recall earlier Sicilian autonomy, and indeed the short-lived Kingdom of the Two Sicilies, and Barcelona, the old independence of Aragon. An alarming number of localities in the southern USSR emerge as independent: paradoxically this is because of their relatively small population size, or rather the late date at which this part of Europe became fully urban.

It is intriguing that when the slope parameter is 0.020, we see what approximates to a return to the Middle Ages (in western Europe) with separate status for former polity centres such as Naples, Valencia, Cordoba, and Seville. In effect the program is now including second-order centres, such as Glasgow and Belfast, and particularly notable is their manner of grouping themselves around the major, first-order centres which already emerge when the slope parameter is 0.006.

Turning now to the first of these maps, with slope parameter .006 we see indeed a Europe of great powers, reminiscent in some ways of the situation at the time of the Napoleonic wars, when Britain and France were the major competitors, yet with the retreat from Moscow clearly implied. Both Waterloo and the battlefields of the Peninsular War (in Iberia) are appropriately under British influence. Athens and Istanbul give us a hint of the Eastern question.

These comments, not all entirely serious, do reflect the important generalization already made in the case of Malta, that alteration in the slope for a given distribution may in some respects mimic the effect of the passage of time.

### Experiment 3: Late Uruk Settlement

To illustrate the approach as applied to archaeological settlement data derived from survey, the program was applied to the Late Uruk settlement system in the Warka area of Mesopotamia. The settlement areas have been conveniently listed by Johnson (1975, 312–14), and location coordinates were measured from his map (ibid. 316). His data are derived from the survey by Adams and Nissen (1972) and we follow him in including 98 of the 118 sites listed by Adams and Nissen. It was necessary to assume an area for Warka itself, since this had not been estimated. In fact separate runs were undertaken for areas of 40, 60, and 80 ha, respectively, and the discussion here relates to that for an area of 60 ha.

*Table 2.* The effect of varying the slope on the number of autonomous centres and on the radii of influence for the Uruk area in the Late Uruk period ($\alpha = 0.5$)

| Slope parameter | Number of autonomous centres | Radius (km) | |
| --- | --- | --- | --- |
| | | For 1 ha | For 100 ha |
| 0.005 | 4 | 7.95 | 79.5 |
| 0.010 | 18 | 3.97 | 39.7 |
| 0.020 | 44 | 1.99 | 19.9 |
| 0.030 | 62 | 1.32 | 13.2 |

The exponent $\alpha$ was held at 0.5 throughout, and the slope parameter was given successive values of 0.005, 0.01, 0.02, and 0.03. The results are seen in table 2. As before, the computer determine which sites dominate others, in terms of their size and location indicating the territory of dominant 'capitals' and the locations of the subordinate settlements. As slope is decreased, all the settlements gradually become subordinate to larger centres, until only the largest is autonomous. As slope is increased, smaller and smaller centres emerge as 'independent.' In an egalitarian political situation the latter may approximate to the political reality. But when the administration is in reality hierarchical, the increase in slope leads to the appearance of subordinate second-order centres as autonomous.

Figure 11 shows the configuration with the slope parameter set at 0.01. The autonomous settlements are indicated by a cross. In addition we have used arrows to indicate the four centres which already emerge as autonomous when the slope parameter is 0.005. Here then we are in effect beginning to use an overlay of the configurations for different slopes to give an indication of internal, hierarchical structure within polities.

It is instructive to compare this with the configuration at which Johnson himself arrived (1975, 332) as a result of his locational analysis (figure 12). By plotting a histogram for area of settlement he divided settlements into four size classes: large centres, small centres, large villages, and villages. Using classical central place theory concepts he regarded the settlement distribution as a modified hexagonal lattice (assigning special significance to sites at which ceramic wall cones have been found, considered as indicating a temple).

Of the five settlements classified as large centres by Johnson, four emerge as autonomous centres at slope parameter 0.005, and the resemblances between the two interpretations are obvious. Our program tends to grant autonomous status to middle-size settlements located far from others, and this has occurred with the two located at the southeast of the area. Likewise, our program underlines the potential significance of the centre at the northwest (Johnson's 'small centre' no. 020). It is difficult to see why this was omitted from his lattice. Moreover, the six centres arranged between it and the two large centres to the south (nos 242 and 125) have very much the appearance of second-order locations in a settlement hierarchy and might well have responded to his central place approach.

Our program does not, in itself, tell us which of the alternative political configurations it produces (according to change in slope) is the most appropriate. This depends on the distance over which a centre of a given size can exert effective influence (see the last column of table 2), which is inversely proportional to the slope. If a given distance (and slope) does effectively lead to a representation of the political reality, steeper slopes will give an insight into a structuring within polities, whereas smaller slopes predict supra-national spheres of influence.

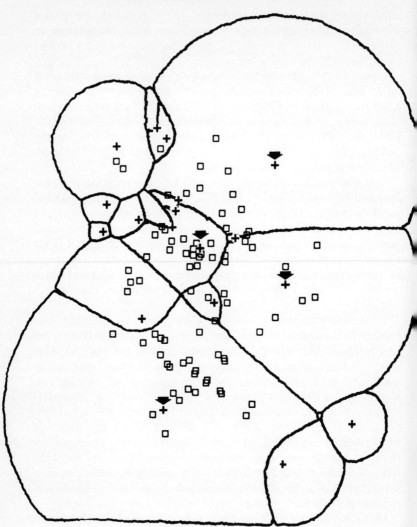

*Figure* 11. Predicted political divisions for the Late Uruk period in the Warka area of Mesopotamia (exponent $\alpha = 0.5$, slope parameter 0.01). Arrows indicate the four centres that emerge as autonomous with slope parameter 0.005. Compare with figure 12, shown on the same scale.

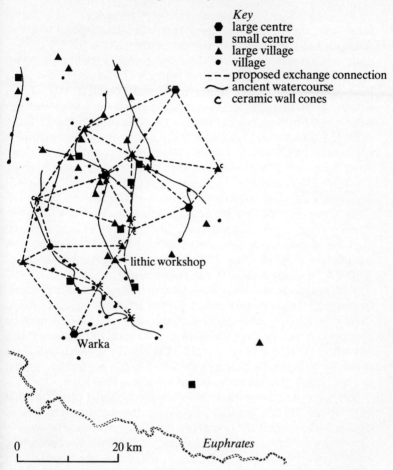

Key
◆ large centre
■ small centre
▲ large village
• village
--- proposed exchange connection
~ ancient watercourse
c ceramic wall cones

← lithic workshop

Warka

0                     20 km            *Euphrates*

*Figure* 12. Settlement structure of the Late Uruk period in the Warka area as analysed by Johnson (1975, 332). Note the similarities with figure 11, which is on the same scale.

## *The XTENT Model as a Framework of Comparison*

Our experiments, which included further examples not cited here, suggest that although a widely appropriate value of the exponent may be found ($\alpha \approx 0.5$), there is no easy or *a priori* means of judging the 'right' slope.

75

We would claim, however, that the very concept of 'slope' in this sense, expressed in absolute terms, may offer a conceptual advance. Accepting for the moment that the appropriate value for the exponent is agreed, we have in the slope a *single* variable which will uniquely determine the political landscape. For convenience we have spoken here using normalized values (such as 0.01, 0.02) without absolute units. But in table 2 the appropriate absolute units were given for the Uruk pattern, and may be compared with those in table 1 for European cities in 1960. Obviously direct comparison is possible only if we know the approximate population in Uruk times for a town whose area was 100 ha (or know the mean area for a town of 100,000 in modern Europe). But if we use, for the basis of argument, an urban population density of 100 ha$^{-1}$ for Mesopotamia in the Uruk period, the last columns of the two tables become directly comparable. Indeed figure 10 (Uruk settlement, with 100 ha seen as influencing a radius of 40 km) may be compared with figures 8c and 8d (Europe 1960, with centres with a population of 10,000 influencing 50 and 35 km, respectively).

Such comparisons can at times be misleading. Transport factors, overall population density, and degree of urbanisation must all have their effects. Moreover, although the exponent $\alpha = 0.5$ may be appropriate as a first approximation, it remains to be tested that a city with a population of one million has in fact a sphere of influence precisely 10 times the radius of a town of 10,000 population, or that town a radius 10 times the radius of a village of 100 ha.

Yet we would argue that these are precisely the questions that have to be asked. To what extent do the same parameters of distance and magnitude operate in the classic Maya lowlands as in Sumer, for instance, or in the Mississippian as in the European Iron Age? It may be that the XTENT model, and others like it, will offer a more rigorous framework for cross-cultural comparisons than has been available hitherto and hence open the way at last to a systematic and diachronic comparative study of human societies.    [1979]

## Acknowledgements

We are grateful to Dr Colin Mercer of the Data Research Centre, Institute of Sound and Vibration Research, University of Southampton, for access to its computer facilities, to Professor Kenneth Cooke for stimulation and encouragement, and to Professor Gregory A. Johnson for permission to reproduce figure 12.

## Bibliography

Adams, R. McC. and H. J. Nissen ( 1972 ) *The Uruk Countryside*, Chicago, University Press.

Berry, B. J. L. ( 1961 ) City size distribution and economic development, *Economic Development and Culture Change*, 9, 573–87.

Christaller, W. ( 1933 ) *Die zentralen Orte in Süddeutschland*, Jena.

Crumley, C. L. ( 1976 ) Towards a locational definition of state systems of settlement, *American Anthropologist*, 78, 59–73.

Evans, J. D. ( 1971 ) *The Prehistoric Antiquities of the Maltese Islands, a Survey*, London, Athlone.

Hodder, I. and Orton, C. ( 1976 ) *Spatial Analysis in Archaeology*, Cambridge, University Press.

Hogg, A. H. A. ( 1971 ) Some applications of surface fieldwork, in M. Jessen and D. Hill, eds., *The Iron Age and its Hillforts*, Southampton University, 105–25.

Johnson, G. A. ( 1972 ) A test of the utility of Central Place Theory in archaeology, in P. J. Ucko, R. Tringham and G. Dimbleby, eds., *Man, Settlement and Urbanism*, London, Duckworth, 769–85.

— ( 1973 ) *Local Exchange and Early State Development in Southwestern Iran* ( Museum of Anthropology of the University of Michigan Anthropological Papers 51 ).

— ( 1975 ) Locational analysis and the investigation of Uruk local exchange systems, in J. A. Sabloff and C. C. Lamberg-Karlovsky, eds., *Ancient Civilisation and Trade*, Albuquerque, University of New Mexico Press, 285–339.

Lösch, A. ( 1954 ) *The Economics of Location*, Yale University Press.

Renfrew, C. ( 1973 ) *Before Civilisation, the Radiocarbon Revolution and Prehistoric Europe*, London, Cape.

— ( 1977 ) Alternative models for exchange and spatial distribution, in T. K. Earle and J. E. Ericson, eds., *Exchange Systems in Prehistory*, New York, Academic Press, 71–90.

— ( 1978 ) Space, time and polity, in J. Friedman and M. Rowlands, eds., *The Evolution of Social Systems*, London, Duckworth, 89–112.

Showers, V. ( 1973 ) *The World in Figures*, New York, Wiley.

Soja, E. W. ( 1971 ) *The Political Organisation of Space*, ( Association of American Geographers, Commission on College Geography, Resource Paper 8 ).

Zadeh, L. ( 1965 ) Fuzzy sets, *Information Control*, 8, 338–53.

# II

## TRADE AND
## INTERACTION

\*

Until the 1960s the discovery of objects in one area which clearly originated from a distant source was frequently used to arrive at inferences about cultural 'influences', and was generally interpreted within a framework of diffusionist explanation. Here, as I showed with several examples in *Problems in European Prehistory* (Renfrew 1979), the source of innovation was generally seen as external to the culture area under study. In Europe, therefore, objects imported from the Mediterranean were viewed as highly significant indicators of the workings of the diffusion of culture. Artefacts supposedly imported from Western Asia and found in India and Pakistan, or even further afield, were assigned a similar significance, and the same patterns of reasoning were applied in other areas of the world. For instance, objects found in pre-Columbian north America which resembled in any way those of Mesoamerica were regarded as indications of the influence of the 'higher' cultures upon the lower, and the detection of actual goods of demonstrably southern origin was regarded as even more significant.

All of this was a product of 'normative' thought, where 'influences' of one area upon another were to be measured in terms of the similarities recognised between artefacts in the two areas. As noted in chapter 1, it fitted very well into the predominantly diffusionist explanations almost universally prevalent at that time.

Increasing scepticism about this broadly diffusionist framework, aided in prehistoric Europe by the collapse of the traditional chronology under the impact of radiocarbon dating (Renfrew 1973) led to a very different outlook. There was now a less ready acceptance of inconclusive evidence for contacts between distant areas, and the mere recognition of similarities between specific artefact forms in each no longer led to automatic assumptions that the two had been in contact. In this more critical atmosphere, positive and incontrovertible demonstration that contact of some kind had taken place was all the more interesting, and it could generally only come from the documentation that specific objects had indeed travelled very far from their place of manufacture or from the original source of the raw material. For this reason the scientific *characterisation* of materials – that is to say the recognition of physical or chemical characteristics by which the constituent material can confidently be ascribed to a specific source – became particularly useful. For now it was possible to call into question the provenance of *any* supposedly imported object, and in favourable cases to receive an unequivocal answer.

The focus of interpretation now shifted away from the simple diffusionist notion of cultural 'influence', even when contact between the two areas in question really could be documented by means of characterisation studies. It moved instead to the social and economic processes which led to and sustained the exchange transactions responsible for the movement of the goods in question, and to the consequences of those processes. These questions could best, it was felt, be approached through a study of the distribution patterns of the traded materials themselves, and in chapter 5 the way in which these can be generated as a result of different patterns of exchange is considered.

What these papers do not sufficiently discuss, however, is the range of social mechanisms within which the trading systems in question operate in specific societies, nor the effects upon the societies of these trading systems within them. One specific model of this kind, for instance, has been widely influential. It stresses the possible control in the trade of prestige goods by the local élite of a region, and the effects of this control in strengthening the position of the high-status individuals forming the élite, and ultimately perhaps in elevating them from a position of petty chiefs to one of much greater power within a more centralised society. This model was first developed by Flannery for the Olmec of Central America (Flannery 1968), and very much the same approach was taken by Frankenstein and Rowlands (1978) for the development of very prominent ranking in the south-central European iron age (see also Wells 1980).

There is a risk of circularity with some of these arguments. In some cases the basic data consist of no more than the existence of rich graves containing a number of imported goods. From this the existence of an élite is quite plausibly inferred, and the suggestion made, often without much supporting evidence, that they controlled the processes by which the exotic materials were obtained. From there it is an easy, but not altogether persuasive step to propose that the élite status of the individuals in question is not only

81

documented by these goods but is actually to be explained by them. Despite these possible difficulties, the merit of this explanation is that it sets out to consider in some detail the social context of the goods exchanged in a specific way, rather than merely considering the quantities of imported materials found (see also Rowlands 1980).

Another recent approach, with which I am less in sympathy, has been to regard the presence in a region of a few traded objects deriving from a more industrially advanced society as indicative of the existence of what Immanuel Wallerstein has rather misleadingly named a 'world system' (Wallerstein 1974). Wallerstein's main example comes from the West Indies in the sixteenth century AD, when the economy of the area was indeed so dependent upon that of western Europe that it is entirely sound to regard them together as forming part of a single economic system. (The term 'world' does however seem misleadingly general, even where transatlantic relationships are under consideration.) But when this model is translated back to the first or even the second millennium BC, and the countries of western Asia are seen as the counterparts in economic domination of sixteenth century western Europe, and the prehistoric lands of Europe are compared with the later West Indies as subservient components of the system, the analogy goes altogether too far. Indeed at this point the reasoning seems to have gone full circle, and we are right back to the diffusionist position of Gordon Childe (1958), with his theory of the economic domination of Europe by Mycenaean Greece. Now as then, the Marxist view of the domination of the natives by colonial and capitalist urban centres requires more than simple assertion: it needs a rather more dispassionate study of the social relations within which the exchange systems were embedded, based upon a thorough review of the actual data. Without this it is no more than resuscitated diffusionism.

A more fruitful approach touched on in chapter 4 is the consideration of information flow alongside the material exchanges which can be documented by characterisation studies. Moreover the thrust of much recent work is to consider the effects of exchanges of information as well as material *within* a given region, and to regard these as potentially at least as important as more far-flung exchange transactions. The idea of the single region containing a number of effectively autonomous social units, already discussed in chapter 2, is relevant here. In the case of early state societies it is sometimes possible to speak of Early State Modules. Work undertaken since this paper was written has suggested that it is the interactions between polities of roughly equivalent size within a region which can be of decisive importance in governing the trajectory of development within it. The significance of such peer polity interactions, as they have been termed (Renfrew 1982, 287) in the development of many early societies, not all of them so complex in their structure as early states, is a matter of current discussion (Renfrew and Cherry, in press).

In this field, as in others, there have been several programmatic articles advocating a 'contextual' or 'structural approach', and arguing, quite reasonably, that a much more detailed understanding of the specific properties of the exchange system in question is desirable in each case (e.g. Hodder 1982). It is easy to share this view, as a general aspiration, and indeed it holds much in common with the broadly neo-Marxist approach of Frankenstein and Rowlands, and the earlier analysis of Flannery, mentioned above. Quite clearly, when it is widely recognised that different commodities are traded in different 'spheres of exchange' (Dalton 1977), it is pertinent to seek some understanding of the relative values assigned by the societies in question to the commodities which they were trading. But this is not a new question, and despite systematic consideration in one of the pioneer works of processual archaeology (Winters 1968), this is not a field where there have been striking insights recently.

The problem is highlighted in chapter 5, where it is shown that in some cases very different exchange mechanisms could produce closely similar patterns of artefacts in the archaeological record. The solution here is not, however, to turn away from careful quantitative analysis, as the advocates of 'Structural archaeology' at times seem to advocate, but rather to seek other categories of information with which to supplement these analyses. The so-called 'contextual examination' of the neolithic trade in stone axes in Britain (Hodder and Lane 1982), apparently advocated by Hodder (1982, 207) as some sort of significant methodological advance over previous analyses, appears instead to me to be closely similar in kind to them. With its careful quantitative consideration of shape and size as well as of distribution, it lies in the mainstream of processual thinking along with many other papers in the useful recently edited volumes on trade and exchange (e.g. Earle and Ericson 1977; Fry 1980; Francis, Kense and Duke 1981; Ericson and Earle 1982). Certainly contemporary archaeology is faced with the problem of 'getting inside' early exchange systems in the sense of understanding something of the value systems upon which they were based, but the onus is upon critics of existing analyses of trading systems to put forward methods of research which take us beyond the already very informative analyses of regional exchange systems which are now available (e.g. Pires Ferreira 1976a and 1976b).

The archaeological study of 'action at a distance' has, in effect, only recently begun, and the two papers here contributed to its inception. The task has, of course, been greatly aided by the availability of appropriate techniques of chemical and physical analysis. This seems indeed to be one of the areas within archaeology where scientific developments in technique have made possible entirely new horizons or interpretation. Trade and exchange can, in consequence, be seen in social terms. This field remains one of the most promising areas of archaeological research.

## Bibliography

Childe, V.G. (1958) *The Prehistory of European Society*, London, Penguin.

Dalton, G. (1977) Aboriginal economies in stateless societies, in T.K. Earle and J.E. Ericson, eds., *Exchange Systems in Prehistory*, New York, Academic Press, 191–212.

Earle, T.K. and J.E. Ericson, eds. (1977) *Exchange Systems in Prehistory*, New York, Academic Press.

Ericson J.E. and T.K. Earle, eds. (1982) *Contexts for Prehistoric Exchange*, New York, Academic Press.

Flannery, K.V. (1968) The Olmec and the Valley of Oaxaca: a model for inter-regional variation in Formative times, in E.P. Benson, ed., *Dumbarton Oaks Conference on the Olmec*, Washington D.C., Dumbarton Oaks, 79–110.

Francis, P.D., F.J. Kense and P.G. Duke, eds. (1981) *Networks of the Past: Regional Interaction in Archaeology*, Calgary, University of Calgary Archaeological Association.

Frankenstein, S. and M.J. Rowlands (1978) The internal structure and regional context of Early Iron Age society in south-western Germany, *Bulletin of the Institute of Archaeology*, 15, 73–112.

Fry, R.E., ed. (1980) *Models and Methods in Regional Exchange*, (SAA Papers no. 1), Washington D.C., Society for American Archaeology.

Hodder, I. (1982) Toward a contextual approach to prehistoric exchange, in J.E. Ericson and T.K. Earle, eds., *Contexts for Prehistoric Exchange*, New York, Academic Press, 199–212.

Hodder I. and P. Lane (1982) A contextual examination of neolithic axe distribution in Britain, in J.E. Ericson and T.K. Earle, eds., *Contexts for Prehistoric Exchange*, New York, Academic Press, 213–36.

Pires-Ferreira, J.W. (1976a) Shell and iron-ore mirror exchange in Formative Mesoamerica, with comments on other commodities, in K.V. Flannery, ed., *The Early Mesoamerican Village*, New York, Academic Press, 311–28.

Pires-Ferreira, J. W. (1976b) Obsidian exchange in Formative Mesoamerica, in K. V. Flannery, ed., *The Early Mesoamerican Village*, New York, Academic Press, 292–305.

Renfrew, C. (1973) *Before Civilisation*, London, Cape.

— (1979) *Problems in European Prehistory*, Edinburgh, University Press.

— (1982) Polity and power: interaction, intensification and exploitation, in C. Renfrew and J. M. Wagstaff, eds., *An Island Polity: the Archaeology of Exploitation in Melos*, Cambridge, University Press, 264–90.

Renfrew, C. and J. F. Cherry, eds., in press, *Peer Polity Interaction and the Development of Sociopolitical Complexity*, Cambridge, University Press.

Rowlands, M. J. (1980) Kinship, alliance and exchange in the European bronze age, in J. Barrett and R. Bradley, eds., *Settlement and Society in the British Later Bronze Age*, (BAR British Series 83), Oxford, British Archaeological Reports, 15–55.

Wallerstein, I. (1974) *The Modern World-System*, New York, Academic Press.

Wells, P. S. (1980) *Culture Contact and Culture Change: Early Iron Age Central Europe and the Mediterranean World*, Cambridge, University Press.

Winters, H. D. (1968) Value systems and trade cycles of the Late Archaic in the Midwest, in L. R. and S. R. Binford, eds., *New Perspectives in Archaeology*, Chicago, Aldine, 175–222.

# 4

## TRADE AS ACTION
## AT A DISTANCE

\*

In recent years, trade has become one of the principal foci of archaeological research. There are two reasons for this. The first is pragmatic: trade can be studied. The objects of trade, or at least the imperishable ones, can frequently be found, modern analytical techniques allow the determination of the source, and quantitative methods inspired by geography permit generalisations about distribution patterns. The second reason is theoretical: in the past, the development of human culture and cultures has often been seen primarily in material terms (subsistence, technology, economy – for instance by Childe) or primarily in spiritual terms (social relations, religion, knowledge of the world – for instance by Frankfort). Recently the relationship between these two arbitrarily separated areas has been more fully appreciated, as we have become aware of their total and integral interdependence.

Trade is an activity which closely relates these two groups of sub-systems; it requires organisation as well as commodity, and it implies criteria of value and measure. The crucial importance of the study of trade today is that it offers a practical way of investigating the organisation of society in social terms as well as purely in economic ones.

Trade, a term synonymous with exchange, has been defined as 'the mutual appropriative movement of goods between hands' (Polanyi 1957, 266). The movement need not be over any great distance, and may operate within social or spatial units (internal trade) or between them, across cultural boundaries (external trade). In what follows, the notion of *movement*, in the sense of change of location, is crucial as the generator of spatial distribution. And *between hands* introduces at the outset the theme of human interactions.

This is why trade offers one of the most convenient approaches to

86

the origins of civilisations or of states. For however these terms are defined, they imply an organisation, a specialised administration, which regulates human activities both in terms of procurement (movement of goods including raw materials) and of social relations (human encounters with exchange of information and goods). 'The essence of a social system is interdependence, and the essence of interdependence is men's investment of themselves in other men' (Coleman 1963). The degree of organisation and its evolution, and of the evolution of civilisation itself, may be understood in the light of the exchanges within a civilisation. In this chapter I should like to examine more closely some of these interactions, of which trade is among the most important, and to suggest that we have not yet understood their complexity, nor the range of interpretive uses to which the archaeological record may be put.

In the first part of what follows I shall outline a general approach to civilisations and their formation, and discuss the role of inter-actions within and between them. The second part of the chapter is concerned with the pragmatic archaeological problems involved in the study of trade.

## Interaction and Organisation

### Trade as Local Interaction

Marcel Mauss (1954) was the first fully to stress that in circum-stances of relative self-sufficiency, many exchanges of goods take the form of gifts, and that such gifts have far more than a purely economic significance. They are social acts, prestations, in which the material aspect may have a subsidiary importance. Anthro-pologists from Malinowski to Sahlins have held this view, stressing the embeddedness of the economy within a social matrix among communities of band or tribal organisation. An exchange of goods in such communities is primarily an act reinforcing a social relation-ship, and material exchange is an important aspect of the adjust-ment of the individual's relationship with others in his social en-vironment, and in the adjustment of the band's or tribe's relation-ships with its neighbours.

Sociologists have taken the idea of exchange further to describe all interpersonal contacts, viewing all social behaviour as an ex-change of goods, nonmaterial as well as material (Homans 1958). In this perspective, the cohesiveness of a group, defined as anything that attracts people to take part in a group, is a value variable, referring to the degree of reinforcement that people find in the activities of the group. Communication or interaction is seen as a frequency variable: a measure of the frequency of emission of valuable and costly verbal behaviour. The more cohesive a group is, and the more valuable the sentiment or activity the members exchange with one another, the greater the frequency of interaction among its members.

The anthropologist studying trade can profit from this approach, although he will interpret value rather differently and will broaden the discussion from the primarily verbal interactions which the sociologist may have in mind. For all human action may be viewed at a distance as exchange, both of material and of nonmaterial goods. We can measure the intensity of the interaction either in terms of frequency, as Homans suggests, or in terms of quantity of goods transferred. This is a simple enough concept for material goods, a more difficult but potentially useful one in the field of information. When the exchange habitually takes place at a specific location, we may describe that location as a central place, which will then take on a special significance for the cohesiveness of the group.

Let us for the moment divide the totality of 'goods' exchanged over a given period into material goods (among which 'energy' – i.e., work or services – is here included) and information, defined as a constraint or stimulus upon present or future behaviour. The total interaction, $A$, between two individuals is then the sum of the exchanges of goods, $G$, and information, $I$.

$$A = A_{12} + A_{21} = G_{12} + G_{21} + I_{12} + I_{21}$$

And the total interactions in a group of $N$ individuals is

$$A = \Sigma A_{ij} = \Sigma G_{ij} + \Sigma I_{ij}$$

This approach leads us to contrast two extremes: exchange of goods without a wide range of accompanying information, and exchange of information without goods. The first is clearly the intention of 'silent trade' (although even here information bearing on the future conduct of the trade itself is transmitted, for instance in the acceptance or not of the goods laid out). It is also a feature of market trade, where contacts can be at their most impersonal. The second extreme applies to any contact which we may identify as purely social or purely religious, although on examination many which we might so describe involve the exchange of material goods.

*Information* is not being used here in the special sense used in information theory. Yet the observation holds in that sense also. For quantity of information there indicates the magnitude of the set of possibilities of different messages: information conveyed is not an intrinsic property of the individual message. As Weaver (1949, 12) remarks, 'The word information relates not so much to what you *do* say, as to what you *could* say.' In this special sense the silent trade and its modern equivalent, the supermarket, are also devices which restrict information.

For the archaeologist, the study of trade is central to the study of society because of the association of goods and information in most exchanges, an aspect of the embeddedness of the economy. Indeed, one might go a step further and claim that this association of material and social, of goods and information, this embeddedness, is the *normal* state of society, that is to say the basis upon which human interaction functions in the absence of special mechanisms. From this standpoint the introduction of money and the use of markets are devices of some sophistication to allow the separation of functions, a differentiation overcoming the 'normal' association or embeddedness. Coinage is a further sophistication, as are deferred payment, credit facilities, and the like. The associative embeddedness can only be avoided by the formulation of specific rules and conventions, both in the economic field and in the socioreligious one, where the renunciation of material things allegedly practised in some sectarian groups completes the dissociation, with separate renditions on the one hand to God and on the other to Caesar or to Mammon.

It is appropriate now to set these interactions in spatial terms. In a uniform plain, with a dispersed settlement pattern, we can visualise each nuclear family as a point. If his home is fixed and his economy sedentary, the movements of the individual may be restricted to forays of a few kilometres' distance. Since the plain is uniform he may have minimal contact with his neighbours in adjacent territories. Such an individual or family, living alone, independent and self-sufficient, isolated from other humans, is the antithesis of civilisation. Our interest is in the interactions that can make this individual, without change of local residence, a part of a functioning civilization. (Sedentary settlement is here under discussion: the position of mobile groups, including nomads and transhumant pastoralists may require a different treatment. For convenience a sedentary settlement will be defined as one in which no less than 90 per cent of the annual man-nights of the population are spent at home, in the permanent residence, or in fields not more than a few kilometres from it.)

This picture of minimum interaction is the very antithesis of civilisation. Nor is the presence or absence of dispersed or agglomerate settlement in itself the crux of the matter. For agglomerate settlement does not in itself define civilisation, although it must bring with it some measure of interaction. Indeed, we can visualise an agricultural population, every family of which is entirely self-supporting, in which the houses are clustered. This is in fact approximately the case in many early farming villages, some of which reach almost urban size without reflecting an urban organisation. Çatal Hüyük is an example. The size of such communities is limited by two parameters: the carrying capacity $C$ (expressed as number of persons per unit area) and the maximum distance from the centre of land that is farmed, given the available transport facilities. The maximum population $P$ is $320R^2C$, where $R$ is in kilometres and $C$ in persons per hectare. A radius of 5 km and Allan's figure of 0.5 for $C$ in modern Anatolia (Allan 1972, 225) gives a notional population of 4,000. This figure is indeed exceeded by the agricultural 'towns' of southern Italy (Chisholm 1968, 114), and both early neolithic Jericho and Çatal Hüyük may have housed comparable populations. There is no justification for taking a population figure of this order as an indication in itself of civilisation or of cities: degree of interaction is not determined by population density or size of settlement unit, although both are among the determining factors.

High population need not be permanently associated with a central place, and indeed at periodic central places there is frequently no population. The Siassi-Gomlongon market described by Harding (1967, 150) is at one extreme here; purely religious centres, such perhaps as Stonehenge, are at the other; and between is the whole range of periodic tribal central places which are distinct from residential locations. Residential locations can of course themselves be periodic central places; examples are the circulation markets of the Yoruba or in China, or at the other extreme and in our own society, a circus travelling from village to village.

These different interactions or exchanges, with their flow of goods and of information, are what remove the individual in his Crusoe-like isolation, suggested above, from a condition of brute independence, making him part of a functioning society of a kind we term civilisation, with a high degree of interaction and specialisation.

It was Karl Polanyi who made a fundamental distinction, about human affairs in general as well as about the economy, when he isolated for discussion both reciprocity and redistribution. Their importance can be tabulated as follows:

## Trade as Action at a Distance

| Perspective | Reciprocity | Redistribution |
|---|---|---|
| Configuration | Symmetry | Centricity |
| Geographical | No central place | Central place |
| Affiliation | Independence | Central organisation |
| 'Solidarity' (Durkheim) | Mechanical | Organic |

Reciprocity can of course work as a distributive mechanism, even with specialist manufacture. If we imagine village A making water jars and fine pottery, village O producing fibres and poultry products, and village Z salt, flowers, and maize we can imagine each exchanging its products for those produced by the other. If the number of production points is $N$, each producer will need to visit or be visited by $(N-1)$ village representatives from other villages to effect full distribution, with a consequential $[N(N-1)]/2$ journeys.

If, on the other hand, a system of redistribution operates, and one village functions as a central place as well as a small production location, inhabitants of the surrounding villages will have to travel only to the central one, and its inhabitants will not need to travel at all, so that the total of journeys will be $N-1$ (figure 1). As the number of participating production centres increases and also the proportion of the produce of each that is exchanged, the institution of the central redistributive agency becomes overwhelmingly more efficient in terms of transport cost.

This, then, is a purely economic reason for the emergence of central places as the exchange of goods develops. In cases where there is also marked local diversity, with ecological variations within the region, a desire to obtain the products of a neighbouring niche will inevitably promote exchange, which in turn will favour the development of central places.

The counterpart of the exchange of goods, namely the exchange of information, is no less important. And underlying any analysis of human society must be the recognition that public meetings take place in nearly all cultures, whether or not they are viewed as adaptively useful in stimulating solidarity and in reducing conflict. One convenient solution is for meetings to take place at each village in succession, which brings some of the benefits of centricity without long-term loss of symmetry. This solution has indeed been adopted by many band and tribal societies, of which the Kyaka of New Guinea are a good example (Bulmer 1960). But the provision of an impressive permanent facility for the occasion, such as a magnificent temple, becomes prohibitively expensive if it has to exist at each settlement. Again a central place is an obvious solution, this time for the exchange of information.

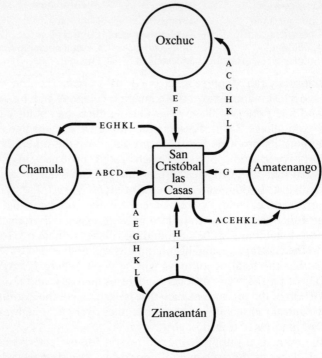

Chamula
A  Musical instruments
B  Firewood and charcoal
C  Woollen fabrics
D  Oranges from Tenejapa
Oxchuc
E  Fibres and cordage
F  Eggs, poultry and pigs
Amatenango
G  Water jars and fine pottery

Zinacantán
H  Salt from Ixtapa
I  Flowers
J  Maize

San Cristóbal las Casas
K  Ceremonial paraphernalia
L  Tools and equipment

*Figure* 1. Transfer of goods by redistribution. In spatial terms this does not differ from market exchange, and the example is based on the market centre of San Cristóbal las Casas, south Mexico (after Siverts 1969).

Just as craft specialisation offers advantages in quality of product and in economics of scale, so specialisation in communication, by priests and leaders controlling a central administration, is efficient and offers an attractive product. These full-time specialists at the centre of redistribution are paid for by the goods of those who come to interact: it is an exchange of information against material goods. Redistribution is therefore simply an exchange of this kind, which, like the exchange of purely material goods, operates most efficiently at a central place.

This perspective allows us to see market exchange, Polanyi's third category along with reciprocity and redistribution, more clearly. For market exchange, seen in spatial terms, does not differ from redistribution. Indeed, figure 1, used above to illustrate redistribution, is taken from an article on market exchange in south Mexico (Siverts 1969, 106), and the central place is not a redistribution centre but the market of San Cristóbal las Casas in Chiapas. The difference, of course, is that accompanying the exchange, in the case of redistribution, is a central organisation within whose functioning the economic function is embedded. In the physical sense, redistribution implies the physical reception and disbursement of the goods by the central authorities and hence the provision of considerable storage facilities, as in the Minoan-Mycenaean palaces (Renfrew 1972, 291–97). But increasingly sophisticated devices make possible a system of redistribution, involving the bulk of the produce not consumed by the producer, without its physical possession – first by nominal possession, although not under the direct control of the central authority, and then by more complicated accounting procedures. There is thus some formal equivalence between redistribution and market exchange which may make it difficult to distinguish between them in archaeological terms.

Moreover, Polanyi did not sufficiently stress that all marketing implies some kind of order, of security – ultimately, indeed, in the case of permanent markets, of jurisdiction. So that while the economic activity is to the fore, there *is* a social relationship (although not necessarily much active interaction) between those exchanging and the central authority ordering the central place. In this sense, market exchange may be regarded as redistribution with a dissociation of the central authority from the material transaction. Market exchange cannot take place without such order, either reigning precariously as in some tribal market exchange, or maintained by central authority, itself normally sustained by taxation (a monetary form of redistribution). The position of the port of trade, originally discussed by Polanyi and more recently by Rathje and Sabloff (cf. Rathje and Sabloff 1972) is an interesting one, for where the trade is at a level of fairly sophisticated market exchange, order is maintained by what may be viewed as reciprocity.

The foregoing discussion makes clear why there can be no civilisation without permanent central places. The city has been well described as a 'communication engine,' and this description applies as much to low-population central places, such as some of those of Egypt or Mexico, as to great cities like Warka or Tenochtitlán. In studying the origins of civilisation we are considering the rise of such central places. The consideration of exchange, of both information and material, reveals why population size is a secondary parameter.

In this section the rise of civilisation has been equated with the development of interpersonal interactions among the population of an area, many of these persons being necessarily at a distance from each other. It has been suggested that with the development of such interactions central places arise and that these need not be large centres of population. Before examining alternative models for the formation of civilisation, it will be useful to consider some features of the spatial organisation of many early civilisations.

## The Administrative Module in Early Civilisations

A permanently functioning central place is a feature of every civilisation. The central place may also be a major population centre, or it may not have a large resident population. It serves as a focus for the material and informational exchanges that make up the interactions characteristic of civilisation, and the permanent existence of the central place and its function as such is one of the features distinguishing civilisations from chiefdom societies, such as those of Polynesia. For even in the most stable of these chiefdoms, with a centre functioning as the permanent seat of a chief, the central place actually operated as a major redistributive centre – for both material and social exchange – only on one or two occasions during the year. (The ceremonial centre of Mu'a in Tonga is a good example (McKern 1929, 95), for major redistribution took place there only on one or two occasions during the year, notably at the great *inasi*, the annual first-fruits ceremony: see p.212.)

I would like to suggest that in most, possibly in all, early civilisations a pattern can be discerned which has not clearly been distinguished hitherto. Perhaps this is because it is a spatial pattern, while the state and civilisation (and even urbanism) are generally defined in terms of human specialisation and organisation, rather than spatially. But of course spatial order is an inescapable aspect of all organisation, and the rise or origin of civilisation can profitably be considered in terms of the genesis of that spatial organisation. The recognition of this general pattern allows a discussion of the ques-

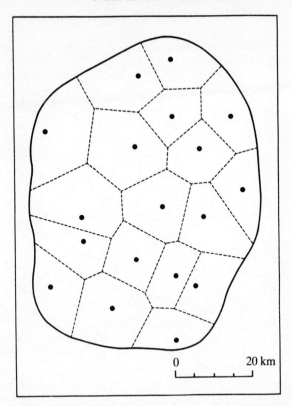

*Figure* 2. Idealised territorial structure of early civilisations, showing the territories and centres of the ESMs within the civilisation (i.e. area of cultural homogeneity).

tion which is not predicated upon an analysis of 'cities' or 'urban centres,' since the central places in question are not necessarily of a character which would universally be accepted as urban. A firm distinction must be made here between the 'civilisation' – viewed as a 'culture' (possessing a distribution in space and time) of a certain complexity – and the organisational units ('states') that comprise it.

1. In most, perhaps all, early civilisations there functions a number of autonomous central places which, initially at least, are not brought within a single unified jurisdiction. It is such autonomous territorial units, with their central places, which together constitute what we would all term a civilisation. They may be recognised as iterations of what I propose to call the *early state module* (ESM).

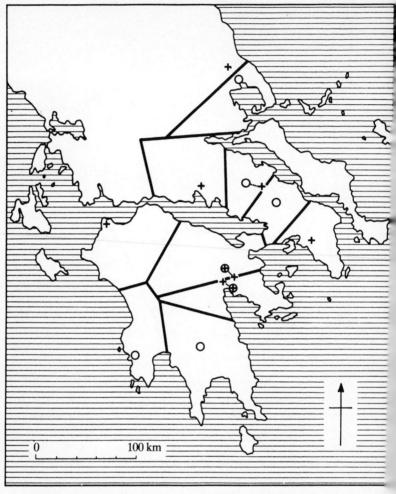

*Figure* 3. The early state module in Mycenaean Greece, showing palaces (circles), major strongholds (crosses) and hypothetical territorial boundaries.

If the territorial extent of any early civilisation is marked on a map, the higher-level organisation pattern will take the configuration seen in figure 2 – fairly evenly spaced autonomous central places set in territories which may notionally be indicated by means of Thiessen polygons. At the level of the early civilisation or early state, these are the largest central places found. And when archaeo-

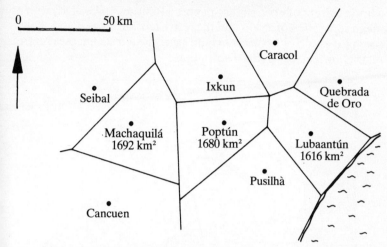

*Figure* 4. The early state module in the Maya lowlands: realms in the south-eastern Petén (after Hammond 1972).

logists claim to speak of the origins of early civilisations, they are usually found to be speaking of the development of these ESMs and of the less permanent and less active central places which preceded them. A central place, as considered here, is not, of course, merely an agglomeration of population; indeed its population may be small. This point is considered further in the next section.

2. The ESM apparently falls within a restricted size range. Frequently the modular area is approximately 1500 km² with a mean distance of about 40 km between the central places of neighbouring modules. Special environmental or social factors may reduce this distance to about 20 km, while intervening parcels of uncultivable land may increase it to at least 100 km.

3. Many early civilisations comprise, before subsequent unification, about 10 of such ESMs, although the number may vary by a factor of at least 2, and cases are known where the number is higher.

Mycenaean Greece may be taken by way of example (figure 3). The results of site survey (Hope Simpson 1965) indicate 14 palaces or major fortresses, of which perhaps 2 (Gla and Mideia) may not have been permanently occupied. Unweighted Thiessen polygons (Dirichlet regions) have been drawn to show the notional boundaries of the ESMs. Taking only adjacent territories (with a common terrestrial boundary), the centres have a mean separation of 76 km, partly in consequence of the rugged terrain between some of them.

Minoan Crete offers a similar picture (Renfrew 1972, 258), with a mean separation of 35 km, but the restricted size of the island allows room for only 5 or 6 places. In both cases the terrain imposes severe restrictions on the spatial distribution.

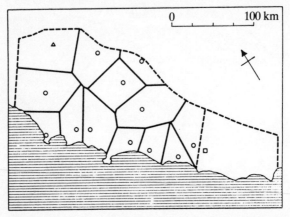

*Figure* 5. The early state module in Etruria: the twelve cities of ancient Etruria (circles) with hypothetical territorial boundaries. Rome is indicated by a square and Fiesole by a triangle.

The pattern is seen again in the Maya area (figure 4) where, in the south-east Petén, Hammond (1972, 784) has identified 'realms' (ESMS) approximately 1600 km$^2$ in area. In Mesopotamia a similar modular organisation can be identified: here the Predynastic and Early Dynastic city-states are the central places of the modules, of which more than a dozen have been identified. A similar pattern may be recognised among the Hausa states of northern Nigeria (Magobunje 1968, 51, fig 3). For classical Greece, Doxiadis (1971) has proposed an area of 1471 km$^2$ for the territory of a city-state. Early Etruria (figure 5) offers another instance of an arguably 'pristine' civilisation, which emerged into history as a hegemony of 12 city-states. The mean distance between neighbours (with common terrestrial boundaries) is 56 km. Egypt, of course, is something of an exception to this schema, since the Nile imposes a linear arrangement, and little is known of the settlement pattern or administrative organisation before the unification at the outset of the Old Kingdom. The discussion here, furthermore, is restricted to sedentary agricultural societies; more mobile units are discussed later.

The possibility of some uniformity in the size and spacing of these ESMS is particularly interesting, since the central places of one civilisation are evidently different in size from those of another, as are the population densities. Brush and Bracey (1955) have, however, made a similar observation, although at a lower administrative level, in their comparisons between modern southwestern Wisconsin and southern England, where they found a spacing of about 21 miles between higher-order centres, about 7 miles between lower-order ones, and about 5 miles between the lowest-order centres. The interest here lies not in the absolute figures but in the existence of modular units which appear in this case also to be of the same order in quite unrelated rural regions.

Settlement hierarchies have been recognised in a number of early civilisations, but the mean distances between adjacent centres of autonomous units have not been reported. Hodder (1972), writing of the hierarchy of settlement in Roman Britain, reports a distance of 6.5 miles between minor settlements, of 13 miles between major unwalled settlements, and 26 miles between walled settlements. His interest, however, is in the Roman period, and not in the pre-Roman Iron Age, when south Britain was composed of effectively autonomous tribal units. The Roman cantonal capitals approximate those of the previous period, and using Rivet's map (1964, fig. 9) I have calculated the mean distance between centres with common territorial boundaries in south Britain. For this purpose a line was drawn between the Wash and the Bristol Channel, and all *civitates* or *coloniae* south of the line, other than London and Glevum, were included. This gave a mean distance of 52 Roman miles, or approximately 76 km. Iron Age Britain was not of course organised at the state level, but it has been widely recognised that the major hill forts and oppida were central places which one might term proto-urban, although the Roman conquest radically altered the course of subsequent development. It would be particularly interesting to know how this mean distance changes during the transition from chiefdom to early state; my suspicion is that it decreases more often than it increases. I have not attempted any detailed cross-cultural survey of early civilisations that would test the extent to which (a) the cellular pattern of ESMS and (b) their modular size are universal. But certainly many other early instances could be found: Wheatley and Chang have both (in seminar comments) discussed the spatial organisation of Shang China in this way, and the forerunner of the Hittite Empire is amenable to similar treatment.

If this concept of ESM is accepted, it throws into relief a much-neglected feature of early civilisations. For while the external, long-distance trade of such civilisations is much discussed, and the internal trade, within the modules – that is to say the redistributive organisation, with some residue of reciprocal exchange – has been well considered, the flow of goods and information *between* the ESMS, what we may term the *intermediate trade*, is rarely discussed. Yet this is the exchange whose effect must have been to produce and maintain the uniformity of culture or civilisation as a whole. This question of uniformity or similarity has never been adequately considered for the state or civilisation level of organisation. D.L. Clarke (1968, chap. 9) has given an interesting discussion of spatial similarity patterns among tribes, but nowhere in the literature is there a careful investigation of the exchange mechanisms underlying them, other than vague reference to 'pan-tribal sodalities' and the like.

Here one aspect of exchange must be discussed for its substantial impact on information flow: exogamy with respect to the territorial unit. There is no doubt that the most influential form of interaction at a distance takes place when the 'distance' is permanently negated by change in place of residence. This simple truth underlies much older migrationist reasoning, but only in a few studies, such as those of Deetz (1965) and Hill (1966), has it been applied to a 'steady state' situation. One can see that any perceived division into 'them' and 'us' is likely to lead, within the restrictions of the society's marriage rules, to a higher degree of intermarriage among 'us' and hence a greater information flow, leading to an effective, operational difference in the culture of 'them' and 'us' which will reinforce the perceived distinction. The extent to which ESMs function as exogamous entities is relevant, therefore, to an understanding of the homogeneity of the culture of the ESMS within the civilisation as a whole, although it does not diminish the significance of other kinds of exchange.

The initial autonomy of the ESMS implies that trade between them will be reciprocal, primarily between the major central places. Indeed, when there is a shift from reciprocity to redistribution, implying the emergence of a higher-order central place, the civilisation is consequently unified to form an empire. Alternatively, when the reciprocity breaks down, giving rise to hostility, unification may again be the consequence. This is the phenomenon implied in Julian Steward's term 'Era of Cyclical Conquests' (Steward 1955, 196). (Attack from outside may bring a measure of unification, very much like that seen in a segmentary lineage system

100

(Bohannan 1954).) On occasion such unification processes have been identified with state formation itself (cf. Krader 1968, chaps. 3, 5, and 6), but there is in such cases a confusion between organisation and perceived ethnic identity over a wide area. My focus here is on aspects of organisation and interaction without which no civilisation or state can function, and on sedentary rather than nomad societies.

The ESM for various early civilisations clearly falls within a limited size range, and the maximum distance from centre to territorial boundary must be related to the means of transport available. For the Etruscan city territories the maximum is about 50 km; for the Mycenaean centres, with their uncultivable intervening terrain, about 70 km. In none of the early civilisations we are discussing was the horse widely used (although horses were ridden in Etruria); the ox-drawn cart was significant in some. So the boundaries of the module were generally no more than one or two days' march from its centre. The distance from chief centre to boundary for a civilisation-empire could clearly be much larger, and effective military control must have been a crucial factor, implying a military hierarchy, with local governors and often local garrisons, and with the development of the totalitarian structure that some authors consider typical of the state. I suggest, however, that effective control – if less obviously militaristic – will have come first at ESM level.

The exchange situation implied by this model is seen in figure 6. Within an ESM, the internal exchange is by redistribution with some reciprocity (redistribution including the possibility of market exchange). Among ESMs there is intermediate exchange on a basis of reciprocity. And between ESMs and the outside world there is external exchange. Dotted lines indicate the possibility of the amalgamation of the ESMs into an empire, with the development of a higher-order central place (or the emergence as such of the centre of one of the ESMs).

*Trade as Remote Interaction*
The interactions associated with exchange within the system, specifically within the ESM, have already been mentioned, with redistribution taking a major part (with or without the agency of market exchange), reciprocity a subsidiary position, and marriage exchange a significant role. Intermediate exchange between ESMs, but within the culture or civilisation, still awaits adequate analysis. But again marriage exchange must be an important factor. It is now exchange across the boundaries of the culture or civilisation –

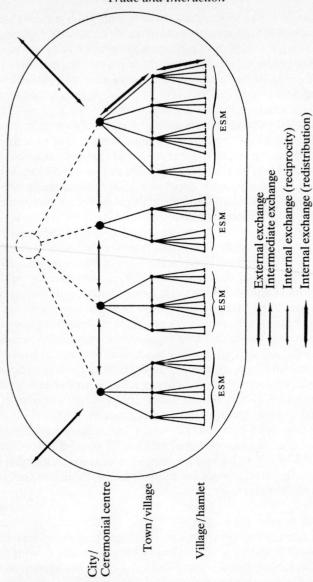

*Figure* 6. Modes of exchange for an early civilisation, indicating the place of the E S M s within it and the scope of internal, intermediate and external trade. Dotted lines indicate the organisational unification occurring when the E S M s of the civilisation merge to form a single empire or civilisation-state.

external exchange – that concerns us.

Our interest is in the effects of this exchange upon a culture which, in terms of organisation, of hierarchy, of volume of internal exchange, is *less* highly differentiated than its neighbour. The possible effects of the internal organisation arising with the development of an export trade are indicated in the next section; our interest focuses here not so much on purely economic organisation as on the effects upon the system of the flow of information reaching it from its more highly organised neighbour, the process numbered 6, *Emulation* (below, p.113).

It should be explained at this point that exchange between major regions with very different resource patterns has not been singled out for special mention. For I take it as axiomatic that any early civilisation must control, normally within its boundaries, such resources as are altogether essential for its survival. In cases where there is a very heavy interdependence between them, developments may occur as in process 3, *Intraregional Diversity* (below, p.109), and the boundaries of the civilisation may develop (as a consequence of the strong interactions between the regions) so that the ecological diversity is an internal one.

Our interest in remote interactions was well expressed by Flannery (1972, 135): 'It might provide a great deal of unexpected fun if future studies used such exchange as a window into each society's explosively evolving ability to collect and process information about neighbouring societies.'

Exchange of goods between A and B through intermediary or intermediaries C can effect the transmission of information in three ways:

(i) *Commodity*. The traded material itself, at its place of receipt, and independent of the means by which it reached that place, may convey meaning. In information theory terms it can be both signal and message (whether or not the transmitter or the receiver had a prior intention of transmitting or receiving). In what it *is*, if this is something new, it is a message with appreciable semantic content. A cup made of gold, to a person who has not previously seen gold, imparts information about the world. From the standpoint of the receiver it is a message.

Secondly the object itself may function as signal, which requires decoding before yielding any recognisable semantic content. Let us take as an example here the remarkable steatite carvings of Tepe Yahya (Lamberg-Karlovsky 1972b). In the hands of a person (destination) who is familiar with the symbolism involved, these carvings are, for instance, religious scenes making sense to a participant in Sumerian civilisation: he can decode the signal. In the hands of someone who does not have the code, they are just odd carvings.

The extent to which meaning and hence information is conveyed by objects is a complicated one. The complexity arises, as so often in the attempt to apply information theory in an unrestricted human context, because many channels of communication are in operation, and more are continually being opened. The process does not easily lend itself to analysis, since the bandwidth can never be regarded as fixed.

Objects themselves, in isolation, can convey information, and this process is precisely what Kroeber (1940) meant by the term 'stimulus diffusion.'

(ii) *Association with commodity*. Inherent in the act of exchange between intermediary C and recipient B is a complex of mutual understandings, which have to be common to B and C and which will be conveyed from B to C or vice versa before the transaction can be completed. Some, in turn, may have been transmitted to C on the occasion of his interaction with A. These understandings include concepts of number and of unit of measure (weight, capacity, and so forth), as well as the means of measuring these (scales, graded capacities, and the like). Inherent in the exchange is the very concept of exchanging the two commodities in question, as well as the valuation systems by which quantities are established. (Here, after all, was what motivated much of early European trading endeavour in the Middle Ages: the search for El Dorado, where the streets would be paved with gold bricks, was the search for a land not only with a supply of the desired commodity but also with a favourable value system.) Accompanying the exchange also may be the concept of currency, and possibly some system of recording. It is within this constellation of information types that the regulating effect of exchange over the supply of desired commodities operates (Wright and Zeder 1977, Rappaport 1967).

(iii) *Verbal exchange*. The intermediary C can tell the recipient B what he knows of A and of his culture. A large quantity of information can be transmitted in this way.

The trade situation is an exchange situation, and an exchange situation is an information flow situation. For this reason the analogy seen in figure 7 between a communication system (Weaver 1949) and a trading system is only in part analogy; in part it is descriptive. The reciprocal nature of all trade and exchange is indicated, or more strictly the cyclical nature.

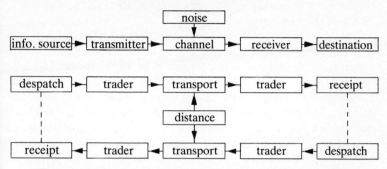

*Figure* 7. Exchange as information flow: the structural homology between the transmission of a signal and the trade of goods.

The enormous complexity of the communication of information during trading exchanges makes it understandable that in the past the whole process has been swept under the carpet by using the term *diffusion*. Progress, however, will only come when different categories of information, conveyed by different channels, are distinguished.

### Alternative Models for Civilisation Formation

The origin of the early civilisation or the state, whatever its subsequent career, has been identified above with the emergence of ESMs, each with a stratified organisation for exchange. This central place exchange, and the permanency and permanent functioning of the central places, underlie the interdependence of ESM society, in contrast to the relative independence of local units linked only by reciprocal exchanges.

One obvious concomitant of central places, not yet discussed here, is *central persons*. These are the individuals upon whom the exchange of goods and of information focuses. The hierarchy of central places thus carries with it a hierarchy of central persons, who may themselves be singled out by great prestige and wealth. While this may be the case, however, it is not a necessary part of their function (even if display, sumptuary rules, and conspicuous consumption often have an adaptive role in facilitating that function). Archaeologists often assume that a pronounced hierarchy of personal wealth and conspicuously asserted prestige is a necessary accompaniment of early civilisations. This, however, is not so. In both the Greek city-states and Republican Rome, a different set of values soon developed – although it could be argued that these democratic, antiroyal values were not a feature of the first emergence of the ESM.

I have often thought how singular the Indus Valley civilisation is in this respect. For it possesses very large urban centres with a rectangular layout more impressive than any in Early Dynastic Mesopotamia, and worthy of comparison with Teotihuacan. The centres have 'citadels' with large granaries which were clearly the nub of a complex redistributive exchange system. A range of traded materials is seen. Yet nowhere, on the basis of the archaeological record at present available, is there the superabundant personal wealth so characteristic of the early civilisations of Egypt, Mesopotamia, and China. Nor has there been found the exceedingly complex and monumental religious symbolism characteristic of the Mesoamerican early state modules. Nor yet, despite the existence of a script, is there the vainglorious assertion of personal power, expressed in colossal monuments or inscriptions, that we see in Egypt and Mesopotamia. The Harappan civilisation does not reveal to the world any Ramses, any Hammurabi, nor yet any Gudea of Lagash. Indus exchange evidently functioned without such emphatically assertive statements about the prestige and power of the central person.

I should like to identify now six different *processes* which may lead to the formation of central places serving ESMs. In most real instances a number of these processes will be in operation, but they can be separately distinguished. Indeed, different 'mixes' of these processes can be seen to generate a typology of early centres which approximates the range recognised by archaeology today. All these processes centre upon exchange 'at a distance' – at a central place – whether of information or of goods. The first three involve internal exchange, and only one of these calls for marked ecological diversity within the ESM. The three processes of internal exchange will first be outlined.

*Endogenous Growth*

1. *Social and religious exchange predominating.* With an initial distribution of dispersed settlement in farmsteads, hamlets, or small villages, a *periodic* central place emerges, for seasonal ceremonies related either to the identity of the community (i.e. the common affiliation of the participants), in some cases focusing on the person of the chief, or to projections of the seasonally changing world, or

106

both. The Kyaka meetings of New Guinea are instances of such functioning at tribal level, and nearly all chiefdoms have such periodic central places. Mention has already been made of Mu'a on Tongatapu, which was the scene of the annual presentation of first fruits to the Tu'i Tonga. Sahlins and others have stressed the material redistribution of such occasions, which was certainly impressive, but an annual feast can have little long-term impact on subsistence. The importance of the occasion was in terms of information – as a meeting. The ceremonial centre of Orongo on Easter Island is particularly interesting because the business of awaiting the migratory arrival of the sacred bird necessitated the prolonged occupation of the site. It seems likely that some of the central places of the British Neolithic (Renfrew 1973) were periodic central places of this kind (see chapters 7 and 8).

At the point that such a periodic central place becomes a permanent central place, the territorial unit may be regarded as an ESM. It is not sufficient, however, that the location be inhabited throughout the year; it must continue to fulfil its central function as well. And the specialists who control that function must be full-time specialists. This implies, of course, that the exchange includes a measure of foodstuffs and other goods to sustain these central persons, in return for the information they impart.

A multiplier-effect interaction is here possible between the subsistence and projective systems. For the calendric expertise offered at the central place may be of real significance in the scheduling of subsistence activities in relation to the seasons, and the successful development of the subsistence subsystem may thus be linked to that of the projective one.

Naturally such central places become the foci also of other types of exchange. Yet the process described may be seen in operation. I suspect that this exchange model is applicable to a number of Mesoamerican developments. Prototypes for the ESM centre are to be seen in many chiefdom periodic central places. The population of the central place on this model can be very small – little larger than that of the various residence units which it serves.

2. *Population agglomeration and craft specialisation.* On this model, the population accumulation, at a local agricultural village/town location, of an agglomerate population distribution makes possible economies of scale. It was indicated above that in parts of the Old World, villages of up to 4,000 persons are possible, without any of these being supported in exchange for the discharge of central-person functions. In reality, of course, 4,000 persons living

together at one location do interact and do participate in exchanges, even if theoretically they could live as independently as if their settlement pattern were dispersed.

Population size itself may lead to the development of specialist occupations – potter, leather worker, weaver, and so forth – so that the society becomes differentiated, and a redistributive system develops. This is possible without any marked ecological diversity in the territory.

With the emergence of a redistributive system, some central regulation or control is likely to develop. and this can actively *organise* aspects of the specialisation. For instance, irrigation works can be regulated centrally with far greater efficiency than that of persons acting together on an essentially reciprocal basis of mutual agreement.

As the benefits of specialisation are seen, the centre becomes a point of attraction for a larger territory and can act as an exchange centre for goods made elsewhere. For instance, if one neighbouring village is effective at pottery manufacture, and another at weaving, the centre will become the locus of exchange of these products (figure 1).

It should be noted that specialisation of this kind need not rely in any way upon diversity of resources; it can arise simply from the local development, over a long period, of specialist skills. For instance, in the well-organised – but not central place-based – trading system of the Vitiaz Strait, the production of some goods is, of course, environmentally determined. For other products, however, this is not so. 'For example, Sio lacks neither the resources nor skills required to produce mats, ornaments of cowrie shell, and tambu shell as sago. Why import these goods from Siassi?' (Harding 1967, 54).

An answer to this question can be offered at several levels. At that of personal motivation may be the desire for prestige through the ownership of goods, which are obtained through successful trade. Wright and Zeder (1977) have stressed a suggestion by Rappaport (1967) that the real, operative function of the trade of some 'ritual' artefacts may be to regulate exchange systems of goods essential to the maintenance of life. Harding's question may perhaps be answered along these lines. In any case, devices such as those described by Harding and Rappaport do ensure the existence of a permanent trade at a tribal level, rather than the periodic exchange occurring in the earlier stages of model 1 above.

The central place of the ESM likewise regulates such exchange.

whether or not by the use of prestige commodities. In the long term it is to the advantage of a village entirely independent in terms of subsistence commodities and with a temporary sufficiency (or 'surplus') of others to go on trading. For to fail to do so would endanger the survival of trading partners who are not self-sufficient in subsistence terms and would hence jeopardise the long-term supply of the imports currently in surplus.

Of course in most real cases prestige commodities will also be involved, their prestige deriving from an ascribed value in the social or projective subsystem. The case which does not rest heavily on prestige commodities is, however, worth stressing so that the validity of this second model can be recognised, even if it usually works in association with other processes.

Prototypes for such ESM centres may be recognised in such early population centres as Jericho and Çatal Hüyük. The central-place activities here outlined, in the absence of ecological diversity, are very much those of classical central-place theory.

3. *Intraregional diversity.* Consider a region no more than 1,000 km$^2$ in area with four subregions, in each of which the same four different crops may be grown but with differing yields per unit area. Suppose that each subregion can grow one of these crops with a higher yield per unit area than the three other subregions. Clearly it is possible for an individual in one region to live independently and have a supply of all four crops, homegrown. His total yield, however, will be increased if he can specialise in the one crop at which he is most efficient and exchange a portion of his harvest for supplies of the other three crops.

The advantages of redistribution over reciprocity, in terms purely of efficiency, as indicated above, when a large proportion of the total per capita produce is to be exchanged, are considerable. In such a case a redistributive centre is to be expected, located at or near the point of intersection where three of the four, or if possible all four, subregions meet.

The same arguments apply with even greater force when key resources are very highly localised, as in the case of metals, precious stones, and other minerals.

These ecological circumstances thus favour the development of a major exchange centre, the subsistence subsystem developing a multiplier effect with the communications subsystem. Flannery and Coe (1968) have described this process in their discussion of the development of social organisation in symbolic areas of ecological diversity. I have similarly stressed the crucial significance for early

Aegean civilisation of Mediterranean polyculture (Renfrew 1972, 297–307). The development of viticulture and the cultivation of the olive made effective what was formerly only a potential diversity in the environment, and led in the third millennium BC to the form-ation of small proto-urban settlements, which were succeeded in the second millennium by the palace centres of the Minoan-Mycenaean civilisation (figure 3). Yet the population of many of the ESM central places was no larger than Early Neolithic Çatal Hüyük.

These three entirely endogenous processes can be imagined as working in isolation, but in reality each carries with it something of the others. The process of city formation in terms primarily of these three processes is seen schematically in figure 8. The starting point is a small, noncentral place with small population – a hamlet. The three processes are seen at work, generating (1) a proto-urban centre indicating a periodic central place (Stonehenge, perhaps): (2) a centre of population with few urban functions (such as Jeri-cho); and (3) a redistribution locus regulating intraregional divers-ity (such perhaps as Early Bronze Age Lerna in the Aegean, with the central store, the House of the Tiles, and associated sealings).

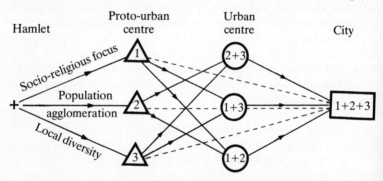

*Figure* 8. Alternative paths for the formation of the urban centre and the city. Three processes, all endogenous, are singled out: increase of population, exchange arising from local diversity, and the develop-ment of a social or religious focus. In each case the proto-urban centre will be of a different type. The city is always the product of the operation of all three processes.

If these processes continued unchecked they would reach more extreme situations (not shown on figure 8). For instance, process 1 would result in colossal ceremonial centres without any sizeable permanent population or any significant role as an exchange centre

110

for goods. Probably Monte Albán or Angkor Wat come as close as any human centre to this extreme. Process 2 would result in massive urban centres of population, with limited social or religious significance and without much local diversity. The Indus Valley cities could be caricatured to fit this role, but there is probably no real case to fit it. Process 3 would result in centres for local redistribution, or in markets, which have only a low population and little symbolic or socio-religious function. Again it would be difficult to find real cases to fit this extreme – ports of trade are excluded here since they do not exist until well after the development of ESMs. But one of the main points of the earlier argument was that redistributive functions imply central persons, and hence usually social actions centred upon them.

Figure 8 indicates six paths by which the three notional forms of urban centre which reflect the working of two of these processes may be reached. The circle labelled 1 + 3 designates those centres where redistribution and social and religious functions take place but which have limited permanent population. This is the well-known phenomenon of 'civilisation without cities', where the degree of urbanisation (calculated on the basis of the number of 'urban' dwellers) is much lower than in an agglomerate population distribution whose centres nonetheless lack urban functions.

The final stage envisaged is the emergence of the city with its full complexity. In reality few cities have emerged without a contribution from all three processes, and ultimately the systemic model which considers all three at a time, mutually operating, is closer to reality. To distinguish discrete paths, as in figure 8, may not be entirely warranted, but it does allow a typlogy of central places to arise, generated by the varying operation of these processes.

In discussing such endogenous change, no mention has been made of the operation of external trade or of other input from outside the civilisation territory. Yet external factors can play a significant role in morphogenesis without making the process itself an exogenous one; an exogenous civilisation, that is one that is secondary or derived, can only arise through contact with an existing earlier civilisation. But neither external trade nor conflict at the borders of the civilisation need imply contact of this kind. Such factors are:

(a) External trade. When conducted with *less* centralised communities, external trade may nonetheless play a significant role: the goods traded may be such as will readily appear prestigious within the civilisation boundary. Central persons who control the supply of

111

these goods may thus achieve added power and status. This is not, however, the process described by Flannery (1968), where trade was heightening a hierarchy of a *less* ordered society, in trading contact with a *more* highly ordered one. And in the instance from the central Maya lowlands discussed by Tourtellot and Sabloff (1972), it was again supposed that a ranked society emerged, partially as a consequence of trade in prestige goods, these being supplied by a more highly ranked society whose values were in some way adopted along with the goods.

(b) *Hostilities*. Armed conflict has not been considered here as a major process leading to the formation of central places. It may indeed favour aggregation behind a wall, as at Jericho, but that is little more than a preliminary for process 2. A Çatal Hüyük or a Jericho need display no more than a mechanical solidarity. Similarly, conflict on the fringes of the civilisation may act in this way as an agglomerative factor, but this need not imply that the external disruptive force is as organised as the culture under attack.

*Exogenous Growth.*
There are three evident ways in which civilisation can grow up in a region as a consequence of interaction with an existing, more highly structured civilisation nearby.

4. *Urban imposition*. As noted earlier, one of the most efficient forms of communication among humans is change of location. When this is accompanied by armed conflict, the entire information-carrying system of one area can be imposed upon the other. This may not result in instant urbanisation, but centralising processes can then be initiated which will be self-sustaining. The Roman conquest of the British Isles is a good example. The early Roman centres were primarily military, but they soon developed the other features of centrality described. Even after three centuries of continuous functioning, however, they collapsed when the external contact with Rome came to an end.

5. *Implantation*. A colonial enclave is conceived here as an intrusive community – one whose inhabitants are foreigners with respect to their neighbours – which continues to interact strongly with its parent community. A major component of this interaction is frequently an intensive trade. This intensive trade has a major effect on the activities of the indigenous inhabitants, amongst whom an economic organisation develops with increasingly more intensive interactions. This can lead to the development of civilisation without any extensive adoption of the technology, customs, or beliefs of

the colonial newcomers.

6. *Emulation*. External trade brings exotic prestige artefacts that confer status on those individuals controlling the supply. A prominent hierarchy can thus emerge in what was formerly only a partly stratified society. In this case the society supplying the goods is already highly organised and stratified, and with the goods comes information, a set of values and social procedures which are more readily adopted because of the sophistication of the source society's products and the prestige in which they are held. This process has been admirably described by Flannery (1968) and by Tourtellot and Sabloff (1972). It contrasts with the process of external trade discussed above (3(a), p.111), for there the information component of the exchange was not a significant one. Here, ideas, values, and technological innovations are being transmitted from the parent society. This is the process that earlier writers termed *diffusion*.

In reality, once again, processes 5 and 6 are not readily separable. For in most real cases, the structurally significant economic effects (of 5) are indeed accompanied by the adoption of the technology and values of the more 'advanced 'colonists (of 6). Yet the processes can usefully be distinguished.

Gordon Childe, the most systematic and persuasive advocate of 'diffusion' in recent decades, used a compound of these two processes, which I have termed *implantation* and *emulation*, to explain the diffusion of civilisation in the Old World outside the 'primary centres' of Egypt, Mesopotamia, and the Indus. His argument is so coherent that it is worth repeating at length (Childe 1936, 169–70):

> But once the new economy had been established in the three primary centres it spread thence to secondary centres, much like Western capitalism spread to colonies and economic dependencies. First on the borders of Egypt, Babylon and the Indus valley – in Crete and the Aegean islands, Syria, Assyria, Iran and Baluchistan – then further afield, on the Greek mainland, the Anatolian plateau, South Russia, we see villages converted into cities and self-sufficing food-producers turning to industrial specialisation and external trade. And the process is repeated in ever widening circles around each secondary and tertiary centre. . . . The second revolution was obviously propagated by diffusion; the urban economy in the secondary centres was inspired or imposed by the primary foci. And it is easy to show that the process was inevitable. . . . In one way or another Sumerian trade and the imperialism it inspired were propagating metallurgy and the new economy it implies. . . .

113

These secondary and tertiary civilisations are not original but result from the adoption of traditions, ideas and processes received by diffusion from older centres, and every village converted into a city by the spread became at once a new centre of infection.

This is a powerful model, an evocation of the way a new, secondary civilisation can be 'called into being' (Childe 1958, 163) through trading contact with an existing primary civilisation. The distinction between the purely economic effects and the impact of new activities and ideas has been drawn above. The latter will be examined further in the next section. The magnitude of this impact in some cases cannot be denied, although the mechanisms are sorely in need of elucidation so that the meaningless term *diffusion* can be circumvented.

At this point, however, what must be stressed is that Childe was demonstrably wrong in many of his applications of this impressive model. Elsewhere (Renfrew 1972) I have established at length that the situation in the Aegean was almost the converse of the one which Childe described, and that the Aegean civilisation must be explained primarily in local terms. More recently, the widespread application of his model to other aspects of European prehistory has been criticised. In my view, the distinctions which in practice have been drawn between many 'primary' or 'pristine' civilisations, and others which are supposedly 'secondary' or 'derived,' are totally without value. Many discussions of the origins of civilisation have been cripplingly limited in scope by their restriction to some received list of *the* five or six, or whatever, 'primary' civilisations. I do not doubt, as the preceding discussion will have shown, that the origin of some civilisations can be seen as fundamentally modified through contact with another civilisation. But with the exception of a few recent writings about Mesoamerica, there has been no adequate attempt to consider mechanism, or to set up valid criteria by which 'primary' and 'secondary' can be distinguished. If *total* absence of contact were a condition for primacy there would only be two 'primary' civilisations in the world, or perhaps only one, and the course of Human History would be very much as Elliot Smith, with his Egyptocentric belief in the absolute primacy of a single civilising centre, described it (1930).

*Trade and the Culture System*

Civilisation implies the development of a highly structured and differentiated society, with specialist production (craftsmen), a permanent controlling organisation disposing of a significant proportion of produce (government), and a developed, explicit set of shared beliefs (cognitive structure), sometimes with large aggregations of population. (Partial or periodic manifestation of these features is characteristic of chiefdom society.)

Complex societies of this kind cannot be characterised in terms of a single variable, whether it relates to population, subsistence (e.g., irrigation), technology, social organisation (e.g., places), or the cognitive structure (e.g., writing). In much of what I have written above, human culture is being viewed from the standpoint of trade. The choice of perspectives for the investigation of culture change is, of course, entirely up to us, but when all the variables in the inquiry are interdependent, to single out any one for heuristic purposes as the independent variable is obviously arbitrary. To do so, however, need not imply any reliance on monocausal explanations, and I suggest that it is useful to have in mind some general model of society to cope with its multivariate complexity. At present a systems model does allow a rounded, qualitative view, and the framework offers the possibility of eventual quantification.

Such a general model for the growth of civilisation is relevant here in offering an insight into the importance of trade in early civilisations. For it emphasises that trade will only be a major force for change if it enters into this kind of positive relationship with another subsystem of the society.

Both the explanations offered by Flannery (1968) for the growth of trade between the Olmec and the Valley of Oaxaca and the analysis by Tourtellot and Sabloff (1972) of the development of trade in the Maya lowlands can be seen in these terms. In each case the interaction between the two subsystems produced coupled development through the multiplier effect.

It is important to note that such interaction is possible only when the traded commodity achieves a value or importance in the social system, often in terms of prestige. This is an instance of the symbolic equivalence of material and social values (see pp.302–7 below) which lies at the root of many applications of the multiplier effect. For not all trade works this way. The obsidian trade in the Aegean, for instance, involved transport by sea already in the seventh millennium without striking social consequence, and declined dramatically when a more useful and more prestigious commodity – bronze – came into use.

Through the operation of the 'law' of supply and demand, an equilibrium will normally be reached whereby the flow of a given commodity settles down to a stable rate. The development of a social system is just one of the ways, however, by which sustained growth in the volume of trade may occur. Multiplier-effect interaction can occur with other subsystems: in the third millennium Aegean, the technological interaction was particularly strong. There the innovation of bronze metallurgy (which did not take place overnight, and can itself be analysed in these terms) naturally resulted in a trade in bronze goods. The bronze trade did not, however, stabilise at a given level, with a steady supply of daggers or axes. For at each stage the increasing flow of trade, related to increasing production, seems to have produced a spin-off of innovation. The new forms of artefact thus produced (such as metal vessels and swords) became new commodities for trade without necessarily competing with the older ones. Again, the increasing bulk of material manufactures seem to have led both to economies of scale and to further technological innovation. A period of technological and commercial growth ensued which lasted for well over a millennium (figure 9) and terminated only when other factors (probably demographic and social) brought about a system collapse and the Greek Dark Age.

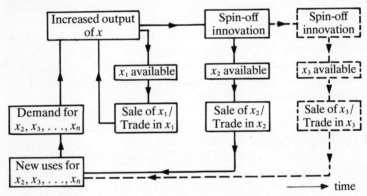

*Figure* 9. The dependence of sustained growth upon the interaction between subsystems: the multiplier effect. In this example growth in trade is related to technological innovation, and vice versa. (Note that *demand* and *new uses* relate also to the social subsystem.)

In general terms, therefore, the importance of trade for the development of early civilisation will be understood fully only in the context of its impact upon other subsystems of the culture system.

## Questions of Archaeological Analysis

Hypothetical analyses such as those drawn in the last section, and considerations of information flow, can be of practical use to the archaeologist only if they allow him to seek and find (or disconfirm) patterns among the real data. Progress has been made in this direction; there is scope for much more.

## Documentation of Action at a Distance

The most striking advance of the past decade in the study of trade has been the development of characterisation studies reliably establishing, by scientific means, the source of traded materials found far from their origin. Generally speaking, this can most readily be accomplished for minerals, but techniques exist also for organic products such as amber (by infrared absorption spectroscopy: Beck *et al.* 1965) and marine shells (by oxygen isotope analysis: Shackleton and Renfrew 1970). In general, however, the spatial discrimination that can be achieved by these means for plant and animal products is no finer than the spatial discrimination arising from their differential distribution in different ecological zones or niches. The most obvious such ecological distinction is sea versus land, allowing firm although rather unspecific conclusions to be drawn from marine finds on land.

Among the discriminatory methods listed in an earlier survey (Renfrew 1969) were examination of thin sections by the petrological microscope, x-ray diffraction, trace-element analysis by optical spectroscopy, trace-element analysis by x-ray fluorescence spectroscopy, and trace-element analysis by neutron activation. Other well-established methods are atomic absorption spectroscopy and analysis by gamma-ray back-scatter. Descriptions of these and other techniques will be found in the periodical *Archaeometry*.

Other characterisation methods recently employed include fission track analysis (Durrani *et al.* 1971), cathode luminescence (Renfrew and Peacey 1968), Mössbauer spectrography (Pires-Ferreira 1973), and mass spectrometry for metal isotopes (Brill and Wampler 1967).

Among important recent developments based on existing methods have been the characterisation of traded objects in the Pacific area (Ambrose and Green 1972) and the much more systematic and effective use of petrological methods (including heavy mineral analysis) to study early ceramics (Peacock 1970).

117

Finally, the use of explictly statistical procedures to handle the results of these analyses (e.g. Newton and Renfrew 1970) has made the resulting discrimination both finer and more reliable. In some fields, however – for instance the characterisation of metals by trace-element analysis – problems of interpretation sometimes make the results of doubtful validity.

*Spatial Analysis*
Until recently the effect of different modes of exchange upon spatial distribution of traded goods has been neglected. In consequence, the possibility of learning about exchange modes from the archaeological distributions recovered has not been explored.

There are three obvious complications. The first is that only some classes of traded commodity are sufficiently durable or distinguishable to be reflected as such in the archaeological record. A trade in slaves, for instance, would be extremely hard to detect.

Secondly, the distributions recovered come in the form of what is found – that is to say in the form of materials that left the trading system. The record covers either use of the goods resulting in burial or loss of goods resulting in burial. The archaeologist studying trade is thus in the same position as the archaeologist using frequencies of tools recovered to gauge frequencies of utilisation (cf. Binford, 1973). Archaeological recovery results from the ancient civilisation's failure to keep things and is therefore not a direct measure of frequency of use. Burial of goods with the dead will, of course, normally be a deliberate act, but does not necessarily give a representative inventory of the full range of the dead person's possessions.

Thirdly, a spatial distribution of finds never represents a situation at a single point in time. It represents a series of events over a definite time span; it is a palimpsest of activities.

All these restrictions imply that the archaeologist cannot use the geographical techniques of locational analysis unthinkingly, despite their potential value. On the other hand, the presence of more than one characterisable commodity within a trading network offers a much wider range of approaches. The work of G. A. Wright (1969), H. T. Wright (1972), and Pires-Ferreira (1973) makes pioneering steps in this promising direction.

One of the problems bearing on the analysis of trading distribution is that it must be quantitative in nature, and this places greater weight on the recovery techniques of excavators than many are able to sustain. For instance, no meaningful figure for the absolute weight of a commodity found at a site or part of a site, whether expressed in weight or in weight per unit volume, can be given without an efficient sieving (screening) procedure. Recent studies have shown how vulnerable such results are to variations in mesh size. An alternative is to use dimensionless quantities – i.e., ratios (for instance sherds of one fabric per 1,000 sherds recovered, or number of pieces of obsidian against number of flint) – in the hope that recovery of the two classes compared will be efficient or inefficient to approximately the same degree.

## *Modes of Trade: Spatial Aspects.*

In what has been said so far a number of different modes of exchange are implied, each differing as to where the transfer of goods takes place, and between whom. Our interest here is in the extent to which they may differ in *operational* terms, that is to say in their impact upon the flow and distribution of goods, and hence upon the pattern of artefacts discovered. An implicit and dangerous assumption here, already questioned above, is that there is a close linear relationship between intensity of use at a location and intensity of loss or burial and hence of archaeological discovery. This proposition certainly does not hold good in all cases, but I am using it as a simplifying assumption here. In all real cases it requires investigation.

In figure 10 an attempt is made to indicate the spatial implications of ten of the various modes of trade frequently discussed by archaeologists and anthropologists. The purpose of this classification is not to set up a typology for its own sake but to clarify the implications of some of the concepts in use and to examine how they differ in spatial terms. The modes of exchange to be distinguished are:

1. Direct access. $B$ has direct access to the resource at $a$ without reference to $A$. If a territorial boundary exists, he can cross it with impunity. There is no exchange transaction.

2. Home-base reciprocity. $B$ visits $A$ at $A$'s home base ($a$), and exchanges the special product of $b$ for that of $a$.

3. Boundary reciprocity. $A$ and $B$ meet at their common boundary for exchange purposes.

4. Down-the-line trade. This is simply reduplicated home-base or boundary reciprocity, so that the commodity travels across successive territories ($k, l$) through successive exchanges.

5. Central place redistribution. $A$ takes his produce to $p$ and renders it to $P$ (no doubt receiving something in exchange, then or subsequently). $B$ takes his produce to $p$ and receives from $P$ some of

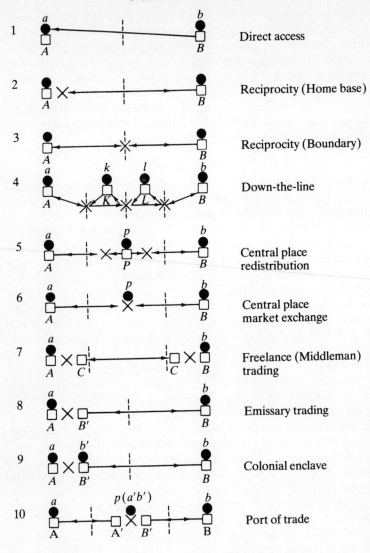

*Figure* 10. Modes of trade and their spatial implications. Circles *a* and *b* indicate respectively the point of origin and the place of receipt of the commodity, squares *A* and *B* the person at the source and the recipient. Circle *p* is a central place, square *P* a central person. Exchange transactions are indicated by a cross, and territorial boundaries by a broken line.

120

*A*'s produce.

6. Central-place market exchange. *A* takes his produce to *p* and there exchanges it directly with *B* for produce from *b*. The central person *P* is not immediately active in this transaction.

7. Middleman trading. The middleman *C* exchanges with *A* at *a* and with *B* at *b*. *C* is not under the control of *A* or *B*.

8. Emissary trading. *B* sends his emissary *B'*, who is his agent and under his jurisdiction, to *a* to exchange goods with *A*.

9. Colonial enclave. *B* sends his emissaries *B'* to establish a colonial enclave *b'*, in the close vicinity of *a*, in order to exchange with *A*.

10. Port of trade. Both *A* and *B* send their emissaries *A'* and *B'* to a central place (port of trade) which is outside the jurisdiction of either.

It should be noted that under 7, 8, 9, and 10, place *b* is itself likely to be a central place, since organisation of this kind implies that place *b* will operate a distribution system for some of the goods acquired, although the mechanism implies that place *a* is not within the jurisdiction of its own system of redistribution.

Five of these modes, numbers 4, 7, 8, 9, and 10, transport goods over very great distances.

Although there is no prescription which says that one of these modes will develop from or give rise to another, the sequence as listed can be an evolutionary one. Mode 1 is a very simple one, where *A* does not have territorial jurisdiction over the produce in his own neighbourhood. It has been suggested that the early obsidian trade of the island of Melos in the Aegean was of this kind (Renfrew, Cann and Dixon 1965). Strictly this is not trade or exchange, but simply transportation.

As soon as the people at place *a* were prepared to assert their right to locally produced materials, mode 1 would develop into mode 2. There are many ethnographic instances of inhabitants of one village visiting another for the purpose of trade. It may be more satisfactory that an intermediate place be chosen (cf. Harding 1967, 150), in which case mode 3 applies.

When the produce acquired by the people of *b* is further exchanged with their other neighbours (down the line), mode 4 applies. It has been suggested that the obsidian trade in the Near East was of this form (Renfrew, Dixon and Cann, 1968).

As discussed earlier, central-place trade is in some senses more efficient than reciprocal trade. Regional diversity, for example, will favour the development of a redistributive system (mode 5). With the development of more sophisticated exchange mechanisms, including money, the exchange becomes less embedded, less integrally related to the social organisation. This differentiation allows the growth of market exchange (mode 6).

The increasing importance of long-distance trade, and the increasing bulk, implies that mode 4, with its many changes of hands, is inefficient. The number of changes of hands can be reduced if one carrier or middleman has the means of transport (and can assure security over intermediate territories) to cover the entire intervening distance between $a$ and $b$ (mode 7). Both security and transport are facilitated by riverine or marine travel, and waterborne trade was a favourite mode for ESMS. Trade between the Aegean and the East Mediterranean in Middle Minoan times may have been of this kind (Renfrew 1972, 468–70), as was the trade in Homeric times described by Hesiod (Knorringa 1926, 2–15).

The increasing external trade of ESMS made desirable a closer control over the activities of traders, so that much of the trade became state organised (mode 8). This was apparently the mode which developed in early dynastic Mesopotamia (Mallowan, 1965). As the bulk of trade increased and the power of the ESM was assimilated within the greater power of the empire capital, remote trading stations could be set up, colonial enclaves in a distant land (mode 9). The famous Assyrian settlement at Kültepe in Cappadocia is a well-known example. Finally, at this much more highly organised level, where we are speaking of exchange between ESMS or empires, higher-order central places again emerged, analagous in some ways to mode 6. But in mode 10 we are dealing with long-distance trade between more powerful and highly organised units, so that the port trade has its own special characteristics (cf. Revere 1957, Chapman 1957).

In historical terms it is probably fair to present this as a possible evolutionary sequence. In terms of interaction, however, some modes allow a much greater flow of information than do others. For instance, in spatial terms there is a close formal similarity between modes 2, 8 and 9. In each case persons from $b$ travel to $a$. These persons will learn far more about $a$, and communicate it to $B$ more efficiently, than under any other mode. Moreover, in mode 9, the population of $a$ stands to learn much more about the culturally patterned activities of $b$ from the colonial population living at $b'$.

There is likewise a formal similarity between modes 3, 6, and 10, where the exchange takes place on the borders of or outside the territories of both $a$ and $b$. As indicated earlier, the silent trade (which operates under mode 3), market exchange, and the port of trade are all devices which maximise the flow of goods while minimising the flow of information that accompanies the exchange.

These different modes of trade are distinguished here in spatial terms. But there are, of course, other criteria indispensable to the generation of an adequate typology of trading types.

In the first place, absolute distance and the transport facilities available are of central relevance. Marine trade virtually excludes certain modes, such as mode 4, and it is a truism that rivers or seas, or indeed deserts, may be regarded either as barriers or as easy channels of communication according to the transport available.

The distinctions made here carry with them some implications for the organisation of the trade, but none for the nature of the commodity carried. It may be transported in bulk or in smaller quantities; it may be productive, in the sense of facilitating subsistence or technology, or unproductive (this is the same distinction as that drawn by Tourtellot and Sabloff (1972) but avoids the paradox of using *functional* as the antithesis of *useful*). It may be destined for circulation freely or only among a segment of the recipient population; and it may or may not have ascribed to it high value, or confer prestige upon its owners.

This last is an important distinction, since in a society where currency is not used in all cases, it may be that certain classes of goods are not exchanged for other classes. Such distinctions apply even in our own monetised society: invitations to certain social functions may not be acquired even in exchange for dollars. Certainly in Britain the sale of honours, such as peerages, for mere money, even in large quantities, has always been deplored, and occasional suggestions that such traffic has taken place have been met with passionate denials. These are different 'spheres of conveyance'. Firth (1939, 340) describes three 'spheres of exchange' among the Tikopia, and Malinowski (1922) earlier indicated the different commodities appropriate to the *kula* (ceremonial) and *gimwali* (barter) exchanges of the Trobriand Islanders. Evidently these different kinds of exchange involve not only different goods, but also different exchange partners of different distances and differing attendant circumstances governing the flow of information in the exchange.

The information-minimising aspects of some modes of trade have already been emphasised. It is clear also that the number of exchange transactions between $A$ and $B$ has an attenuating effect on the flow of information between them: each intervening exchange transaction is a source of 'noise.'

The distinctions drawn here, carrying with them certain spatial implications, should to some extent be reflected in archaeologically recoverable artefact patternings. The next sections make some suggestions in this direction (see also chapter 5).

*Reciprocity*. The obsidian trade in the Near East has been examined spatially in terms of distribution (Renfrew, Dixon and Cann 1968), and Ian Hodder of the University of Cambridge has made quantitative studies of the distribution of other commodities traded in early times. The Near Eastern obsidian showed that within a 'supply zone' radius of 200 or 300 km from the source, the proportion of obsidian in the total chipped stone industry fell only gradually, to a figure above 80 per cent. The suggestion offered to explain this was that mode 1 was in operation, or mode 2, or 3 *within* a culture region; this is conceived as an internal trade with high frequency of interaction. Outside this radius, in the contact zone, the proportion fell off rapidly, falling to around 0.1 per cent at a radius of 600 km. The device of plotting the percentage on a logarithmic scale (the distance remaining linear) showed the fall-off to be exponential (figure 11).

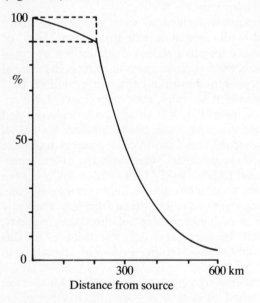

*Figure* 11. Down-the-line trade: fall-off in abundance of commodity with distance from source.

124

It was further suggested that this pattern was the result of down-the-line trade, mode 4, the result of a large number of exchanges. It can be shown (Renfrew 1972, 466) that precisely this distribution, described by the formula $y = Nk^{x/l}$, will occur with a village spacing of $l$, where $y$ is the percentage of obsidian in the chipped stone industry received at distance $x$ from the edge of the supply zone, $N$ the proportion at the edge of the supply zone, and $k$ the proportion of that which it receives passed on by each village. However, a regular spacing of villages or exchanges is not a necessary part of theory; the crux of the theory is a long series of successive exchanges of material from a point source. Comparable distributions for coins have been obtained using the theory of random flights (Hogg 1971). In both cases, however, reciprocal exchange as shown in mode 4 is envisaged. An excavation at any location should thus yield a lower proportion of the traded commodity than at any point closer to the source. Points equidistant from the source should have the same proportion, thus maintaining the symmetry which Polanyi suggested was a basic feature of reciprocity.

*Central-Place Redistribution.* The existence of a central place will fundamentally distort this picture. For if we make the necessary assumption that the quantity recovered at any location bears some regular relationship to the quantity passing through it, the high intensity of interaction at a central place destroys this symmetry, producing the centrality which Polanyi recognised in central places, and which, as I have suggested above, is also a feature of places of market exchange.

If the vertical axis in figure 12 now indicates total quantity recovered, rather than proportion, the asymmetry surrounding the central place at location $B$ is clearly seen. This corresponds to modes 5 and 6. Indeed figure 12 could be modified so that, within the territory served by the central place, the fall-off with increasing distance from it could be exponential but much less steep than the generally prevailing fall-off. (It should be noted, however, that the *proportion* of the commodity under consideration recovered at the central place will be higher in this way only if that commodity is more intensively traded there than elsewhere with respect to the commodities with which it is compared. This assumption may well hold when the commodity is brought by long-distance trade and the others are widely and locally produced.)

*Free-Lance Trade.* Spatial analysis can be expected to reveal a further trading mechanism: free-lance (middleman) trading. For the effect of a middleman trader is to make much more impact upon

125

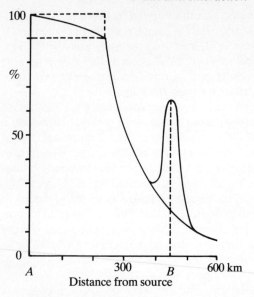

*Figure* 12. Directional trade (redistribution): fall-off in abundance with distance from source.

the distribution of the commodity than is seen under down-the-line reciprocal exchange, *within the locus of his activity*. Any middleman has an effective area of operation, outside of which he does not normally travel. Within this area, in the absence of any preferential service for central places, the fall-off of the commodity with distance from source will be much less rapid (figure 13, where point *C* represents the outer boundary of the region served by the trader). This corresponds to mode 7.

These suggestions, at least in favourable cases, allow the distinction of modes 2, 3, and 4 from modes 5 and 6, and of both these groups from mode 7. Modes 8–10 and the distinction between modes 5 and 6 will be considered in the next section. (Mode 4 is, of course, simply the aggregation of repeated transactions of the type seen in modes 2 and 3: I see no way of distinguishing archaeologically between 2 and 3 if the place of exchange under 3 is always a different one.) Mode 1 could presumably be recognised by the dearth at place *b* of objects originating at place *a*, since the transaction works only to the favour of *a*.

Once again, no consideration has been given here to the nature of the commodity traded or the manner of the exchange. I have

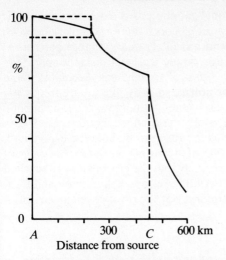

*Figure* 13. Free-lance trade: fall-off in abundance with distance from source.

suggested, however (Renfrew 1972, 467), that goods carrying high prestige or value and exchanged reciprocally under mode 4 in fact produce a distribution differing in one respect from figure 11 (figure 14). In such 'prestige chain' exchange the effective parameter $l$ is

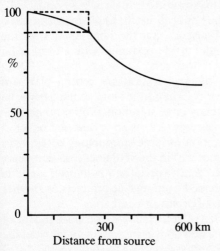

*Figure* 14. Prestige-chain trade: a modification of down-the line trade (see figure 11).

127

lengthened, and the fractional parameter $k$ is closer to unity. In the first place, the transfer of prestige goods often takes place between specific notable persons, and it is likely that exchange partners at this level will, on the average, reside a greater distance apart than the average for ordinary (*gimwali*) exchange. Secondly, these goods are not expended or utilised in daily life but are frequently handed on in subsequent exchanges – Malinowski's fundamental point about the kula ring. Both these effectively increase $k$ to a figure nearer unity. This has the result of making the exponential fall-off more gradual, and thus of increasing the detectable range of travel of the goods. It seems likely that the great distances reached by the Spondylus trade of neolithic Europe (Shackleton and Renfrew 1970) were the consequences of the prestige-chain variant of mode 4.

## Evidence of Organisation

The most neglected feature of prehistoric trade is organisation, in its nonspatial aspects. Not until the emergence of written records in Mesopotamia and Crete, which give explicit (cognitively predigested) information on this count, has the evidence been systematically exploited by archaeologists. So it is that, despite the thousands of seals and hundreds of sealings from Crete and mainland Greece which archaeologists have studied from the standpoint of typology and style, there remains to be written an article systematically considering their use and the implications they hold for the organisation of Minoan society. I suspect that the same applies for the numerous cylinder seals found in Mesopotamia dating from as far back as predynastic times.

The two obvious fields of investigation are central places of exchange and central authority. The former may in themselves be difficult to recognise, but clearly large storehouses offer *prima facie* evidence of redistribution – as indeed does any evidence from craft specialisation. The investigation of large storehouses necessitates excavation at a particular spot within the settlement, so that negative evidence has little force. Craft specialisation in itself, and the extent to which it can be inferred from specific products, is another of the much-neglected fields of prehistoric research.

Fortunately, however, size of settlement is not independent of centrality, although, as discussed above, they are very far from the same thing. Archaeologists are now starting to study spatial distributions of settlements with particular reference to their size and the existence of fortifications (e.g., Hodder and Hassall 1971), and such studies can certainly give evidence for the existence of central places. In doing so they need not imply any adherence to 'Central Place Theory' in its more abstruse forms, where a determination to find hexagons where none exist approaches the fervour of Ptolemaic astronomers adding epicycles to 'save the Phenomena' of the celestial spheres. As Hodder justly remarks (1972, 889): 'It is the various characteristics of spatial behaviour that underlie the model that are really being considered.' Evidently the study of settlement distribution can give clues about the organisation of trade, even if these will need corroboration by other evidence of organisation and by the traded goods themselves.

Central authority, crucial to the understanding of trading organisation, may be revealed in the first place by any insignia or symbols of authority. Seals, sealings, and bullae fall in this class. Wright (1972) based his rejection of the hypothesis that interregional exchange alone causes state development on the find of a bulla at his site in levels prior to those indicating a transformed exchange network. His major conclusion is no doubt correct, as indeed may be his interpretation of the crucial bulla; my point is simply to emphasise its critical value and, indeed, the value of all such finds, which reveal the informational component of the exchange.

A further field, sadly neglected by economic anthropologists, is the archaeological evidence for currency. Recent studies have at last begun to study minted coinage from the anthropological rather than the numismatic standpoint (Collis 1971). The presence of coins in a civilisation is a crucial one, and Collis has shown convincingly in one case that while gold and silver coinage might there have had a prestige value, being employed in conditions of reciprocity, a bronze coinage was employed for market exchange. I think one can risk the generalisation that the existence of any low-denomination coinage, used within the jurisdiction of the issuing authority, is an indication of market exchange. Indeed Polanyi, with his scepticism concerning early market exchange in the Old World, very nearly implied the converse, that there was no market exchange without coinage. Certainly market exchange would be unthinkable without some established currency.

*Evidence for Information Flow*
In this chapter an attempt has been made to stress the importance of trade within the broader meaning of the term *exchange*. All interactions imply information flow, so that continuous spatial distributions of any class of artefact imply repeated interaction and effective

information flow. In the past, artefact counts at different locations have been used to give a measure of 'similarity' between them. Yet this lumping together of features implies a holistic approach to culture, and there is a risk that to lump all interactions together as an exchange of 'information' falls into the same error. For unlike the cyberneticist or the information theorist, the archaeologist must ask, 'Information about what?' One of the most significant contributions to archaeology in the past two decades has been Lewis Binford's investigation of this question (cf. Binford 1972, 329–41); indeed, all his work could be regarded as just this: the examination of the significance of artefact variability. When we are examining the emergence of early civilisations, therefore, it is particularly relevant to ask wherein lies the unity of the particular civilisation which justifies the use of the term *civilisation*. And when using Joseph Caldwell's helpful term *interaction sphere* (1964) we must ask what kind of interaction this embraces, and what it includes.

The consequence of this line of thought is that it will be profitable to examine – together with the distribution of traded materials documenting commodity exchange – the distribution of stylistic and symbolic materials indicating information exchange. In terms of the discussion here, the former should extend across cultural boundaries, the latter be more intense within them. Finds like the steatite carvings of Tepe Yahya (Lamberg-Karlovsky 1972b) take on a crucial significance, since they document an exchange both of commodity (originating near that site) and of information (apparently originating in Mesopotamia). If the information did originate in Mesopotamia, I wonder whether the exchange had any great relevance for the emergence of civilisation (itself here conceived as an exchange organisation) *within* Mesopotamia; clearly it has many implications for Iran. Can this have been trade of mode 9 – was there a Sumerian colony at Yahya? If not, how do we explain Sumerian symbolism on its products?

Attention to the role of trade in early civilisation has so far focused upon three areas – Mesopotamia, Mesoamerica, and the Aegean. But what about the Indus, Egypt, China, and Peru? And what indeed of those second-class citizens, separate but not equal, the 'secondary' civilisations? If our interest is in the working of culture process, why arbitrarily exclude a major part of the available sample? In each case it is the nature of the interactions between members of the civilisation which is crucial, whatever the influence of outside forces upon these internal interactions. Trade, because it is at once the motive and the indication of such interactions, offers a most promising field for their investigation.

[1975]

## Bibliography

Adams, R. M. (1966) *The Evolution of Urban Society*, Chicago,
  University of Chicago Press.
Allan, W. (1972) Ecology, Techniques and Settlement Patterns, in
  *Man, Settlement and Urbanism*, eds. P. J. Ucko, R. Tringham
  and G. W. Dimbleby, London, Gerald Duckworth.
Ambrose, W. R. and R. C. Green (1972) First Millennium BC
  Transport of Obsidian from New Britain to the Solomon Islands,
  *Nature* 237, 31.
Beck, C. W., E. Wilbur, S. Meret, M. Kossove and K. Kermani
  (1965) The Infrared Spectra of Amber and the Identification of
  Baltic Amber, *Archaeometry*, 8, 96–109.
Binford, L. R. (1972) *An Archaeological Perspective*, New York:
  Seminar Press.
— (1973) Interassemblage Variability – the Mousterian and the
  'Functional' Argument, in *The Explanation of Culture Change
  Models in Prehistory*, ed. C. Renfrew, London, Gerald
  Duckworth.
Brill, R. H. and J. M. Wampler (1967) Isotope Studies of Ancient
  Lead, *American Journal of Archaeology*, 71, 63–77.
Brush, J. E. and H. E. Bracey (1955) Rural Service Centres in
  Southwestern Wisconsin and Southern England, *Geographical
  Review*, 45, 558–69.
Bohannon, P. (1954) The Migration and Expansion of the Tiv,
  *Africa*, 24, 2–16.
Bulmer, R. (1960) Political Aspects of the Moka Ceremonial
  Exchange System among the Kyaka People of the Western
  Highlands of New Guinea, *Oceania*, 31, 1–13.
Caldwell, J. R. (1964) Interaction Spheres in Prehistory, in
  *Hopewellian Studies*, ed. J. R. Caldwell and R. L. Hall. Illinois
  State Museum Papers 12, no. 6.
Chapman, A. (1957) Port of Trade Enclaves in Aztec and Maya
  Civilizations, in *Trade and Market in the Early Empires*, eds.
  K. Polanyi, C. M. Arensberg and H. W. Pearson, New York,
  Free Press.
Childe, V. G. (1936) *Man Makes Himself*, London, Franklin Watts.
— (1958) *The Prehistory of European Society*, Harmondsworth,
  England, Penguin Books.
Chisholm, M. (1968) *Rural Settlement and Land Use*, London,
  Methuen.
Clarke, D. L. (1968) *Analytical Archaeology*, London, Methuen.
Coleman, J. S. (1963) Comment on the Concept of Influence, *Public
  Opinion Quarterly*, 27, 63–82, quoted by W. Buckley, *Sociology
  and Modern Systems Theory*, Englewood Cliffs, N.J., Prentice-
  Hall, 139.
Collis, J. R. (1971) Markets and Money, in *The Iron Age and Its Hill
  Forts*, eds. D. Hill and M. Jesson, Southampton, England,
  Southampton University Archaeological Society.

Deetz, J. (1965) *The Dynamics of Stylistic Change in Arikara Ceramics*, Illinois Studies in Anthropology 4, Urbana, University of Illinois Press.

Doxiadis, C. A. (1971) Ancient Greek Settlements, *Ekistics* 182, 4–21.

Durrani, S. A., H. A. Khan, M. Taj and C. Renfrew (1971) Obsidian Source Identification by Fission Track Analysis, *Nature* 233, 242–45.

Elliott Smith, Sir G. (1930) *Human History*, London, Jonathan Cape.

Firth, R. (1939) *Primitive Polynesian Economy*, London, Routledge & Kegan Paul.

Flannery, K. V. (1968) The Olmec and the Valley of Oaxaca: A Model for Interregional Interaction in Formative Times, in *Dumbarton Oaks Conference on the Olmec*, ed. E. P. Benton, Washington, D. C., Dumbarton Oaks Library.

— (1972) Evolutionary Trends in Social Exchange and Interaction, in *Social Exchanges and Interaction*, ed. E. N. Wilmsen, University of Michigan Museum of Anthropology, Anthropological Papers no. 46, Ann Arbor.

Flannery, K. V. and M. D. Coe (1968) Social and Economic Systems in Formative Mesoamerica, in *New Perspective in Archaeology*, eds. L. R. and S. R. Binford, Chicago, Aldine Atherton.

Hägerstrand, T. (1967) *Innovation Diffusion as a Spatial Process*, Chicago, University of Chicago Press.

Hammond, N. D. C. (1972) Locational Models and the Site of Lubaantún, A Classic Maya Centre, in *Models in Archaeology*, ed. D. L. Clarke, London, Methuen.

Harding, T. G. (1967) *Voyagers of the Vitiaz Strait*, Seattle, University of Washington Press.

Hill, J. N. (1966) A Prehistoric Community in Eastern Arizona, *Southwestern Journal of Anthropology*, 22, 9–30.

— (1970) School of American Research Advanced Seminar, *American Anthropological Association Newsletter*, 13.

Hodder, I. R. (1972) Locational Models and Romano-British Settlement, in *Models in Archaeology*, ed. D. L. Clarke, London, Methuen.

Hodder, I. R. and M. Hassall (1971) The Non-random Spacing of Romano-British Walled Towns, *Man*, 6, 391–407.

Hogg, A. H. A. (1971) Some Application of Surface Fieldwork, in *The Iron Age and Its Hill Forts*, eds. D. Hill and M. Jesson, Southampton, England, Southampton University Archaeological Society.

Homans, G. C. (1958) Social Behavior as Exchange, *American Journal of Sociology*, 63, 597–606.

Hope Simpson, R. (1965) *A Gazetteer and Atlas of Mycenaean Sites*, Institute of Classical Studies, Bulletin Supplement 16, London.

Knorringa, H. (1926) *Emporos, Data on Trade and Trader in Greek Literature from Homer to Aristotle*, Amsterdam, Hakkert.

Krader, L. (1968) *Formation of the State*, Englewood Cliffs, N. J., Prentice-Hall.

Kroeber, A. L. (1940) Stimulus Diffusion, *American Anthropologist*, 42, 1.

Lamberg-Karlovsky, C.C. (1972a) Trade Mechanisms in Indus-Mesopotamian Interrelations, *Journal of the American Oriental Society*, 92, 222–29.
— (1972b) Tepe Yahya 1971, Mesopotamia and the Indo-Iranian Borderlands, *Iran*, 10, 89–100.
McKern, W.C. (1929)) *Archaeology of Tonga*, Berenice P. Bishop Museum Bulletin, 60.
Magobunje, A.L. (1968) *Urbanization in Nigeria*, London, University of London Press.
Malinowski, B. (1922) *Argonauts of the Western Pacific*, London, Routledge & Kegan Paul.
Mallowan, M.E.L. (1965) The Mechanics of Trade in Western Asia, *Iran*, 3, 1.
Mauss, M. (1954) *The Gift*, London, Cohen.
Meadow, R.H. (1971) The Emergence of Civilisation, in *Man, Culture and Society*, ed. H.L. Shapiro, Oxford, Oxford University Press.
Meier, R.L. (1962) *A Communications Theory of Urban Growth*, Cambridge, Mass., M.I.T. Press.
Newton, R.G. and C. Renfrew (1970) British Faience Beads Reconsidered, *Antiquity*, 44, 199–206.
Oppenheim, A.L. (1954) The Seafaring Merchants of Ur, *Journal of the American Oriental Society*, 74, 6–17.
Peacock, D.P.S. (1970) The Scientific Analysis of Ancient Ceramics – A Review, *World Archaeology*, 1, 375–89.
Pires-Ferreira, J.W. (1973) Formative Mesoamerican Exchange Networks, Ph.D. dissertation, University of Michigan.
Polanyi, K. (1957) The Economy as Instituted Process, in *Trade and Market in the Early Empires*, eds. K. Polanyi, C.M. Arensberg and H.W. Pearson, New York, Free Press.
Rappaport, R.A. (1967) *Pigs for the Ancestors*, New Haven, Yale University Press.
Rathje, W.L. (1971) The Origin and Development of the Lowland Classic Maya Civilization, *American Antiquity*, 36, 275–85.
— (1973) Models for Mobile Maya, in *The Explanation of Culture Change: Models in Prehistory*, ed. C. Renfrew, London, Gerald Duckworth.
Rathje, W.L. and J.A. Sabloff (1972) Ancient Maya Commercial Systems: A Research Design for the Island of Cozumel, Mexico. Paper read at the annual meeting of the American Anthropological Association, Toronto, December 1972.
Renfrew, C. (1969) Trade and Culture Process in European Prehistory, *Current Anthropology*, 10, 151–69.
— (1972) *The Emergence of Civilisation*, London, Methuen.
— (1973) Monuments, Mobilisation and Social Organisation in Neolithic Wessex, in *The Explanation of Culture Change: Models in Prehistory*, ed. C. Renfrew, London, Gerald Duckworth.
Renfrew, C., J.R. Cann and J.E. Dixon (1965) Obsidian in the Aegean, *Annual of the British School of Archaeology at Athens*, 60, 225–47.
Renfrew, C., J.E. Dixon and J.R. Cann (1968) Further Analysis of Near Eastern Obsidians, *Proceedings of the Prehistoric Society*, 34, 319–31.

Renfrew, C. and J. S. Peacey (1968) Aegean Marble – A Petrological
    Study, *Annual of the British School of Archaeology at Athens*,
    63, 45–66.
Revere, R. B. (1957) 'No Man's Coast': Ports of Trade in the Eastern
    Mediterranean, in *Trade and Market in the Early Empires*, eds.
    K. Polanyi, C. M. Arensberg and H. W. Pearson, New York,
    Free Press.
Rivet, A. L. F. (1964) *Town and Country in Roman Britain*, London,
    Hutchinson Publishing.
Rowlands, M. J. (1973) Modes of Exchange and the Incentives of
    Trade with Reference to Later European Prehistory, in *The
    Explanation of Culture Change: Models in Prehistory*, ed.
    C. Renfrew, London, Gerald Duckworth.
Sahlins, M. (1972) *Stone Age Economics*, Chicago, Aldine
    Atherton.
Shackleton, N. and C. Renfrew (1970) Neolithic Trade Routes
    Realigned by Oxygen Isotope Analysis, *Nature*, 228, 1062–65.
Siverts, H. (1969) Ethnic Stability and Boundary Dynamics in
    Southern Mexico, in *Ethnic Groups and Boundaries*, ed.
    F. Barth, London, George Allen & Unwin.
Steward, J. (1955) *Theory of Culture Change*, Urbana, University of
    Illinois Press.
Struever, S. and G. L. Houart (1972) An Analysis of the Hopewell
    Interaction Sphere, in *Social Exchange and Interaction*, ed. E.
    Wilmsen, University of Michigan Museum of Anthropology,
    Anthropological Papers no. 46, Ann Arbor.
Tourtellot, G. and J. A. Sabloff (1972) Exchange Systems among the
    Ancient Maya, *American Antiquity*, 37, 126–35.
Weaver, W. (1949) The Mathematics of Communication, *Scientific
    American*, 181, 11–15.
Wheatley, P. (1971) *The Pivot of the Four Quarters*, Edinburgh,
    Edinburgh University Press.
Wood, W. R. (1972) Contrastive Features of Native North American
    Trade Systems, *University of Oregon Anthropological Papers*, 4,
    153–69.
Wright, G. A. (1969) *Obsidian Analyses and Prehistoric Near
    Eastern Trade: 7500 to 3500 B. C.*, University of Michigan
    Museum of Anthropology, Anthropological Papers n. 37,
    Ann Arbor.
Wright, H. T. (1972) A Consideration of Interregional Exchange in
    Greater Mesopotamia: 4000–3000 B C, in *Social Exchange and
    Interaction*, ed. E. Wilmsen. University of Michigan Museum of
    Anthropology, Anthropological Papers no. 46.
Wright, H. T. and M. A. Zeder (1977) The Simulation of a Linear
    Exchange System under Equilibrium Conditions, in *Exchange
    Systems in Prehistory*, eds. T. K. Earle and J. E. Ericson, New
    York, Academic Press.

# 5

## ALTERNATIVE MODELS
## FOR EXCHANGE AND
## SPATIAL DISTRIBUTION

*

Characterisation methods and the development of efficient field recovery procedures have now made possible the quantitative investigation of trade or distribution patterns in a detailed manner. The most obviously suitable subjects for such studies are classes of artefact, such as pottery or chipped stone, which are of relatively frequent occurrence at the sites where they do occur so that quantitative measures, in terms of frequency (whether absolute or relative) or quantity recovered per unit volume, can be established. The focus of investigation has thus moved beyond simply the identification of the source of origin for individual finds and hence the demonstration of contact. Instead the underlying regularities in the patterns observed are being sought, with the aim of understanding the mechanisms of exchange involved and hence of gaining an insight into the economic and social processes at work in the society in question.

It is the aim of this paper to draw attention to some of the regularities that are now becoming apparent and to ask to what extent we are justified in associating these with specific kinds of trade or exchange. (Exchange is here interpreted in the widest sense; indeed in the case of some distributions it is not established that the goods changed hands at all. Trade in this case implies procurement of materials from a distance, by whatever mechanism.)

In particular two different models for the traffic in goods are shown to produce distributions of the same form. Their coincidence raises questions of a more general nature.

### The Law of Monotonic Decrement

When a commodity is available only at a highly localised source or sources for the material, its distribution in space frequently con-

135

forms to a very general pattern. Finds are abundant near the source, and there is a fall-off in frequency or abundance with distance from the source. This pattern is observed in many archaeological instances, and fall-off patterns of this kind are familiar to geographers. Frequency of occurrence declines with distance. That this should be so is not unduly surprising, since, in general, the transport of goods from a source requires the input of energy and, other things being equal, the greater the distance the greater the energy input required. The generality, that there is a fall-off in frequency or abundance with distance from source, shows sign of implying further and more interesting regularities. Moreover, departures from it are likely to be of interest and significance. It can be stated as follows:

> In circumstances of uniform loss or deposition, and in the absence of highly organised directional (i.e., preferential, non-homogeneous) exchange, the curve of frequency or abundance of occurrence of an exchanged commodity against effective distance from a localised source will be a monotonic decreasing one.

This implies little more than that frequency decreases with increasing distance. The first proviso is an important one (see Ammerman *et al.* 1978). And we are dealing here with *effective* distance, which is not necessarily the same as the distance between points, since the ease of traversing terrain has to be considered. Deserts and mountains, acting as barriers or impediments, will increase effective distance. In certain circumstances rivers and sea will decrease it, depending always on the transport available. Effective distance may indeed be regarded as a measure of the energy required to move goods between two points, and it is crucially dependent upon the mode of transport available. The development of new travel technologies – the inception of long distance maritime travel or the use of the camel in desert lands – fundamentally alters effective distance.

The absence of directional exchange is a crucial point, and on the adequate definition of it rests the status of the law. For if directional trade were recognised solely by departure from the regularity, the 'law' would become a tautology. Directional exchange and concentration effects are discussed below.

The geographical literature about distance decay effects is already extensive (cf. Haynes 1974, Claeson 1968, Olsson 1965). It embraces many aspects of the spatial distribution of human interaction and offers stimulating insights for the archaeologist. But while we stand to learn much from the rigour with which some geographers have approached their data, the models offered should not be accepted without some consideration of the underlying theory.

Various approaches have now been made toward a regression analysis of the fall-off with distance of traded commodities (cf. Renfrew *et al.* 1968, Hodder 1974). In each case some measure of abundance or frequency is plotted against distance from the source in question. The choice of the measure of abundance used is an important one. Naturally it is preferable to select a measure that is not massively biased by recovery techniques in the field, where so often a high frequency is a measure of intensity of archaeological activity rather than of real variations in the archaeological record itself. In operational terms the choice of an appropriate measure is crucial.

It is the possibility of reaching general conclusions of wider application that makes this field of research such an interesting one at present. Demonstrable regularities conforming to mathematically simple forms are still disappointingly few in archaeology, and their analysis raises new and interesting questions. For there is hope that many archaeological distributions from different times and places, and entirely independent in the circumstances of their formation, can be expressed in this way. If it is the case that these distributions share basic, simple properties, the same may be true also for the processes generating them. And the understanding of these cultural processes is the ultimate goal of our investigation.

## *Shape of Fall-off*

Three principal classes of curves have, up to the present time, been considered relevant as possible approximations for the distance regressions observed. In each the variation of some measure of frequency or abundance $I$ (whether expressed in occurrence per unit area or ratio of occurrence to that of some other material) at a point is related to the distance $x$ of the point from the source locality:

$$I = f(x) \tag{1}$$

### A. The Pareto Model
The first of these is a power function known as the Pareto model (see figure 1).

$$I = mx^{-k} \tag{2}$$

137

where $k$ and $m$ are constants. To those reared on Newtonian mechanics and the inverse square law, such a formulation seems a natural one to describe action at a distance. But there is no clear theoretical basis for the application of such an expression to human interactions, and geographers have in general found that it does not fit their data well.

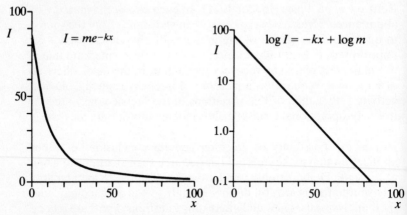

*Figure* 1. The Pareto model. On the left, interaction and distance are both on a linear scale; on the right, both are on a logarithmic scale.

To investigate such a relationship, logarithmic plotting may be used. For

$$\log I = -k \log x + \log m \tag{3}$$

so that when a power relationship holds, the logarithm of interaction plotted against the logarithm of distance on log–log paper will give a straight line with slope $-k$ and intercept $\log m$ on the ordinate. Wright (1970) has used such a plot for obsidian in the Near East.

*B. Exponential Distance Decay*

$$I = m \cdot e^{-kx} \tag{4}$$

$$\log I = \log m - kx \tag{5}$$

In this case $e$ is the base of the natural logarithms, and fall-off is dependent on $e$ raised to the power of the distance. When an exponential relationship holds, log (interaction) plotted against distance – *not* against the logarithm of distance – will give a straight line

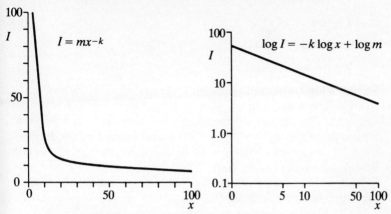

*Figure* 2. Exponential distance decay. On the left, interaction and distance are both on a linear scale; on the right, interaction is on a logarithmic scale, distance on a linear one.

of slope $-k$ and with intercept $\log m$ on the ordinate (see figure 2).

## C. Gaussian Fall-Off
Since the work of Pearson and Blakeman (1906), Gaussian (normal) fall-off has been associated with the idea of random flights (see figure 3).

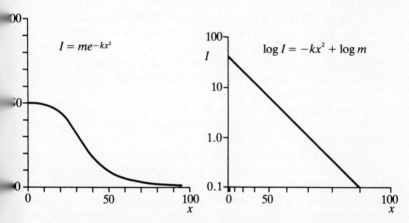

*Figure* 3. Gaussian fall-off. On the left, interaction and distance are both on a linear scale; on the right, interaction (on a logarithmic scale) is plotted against the square of distance.

139

$$I = m \cdot e^{-kx^2} \tag{6}$$

It follows that

$$\log I = \log m - kx^2 \tag{7}$$

So that if $\log I$ is plotted on the ordinate against $x^2$ on the abscissa, a straight line will result, of slope $-k$ and intercept $\log m$ on the ordinate. The idea of random flights was first applied to archaeological distributions by Hogg (1971) when considering the distributions of Iron Age coin types in Britain and the distance of the findspot from the issuing mint.

It should be noted that equations (4) and (6) are specific cases of the more general relationship

$$I = m \cdot e^{-kx^\alpha} \tag{8}$$

where $\alpha$, the exponent, is a constant. Its value is 1 in the exponential case and 2 in the Gaussian.

Other fall-off patterns may yet be sought in the data; log normal, Pareto exponential, and square root exponential have been considered by geographers (Morrill 1963, Morrill and Pitts 1967).

## Steepness of Fall-off

The shape of the fall-off curve is discussed further below. Clearly, in the expressions given, it depends first on whether a power or exponential relationship is chosen and secondly on the value of the constant $k$, which in equations (5) and (7) determines the slope of the line produced when the transformed variables are plotted.

It is in fact intuitively fairly obvious that some commodities will travel farther than others, and this has been confirmed in quantitative studies by geographers, demonstrating the greater travelling power of high-value goods.

This relates in some cases to the distinction between what I have called down-the-line exchange and prestige-chain exchange (Renfrew 1972; see pp.125–7 above).

The underlying idea is that the commodity or artefact has reached its destination as a result of a number of exchange transactions. The two models in question envisage a chain of exchange transactions by which the artefact finds its way from the source to the place where it finally enters the archaeological record. Four features of the latter were put forward (Renfrew 1972, 465–8).

That formulation fails to do justice to the complexity of the situation and the number of factors operating, nor does it follow that high-value goods are necessarily prestige goods, which amount to what George Dalton calls 'primitive valuables' (by implication belonging to a different sphere of exchange), although this is often the case. Among the relevant factors governing the distance a given object travels are mean distance transported between exchange transactions (in prestige exchange, it is expected that the distances are greater); transportability (expressed as a ratio of value to weight and breakage rate in transit) and effective life, considering frequency of use, breakage rate in use, reuse-discard after breakage, loss-recovery rate, and deliberate burial.

A consideration of these factors – and no doubt there are others – makes it clear that 'high-value' commodities will have a smaller slope than others. The exchange of prestige goods involves at least two further considerations: namely, a restriction in the number of those for whom it is appropriate to have them, and the existence of 'spheres of conveyance' restricting the free exchange of one class of good for another. The exchange of *Spondylus* shells in neolithic southeast Europe may be one such instance. Hammond et al. have discussed the Maya jade trade in comparable terms, and Pires-Ferriera (1973, 257) has considered iron ore mirrors in Oaxaca in this way.

### The Down-the-Line Model:
### Linear Attenuation and Exponential Fall-off

In 1968, when working with obsidian data from the Near East (Renfrew *et al.* 1968, figure 2), I noticed that an approximately linear pattern was obtained by plotting the percentage of obsidian in the total chipped stone industry on a logarithmic scale (distance being plotted on a linear scale). As indicated above, this implies an exponential fall-off. A possible generating model was proposed as follows (cf. Renfrew 1972, 446).

Imagine a line of villages linked in a trading network in a linear manner and equally spaced a distance $l$ apart. Each receives a supply of a particular commodity from its neighbour nearer the source, retains some for its own use (which ultimately finds its way into the archaeological record as debris, etc.), and passes the remainder on. If each village passes on a proportion $k$ of what it receives ($k$ being less than 1), then

Village 1 at distance $l$ passes on $Nk$
Village 2 at distance $2l$ passes on $Nk^2$
Village 3 at distance $3l$ passes on $Nk^3$
Village $n$ at distance $nl$ passes on $Nk^n$

At distance $x$ the amount passed on is $N \cdot k^{x/l}$. An exponential fall-off is generated by this series of exchange transactions.

The assumption of a chain of villages at uniform spacing is, however, a needlessly special case of a more general condition for exponential decay, namely a uniform distribution of population. Assume first that reduction in number of artefacts or quantity of material is proportional to the number or quantity left at the point in question, namely $l$. Assume further that this population is uniformly distributed and takes a constant fraction before passing the remainder on.

$$-dI \propto I\,dx$$

$$\int \frac{dI}{I} = -\int k \cdot dx \qquad \text{where } k \text{ is constant}$$

$$\log I = -kx$$

$$I = I_0 e^{-kx} \qquad \text{where } I_0 \text{ is constant} \tag{9}$$

This model makes no statement about a number of transactions but states simply that there is a continual attrition or attenuation proportional to the flow of goods at the point. Exponential distance decay has been well discussed by Haynes (1974). He is using a slightly different model, that of the journeys or trips from the source along a line away from the source.

The key condition here is that the reduction is proportional to the number or quantity at the point in question. If this assumption were modified so that the reduction were independent of the number left but dependent only on change in distance, we would have (in one dimension) simply a linear fall-off:

$$-dI \propto dx$$

$$\int -dI = \int k \cdot dx \qquad \text{where } k \text{ is constant}$$

$$I - I_0 = -k \cdot x \qquad \text{where } I_0 \text{ is constant}$$

$$I = I_0 - kx \tag{10}$$

### Random Walk or Flight. Gaussian Fall-off

Pearson (1906) was faced with the problem of the infiltration of a species into a new habitat. He therefore conducted a mathematical analysis of the distribution of mosquitoes departing from a point source. For the archaeologist the analogy is that of transactions involving the transport of commodities, each period of ownership being the counterpart of a single flight, an exchange transaction terminating one flight and starting another. When a large number of transactions (flights) are included, the situation is clear. Pearson's expression is

$$\phi(r^2) = \frac{N}{2\pi\sigma^2}\exp-\left(\frac{r^2}{2\sigma^2}\right) \qquad (11)$$

where $\phi$ is the frequency of individuals in a small area distant $r$ from the centre of dispersion, $N$ is the number of individuals starting from that centre, and $\sigma^2 = 2nl^2$, where $l$ is the length of each flight and $n$ the number of random flights.

Although containing more constants, this is of the same form as our equation (6):

$$I = m \cdot e^{-kx^2}$$

since $r$ is the equivalent of $x$.

When $n$ is fairly small, the concentration is near the centre of dispersion. But when $n$ is much larger, the distribution is more widely dispersed.

This generative model indicates clearly how a Gaussian distribution may occur in many cases analogous to the random flights of mosquitoes. It should be noted, however, that in this case the term 'random' refers only to the direction of flight. The model is highly nonrandom in other respects, for each mosquito is constrained to undertake precisely $n$ flights, each of length exactly $l$. In most real cases, however, the length of flight is not fixed but could be given by a frequency distribution. More seriously for the archaeological cases likely to be encountered, the objects in question certainly do not undertake the same number of flights or walks. The archaeological record is in fact the sum of the random walk functions for $n = 1$, $n = 2$, and so on up to a high value for $n$. Once again a frequency distribution could be constructed for the number of flights. A further necessary modification may be to allow the source to produce further individuals as the successive flights of existing individuals take place.

The essential point here remains that a large number of unco-ordinated events will, in certain circumstances, produce a coherent, quantifiable fall-off curve in this way. The world offers many examples of such behaviour – Brownian motion is one – and there are analogies here for the diffusion of innovation as well as for the exchange of goods.

## *Attenuation in Two Dimensions*

In an earlier section, fall-off along a line was discussed for the situation in which reduction of goods at each point is proportional to the quantity/frequency of goods at the point in question. The result was an exponential fall-off. It is interesting to extend this assumption to exchange in two dimensions, making the same assumptions as in the one-dimensional case. This, then, is the general situation of diffusion or attenuation in two dimensions. As Dr R. H. Dean has kindly indicated to me, the result is once again a Gaussian distribution. Assume

1. That the reduction at a point is proportional to the number or quantity left, $I$.

2. That the population is uniformly distributed and takes a constant fraction

$$-dI \propto I \cdot 2\pi x \, dx$$

i.e. $\quad \int -dI/I = \int 2kx \, dx \qquad$ where $k$ is constant $\qquad$ (12)

$$\log I/I_0 = -kx^2$$

or $\quad I = I_0 e^{-kx^2}$ $\qquad\qquad$ (13)

This is an important result, since it takes the same form as equation (6), although the generating model is a very different one.

In order to complete the examination of random walk, uniform attenuation, and constant fall-off in one and two dimensions, two other cases should be considered at this point. Again I owe their formulation to Dr Dean.

(1) *Reduction independent of number left; two dimensions.* Here we are making the same assumption that led, for one dimension, to equation (9). The reduction in number or quantity is independent of the number or quantity left.

$$-dI \propto 2\pi x \, dx$$

i.e. $\quad \int -dI = \int 2kx \, dx \qquad$ where $k$ is constant

$$I - I_0 = kx^2$$ $\qquad\qquad$ (14)

This is parabolic.

(2) *Random walk in one dimension.* A particle or object has an equal probability of going to the right or to the left at each decision. After $N$ steps let it be dispaced $n$ steps to the right. What is the probability of this? The total number of choices is $2^N$. The 'successful' number (i.e., the number of ways of producing a shift of $n$) is

$$^{N}C_{(N+n)/2} = \frac{N!}{\left(\dfrac{N+n}{2}\right)! \left(\dfrac{N-n}{2}\right)!}$$

Therefore the probability is

$$\frac{N!}{\left(\dfrac{N+n}{2}\right)! \left(\dfrac{N-n}{2}\right)! \; 2^{N}}$$

If there are many steps, this becomes

$$\text{Probability} = \left(\frac{2}{\pi N}\right)^{\!1/2} \exp -\left(\frac{n^2}{2N}\right) \tag{15}$$

This is again a Gaussian expression.

We are thus in a position to summarize the shape of fall-off curves obtained for each of the three models in one and two dimensions, assuming that the distribution of population is uniform (see table 1).

*Table* 1. The shape of the curves resulting from distance fall-off effects from a point source, along a line, and on a plane, with a uniform distribution of population.

| Model | One dimension | Two dimensions |
|---|---|---|
| Reduction in number independent of number left | linear (10)* | parabolic (14) |
| Reduction in number proportional to number left | exponential (9) | Gaussian (13) |
| Random walk | Gaussian (15) | Gaussian (11) |

* Figures in parentheses refer to equations in the text

## Equifinality and the Choice of Models

In earlier sections two different models for prehistoric exchange are discussed that might explain fall-off effects. The first represents exchange transactions in two dimensions in terms of random flights, where the direction of travel is random although other features (length of flight, number of flights) are fixed. The second postulates exchange transactions in two dimensions originating from a point source, the quantity of commodity retained at any location being a given constant proportion of that which reaches it. The remarkable circumstances is that the shape of the two distributions is identical: it is Gaussian.

Dr Dean has kindly pointed out another case. We have assumed throughout that the distribution of population is uniform. To modify this assumption varies the results. For example in equation 12, we have

$$-dI \propto I \cdot 2\pi x \, dx$$

But if the population density falls off as $1/x$ from the centre of distribution or dispersal, this becomes

$$-dI \propto I \cdot 2\pi \, dx$$

which again gives rise to equation (9), the exponential case.

The circumstance in which different initial conditions and different processes lead to the same end-product in the archaeological record suggests at first the notion of equifinality in general systems theory. There is no difficulty, of course, in defining the formation processes and preservation process of the archaeological record as a *system*. As Kast and Rosenzweig (1972, 23) express it:

> In physical systems there is a direct cause and effect relationship between the initial conditions and the final state. Biological and social systems operate differently. The concept of *equifinality* says that final results may be achieved with different initial conditions and in different ways. This view suggests that the social organisation can accomplish its objectives with varying inputs and varying internal activities. Thus the social system is not restrained by the simple cause and effect relationship of closed systems.

Equifinality is a fascinating concept because of the great scope of the cases to which it is applicable (cf. Von Bertalanffy 1950, 157f.). But I am not sure that it is applicable here, or rather that it relates to the behaviour of the culture system, which is the focus of our interest. For there is no suggestion that the culture system in the cases under discussion did in fact reach a final, steady state to which the term equifinality could be applied. In a sense, I suppose, the formation processes did reach a steady state, namely the state in which we find the archaeological record. But this realisation does not help us in the choice between two models, both producing the same patterning in the data. A more effective resolution must be to seek for independent tests for the different assumptions on which those models rest.

146

## Comparisons of Fall-off Data

The most systematic investigation to date of distance decay data from archaeological contexts has been undertaken by Ian Hodder (1974). In his thoughtful and wide-ranging survey he has for the first time collected sufficient instances to make the distinctions discussed above of more than academic interest. At the same time, the treatment given above of the models generating the different patterns puts some of these real cases in a new light.

Hodder used the very general expression, equation (8) above, in the form

$$\log I = a - bD^{\alpha} + c \qquad (16)$$

His method was to use a computer program to calculate the best fit regression line, performing the calculation for several values of $\alpha$ in succession (varying in steps of 0.1 from $\alpha = 0.1$ to $\alpha = 2.5$). As we have seen, in the exponential case, $\alpha = 1$; in the Gaussian case, $\alpha = 2$.

Hodder reported that his data fell into two groups, and such a division is reflected in the work of geographers studying distance decay effects. In the first group $\alpha$ was around 1 or greater. He cites Anatolian obsidian ($\alpha = 0.9$), Dobunnic coins ($\alpha = 1.3$), Roman fine ware from Oxford and Hampshire ($\alpha = 1.0$ and 1.3), neolithic pottery from Cornwall ($\alpha = 1.6$), and neolithic axes ($\alpha = 2.5$) (cf. Hodder 1974, figure 17).

In the second group are materials whose fall-off shows a very low $\alpha$ value, between 0.1 and 0.6. Examples are Roman roofing tiles, Roman coarse pottery, and Middle Bronze Age palstaves.

In the discussion it must be remembered that the value of $\alpha$ determines the shape of the curve and hence the nature of the model. It is not merely some expression for the value of a constant in an equation.

The first group, with value of $\alpha$ around 1, suggests some conformity with the exponential decay situation. Higher values of $\alpha$, around 2, indicate Gaussian fall-off. It is not correct to suggest that a figure near unity ($\alpha = 0.9$) for Anatolian obsidian may be seen as the result of a random walk process. The very thrust of Hodder's elegant regression analysis must be to show that, for a random walk, $\alpha = 2$.

The analysis tends to suggest exponential rather than Gaussian fall-off for some commodities, and our models indicate that this implies some linear patterning. Attenuation down a line produces exponential decay, while attenuation in two dimensions or random walk along a line produce Gaussian fall-off ($\alpha = 2$). Down-the-line trade of this kind has to be seen in terms of trading chains and trading *networks*.

Hodder's second group suggests to me something very different. When $\alpha$ is near zero, neither exponential decay nor random walk can apply at all. He had documented that many of the goods in question are common, bulky, and supplied in a limited area: for instance, Roman roofing tiles near Cirencester. In some cases the slope of the regression line is also very steep. This leads me to suggest that the models discussed above, which are framed in terms of repeated transaction, do not apply in such cases. In some of them the pattern may not be very far from the linear one described above (equation (10)) or even the parabolic (equation (14)).

I suggest that this is *supply zone* behaviour (Renfrew *et al.* 1968, 327), where we are dealing with a pattern arising largely from single journeys. In many cases the user is travelling direct to the source or manufacturing centre, or the producer is travelling with his goods direct to the purchaser. The result is an extreme localisation in the distribution of the product that is not in general handed on in subsequent transactions. There is a radius beyond which the specific product is very rarely found, and this radius is usually the length of a single journey that the producer or user will normally undertake to sell it or to fetch it. In some cases there may be an intermediate transaction at a local market. But in general, within the supply zone, the goods are distributed by means of a single exchange transaction. This is mode 2 of a recent formulation of trading types (Renfrew 1965, 42).

This is to be contrasted with *contact zone* behaviour, where commodities are worth exchanging beyond the limits of the supply zone (although the distance travelled may be limited by the effect of competing sources – cf. p.150ff.). Often they are distributed by down-the-line exchange. As Hodder well brings out, these are usually either more desirable, or easier to transport, or both.

## Concentration Effects and Directional Trade

We have discussed so far distributions in which the exchange is taking place from hand to hand in a homogeneous population. That is to say, no one individual or place is particularly distinguished from any other. In these circumstances any location will receive less of a commodity than its neighbour nearer to the source.

Not infrequently, however, this principle, the law of monotonic decrement, is violated, and a more distant source obtains not only

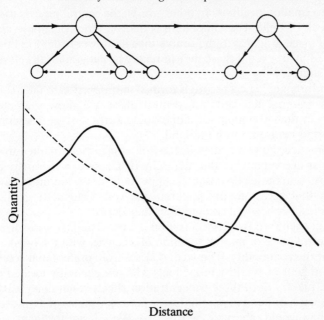

*Figure* 4. Directional trade: the effect of central places (*above*) on the fall-off. The dashed curve (*below*) shows down-the-line exchange: exponential fall-off generated by exchange in a linear chain (quantity and distance on linear scales).

more of the commodity but a greater *per capita* frequency of it. This can only mean that it is being supplied preferentially (with respect to its neighbours), and it is here that the term directional trade is appropriate.

In the first place, it is relevant to see in this the development both of larger centres of population and of central places. A large centre of population, whatever its nature, will attract a large absolute quantity of any commodity (see p.126ff.). But this will not of itself guarantee any larger quantity *per head* of population.

The concept of 'central place' implies, however, more than simply larger size. The central place is a locus for exchange activity, and more of any material passes through it (per head of population) than through a smaller settlement (see figure 4).

The hierarchy of settlement is here accompanied by a hierarchy of exchange activity. Suppliers from a distance bring their goods first to the central place, and they are disseminated from the central place to smaller localities. In other words, the central place is used for break of bulk. The effect here is that, in terms of supply, the central place is nearer to the source than are lower-order localities supplied by it, even if these may in reality be geographically closer to the source.

If the archaeological record is formed in proportion to the quantity of material handled, the central place will show a greater frequency than its population alone would warrant, since it is acting as a supply centre for its hinterland.

In practice, however, the effect is sometimes more marked than this. For accompanying the hierarchy of places is a hierarchy of persons. And those persons in the upper parts of the hierarchy have preferential access to the material and will accumulate greater quantities, per head, of commodities they desire.

Here, then, are two concentration effects. The first arises from the central place or market function of a centre, with the break of bulk of the commodity. The second arises from preferential access of prominent or wealthy individuals who are generally located at central places. Both these concentration effects result in a greater frequency (per head of population or per cubic metre of excavated soil) than would otherwise be the case. Were it not for them, the total of a commodity at a large population centre would be greater than in surrounding settlements, but the frequency would not.

Directional trade is to be recognised by indications of break-of-bulk operations (storehouses, organisational systems, waste materials) and by signs of preferential supply in large quantity. In favourable cases, both of these will result in a higher frequency of finds and hence in a departure from the monotonic decrease effect encountered with nondirectional trade.

This argument has been used (Renfrew and Dixon 1977) to explain the decline in the concentration of obsidian at rural sites in the Near East in the middle and late neolithic period, it being suggested that the emergence of central places was actually impairing the supply of obsidian at lower-order localities. Sidrys has elegantly documented the concentration effect operating for obsidian at Classic Maya ceremonial centres.

### Competing Sources

Care is needed in the use of gravity models for the prediction of traded materials as reflecting interaction with centres of population. For, as implied in the last section, the larger population attracting a larger quantity of material need not result in any greater frequency, expressed in frequency per head or per cubic metre of soil.

The impact of a second source of the same commodity, however, is important. Bradley (1971) suggests that the asymmetrical spread of various pottery products, as well as of obsidian, in the Near East may be interpreted in these terms. An equally interesting case has arisen in the obsidian distribution of the Sardinia, Lipari, and Parmarola sources of southern Italy (Hallam *et al.* 1976).

If we use a modification of the Law of Retail Gravitation (Reilly 1931), this impact can be explained. Let the material traded have a desirability factor or attractiveness $A_1$. Then source $S_1$ will supply a quantity $Q_1$ directly proportional to its attractiveness $A_1$ and inversely proportional to some function of the distance $D_1$ from the source. (In this formulation the square of the distance is used.) That is

$$Q_1 \propto A_1/D_1^2$$

When dealing with two sources

$$Q_1/Q_2 = A_1/A_2 \times D_2^2/D_1^2 \qquad (17)$$

And if we take the locus of equal interaction, $Q_1 = Q_2$, and

$$A_1/A_2 = D_1^2/D_2^2 = k^2 \qquad (18)$$

where $k$ is the ratio of the "attractiveness" of the sources. If $d$ is the effective distance of separation of the sources, then it is easy to show that the locus of equal interaction is a circle of radius $kd/(1-k^2)$ with a centre lying on the line joining the landfalls and displaced a distance $k^2d/(1-k^2)$ from the least attractive source (see figure 5).

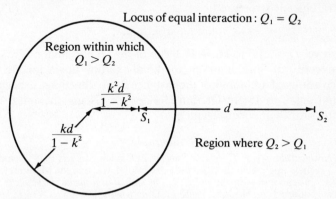

*Figure* 5. The locus of equal interaction for two competing sources $S_1$ and $S_2$ (after Hallam *et al.* 1976).

## Trade and Interaction

It is quite possible for two sources a distance $x$ apart to give rise quite independently to fall-off patterns, which taken together might suggest the behaviour of competing sources discussed here. The two patterns superimposed, as if they were contemporary, will give a first approximation to that predicted by the Law of Retail Gravitation. It is therefore necessary to distinguish the effect of straightforward, independent distance fall-off from that of sources simultaneously in competition. A 'test' of the model, apparently supporting its application, would be of little worth. Moreover, it is probably inappropriate to use an inverse square relationship for distance, as explained in much of the preceding discussion. Until these problems have been carefully thought out, applications and modifications of the Reilly formula should perhaps be viewed with suspicion.

## Modes of Exchange

A recent attempt (see p.120, figure 10) to identify the spatial correlates of various specific modes of trade, in the vocabulary of Polanyi, must be viewed with some sobriety in the light of the foregoing discussion.

Central place redistribution and central place market exchange are spatially identical (although concentration effects are facilitated by redistributive control or by tax).

These two modes should, however, be distinguishable from symmetrical, homogeneous, reciprocal exchange networks. I suggest that a useful field for further study will be the range of organisational devices through which the law of monotonic decrement is circumvented by human exchange systems, particularly those that are hierarchically structured.                                    [1977]

## Acknowledgements

I am very grateful to Dr R. H. Dean of the Department of Physics, University of Southampton, for kindly setting down for me the derivations of a number of the distance decay functions, especially equations 2 to 15; to Dr. Ian Hodder for discussion; and to the editors for their encouragement.

## Bibliography

Ammerman, A. J., C. Matessi and L. L. Cavalli-Sforza (1978) Some new approaches to the study of obsidian trade in the Mediterranean and adjacent areas, in *The spatial organisation of culture*, editor I. A. Hodder, London, Duckworth, 179–96.

Models for Exchange and Spatial Distribution

Bradley, R. (1971) Trade competition and artefact distribution. *World Archaeology*, 2, 347–52.

Claeson, C. F. (1968) Distance and human interaction, *Geografisker Annaler B*, 50, 142–61.

Hallam, B., S. Warren and C. Renfrew (1976) Obsidian in the West Mediterranean, *Proceedings of the Prehistoric Society*, 42, 85–110.

Haynes, R. (1974) Application of exponential distance decay to human and animal activities, *Geografisker Annaler B*, 56.

Hodder I. (1974) Regression analysis of some trade and marketing patterns, *World Archaeology*, 6, 172–89.

Hogg, A. H. A. Some application of surface fieldwork, in *The Iron Age and its hillforts*, edited by M. Jesson and D. Hill, Southampton, England, University of Southampton Press.

Kast, F. W. and J. E. Rosenzweig (1972) The modern view: a systems approach, in *Systems behaviour*, edited by J. Beishon and G. Peters, London, Open University.

Morrill, R. L. (1963) The distribution of migration distances, *Papers and Proceedings of the Regional Science Association*, 11, 75–84.

Morrill, R. L. and F. R. Pitts (1967) Marriage, migration and the mean information field: a study in uniqueness and generality, *Annals of the Association of American Geographers*, 57, 401–22.

Olsson, G. (1965) Distance and human interaction: a review and bibliography, *Regional Science Research Institute Bibliography Series*, 2.

Pearson, K. (1906) A mathematical theory of random migration, *Drapers Company Research Memoirs, Biometric Series*, 3, 3–54 (with J. Blakeman).

Pires-Ferreira, J. W. (1973) *Formative Mesoamerican exchange networks*. Ph.D. dissertation, Ann Arbor, Michigan, University of Michigan.

Reilly, W. J. (1931) *The law of retail gravitation*, New York.

Renfrew, C. (1972) *The emergence of civilization: the Cyclades and the Aegean in the third millennium B C*, London, Methuen.

— (1975) Trade as action at a distance: questions of integration and communication, in *Ancient civilization and trade*, edited by J. A. Sabloff and C. C. Lamberg-Karlovsky, 3–59, Albuquerque, New Mexico, University of New Mexico Press.

Renfrew, C. and J. Dixon (1977) Obsidian in western Asia: a review, in *Studies in economic and social archaeology*, edited by I. Longworth and G. Sieveking, 137–50, London, Duckworth.

Renfrew, C., J. E. Dixon and J. R. Cann (1968) Further analysis of Near Eastern obsidians, *Proceedings of the Prehistoric Society*, 34, 319–31.

Von Bertalanffy, L. (1950) An outline of general system theory, *British Journal of the Philosophy of Science*, 1, 134–65.

Wright, G. A. (1970) On trade and culture process in prehistory, *Current Anthropology*, 11, 171–73.

# III

## MONUMENTS AND
## THE STRUCTURE
## OF PRE-URBAN
## SOCIETIES

*

In the development of research it often happens that what seems at first a rather specific, and indeed minor, point soon emerges as a focus for thought and for investigations which later assume a much larger significance. The particular issue in question then comes to be regarded as a specific instance, at the time in question the first of its class to be recognised, of a very much wider and more interesting problem. Such was the case with the monumental burial and henge monuments of Britain, whose study opened the way to the discussions of the social organisation of those societies showing some degree of complexity, yet not at that time attaining the level of organisation seen in urban societies or states. Just as the consideration of comparable societies in Polynesia led to the development of the concept of the 'chiefdom' in anthropology, and to much wider discussion of the general issues surrounding it (Sahlins 1958), so the reconsideration of the European monuments was a step towards the broader consideration, on the basis of actual archaeological data, of the structure of ranked societies (e.g. Renfrew and Shennan 1982). The work of many writers who have contributed to this discussion, some of them mentioned in this introductory paper, although focusing primarily upon archaeological issues within the prehistory of Britain, is in reality of much wider significance. It develops for the first time some important general issues in the archaeology of pre-state, or rather non-state, societies.

When I first began to read archaeology seriously, one of the most intriguing problems for the prehistorian was presented by the various impressive monuments from the remote past which obviously pre-dated the development of urban life in the areas in question. In Britain, Stonehenge is the most famous of these, and the whole range of megalithic tombs which are of widespread distribution in western Europe. The northern United States have their major monuments too, and many other places, from Polynesia to Malta have comparable constructions. Initially these sites were usually explained in diffusionist terms as the result of some colonial-

156

ist expansion from the homelands of the major early civilisations. Great Zimbabwe, for instance, was first seen as the result of activities originating in western Asia, and only more recently has its fundamentally African inception been widely recognised.

These major works of construction are the very obvious products of groups of people who are otherwise archaeologically much less conspicuous. They are, moreover, very often *collective* works, the products of the labour of larger groups than might at first sight be expected to have cooperated together at the time in question. And the ultimate issue which they raise is the appropriate method of approaching archaeologically those societies which are structured above the household level, but which are not to be considered as state societies. The old distinction between kingdoms and acephalous societies (Fortes and Evans-Pritchard 1940) is seen, in the light of this approach to be a considerable over-simplification. Instead we find ourselves contemplating the whole range of social formations displayed by non-state societies.

The first of these papers to be written (chapter 8) was conceived in response to a specific need of the time. The radiocarbon revolution was just confirming what some of us had long suspected, namely that the megalithic monuments were a good deal earlier than their supposed precursors in the East Mediterranean, and that the existing and widely accepted views of their origin would have to be scrapped entirely. At that stage the necessity was not so much to arrive at an entirely satisfactory explanation for them as to show at least that an explanation in social rather than diffusionist terms was a possibility at all. To undertake this task effectively it was necessary to set the argument into some kind of coherent context of thought.

The obvious framework readily available was that constructed by Sahlins (1958) and by Service (1962), where beside the rather standard ethnographic and archaeological concepts of the tribe and the state, they added the chiefdom. Although these terms are often called 'neo-evolutionary'. I have never seen any force in the criticism that they imply some necessary progression: the archaeological record is full of chiefdoms which did not turn into states, and of societies at a tribal level of complexity which did not change into chiefdoms. There is no implication here of some prescribed unilineal path in evolution. Indeed in my own view there is little justification for the present fashion of categorising the terms 'band', 'tribe', 'chiefdoms' and 'state' as evolutionary or 'neo-evolutionary'. They are simply descriptive or taxonomic categories of social forms, and carry with them no necessary evolutionary connotations.

A much more relevant criticism today is that simply to designate a prehistoric society as a chiefdom does not in itself advance matters very much. A broad taxonomy of social groupings, classed as 'chiefdoms' or as 'states' may be convenient for some purposes, but we are not very much the wiser about a society simply by agreeing that it can properly be termed a 'state' within our definition of that concept. Binford (1983, 390) has recently made this point: 'Many may recognise the methodological bind that these tactics forced on the archaeologist. All argument from archaeological facts is of necessity an argument of relevance. All that can be judged is the appropriateness of the model to the case in question.' This point, applied to chapter 8 here, certainly has some force. Simply to apply a taxonomic term to a specific case does not in itself achieve much. But to say this may overlook the point that the purpose of such a taxonomy is to facilitate research at a particular stage in the development of the discipline, not to attain some ideal of classificatory perfection. Nor has the concept of chiefdom yet outlived its usefulness (Carneiro 1981): it is not uncommon for writers attempting to deal with the problem of the origin of the state to claim as state societies communities which on the criteria discussed here would more readily be classed as chiefdoms (e.g. Haas 1982, 213). To do this risks falling back into the old, over-simple dichotomy between 'acephalous' and state societies, which the introduction of the term 'chiefdom' was specifically designed to overcome.

The use of such terms opened the way to the comparison of prehistoric societies showing some degree of centralised organisation with more recent societies, such as those of parts of Polynesia, as undertaken in chapter 7. The purpose of such analogies in my view is not precisely what is often claimed for them. It removes the discussion from the specific single case to a more general level, and allows the actual case in question to be seen as possibly a specific instance of a more general process or phenomenon. For me the purpose of comparing Tonga with neolithic Britain, and the monuments of Easter Island with some of the European megaliths, was not to compare this or that specific feature with the intention of establishing some kind of equation between them. At the more superficial, heuristic level it demonstrated usefully that major monuments, analogous in scale to those of prehistoric Europe, certainly could be produced and have been produced by non-urban societies without the benefits of any very advanced technology, and that the social organisation of such societies is to a considerable extent known to us today. More interestingly it suggested whole further fields for investigation. The possible spatial regularities in the distribution of the south-British long barrows or henge monuments could be grasped, in the light of the spatial organisation of the Easter Island tribal groups and of their ceremonial centres, as possible instances of more general organisational principles. They highlighted and confirmed the fruitfulness of a territorial approach to the problem. In this way, and in others, the analogy serves as a stepping stone to more coherent theoretical formulations. I do not see ethnographic analogy as an end in itself. At the superficial level it can lend plausibility to suggested explanations, by showing that in other and better understood cases such explanations can and do indeed work. At the general level the analogy is a means towards the formulation of hypotheses and of theories.

The issues which arise from these specific cases are very wide ranging (see Gilman 1981). The most obvious is the whole question of 'ranked societies', to use the term favoured by Fried (1967), although it too inevitably suffers from the limitations inherent in any attempt to classify human societies in a simple and coherent way. That question was dealt with in an influential and wide-ranging paper by Peebles and Kus (1977), where the possible archaeological correlates of ranked societies were reviewed. Much recent work on the analysis of funerary assemblages, especially those arranged in cemeteries of single graves (e.g. Shennan 1975) has focused on the same problem. There is now the growing realisation that the degree of prominent ranking is only one of the relevant issues. Another, well developed by Earle (1977), is the extent to which the central figure in such a society, who commands greatest prestige and power, really does act as a redistributive agency in the manner proposed by Sahlins (1958), and thus increase the overall efficiency of the social group by the redistribution of agricultural and other production. This image of the friendly chief has been attacked by some as the product of a western capitalist society, all too ready to believe in the economic benefits bestowed by corporate institutions, on much the general principle that 'What's good for General Motors is good for America'. The most prominent alternative view is to see the chief as perpetrating a 'rip-off', and manipulating the symbols of his exalted status in order to hoodwink the masses, in a classic Marxist exemplification of exploitation in a pre-class society.

There is now a general consensus (Smoothy 1981) that, at least in south Britain, the monuments represent at least two developmental stages, reflecting significant social transformations, and that towards the end of the neolithic period there were further significant social developments associated with the emergence of exchange networks furthering the acquisition of prestige goods. It is now widely acknowledged that the megalithic tombs, as indicated in chapter 6, served as territorial markers for segmentary societies (Darvill 1979 and 1982; Chapman 1981; Renfrew 1981), and as such had both social and symbolic significance. Tilley (1981, 381) in an interesting paper has gone further, suggesting that the megalithic tombs 'may be the material manifestations of a system of social control . . . designed to bolster and represent as pre-ordained a hierarchical system of social control and established social order.' This is an interesting extension of the Marxist agonistic model applied to a very simple level of society. For it is not claimed by Tilley that the societies building the megalithic tombs were ranked societies or chiefdoms such as were responsible for the great henge monuments. Instead Tilley (in press) argues, with an acknowledgement of the debates among neo-Marxist anthropologists as to whether 'exploitation' can appropriately be seen in such simple, segmentary societies (Kahn 1981), that the megaliths can be viewed as the product of, and to some extent the means of, exploitation of the younger members of the group by their elders. These ideas have not yet been widely assessed, but it is clear that they raise interesting new questions for the relatively simple, segmentary societies of the kind discussed in chapter 6. Hodder has also written recently about the symbolic significance of constructions such as the megalithic tombs (Hodder 1982, 218), drawing upon recent fieldwork in the Orkney islands (Renfrew 1979). In the application of a structuralist approach he was, however, anticipated by Kinnes (1975), who showed how the typology of such monuments may usefully be seen in terms of some rather simple general principles of design (see also Fleming 1972). Other symbolic aspects of the use of the monuments have been considered by Shanks and Tilley (1982) and by Hedges (1983).

The second major developmental stage, represented by the emergence of larger centres, including the henge monuments, is discussed in chapter 8. Recent work has quite properly moved on from the concept of chiefdom which, while remaining descriptively appropriate, soon has little more to add to the discussion, and has stressed their function as ritual centres. The manpower estimates outlined in Chapter 8 have been subjected to revision (e.g. Startin and Bradley 1981), but the essential point remains valid that the causewayed camps of south Britain are an order of magnitude greater in their manpower requirements than the average megalithic tomb or long barrow, and the large henges (or 'megahenges') an order of magnitude larger again. One question not yet adequately resolved is the wider range of contacts implied at this time by the distribution of the henge monuments themselves, and by the specific ceramic form, Grooved Ware, which is often found with them (Whittle 1981). In an interesting paper (Bradley and Chapman, in press), the notion of peer polity interaction has been extended to illuminate this question, and it is clear that the symbolic aspects of the monuments and of their accompanying artefacts will be crucial in reaching some explanation of their very widespread distribution.

It is also now very widely accepted that, at the end of the neolithic period, there was a further major social change, associated with the decline in the major ritual centres and with the development of single burials accompanied by prestigious gravegoods. The earlier of these include finely made ceramic beakers and later, in the so-called Wessex culture, there is a broader range of prestige materials. This shift now seems of very much wider significance (Renfrew 1974, 74):

> At one extreme lie societies where personal wealth in terms of valuable possessions is not impressively documented but where the solidarity of the social unit was expressed most effectively in communal or group activities. And at the other are societies where a marked disparity in personal possessions and in other material indications of prestige appears to document a salient prestige ranking, yet often without evidence of large communal meetings or activities.
>
> Societies of the first kind may be termed *group-oriented*. Those of the second kind are here termed *individualising*, since the role of the individual is so much more marked: one might alternatively have termed them personalising or aggrandising.

These changes have been fruitfully considered by a number of writers(e.g. Burgess and Shennan 1976, Shennan 1982, Thorpe and Richards 1982), and from their work there emerges the notion of a broad network of exchanges. The prestige goods which passed along this network are seen as legitimising and enhancing the status of the individuals situated at its nodes. At this point the neo-Marxist (e.g. Rowlands 1980) and structuralist (e.g. Hodder 1982) strands of contemporary thought do, to a considerable extent, merge with the processual views presented here. There is agreement that the ritual means of sustaining solidarity among the social group, reflected in the henges, was largely superseded by a system of personal prestige, where the position of high-status individuals was enhanced by the ownership of prestige goods. This emphasis upon the social significance of material goods (Douglas and Isherwood 1978) is considered again in relation to the Aegean in chapter 10.

## Bibliography

Binford, L. R. (1983) *Working at Archaeology*, New York, Academic Press.

Bradley, R. and R. Chapman (in press) The nature and development of long distance relations in later neolithic Britain and Ireland: the end of the peer show?, in C. Renfrew and J. F. Cherry, eds., *Peer Polity Interaction and the Development of Sociopolitical Complexity*, Cambridge, University Press.

Burgess, C. and S. Shennan (1976) The beaker phenomenon: some suggestions, in C. Burgess and R. Miket, eds., *Settlement and Economy in the Third and Second Millennia B. C.*, (BAR British Series 33), Oxford, British Archaeological Reports, 309–26.

Carneiro, R. L. (1981) The chiefdom: precursor of the state, in G. D. Jones and R. R. Kautz, eds., *The Transition to Statehood in the New World*, Cambridge, University Press, 37–79.

Chapman, R. W. (1981) Emergence of formal disposal areas and the 'problem' of megalithic tombs in prehistoric Europe, in R. W. Chapman, I. A. Kinnes and K. Randsborg, eds., *The Archaeology of Death*, Cambridge, University Press, 71–82.

Darvill, T. C. (1979) Court cairns, passage graves and social change in Ireland, *Man*, 14, 311–27.

— (1982) *The Megalithic Chambered Tombs of the Cotswold-Severn Region*, Highworth, Wilts., VORDA Publications.

Douglas, M. and B. Isherwood (1978) *The World of Goods, Towards an Anthropology of Consumption*, London, Allen Lane.

Earle, T. K. (1977) A reappraisal of redistribution: complex Hawaiian chiefdoms, in T. K. Earle and J. E. Ericson, eds., *Exchange Systems in Prehistory*, New York, Academic Press, 213–32.

Fleming, A. (1972) Vision and design: approaches to ceremonial monument typology, *Man*, 7, 57–73.

Fortes, M. and E. E. Evans-Pritchard, eds. (1940) *African Political Systems*, Oxford, University Press.

Fried, M. H. (1967) *The Evolution of Political Society*, New York, Random House.

Gilman, A. (1981) The development of social stratification in bronze age Europe, *Current Anthropology*, 22, 1–8.

Haas, J. (1982) *The Evolution of the Prehistoric State*, New York, Columbia University Press.

Hedges, J. W. (1983) *Isbister, a Chambered Tomb in Orkney*, (BAR British Series 115), Oxford, British Archaeological Reports.

Hodder, I. (1982) *Symbols in Action*, Cambridge, University Press.

Kahn, J. (1981) Marxist archaeology and segmentary societies: a review of the literature, in J. Kahn and J. Llobera, eds., *The Anthropology of Pre-Capitalist Societies*, London, Macmillan.

Kinnes, I. (1975) Monumental function in British neolithic burial practices, *World Archaeology*, 7, 16–29.

Peebles, C. S. and S. M. Kus (1977) Some archaeological correlates of ranked societies, *American Antiquity*, 42, 421–48.
Renfrew, C. (1974) Beyond a subsistence economy: the evolution of social organisation in prehistoric Europe, in C. B. Moore, ed., *Reconstructing Complex Societies* (Supplement to the *Bulletin of the American Schools of Oriental Research* 20), 69–96.
— (1979) *Investigations in Orkney*, (Reports of the Research Committee of the Society of Antiquaries of London 38) London, Thames and Hudson.
— (1981) The megalith builders of western Europe, in J. D. Evans, B. W. Cunliffe and C. Renfrew, eds., *Antiquity and Man, Essays in Honour of Glyn Daniel*, London, Thames and Hudson, 72–81.
Renfrew, C. and S. Shennan, eds. (1982) *Ranking, Resource and Exchange*, Cambridge, University Press.
Rowlands, M. J. (1980) Kinship, alliance and exchange in the European bronze age, in J. Barrett and R. Bradley, eds., *Settlement and Society in the British Later Bronze Age*, (BAR British Series 83), Oxford, British Archaeological Reports, 15–55.
Sahlins, M. (1958) *Social Stratification in Polynesia*, Seattle, University of Washington Press.
Service, E. R. (1962) *Primitive Social Organisation*, New York, Random House.
Shanks, M. and C. Tilley (1982) Ideology, symbolic power and ritual communication: a reinterpretation of neolithic mortuary practices, in I. Hodder, ed., *Symbolic and Structural Archaeology*, Cambridge, University Press, 129–154.
Shennan, S. (1975) The social organisation at Branc, *Antiquity*, 49, 279–88.
Shennan, S. J. (1982) Ideology, change and the European early bronze age, in I. Hodder, ed., *Symbolic and Structural Archaeology*, Cambridge, University Press, 155–61.
Smoothy, M. D. (1981) Socio-political development in the British neolithic. Unpublished B. A. dissertation, Department of Prehistory and Archaeology, University of Sheffield.
Startin, B. and R. Bradley (1981) Some notes on work organisation and society in prehistoric Wessex, in C. L. N. Ruggles and A. W. R. Whittle, eds., *Astronomy and Society in Britain during the period 4000 to 1500 B. C.*, (BAR British Series 88), Oxford, British Archaeological Reports, 289–96.
Thorpe, N. and C. Richards (1982) The decline of ritual authority and the introduction of beakers into Britain, unpublished paper delivered at the 4th meeting of the Theoretical Archaeology Group, Durham, December 1982.
Tilley, C. (1981) Conceptual frameworks for the explanation of sociocultural change, in I. Hodder, G. Isaac and N. Hammond, eds., *Patterns of the Past: Studies in Honour of David Clarke*, Cambridge, University Press, 363–86.
— in press. Ideology and the legitimation of power in the middle neolithic of southern Sweden, in C. Tilley and D. Miller, eds., *Ideology, Representation and Power in Prehistory*, Cambridge, University Press.

Whittle, A. (1981) Later neolithic society in Britain: a realignment, in C. L. N. Ruggles and A. W. R. Whittle, eds., *Astronomy and Society in Britain during the period 4000 to 1500 B. C.*, 297–342.

# 6

## MEGALITHS, TERRITORIES
## AND POPULATIONS

*

For more than a century the stone-built monuments of northwestern Europe, belonging as we now know to the fourth and third millennia BC, have been regarded as a unitary phenomenon, the product of a single sequence of events. They have always presented a special problem, since they represent in skill, in organisation and in manpower a level of achievement not surpassed in some areas until Roman times or the Middle Ages. Basic similarities in form and technique among the 'rude stone monuments' of western Europe, as well as those of north Africa and India, were brought out in 1872 by Fergusson in a masterly survey. And since that time it has come easily to scholars to see these structures, or the European ones at least, as linked by a single historical process. That is to say that their derivation, in form and in function, could be traced back ultimately to a single region of origin. Their appearance in a given area was then the product either of imposition – the direct introduction of new forms and practices by an intrusive population – or of acculturation, the borrowing of such customs by an existing population from an intrusive one. The notion of a 'spread' of megalith builders, or at least of 'the megalithic idea', was set out authoritatively by Montelius and further analysed in impressive detail in several works by Childe (1925, 1957). Early suggestions of a European genesis for the entire phenomenon did not find wide acceptance. But the general notion of a megalithic spread or colonisation did not prevent the detailed discussion of regional variants, or the full elaboration of a typology capable of comprehending the wide varieties of form (e.g. Daniel 1958). So the attractive simplicity of a unitary explanation did not necessarily render it a simplistic one.

Already, before the full impact of radicarbon dating was felt, and then the calibration of the radiocarbon calendar, a fundamental

165

tenet of the original 'single spread' concept was undergoing critical examination. For since the time of Montelius (1899) it had been axiomatic that the ultimate source for the practice of collective burial in monumental tombs built of stone was the eastern Mediterranean:

> One does not have to probe deeply into the study of the conditions here in the north during the stone age... to see that the original homeland of the dolmens cannot be sought in north Europe. They could not have spread from here to the southern shores of the Mediterranean, to Palestine and to India. The entire discussion here shows that this would be absurd. So powerful a movement, able to influence the burial customs of so many and widely distributed peoples, simply cannot have originated here, thousands of years before our era. It is indeed remarkable enough that, originating in the Orient, it should already have reached us here at so early a date.

The traditional picture, taking up the idea of Montelius, became the arrival of east Mediterranean colonists (Blance 1961) or at least influences, in Spain. From here, and also from south France the custom of building megaliths supposedly spread northwards along the Atlantic seaboard as far as Britain and ultimately Scandinavia.

A central and fundamental element of this view is that the communal burial practices of Iberia had an east Mediterranean origin. In 1965 this was called into question (Renfrew 1965 and 1967) on traditional archaeological grounds. And indeed the wider application of radiocarbon dating makes it now chronologically untenable (Renfrew 1973a). This is of course true whether we are dealing with simple radiocarbon dates, or using dates calibrated by the bristlecone-pine dendrochronology. The tree-ring calibration in one sense simplifies the picture by permitting us to speak, at least approximately, in calendar years. But it is quite sufficient simply to use uncalibrated dates for the east Mediterranean and for western Europe in order to show that the Montelian view is erroneous.

We are forced, therefore, to contemplate a European origin or origins for the neolithic monuments. Much of the traditional pattern of explanation can, however, still be preserved if we retain a unitary view, postulating a single place or region of origin, and if we situate that seminal area in Iberia. For then the remaining diffusionist picture of the spread north from Iberia can be retained with a minimum of modification. But alas, the radiocarbon dates from Brittany are so far the earliest available, and it looks as if, should we desire a seminal centre from which all the European megaliths are to be derived, Brittany is a stronger candidate.

The objective of this paper, however, is to question whether a single origin, in this restricted sense of a single seminal centre of diffusion, is in fact an appropriate model for the European monuments. In the next section it will be argued that we can detect indications of innovation in several different areas. It will be argued that these should be explained in terms of factors operating locally (whether or not there may have been some measure of contact between any or all of the areas in question).

Indeed it is relevant to ask whether there is really any unified distribution of 'megalithic tombs' in western Europe, despite the admitted concentration of monumental stone structures at the west of the continent, and their rarity or absence in central and eastern Europe. If the monuments in each area are to be explained in terms of factors operating locally, may not these various factors be different ones in many cases? And are we not perhaps too hasty in terming all of these monuments 'tombs'? It has often been suggested that some may have had a significance that was not primarily funerary. Indeed already earlier in the century it was realised that some structures, literally megalithic in terms of their construction, should be considered apart – the stone circles of Britain for instance, and the temples of Malta. Somewhere along the line the tombs of Sardinia and the Balearic Islands were also dropped from the discussion, and for reasons not entirely clear are considered less 'megalithic' than the passage graves of Brittany or Iberia, many of which are built of small stones. Certainly today there can be no easy assumption that simply by selecting monuments in different parts of Europe, that happen to be approximately contemporary, and labelling them 'megalithic tombs', we therefore make them a part of some unitary phenomenon. There is no *a priori* reason to expect a single, unitary explanation. It is important, then, to recognise that it is a taxonomic decision of our own which leads us to apply the term 'megalithic tomb' to monuments as different as the *dysser* of Denmark and the passage graves of Almeria.

And yet, at the same time, it is difficult to escape from the feeling that there *is* a certain homogeneity, both in time and in space, of the distribution of these monuments once so defined. None of them has been convincingly dated yet to before 4000 bc in radiocarbon years (c. 4800 bc in calendar years, according to the calibration proposed by Clark (1975), which is used throughout this paper). And in few cases can the construction of a stone-built chamber for communal burial in the area be set after c. 1800 bc in radiocarbon years (c. 2300

BC in calendar years). Moreover while the distribution of such monuments in western Europe may not be a continuous one, their absence from regions more than c. 300 km from the Atlantic or North Sea coast is striking. Such monuments are simply not found in central Europe.

So it seems reasonable to recognise that there does indeed seem to be a coherence, indeed a measure of unity, underlying the distribution. What we no longer have to accept today, however, is that such a coherence is the result of a single complex of historical events, a single spread from one seminal area – whether in Iberia, or Brittany or Denmark – which stands at the head of all later developments. Such a spread from a single focal area cannot yet be excluded, but nor should it any longer be assumed, now that the notion of east Mediterranean origins can be dropped.

A widespread, Atlantic distribution in the absence of a single colonising movement or megalithic spread need not be a paradox. It requires simply that a particular set of conditions existed in the Atlantic region at this time, conditions which were not seen elsewhere in Europe, and that these favoured the construction of stone monuments by the small-scale societies of the time. Such a general formulation, if it can be achieved, would explain for us the essentially independent genesis of stone monuments, no doubt of widely different forms, in several areas. It might also explain the adoption of similar customs in adjacent areas, and do so in such a way as to give detailed, locally-operating reasons for such an adoption, rather than appealing to migration or diffusion as adequate explanations in themselves. For of course the adoption of an explanation that is, in the traditional sense, non-diffusionist, in no way denies the mutual influence of neighbouring communities.

In what follows a first attempt will be made to offer such an explanation, after a brief statement of the chronological evidence which makes possible the discussion in terms of a number of essentially local and independent developments. The initial step in the argument is to see in these monuments an expression of territorial behaviour in small-scale segmentary societies. The second step is to suggest that such forms of territorial behaviour may be particularly frequent in small-scale segmentary societies of this kind in circumstances of population stress. And finally it has to be shown that there are grounds for thinking that such population stress was in fact experienced along the Atlantic/North Sea seaboard, but was not felt among approximately contemporary communities in central or eastern Europe. I do not claim that the explanation will be an

168

entirely satisfactory one, but it does at least offer a fairly high degree of generality. Among other things it suggests that the construction of such monuments is in some cases likely in remote islands, such as those of the eastern Pacific, where monuments of this general kind are in fact seen.

Crucial to the entire approach are two concepts: continuity and acculturation. For it is suggested here that the genesis of the monuments is to be considered in terms of *local* development, rather than of the direct importation of foreign ideas. At the same time the demographic circumstances which gave rise to these developments arose as a result of the new and imported techniques of farming. In this very real sense the megalithic monuments are thus the result of 'acculturation'; not the passive acceptance of new ideas handed down from a centre of 'higher' culture but a more dynamic working of acculturation processes, where the existing local conditions together with the arrival of new factors work mutually to generate something new and emergent, which was not immanent in either component.

## Chronological Questions

The traditional view of the origins of the stone-built monuments of north-western Europe, developed by Montelius and Childe, was clearly expressed in the late fifties by Childe (1957) and Daniel (1958). As already indicated it proposes an Aegean or east Mediterranean origin for the collective tombs of Iberia, and a derivation from these of the other European monuments. This view can be challenged on traditional archaeological grounds – that there is no good evidence for the initial 'colonisation' of Iberia by the ancestral megalith builders, nor for their movement northwards from Iberia. Indeed perhaps at present we are focusing excessively on chronological questions to the detriment of other classes of evidence. Nonetheless the development of radiocarbon dating, its dendrochronological calibration and the use of thermoluminescence dates, at last offer an objective time scale for European prehistoric interrelationships. It seems to exclude some aspects of the traditional view, and opens the possibility of several independent centres of origin for the monuments.

### The Aegean and the West Mediterranean

The arguments against the 'colonist' view have been set out in a recent book (Renfrew 1973a) and in an earlier paper (Renfrew 1967). The only *points de départ* for the colonists that have been argued with any vigour in recent years are Early Minoan Crete (with the Mesara round tombs as the prototypes for collective burial) or the early bronze age of the Cycladic Islands, or just possibly early bronze age western Anatolia (although there are no prototypes for collective burial as yet at the relevant times in the eastern Aegean).

Probably no serious worker in the field would date the Early Minoan round tombs much before 2800 BC, nor the Keros-Syros culture of the Cyclades as early as that. Nor would the foundation of Troy be set by many before 3200 BC in calendar years, nor the inception of the Cycladic Grotta-Pelos culture much earlier (Renfrew 1972, 221). The Early Bronze 2 period of the Aegean may perhaps be dated by the radiocarbon determinations for the Korakou (EH II) culture at Lerna which range between 2262 ± 56 bc (P-317) and 1887 ± 65 bc (P-312), the approximate equivalent of 2900 BC to 2200 BC in calendar years (following the Suess/Clark calibration).

Already the radiocarbon dates, for what is acknowledged to be a developed phase at Los Millares, make improbable a derivation for the origin of the settlement or its tombs from the instances cited above. For dates of 2345 ± 85 bc (H-204) and 2430 ± bc (KN-72) may be calibrated to between approximately 2960 and 3350 BC (following Suess), which are already too early.

Moreover the dates for the Portuguese dolmen of Carapito I (2900 ± 40 bc: GrN-5110; 2640 ± 65: GrN), together with those from Orca dos Castenairos (3110 bc; 2660 bc; laboratory number not cited: Leisner and Ribeiro 1968) calibrate to between 4200 and 3400 BC. There can be no question of derivation from the Aegean instances hitherto cited in the literature. These arguments of course gain added force when the very early dates for Brittany are taken into consideration.

It should be noted that no undue weight is put here upon the calibration. We may either compare radiocarbon dates with radiocarbon dates for each region, speaking in radiocarbon years bc, or after calibration compare calendar dates in years BC.

*Iberia*

There are as yet rather few radiocarbon dates for Iberian tombs, so that it is difficult at present to build up a plausible chronology for Iberia based on radiocarbon alone. The available data have recently been supplemented, however, by the publication of an important series of thermoluminescent dates for Iberia (Whittle and Arnaud,

1975). In general thermoluminescence (TL) is not considered as accurate a method as radiocarbon dating, and sometimes problems occur with specific sets of material – as may at present be the case with the vexed question of Glozel. But the new evidence is to be taken seriously, and in fact it harmonises tolerably well with the existing radiocarbon dates. It should be remembered that the TL method, not being dependent upon the concentration of radioactive carbon in the atmosphere, is not subject to the same calibration (whatever its other limitations), and the dates are to be regarded as expressed in calendar years BC. TL dates should therefore be compared with calibrated radiocarbon dates, and never with uncalibrated ones.

The TL dates have been used to construct the chart shown in figure 1, to which selected radiocarbon dates have been added, allowing the formulation of four phases for the Iberian neolithic/chalcolithic, preceded by the Portguese middens. It should be admitted that at this stage any such table implies a measure of selection: it is an interpretation, and hence in part subjective. Much more information will be needed before it could be otherwise. Moreover the dates have been set out without a proper concern for the different regions of Iberia, producing five broad phases. Obviously a satisfactory chronology will ultimately have to take account of regional variations.

The most striking point in figure 1 is the harmony between the TL dates and the calibrated radiocarbon dates for the early Portuguese dolmens. Gorginos and Poço da Gateira give TL dates between 4700 and 3800 BC, averaging 4440 and 4510 BC respectively. The radiocarbon dates for Carapito I, Orca dos Castenairos and Seixas, lying between 3110 and 2640 bc (GrN-5110 for Carapito, GrN-5734 for Sexias), calibrating to between 4200 BC and 3400 BC.

These dates may be taken to establish a date range for the developed neolithic. The Cardial neolithic of Coveta del Or establishes the early neolithic, phase I, of c. 5500 to 4900 BC, preceded by pre-neolithic represented by the earlier dates for the Portuguese shell middens.

The succeeding phase III, c. 3400 BC to 2700 BC includes the radiocarbon dates for Los Millares, and the TL dates for Comenda de Igreja and the settlements at Serra das Baútas C ('neolithic'), Castelo do Giraldo and Peñedo de Lexim C ('neolithic'). This I am calling early chalcolithic, since sites like Los Millares may be so regarded, although other contemporary sites will have a more traditional, 'neolithic' aspect.

171

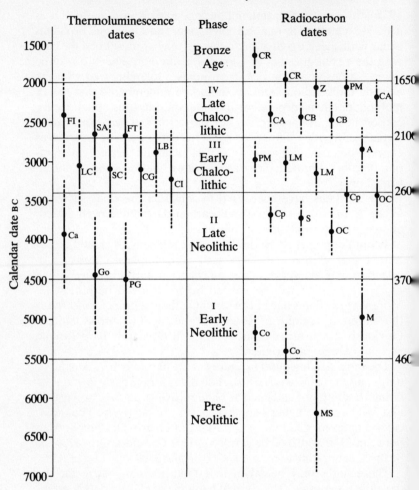

*Figure* 1. Comparison of calibrated radiocarbon dates and thermo-luminescence dates for the Iberian neolithic/chalcolithic.

The radiocarbon dates are plotted in calendar years (i.e. after calibration, using the corrections suggested by Clark (1975)). The corrected date is shown by a dot, the standard deviation is shown by an unbroken line and the second standard deviation by a broken line (so that there is a probability of ~95% that the true date lies within the range indicated by the broken lines). Thermoluminescence dates in calendar years BC (following Whittle and Arnaud 1975) are shown with an associated error of two standard deviations, the second again indicated by a broken line.

This is followed by phase IV, late chalcolithic, from c. 2700 BC to 2000 BC, with TL dates for Farisoa, Serra das Bautas A ('chalcolithic') and Lexim B ('chalcolithic'), and radiocarbon dates for Almizaraque, Praia das Maças, and at the very end of the period Zambujal. The present pattern of radiocarbon dates does not allow us to separate a beaker period from the early bronze age El Argar culture, but more dates may make this possible.

This first crude outline for an Iberian chronology at least allows us to draw some preliminary conclusions about the early tombs. Our Period III, from c 3400 BC to 2700 BC encompasses both the Anta grande da Comenda da Igreja, a large passage grave in the Alentejo, and tomb 19 at Los Millares. This, then, is a period of accomplished passage grave building both in Almeria and in the west.

The preceding phase, c. 4600 to 3400 BC, yields both TL and radiocarbon dates for the simpler Alentejo tombs, including Anta 1 Poço da Gateira and Anta 2 Gorginos. (It should clearly be noted that the calibrated radiocarbon dates do not yet fall earlier than 4100 BC). It seems a reasonable suggestion that the early Almerian round tombs may also date within this period.

It would be fair to say that the radiocarbon chronology implies that the Portuguese dolmens have begun by 4000 BC, and that passage graves such as those of Los Millares were under construction by 3000 BC. The TL dates would set the beginning of each period earlier, quite plausibly by some four centuries.

## Brittany

The radiocarbon chronology, with its tree-ring calibration, has already been the subject of systematic study (Giot 1971), so that it is necessary here only to review the salient points. In the first place

---

It is clear that the early ('cardial') neolithic (Co) was under way by 5500 BC, and that built stone tombs (Go, PG, Cp, OC, S) were being constructed by 4500 BC. The early chalcolithic, associated with the beginning of the Los Millares period (LM), began shortly after 3500 BC, and beakers (Z, CA, CB) in the later chalcolithic around or shortly after 2500 BC. The Argaric bronze age (CR) was under way by about 2000 BC.

Evidently this simple table, which does not attempt the necessary analysis on a more detailed regional basis, is only an outline sketch. But already it is clear that an east Mediterranean origin for the construction of built stone tombs, and probably for the supposedly 'colonist' settlements, is unlikely on chronological as well as on other grounds.

there is a substantial series of dates for passage graves before 3000 bc in radiocarbon years. The series from Barnenez in particular is consistent and impressive (A: 3500 ± 150, Gif-1310; entrance of B: 1250 ± 120, Gif-1311; F, chamber: 3600 ± 140, Gif-1556; F, passage: 3150 ± 140; Gif-1116; G: 3800 ± 150, Gif-1309). If we exclude the late date for the entrance to chamber B as due to later activity, this gives a mean of c. 3500 bc, calibrating to around 4300 BC.

It should be noted that so far the passage grave is the earliest form of monument in Brittany for which a consistent date emerges.

## Great Britain and Ireland

The calibrated dates for the British Isles have been reviewed in a recent volume (Smith 1974; Henshall 1974). We have several dates for earthen long barrows in south England, in Yorkshire and in Scotland (Dalladies) in the time period 3200 to 3000 bc, calibrating to c. 4200 to 3800 BC. Radiocarbon dates for Monamore Cairn (3160 ± 110, Q-675), Waylands Smithy (2820 ± 130, I-1468) and Carnabane (2980 ± 80, UB-534) suggest that chambered cairns in Scotland, England and Ireland respectively were little if any later.

In each area the stone-built tomb takes on its own characteristic form, little resembling either the Portuguese dolmens or the Breton passage graves.

The earliest Irish passage grave date so far is from Knowth (2975 ± 165 bc), and dates for Orcadian passage graves are later than this.

## Denmark

The effect of the tree-ring calibration upon the neolithic chronology of Denmark has been conveniently summarised by Tauber (1972). Passage graves can be dated to before 2500 bc (Jordhøj, 2540 ± 120; K-978), and there is the early date for the non-megalithic long grave of Konens Høj of 2900 ± 100 bc (K-919), calibrating to c. 3600 BC. An evolution in Denmark from langdyss to passage grave seems very probable.

## Discussion

The most important aspect of these dates, from the standpoint of origins, is that each area has its own characteristic early form. Later on, as architecture becomes more grandiose, a more ambitious chamber entered by means of an entrance passage, develops in many, or is introduced.

In Almeria, the round tomb and in the Alentejo the simple

174

dolmen make their appearance in Iberian II, the late neolithic, by 4000 BC, or indeed by 4400 BC if the TL dates are accepted. In Brittany, the Breton passage grave, as exemplified at Barnenez is seen comfortably before 4300 BC. In Britain the unchambered long barrow is seen before 4000 BC, with Clyde cairns in Scotland, court cairns in Ireland and Severn-Cotswold tombs in England at about the same time, or a couple of centuries later. And in Denmark we have the long graves making their appearance by 3600 BC, although the development of the passage grave is later.

In each of these areas, therefore, a case can be made for the independent emergence of burial monuments of stone within a few centuries of 4000 BC in calendar years, just a little before 3000 bc in radiocarbon years. So far the Breton tombs are certainly the earliest known.

The corbelled passage grave first make its appearance in Brittany, but a perfectly good case can be made for its independent invention in Almeria, starting with the Almerian round tomb as prototype. Whether or not a similar case can be made in Ireland for the passage graves remains to be seen: it is quite possible that maritime contacts with Brittany influenced the development of Irish architecture in the direction of corbelled passage graves. Similarly, while a case can be made for the local development of corbelled roofing for the Orcadian passage graves, contacts to the west, ultimately with Ireland are not neccesarily excluded.

The only point which has to be made here is that in each of the four or five regions discussed, a fair case can be made for the local development of burial in stone monuments. No doubt the evidence still allows of different and more traditional interpretations, but there are no grounds for simply assuming them to be correct.

Instead, in what follows, an attempt is made to consider the monuments as representative of the societies which made them, and to consider the circumstances which gave rise to their construction.

## Territory and Segmentary Society

In order to discuss the origin of the monuments, it is necessary to have some idea of what they represented to the societies which built them. This implies an understanding of their function – not just in the sense of the immediate use to which they were put (which in some cases was evidently burial) – but of what they symbolised to the societies in question. Naturally this will have differed from society to society, and as indicated at the beginning of this article, it is not necessarily the case that the megaliths are a unitary phenomenon: their function and meaning could have been entirely different in different areas.

However, there are some underlying similarities in several regions, from Almeria to Jutland, and a generalisation is here risked that may hold for many, although not for all, of the monuments. It is suggested that the monuments functioned as territorial markers for segmentary societies. And in most regions their function as a place of burial, an ancestral resting place, was central to that symbolic expression of territory.

*Territoriality*

Territorial behaviour has been recognised for more than a decade as a fundamental aspect of the adaptation of animal populations to their environment, serving to regulate population densities at a lower level than the theoretical carrying capacity calculated on the basis of the available food supply (Wynne Edwards 1962). And some features of the territorial behaviour of animal species have been recognised in human behaviour, both of individuals and of groups, although it does not follow that this behaviour is instinctive.

Territorial behaviour implies the habitual use of a specific, localised area which constitutes the sphere of influence of the individual or the group. Often foreigners are excluded from this territory and from access to its resources. And one of the concomitants of this territorial behaviour is often a spatial identity, an awareness which membership of the territorial group confers, reflected both in marking of individuals (by characteristic behaviour or apparel) and of the territory. Often there is a territorial symbolism or iconography which may also involve flags or insignia.

A group can show territorial behaviour without its membership being defined in terms of the territory. Indeed it is sometimes suggested that an important feature of state society is that the members of that society are defined as such by their residence within its territorial boundaries. Often in small-scale societies group membership is defined in terms of kinship: they can nonetheless show an acute territorial awareness.

*Segmentary Societies*

Most of the social organisations with which we have to deal in the modern world are hierarchically structured, with chains of command, and related to them a hierarchy of places, with controlling centres. Segmentary societies are not like this: they lack the centralised, hierarchical structure of the chiefdom or state. They are small

176

communities, not usually numbering more than a few hundred persons. As Colin Turnbull (1972) puts it, they are 'smallscale societies', and frequently non-literate. In particular they display segmentary organisation, which implies simply the repetition of equivalent groups. They are cellular and modular: cellular in that the groups are clearly defined and operate in many ways independently, and modular in that they are of approximately equal size. the segments are autonomous, economically and politically, and usually number between 50 and 500 persons. In segmentary societies the primary functioning unit – normally a residential unit, whether a village or an association of dispersed houses – is the primary segment, 'a self-sustaining perpetual body, exercising social control over its productive resources' (Sahlins 1961, 325).

In recognising a segmentary society, whether from archaeological or other evidence, there are two basic criteria to meet:

(i) that the society is indeed composed of permanently functioning small groups of this kind, and

(ii) that the groups are not subordinate parts of an effective and larger political and economic entity whose hierarchical control diminishes the autonomy of its constituent parts.

The latter is an important part, for in the present discussion we are particularly interested in the symbolism of such communities. Permanent membership of a larger functioning unit would no doubt carry with it its own symbolism, allegiances and beliefs.

Normally membership of a segment is determined either by descent or marriage, so that the social component of the segment is some kind of kinship group or kindred.

Archaeologically such societies may be recognised when the two above criteria are fulfilled, together with a third. They can be expressed anew in the following conditions:

(i) that a pattern of simultaneously functioning sites be recognised, whose location indicates spacing rather than clustering, and in this sense mutual repulsion rather than attraction. Any fairly regular spacing of nodes implies a possible division of the space between them into cells around the nodes.

(ii) that the territories so recognised are generated by the activities of the living members of such societies rather than by specialised territorial behaviour of cross-cutting groups.

(iii) that there be no hierarchy of places which can be interpreted as indicating a social and political hierarchy.

It seems likely that most settlement patterns of primary village farming, whether in the New World or the Old, reflect segmentary

177

societies, since they generally, in their early stages, lack any indication of a hierarchical structure.

*Monuments as Territorial Markers*
In many segmentary societies the territorial division of the terrain is given symbolic expression. Membership of the group, and the land occupied are expressed in rituals, which are often focused upon a specific location. Generally this will be in the heart of the territory, in the middle of its 'home range'. It is intuitively easy to see that this focus may be an important one to the group, particularly if the settlement is dispersed, so that there is no secular centre in the territory, but solely this ritual one. Mircea Eliade (1965, 22 f) has stressed the symbolic significance of occupying a territory: 'Pour vivre dans le monde, il faut le fonder. . . L'installation dans un territorie équivaut à la fondation d'un monde.'

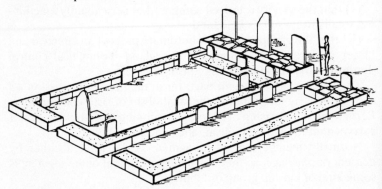

*Figure* 2. *Marae* on the Tuamotu Islands, Pacific. These monuments show a territorial arrangement perhaps typical of segmentary societies (after Emory 1947).

With our modern perspective it is easy to forget that the focal place, the centre of a segmentary society, is for that society quite simply the most important place there is. In a very real sense it is indeed the centre of the world. Whether or not its use is linked with the disposal of the dead, or with communal feasting, or with ceremonial gift exchange or with any of the other important rituals and symbolic acts of many communities, the prime territorial marker in many human societies has a significance by virtue of its symbolism which is not a feature of territorial markers of the territories of other species.

In some societies the central focus is a special natural feature of

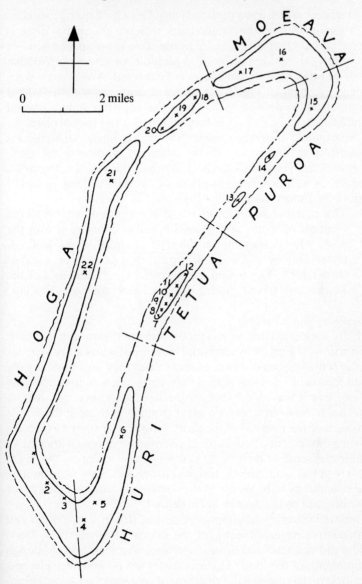

*Figure* 3. Territorial arrangement of *marae* on one of the Tuamotu island groups (after Emory 1947).

the territory which has a particular significance – a spring, perhaps, or a grove. But in other segmentary societies the central place is given added significance by marking it in some special way. A clearing may be kept clear of vegetation, or enclosed. Wooden posts or other striking symbols may be erected. And in some cases stones are heaped together to form a cairn. In societies whose membership is defined by kinship, the ancestors have a special significance, and they may in fact be buried at this special place.

An example of stone monuments serving as territorial markers is offered by several of the Pacific Islands. For instance the stone *marae* of the Tuamotu Islands clearly had this function (figures 2 and 3), as well as serving as places of worship, of feasting and of burial. As Emory has written (1947, 20):

> The maraes, as the property of the kindred, were material symbols of them, and formed a visible connection with the past. Always standing on the land occupied by the kindred, observable by any who might pass, they came to be a seal of ownership. They bound the ancestral spirits and gods of the kindred to the land, putting it under their eternal guardianship.

## The European Megaliths

It is my suggestion that we can profitably view the stone monuments of north-west Europe as territorial markers of segmentary societies in the sense indicated above. In many cases they were undoubtedly used for burial: this was indeed their chief function, in a utilitarian sense. But it was clearly not their chief significance, for there is absolutely no need to erect a great monument to solve the simple problem of the disposal of the dead. However restricted the access to such monuments, both in terms of criteria for burial within them, and in the sense of their being hallowed, *tapu* localities, they were clearly public monuments, designed to be seen. They were built by the community to be visible to the community (and the question of visibility will be touched on again below).

Andrew Fleming has implied a part of this in a thoughtful and provocative paper, 'Tombs for the Living' (Fleming 1973, 188): 'Why did neolithic and bronze age man take such pains to design monuments of this kind? I believe that it was because they played a key role in maintaining the structure of contemporary social organisation'. But it is not necessary to follow him also in seeing them as 'attention-focusing devices, part of a signalling system designed to reinforce the existing patterns of leadership', if he implies thereby that the societies in question already possessed a well-defined hierarchical structure of leadership and command. As we shall see, there is reason to think they were often small, effectively autonomous groups, which need not have possessed permanent leaders. Such small acephalous societies can benefit from the symbolic expression of their identity just as do much larger units where the leadership structure has to be reinforced. In most cases, however, the chambered tombs were collective tombs, and I believe that in general it was collective identity which was symbolised within them. With the rich single grave burials of the early bronze age, on the other hand, for instance in Brittany or Wessex, I believe that we are indeed in the face of individualising chiefdoms (Renfrew 1974), and much closer to what Fleming has in mind.

We are anticipated here by Humphrey Case in seeing some of the megalithic 'tombs' as ritual and territorial centres, rather than as primarily places of burial. After discussing the ritual site of Goodland in County Antrim (Case 1969, 13), he goes on to see analogous functions for the Irish court cairns, the most frequent megalithic monuments of Ireland:

> Such rites have a universal and consolatory role in primitive societies. It is not an idle question to ask therefore whether courtcairns, which were probably prominent in Irish life for more than a millennium, were not shrines of a similar kind, despite the great differences in appearance between the Goodland sites and the often elegant cairns with stone-built chambers and forecourts . . . Unless one assumes almost invariable and complete secondary removal of human remains from court cairns (including numerous small fragments of cremated bones) it does not seem very likely that they were originally intended as mausolea; by no means all cairns were built on acidic soils liable to have destroyed bone. Their frequent contents of what is difficult to interpret as other than redeposited settlement débris justify at least an alternative hypothesis: that they were built less as graves for selected kinsmen or to commemorate great men or calm dangerous spirits than to provide by making rites for the needs of the living, like the Goodland sites. . . . The cairns may thus have been the centres about or before which semi-nomadic communities survived in stable adjustment for several generations.

Clearly many of the megalithic monuments of north-western Europe did indeed serve as mausolea, but this does not diminish their possible ritual function as territorial centres. Indeed the unchambered long barrows of Britain were not open for many years, and thus were not able to act as mausolea over many generations. But there is good reason to think that even when they were no longer used for burial, they continued to have a considerable symbolic significance.

*Testing the Hypothesis*

This hypothesis, that in several regions the European megaliths served as territorial markers for segmentary societies, is an important first step for the argument about their origins to be set out in the next section. It is desirable, however, to put it to the test.

Clearly, if they are such, they should conform to the three conditions set out above.

The third, that there should be no hierarchy of places, is the easiest to consider. In fact, as I have shown elsewhere (see chapter 8) there is indeed a hierarchy of places in neolithic Wessex, although it does not develop until later in the neolithic period. By considering the labour input required for the unchambered long barrows, the causewayed camps, the major henges, and the two superordinate monuments (Stonehenge and Silbury Hill) it is easy to show that there is a hierarchy here, and plausible to suggest that this hierarchy in the social landscape corresponds to a social hierarchy. So it seems reasonable to speak of the emergence of chiefdoms in late neolithic Britain. No doubt something similar is implied for the Mainland of Orkney at the same time, where the building of chambered tombs was superseded by that of henges. Perhaps the alignments at Carnac likewise speak of some centralisation in what was formerly a segmentary society.

In general, however, the scale of the monuments in some areas is fairly uniform, and this condition in those areas is fulfilled. The examples of Arran and Rousay, below, seem to confirm it although in Rousay particularly there is a considerable range of scale. But at the same time the monuments are of essentially the same kind in each area.

The generalisation has, of course, to be tested in each region in turn. It may well not hold for the great mounds of Brittany, although again it could, if these were formed by accretion over several generations. And it may not hold for concentrated cemeteries of tombs such as those of the Boyne: this concentration and centralisation may be the symbolic expression of some centralisation in society.

The first condition, that we should recognise a pattern of simultaneously functioning sites indicative of territorial spacing, seems straightforward enough. But it is, of course, greatly complicated by the requirement of simultaneity. For our chronological control is simply not good enough in most cases to demonstrate simultaneity by accurate absolute dating. On the other hand we are undoubtedly helped by the circumstance that many tombs show a long and apparently continuous tradition of funerary use.

I think, however, we can go further, and suggest that whenever the distribution of tombs does give good indication of territorial spacing, some measure of simultaneity of veneration (if not of construction) is implied. For if a tomb went completely out of use and were entirely forgotten, its location would clearly have no further significance. The chances of a subsequent monument being erected nearby would be no less than those of such a monument being erected further away. In other words the placing of the tombs would be random *with reference to one another*. This is not, of course, to say that it would be random in terms of other terrain factors. Indeed, if tombs were used for a brief period and then

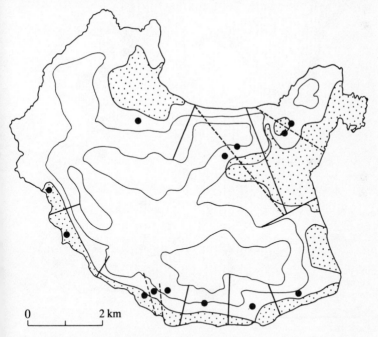

0          2 km

*Figure* 4. Spacing of chambered cairns on Rousay, Orkney, which may reflect teritorial behaviour. (Contours at c.100 m intervals, modern arable land stippled.)

183

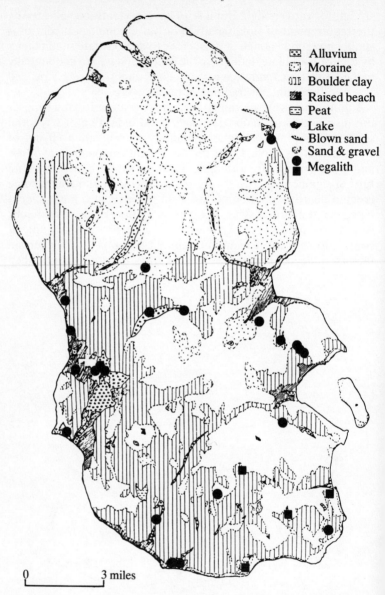

Legend:
- ▣ Alluvium
- ▢ Moraine
- ⁙ Boulder clay
- ▨ Raised beach
- ▤ Peat
- ◆ Lake
- ～ Blown sand
- ● Sand & gravel
- ■ Megalith

0 —————— 3 miles

*Figure* 5. Location of Arran chambered cairns in relation to surface geology, emphasising environmental constraints (after Davies 1946).

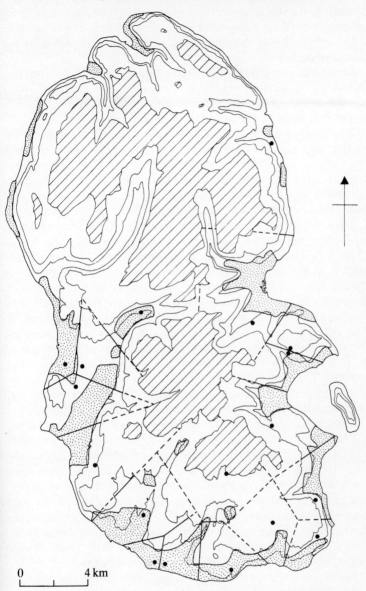

*Figure* 6. Location of Arran chambered cairns with notional territorial divisions (based on equal distance) to emphasise possible social factors. (Contours at c.100 m intervals, modern arable land stippled.)

forgotten, we should expect to find the most fertile areas, or those otherwise most apt for settlement, to be the home of a whole long series of tombs of different date, reflecting occupation in the favoured area.

In practice one tomb was no doubt replaced by another. And that this should be so in no way invalidates our hypothesis. Indeed what we should expect to see is not a simple territorial spacing of single cairns, but of single cairns and of *clusters* of cairns.

I have argued elsewhere (Renfrew 1973a, 135), following the earlier suggestion of Childe (1942) that this is precisely what one does see on the Orcadian island of Rousay. And the territorial argument is made more coherent if we think not simply in terms of equal-distance territories as indicated by means of Thiessen polygons (figure 4) but more carefully about the siting of the tombs.

Turning now to Arran, it is appropriate to refer first to the careful environmental study made twenty years ago by Margaret Davies (1946). Her map (figure 5) elegantly documents her thesis that the settlers in Arran were avoiding the heavier, and probably more thickly forested boulder clays. This environmental analysis is no doubt the first consideration. For it is axiomatic that each territory represents in the first instance the home area of a group of people. The social factors working towards a modular arrangement are therefore subordinate to the environmental ones which may distort it. Even so, however, a simple equal-distance map obtained by drawing Thiessen polygons (figure 6) lends some support to the notion of territorial arrangement. Probably the pair on the east side, and the group of three on the west, might be regarded as clusters of successively used cairns, but this is mere speculation.

I believe that the hypothesis plausibly survives these two tests, and of course it must be further tested in the further regions under consideration. It would of course be desirable to test it more rigorously and formally, perhaps by means of a nearest-neighbour analysis. But it would first be necessary to factor out the environmental considerations, and to allow for irregularities in the terrain. And secondly some further criterion of simultaneity would be desirable. Work is continuing at present on the siting of the Rousay cairns, and it may be that further progress will be made.

Finally, the second condition of the three implies that the territories defined by such a spatial analysis should indeed be territories of living groups, rather than reflecting some other special symbolic arrangement. That the territories are generally those of living groups seems inherently plausible, although societies certainly existed where this is not so. Perhaps in this instance the onus may rest upon whoever wishes to challenge the hypothesis to present another to account for the segmentary pattern observerd?

## Population Stress in Segmentary Societies

The assertion that the stone monuments in several regions of north-western Europe may be regarded as territorial markers in segmentary societies may not seem a very remarkable one: all the ideas which go to make up such a view have been expressed before, although perhaps not quite in this form. At the same time there will be critics particularly aware of the difficulties in demonstrating such a proposition – problems of the contemporaneity of the use of monuments in a given area – and of the various cases to which it does not apply. At least, however, it has the merit of leading us to talk about the social structure and economic basis of the societies themselves, and to assess changes initiated outside in terms of their effects upon those structures.

There are three special features in the environment of these societies which must, I suspect, feature in any explanation of the monuments themselves. All three arise from their situation along what Giot (1963, 3) and Powell (1969, 270) have called the 'Atlantic facade': 'a phenomenon against which westward moving cultures were halted and accordingly modified'. The first is precisely this absence of accessible lands to the west: location on the extreme edge of a major continent establishes a demographic system different to that arising from residence in the middle of the land mass. And secondly, of course, the coastal regions, as well as the lower reaches and estuaries of the major rivers, offered important food resources for the hunting and gathering populations who were flourishing there before the inception of farming. Grahame Clark has recently stressed (1974) the importance of fishing as a major resource for certain Scandinavian groups who were using megalithic monuments, and has, of course, written several studies on the food resources of their predecessors. It was, I think, Gordon Childe (1925, 133) who first indicated the possibility of a significant relationship: 'The great centres of megalithic architecture in Europe are precisely those regions where the palaeolithic survivals are the most numerous and best attested'. And once again it is Humphrey Case, who in an article full of relevant insights (1969, 12), has followed through a possible implication: 'The passage-grave may indeed be an invention of Atlantic Mesolithic communites'.

With these two features go an obvious third, which has been more

187

often stressed in the past: the ease of communication along the Atlantic coasts, along the 'western seaways'. This idea has recently been re-examined by Bowen (1972) in an illuminating way. And of course in stressing the ease of communication along the coasts, and no doubt the frequency of voyages by early fishermen, one need not be thinking in terms of particularly long-distance voyages, although these cannot be excluded.

In its simpler form the model to be proposed does not need to make reference to this existing mesolithic population, or not at least to special features that distinguish it from the mesolithic population of continental Europe. It is necessary first to consider the changes in population density arising from the development of farming techniques in a region formerly only sparsely occupied by hunter-gatherers. (The possible higher density of maritime groups of fishers is considered below.) It is generally accepted that in Europe as in other areas (Braidwood and Reed 1957) the development of farming resulted in substantial population increase, perhaps from a density of 0.1 to around 5 persons per square kilometre, although in the argument that follows the precise figures are not significant so long as a substantial increase is agreed.

Ammerman and Cavalli-Sforza (1973) have put forward a remarkably informative mechanism, a wave of advance model, for the spread of farming in early Europe. In it the speed of spread is related to the pattern of population increase. They visualise a process of 'demic diffusion', where there is modest local migratory activity which is random in direction. When the new mode of production makes possible an increase in population numbers, a wave of population expansion sets in. Their model of the wave of advance is given in figure 7.

For our present purposes, however, it is not the uniformity of this advance which is important, but that the pattern of population growth in each area is likely to be roughly the same. When a population enters a hitherto uninhabited area, or where, as in this case, a new mode of production makes possible a very rapid rate of increase, the pattern of growth is at first exponential (Maynard Smith 1974, 16): the rate of increase of population is proportional to population density.

$$dx/dt = rx \qquad x = x_0 e^{rt}$$

Birdsell (1957) has demonstrated such a growth pattern for instance in Pitcairn Island (figure 8).

However, when the population begins to approach a level that

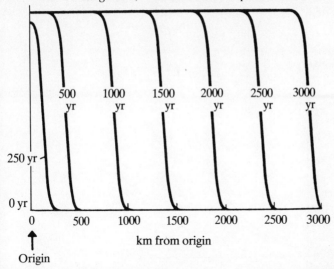

*Figure* 7. Wave of advance model for the spread of farming in Europe (after Ammerman and Cavalli-Sforza 1973). Only one half of a section through the model is reproduced: the full model is generated by rotation through 360° about the vertical axis (i.e. it is symmetrical in distance from the origin).

exhausts the available resources, the rate of increase diminishes, and may reach a steady value. The logistic equation, $dx/dt = ax - bx^2$, describes such a pattern of growth, examples of which are seen in many living populations, from yeast to human (Maynard Smith 1974, 18): figure 9. Naturally the curve will have a different shape, depending upon the growth rate, and the population density at saturation (the 'carrying capacity').

So far this is merely the kind of simplification that is commonly made when speaking of demographic process, and naturally masks the complexity of any real case. It is of course, in the upper part of the logistic growth curve that population stress will arise. In the exponential curve, on the other hand, with no inhibiting environmental limitations, both population and the rate of population growth continue to increase. Such a growth pattern is seen when the death rate and the birth rate are both stable, and the latter greater than the former. In the logistic curve, although the population continues to grow for a considerable period, it ultimately grows more slowly: the rate of increase, although positive, is diminishing (figure 10).

189

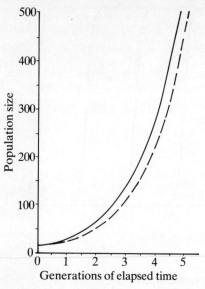

*Figure* 8. Exponential (unrestricted) growth of population, as seen on Pitcairn Island. The initial growth of population in a newly colonised territory takes this form (after Birdsell 1957).

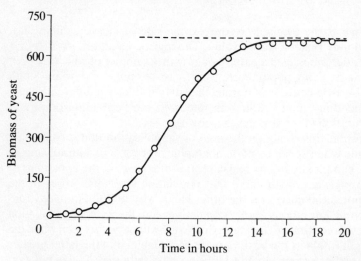

*Figure* 9. Logistic growth curve, as seen in the development of a yeast population. This is the pattern of growth commonly taken when environmental constraints limit the continued growth of population (after Maynard Smith 1974).

190

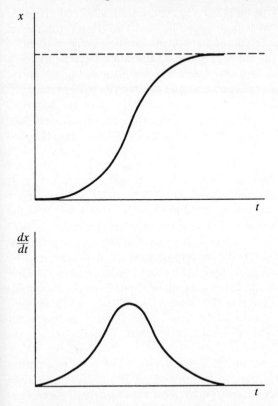

*Figure* 10. Growth of population (*above*) for logistic growth, and *rate* of growth of population (*below*) on the same time axis.

The rate of increase will diminish only if either the death rate is increased or the birth rate reduced. It is here that the notion of population stress is relevant. I am using it here to indicate not so much high population density (although this in itself can cause stress) but the working in society of those processes which inexorably cause a reduction in birth rate, and their accompanying side effects.

The whole field of demographic studies in early societies is a difficult and uncertain one (Spooner 1972), and while the logistic growth pattern has been demonstrated in several cases, the precise mechanism of its operation is not well understood. What has been fairly well established, however, is that the population level, the 'saturation point' at which the growth stabilises, is generally some way below the theoretical carrying capacity of the land (Binford 1968). In other words population in most animal and traditional rural human populations does not go on increasing until mass starvation and deprivation produce a substantial increase in death rate in some Malthusian cataclysm, thereby ensuring that the carrying capacity is not exceeded and that the logistic pattern prevails. Instead the stabilisation is at a lower density, and often seems to come rather from a reduction in the birth rate (or rather infant survival rate), whether through increased age of marriage, reduced conception in wedlock (or out of it for that matter), increase in abortion or infanticide. My point here is that during the period of sharpest decrease in the birth rate, however that reduction is achieved, the adjustments in society will be most painful – more painful, I suggest, than when the birth rate is stable whether at the higher level (with population growth) or at the lower level (with zero growth). For it is *change* in habitual life patterns, in an established pattern of existence, that is most productive of stress.

Now one interesting feature of the wave of advance model, not specifically singled out for comment by Ammerman and Cavalli-Sforza, is that so long as the wave is advancing, while farming continues to be introduced to new lands, there is always a net outflow of population, a leakage, so to speak, from each region on the current periphery, the frontier, as the logistic curve approaches its stable population density. This then permits the approximation to a logistic growth pattern without so rapid a reduction in birth rate. The lands outside the frontier are accepting a small population increase from the agricultural donor lands. The net result may be that while the resultant population in the donor area undergoes logistic growth, the rate of live (and surviving) births need not decrease so rapidly as this would otherwise imply. Some 'overshooting' of the saturation level is possible because the receptor land beyond the frontier takes up the excess (figure 11).

The continuing expansion of the wave of advance, then, cushions the expanding society against some of the effects of the ending of its population growth, and protects it from the necessity of a very rapid cut-back in the birth rate.

Now the interesting thing is that when the wave reaches a barrier that it cannot cross – when a net outward migration of population is no longer possible – this cushioning effect ceases. The society at the end of the line has to undergo an unmodified pattern of logistic growth, including the reduction in birth rate in the later stages, and this more rapidly than previously experienced by neighbouring

192

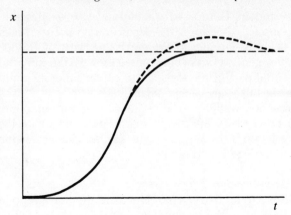

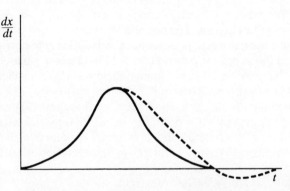

*Figure* 11. Growth of population (*above*) and rate of growth (*below*) when no migration takes place (unbroken line) and when some outward movement takes place at high population density (broken line).

It is suggested that the wave of advance pattern normally proceeds with some outward movement of population (broken line) but that when the wave meets the Atlantic facade this is prevented and the situation is shown with the unbroken line. The rate of population growth (*below*) declines more rapidly in the latter case when the wave meets the facade, creating demographic stress. The stress arises not only from high population density (high $x$) but particularly from the sharp decline in rate of growth (in $dx/dt$).

societies which have already fully accomplished the agricultural transition with all its demographic consequences. The stress in such societies will consequently be higher.

Precisely such conditions apply on the Atlantic facade 'against which westward moving cultures were halted and accordingly modified'. On this model, therefore, the segmentary societies which developed with early farming in the north and west of Europe would, after a few generations of uninhibited growth (the early and almost exponential part of the logistic curve), be suffering population stress as the birth-rate decline set in.

A similar situation would prevail in any situation where population growth proceeds in effectively virgin land, and where the outflow of population is strongly inhibited – as, for instance, in the early colonisation of the Pacific islands.

## Demography and Megaliths

We have suggested so far that at a period shortly after the inception of farming in each area, the inhabitants of the regions of Atlantic Europe may have been subject to social stress arising from the ensuing demographic changes. The first and obvious source of stress may simply have been the high population density, greater than any previously seen in the region. Martin (1972, 443–4) has speculated profitably on the possible effects in human societies when the pace of population growth exceeds that of behavioural adaption:

> Experiments with animals show that certain pathological effects appear at population densities above that for which each species has been adapted, and it is quite conceivable that similar effects may eventually emerge in human societies, such as:
> 1. general individual loss of weight
> 2. digestive disorders and kidney ailments
> 3. circulatory disfunction (e.g. high blood pressure)
> 4. disruption of parental behaviour
> 5. disruption of social behaviour
> 6. decline in fertility
> 7. premature death

In the case in question we are dealing not solely with a fairly high population density (which is by no means a special feature of Atlantic Europe) but of the stress factors arising from a decline in birth rate, or from the more general causes, as yet little understood, of which the birth rate decline is the result.

It is, of course, the behavioural adaptation to the situation which interests us. In some cases a consequence, or at least a correlate, of increasing population density, and perhaps of other aspects of demographic stress, is an increase in specialisation, and a movement towards centralisation, which through greater efficiency permits what in effect is an increased carrying capacity (Dumond 1972, Sherratt 1972). This, by raising the effective ceiling on population growth, alleviates some sources of stress (although not of course stress arising from population density itself).

However, it seems likely that an alternative adaptation operated in Atlantic Europe at this time. For as we have seen, it is only rather later, in certain areas, that the archaeological evidence indicates the possibility of chiefdom society (chapters 7 and 8). There is no evidence in the areas under detailed consideration, for instance in Arran or Rousay, of any early centralising tendency, although as already indicated, it may be relevant that towards the end of the neolithic in Orkney larger public works (the Ring of Brogar and the Stones of Stenness) beyond the scope of the earlier segmentary units were constructed.

Instead of developing larger units, with a central organisation capable of administering specialised production and distribution, the segmentary societies of north-western Europe responded, in some instances at least, by reinforcing their own existing organisation, resisting change rather than exploiting it. In many the group and territorial identity was symbolised in the construction of a ritual centre. And one must no doubt see in this a means of reinforcing traditional norms of behaviour and traditional sanctions, some of which probably were already in existence to exert some kind of control upon the birth rate. When this rate had to be further reduced – as the logic of the logistic curve inexorably demands – existing conventions and sanctions of regulation would have to be more rigorously applied. The alternative, an uncontrolled increase of population beyond the carrying capacity appropriate to the mode of production available, would be a substantial increase in the death rate and with it probably much worse stresses, and possibly the total fragmentation of the social groups.

The pattern of population increase along the Atlantic seaboard was thus very different from that in the centre of Europe, setting up very different pressures upon the segmentary societies which occupied it.

As we saw earlier, there is a further factor which worked to make the demographic system there a special one: the relatively high density of the existing hunter-gatherer-fisher population. In many of the areas earlier discussed which may have seen the independent development of monument building around 4000 BC, there was a substantial population already before the arrival of the first farmers. Based as it was upon the exploitation of marine resources, its

195

population density is likely to have been larger than that seen in inland Europe. In Portugal, as in Brittany, there are shell middens reflecting the activity of this population, and in Britain and Ireland there are abundant traces of mesolithic occupation. The Ertebølle culture of Denmark is likewise well known.

There was thus already a substantial population, with an adequate subsistence base in the area before the arrival of farming techniques. In some areas this population may have resisted change and kept to its traditional economy, while farmers began to practise agriculture and stock rearing inland. Some of the later dates for the Portuguese shell middens may hint as much. But in other areas these fisher-gatherers must themselves have adopted farming practices, while not of course giving up their valuable existing food resources. The result would no doubt be a rapid population increase, at first making unnecessary whatever controls on birth rate operated in these mari-time societies. But soon they would again be called into operation. And the very high population density in these favoured regions, blessed with abundant maritime resources as well as the practise of farming may itself have worked to produce conditions of particular stress.

It is relevant to remember here that these groups will already have had their own identity, and no doubt concepts of territoriality. Moreover the custom of burial in stone graves seen already in Brittany at Hoëdic and Téviec (the former with a date of 4625 ± 300 bc, Gif-227, calibrating to c. 5550 BC) may have had a bearing upon the precise form of territorial marking adopted. Further work is needed to elucidate the social structure of these pre-farming com-munities. It must have had a significant bearing upon that of their agricultural successors.

## Conclusion

In this paper, it has been argued that the stone built monuments of northern western Europe may have had essentially independent origins in several regions. Although the radiocarbon dates cannot be held to establish this, they do at least open the possibility.

The apparent unity of the megalithic phenomenon may instead be the result of factors operating which are special to the Atlantic facade. It is suggested that we should view the monuments as territorial markers in segmentary societies. It is possible to see how population stress was exacerbated in this area by the difficulty of 'overshooting', which was possible in other areas of Europe as the farming population grew towards a notional saturation point. This stress, it is suggested, favoured a stronger territorial expression, and favoured the development of just such territorial markers.

It is relevant to ask, in conclusion what the possibilities may be for testing so general a model. For without the possibility of such testing, the above scenario can be little more than a word picture, plausible enough in itself, perhaps, but difficult to examine constructively.

I hope indeed that some of the ideas here may suggest possibilities of testing. But already some general consequences are clear. In the focal regions of independent development we expect a period of several generations after the adoption of farming practice before the inevitable population stress is felt, and before we expect territorial marking to become prominent. This period of time will depend on the initial density of settlement and on the ultimate carrying capacity. In favourable cases this is a figure for which an estimate can in fact be reached, and compared with the observed lapsed time between first farming and first stone monuments in the region.

Secondly it follows that the stress in question should be widely felt through quite a large region, so that territorial monuments should appear almost simultaneously in quite a wide area.

Thirdly the form of monument adopted in each area will depend very much on local factors. At first there may be little standardisation within the area. If there are local antecedents, as in Brittany, their own form is likely to be influential. If not, a borrowing of architectural devices from adjacent regions would be expected, but with idiosyncratic local modifications.

Any lands first colonised after the development of monumental territorial marking in the homeland are of course likely to reflect similar customs, and there is nothing in the model which excludes the secondary development of monument building in this way. Indeed the colonisation of the Polynesian islands may have been of this kind, since there seem to be strong local similarities in the forms of the territorial customs adopted in each.

It is therefore no part of my argument to deny the frequency of contact between communities along the Atlantic seaboard, or the significance of these contacts for the selection of architectural forms for the solution of specific design problems (cf. Fleming 1972). We have undoubtedly a great deal to learn from a study of maritime interactions in this area. I wish to stress simply that we shall not understand the changes that took place without taking full account also of the locally based factors which determine the dynamics of culture change.                                    [1976]

Monuments and the Structure of Pre-Urban Societies

## Bibliography

Ammerman, A. J. and L. L. Cavalli-Sforza (1973) A population model for the diffusion of early farming in Europe, in C. Renfrew, ed., *The Explanation of Culture Change: Models in Prehistory*, London, Duckworth, 343–58.

Binford, L. R. (1968) Post-Pleistocene adaptations, in L. R. and S. R. Binford, eds., *New Perspectives in Archaeology*, Chicago, Aldine.

Blance, B. (1961) Early Bronze Age colonists in Iberia, *Antiquity*, 35, 192.

Bowen, E. G. (1972) *The Western Seaways*, London, Thames and Hudson.

Braidwood, R. J. and C. A. Reed (1957) The achievement and early consequences of food-production: a consideration of the archaeological and natural-historical evidence, *Cold Spring Harbor Symposium in Quantitative Biology*, 22, 19–31.

Case, H. (1969) Settlement patterns in the north Irish neolithic, *Ulster Journal of Archaeology*, 32.

Childe, V. G. (1925) *The Dawn of European Civilisation* (1st edition), London, Routledge and Kegan Paul.

— (1942) The chambered cairns of Rousay, *Antiquaries Journal*, 22, 139–42.

— (1957) *The Dawn of European Civilisation* (6th edition), London, Routledge.

Clarke, J. G. D. (1974) Megalithic tombs and settlement archaeology in Sweden. Lecture presented to the Society of Antiquaries of London, 14th November 1974.

Clarke, R. M. (1975) An objectively derived calibration curve for radiocarbon dates, *Antiquity*, 49, 251–66.

Daniel, G. E. (1958) *The Megalith Builders of Western Europe*, London.

Davies, M. (1946) The diffusion and distribution pattern of the megalithic monuments of the Irish Sea and North Channel coastlands, *Antiquaries Journal*, 26, 38–60.

Dumond, D. E. (1972) Population growth and political centralisation, in B. Spooner, ed., *Population Growth: Anthropological Implications*. Cambridge, Mass., M. I. T. Press, 286–310.

Eliade, M. (1965) *Le sacré et le profane*, Paris, Gallimard.

Emory, K. P. (1947) *Tuamotuan Religious Structures and Ceremonies* (Berenice P. Bishop Museum Bulletin 191).

Fleming, A. (1972) Vision and design: approaches to ceremonial monument typology, *Man*, 7, 57–73.

— (1973) Tombs for the living, *Man*, 8, 177–93.

Giot, P. R. (1963) *Les civilisations atlantiques du néolithique à l'âge du fer* (Actes du premier colloque atlantique, Brest 1961), Rennes.

— (1971) The impact of radiocarbon dating on the establishment of the prehistoric chronology of Brittany, *Proceedings of the Prehistoric Society*, 37, Part 2, 208–17.

Henshall, A. S. (1974) Scottish chambered tombs and long mounds, in C. Renfrew, ed., *British Prehistory — a New Outline*, London, Duckworth, 137–64.

198

# Megaliths, Territories and Populations

Martin, R. D. (1972) Concepts of human territoriality, in P. J. Ucko, R. Tringham and G. W. Dimbleby, eds., *Man, Settlement and Urbanism*, London, Duckworth, 427–46.

Maynard-Smith, J. (1974) *Models in Ecology*, Cambridge, University Press.

Montelius, O. (1899) *Der Orient und Europa*.

Powell, T. G. E. (1969) Some points and problems, in T. G. E. Powell, J. X. W. P. Corcoran, Frances Lynch and J. G. Scott, *Megalithic Enquiries in the West of Britain*, Liverpool.

Renfrew, C. (1965) *The Neolithic and Early Bronze Age Cultures of the Cyclades and their External Relations.* Unpublished Ph.D. dissertation, University of Cambridge.

— (1967) Colonialism and Megalithismus, *Antiquity*, 41, 276–88.

— (1972) *The Emergence of Civilisation, the Cyclades and the Aegean in the Third Millennium B. C.*, London, Methuen.

— (1973a) *Before Civilisation, the Radiocarbon Revolution and Prehistoric Europe*, London, Jonathan Cape.

— (1973b) Monuments, mobilisation and social organisation in neolithic Wessex, in C. Renfrew, ed., *The Explanation of Culture Change, Models in Prehistory*, London, Duckworth, 539–58.

— (1974) Beyond a subsistence economy: the evolution of social organisation in prehistoric Europe, in C. B. Moore, ed., *Reconstructing Complex Societies* (Supplement to the Bulletin of the American Schools of Oriental Research n. 20), 69–84.

Sahlins, M. (1961) The segmentary lineage, an organisation of predatory expansion, *American Anthropologist*, 63, 322–45.

Sherratt, A. G. (1972) Socio-economic and demographic models for the neolithic and bronze ages of Europe, in D. L. Clarke, ed., *Models in Archaeology*, London, Methuen.

Smith, I. F. (1974) The neolithic, in C. Renfrew, ed., *British Prehistory, a New Outline*, London, Duckworth, 100–136.

Spooner, B., ed. (1972) *Population Growth: Anthropological implications*, Cambridge, Mass., M. I. T. Press.

Tauber, H. (1972) Radiocarbon chronology of the Danish mesolithic and neolithic, *Antiquity*, 46, 106–110.

Turnbull, C. (1972) Demography of small-scale societies, in G. A. Harrison and A. J. Boyce, eds., *The Structure of Human Populations*, Oxford, Clarendon Press, 283–312.

Whittle, E. M. and J. M. Arnaud (1975) Thermoluminescent dating of neolithic and chalcolithic pottery from sites in central Portugal, *Archaeometry*, 17, Part 1, 5–24.

Wynne-Edwards, V. C. (1952) *Animal Dispersion in Relation to Social Behaviour*.

# 7

## ISLANDS
## OUT OF TIME

*

In the year 1722, a vessel captained by the Dutch explorer Jacob Roggeveen sailed round the tip of South America, through the Straits of Magellan, and into the Pacific Ocean looking for a lost island, reportedly sighted by a British explorer and privateer fifty years earlier, and called after him the 'Isle of Davis'. The Dutch expedition never found this legendary land, but instead on 5 April (Easter Day) they sighted a small island. They called this tiny and remote landfall 'Easter Island'.

Remarkably it proved to have a human population. They lived what seemed to the Dutch sailors a simple life, with yams, bananas and fowl for food. But one thing was extraordinary: the large stone statues with which many of their ceremonial places were decorated. These striking monuments were apparently built by the inhabitants of this small island on the easternmost fringe of Polynesia, 1500 miles from the nearest land.

At first sight it may not be obvious what bearing that discovery has upon our own great prehistoric monuments in the British Isles – stone circles such as Avebury or Stonehenge, or megalithic tombs such as the West Kennet long barrow. Certainly it would be nonsensical to think of any direct link between them. Yet we can learn from 'the mystery of Easter Island', the paradoxical occurrence of major building works in a tiny and remote area, with a small population entirely lacking the advanced technology of urban civilisation. For in a sense this is the same problem which has perplexed antiquaries and archaeologists who have tried to explain our own great European prehistoric monuments. How did they do it? Could they have done it without some assistance, if only indirect, from some more advanced technology? The best way to answer these questions, I believe, is for the archaeologists to look across the

200

world to Polynesia, where some of the answers are beginning to emerge.

## The Problem of the Monuments

For centuries the prehistoric monuments of Britain have puzzled and teased the imagination of scholars. Already in the twelfth century Geoffrey of Monmouth mentions Stonehenge in his *Chronicle*, and relates that the stones had been transported from Ireland and erected at Stonehenge by the magic arts of the wizard Merlin. The great architect Inigo Jones visited Stonehenge during the reign of James the First and pronounced it to be of Roman construction, and in the seventeenth and eighteenth centuries scholarly opinion came to favour the Druids, the Celtic priests whom Julius Caesar encountered on his expedition to Britain. But in truth very little was known of such monuments, or of the collective burial chambers, the megalithic tombs, which are common in the British Isles and in other areas of north-western Europe. So it was that the British antiquary Sir Richard Colt Hoare, writing in 1807, could say of the Irish megalithic tomb Newgrange and of these other monuments:

> I shall not unnecessarily trespass upon the time and patience of my readers in endeavouring to ascertain what tribes first peopled this country, nor to what nation the construction of this singular monument may reasonably be attributed, for, I fear, both its authors and its original destination will ever remain unknown. Conjecture may wander over its wild and spacious domains but will never bring home with it either truth or conviction. Alike will the histories of those stupendous temples at Avebury and Stonehenge which grace my native county remain involved in obscurity and oblivion.

Fortunately Colt Hoare was too pessimistic, and gradually archaeology was able to establish a series of facts about these monuments. It soon emerged that they belong to the neolithic period, built that is by the early farming population of Britain, at a time before copper or bronze tools were used.

For many years, indeed until just ten years ago, it was believed that the megalithic tombs of Europe were the result of a movement of colonisation, or at least a wave of influence, from the more civilised lands of the eastern Mediterranean. There monumental stone tombs were being constructed from around 2500 BC. So it seemed likely that the first European megalithic tombs were those of Spain, built perhaps just a little after 2500 BC, and that the techniques of construction, the practice of collective burial, and

201

perhaps the religion which went with them, gradually spread across Europe, reaching the British Isles around 2000 BC or a few centuries after.

This clear picture has been completely disrupted, however, first by the application of radiocarbon dating, and then by the use of tree-ring dates to correct and modify the radiocarbon dates further. It now seems clear that the megalithic tombs of north-western Europe were being built earlier than anything comparable in the east Mediterranean: the earliest of them, in Brittany, before 4000 BC.

So the old idea of the 'diffusion' of culture from the more civilised lands of the Near East can no longer be used to explain the megalithic tomb architecture of Britain. Nor can it explain for us the construction of the even larger and greater monuments, the so-called henges, of which Stonehenge and Avebury are the most famous examples. Until a decade ago it could reasonably be argued that they were the result of some influences from the more civilised cultures of Mycenaean Greece. As one distinguished writer put it: 'Is it then any more incredible that the architect of Stonehenge should himself have been a Myceanean than that the monument should have been designed and erected, with all its unique and sophisticated detail, by mere barbarians?'

Today, however, the barbarians have it. The new dating makes entirely clear that the megalithic tombs are a European phenomenon, built by 'barbarians' – if by that term one means a population with a fairly low level of technology, lacking the use of metal, without writing, and without urban centres. Likewise the great henge monuments, from Mount Pleasant in the south right up to the Ring of Brogar in the Orkney Islands, must be seen as the work of the descendants of the early megalith builders, descendants who at 2000 BC were still (in the same sense) 'barbarians'.

How then did they do it? What special skills did they have? What forces impelled them to invest so many man-hours in such monuments? How could these simple societies marshal the skills and co-ordinate the manpower for such massive undertakings, which represent in some cases millions of man-hours? Perhaps, faced with these difficult questions, it is not surprising that a few writers with uncontrolled imaginations and an eye for the lurid have written of flying saucers, of intelligence from outer space, and of lost and secret lore. But that is the easy explanation, and one without a single shred of sound evidence to sustain it.

The right explanation, demanding the exercise of a more controlled imagination, implies greater respect for the abilities of the human species. It involves the acceptance that 'natives' – whether in neolithic Britain or in Polynesia of just a century or two ago – are not idiots, and that, on the contrary, 'barbarians' differ from us mainly in their lack of advanced technology. It is here that the Polynesian experience has so much to teach us. And we are fortunate that the greatest of all the Pacific explorers, active just two centuries ago, was a man of humane intelligence and curiosity: the 'Great Circumnavigator', Captain Cook.

## The Concept of Chiefdom Society

When Captain Cook visited the Pacific, he found in some of the island groups societies which were highly structured, highly organised. Social relations were ordered by rules of conduct as rigorous (and as courteous) as any in contemporary Europe. And in the Friendly Islands (the modern kingdom of Tonga), in the Society Islands (the modern Tahiti) and in Hawaii (which he himself first discovered for the western world) he described communities with a very coherent system of government. In each the ruler was a chief of very high status, whose person was regarded as sacred and surrounded by taboos as elaborate as in any European monarchy.

Much of this did not, I think, greatly astonish him, for he was of course accustomed to the England of King George III. But it fascinates me, for here we have a direct insight into the working of a society with the simplest of technologies – none of the Polynesian communities knew the use of metal (they were amazed by metal axes, and Cook's sailors could obtain all manner of goods and services in exchange for just a few iron nails).

Cook described for us what modern anthropologists sometimes term a 'chiefdom' society. Societies with a similar structure and social organisation have been described from other parts of the world, including Africa, and they share a number of common features which, I believe, can be of real help to us in understanding those rather remote and mysterious communities of prehistoric Britain which were responsible for the erection of our great monuments. The key to the problem lies in social organisation, in what I like to call Social Archaeology. Unless we can begin to reconstruct the basic features of a prehistoric society – not just its technology (what tools they used, what food they ate), but social aspects too – we shall have no understanding of its capabilities. We need to know how large social groups were. Did they have a central organisation, central leadership? What were their relations with neighbouring communities? How much energy did they invest in religious activities? The Chiefdom Model gives us a very general picture of one kind of structure, which it is profitable to apply to prehistoric Europe.

In chiefdom societies, kinship is a dominating principle. Who you are – your place in life – depends on who you are born, on the status of the parents. But this status is not simply a question of 'class', or of hereditary wealth, as in most state societies. It depends upon kinship in a more subtle way – each individual, whether of high or low rank, is a member of a group, and the groups themselves are ranked and regulated kinship. Those whose heredity links them most closely to the chief are of the highest status.

One such arrangement has been termed by the anthropologist Marshal Sahlins the 'conical clan' – conical because the lineage lines all lead back to the founding ancestor at the apex, whose direct descendant (usually in the male line) is the paramount chief. The hereditary lineage organisation in such a society is reflected in the

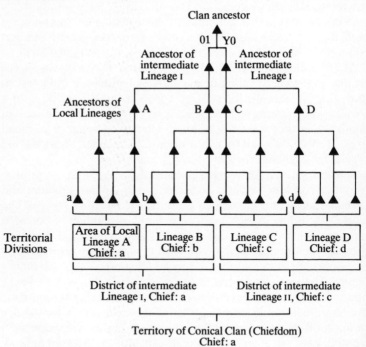

*Figure* 1. Clan genealogy of the 'conical clan' (senior sons to the left) indicating territorial organisation.

204

territorial organisation – in the lands which the different groups occupy.

This kind of analysis was not of course carried out by Captain Cook: it has been set out by anthropologists using Cook's observations among many others. But Cook observed also other features of chiefdom society. The first of these is its harmonious unity. Individuals serve the chief not through repression but because they want to: social respect and prestige comes from correct behaviour. And while the chiefs exercised powers of life and death over their subjects, a more common sanction was the general contempt and disapproval which disrespectful or deviant behaviour would incur.

A second feature of chiefdom society is redistribution: goods and services are offered to the chief. They flow into his hands, and he assigns them, some for his personal use, and others for the common good. This makes possible a third feature: a measure of craft specialisation. The economic device of redistribution allows some craftsmen to specialise in their calling – whether it be boat-building, or carving, or religious practice, or the occupation of chief itself. All are possible because they are supported by society, and more specifically by the chief personally. He in turn assigns their produce in a way which works for the good of society as a whole.

From our point of view this is an important feature of chiefdom society, and so is another: mobilisation. The chief has at his call the entire manpower resources of the community. When some major endeavour is projected, he can ensure that there is the workforce to carry it out.

These then are some of the features of chiefdom society, which make it possible, I think, for us to understand Stonehenge and our monuments without recourse to beings from outer space or other flights of fancy. I have deliberately stated them in a general form, since there is no suggestion whatever that the specific features of any Pacific society can tell us just what happened at Stonehenge. I shall argue below that some of these general features must have been present in neolithic society in south Britain.

But Tonga and Easter Island today offer more than these rather cold and academic generalisations. The Kingdom of Tonga, while a modern state, a member of the United Nations, offering to the visitor all the comforts of the twentieth century, still retains many of those features of a traditional chiefdom society which were encountered by Captain Cook. Easter Island, although its traditions have sadly decayed, still shows in its great monuments the achievements of which such a society is capable. It is still possible, then, to

*Plate* 1. Performance of a night dance before Captain Cook and his party on Ha'apai (engraving after J. Webber).

*experience* at first hand some of the features of chiefdom society. And while the details are different, in escaping from the preoccupations of the western world with its aggressively market economy and its mass production, one is able to see more clearly just how a chiefdom society can work.

## Traditional Tonga

Captain Cook spent several weeks in Tonga during his Third Voyage to the Pacific, arriving in May 1777. His published account, and the detailed journals which he and some of his officers kept, are a precious document of the functioning of a chiefdom society before it was extensively influenced by European culture, indeed the earliest full account of such a society in existence. (Some would claim that the descriptions by Caesar and Tacitus of the iron-age Britons and Gauls could be so designated, but Cook's sympathetic curiosity about the lives and customs of the natives far exceeded theirs.)

Soon after his arrival Cook was entertained by dancing, and he and his colleagues have left detailed descriptions of these occasions, one of which ends with the assessment: 'The dance was musical and harmonious and all their motions were performed with such justness that the whole party moved and acted as one man. It was the opinion of every one of us that such a performance would have met with universal applause on a European theatre.'

Even more valuable than these descriptions are the drawings which Cook's illustrators made, many of which were engraved and published at the end of the Voyage. The finest of these draughtsmen was Webber, who was responsible for most of the illustrations accompanying the account of Cook's Third Voyage. Some of Cook's illustrators have been criticised for romanticising, for drawing what they imagined rather than what they saw, and there is some truth in these accusations. Yet these engravings surpass in quality any earlier ethnographic illustration. Webber's views of the night dances on the island of Ha'apai contain many authentic touches of detail – any European who has had to sit cross-legged for several hours on such an occasion will recognise the rather uncomfortable attitudes of the Europeans in the front row (including Cook himself) with their 'backs to the camera'.

The Christian missionaries who succeeded Cook in Tonga worked consistently to extinguish most that was original and traditional in Tongan life, forcing the natives to conform to European conventions about what was good and moral. Dancing, conceived as a pagan activity, was stopped altogether for a while, until the natives

*Plate* 2. Modern dancers in Makave perform the *lakalaka*.

'invented' some new dances which, lacking the pagan associations of the earlier ones, were seen as acceptable. Happily the newly-invented dances seem in fact to have much in common with those seen by Cook, with the same emphasis on a whole line of figures moving together in harmony and the same exquisitely graceful movements of the hands. The modern *lakalaka*, where the dancers sing in harmony as they move, still gives the observer an authentic glimpse of the harmony and perfection of traditional Tongan song and dance, a reminder of the consummate artistry of which technologically simple societies are capable.

The same sense of continuity, of the old not fundamentally changed beneath the surface of the new, is seen in other aspects of Tongan society. The King of Tonga today, His Majesty King Taufa'ahau Tupou IV, receives much the same traditional respects as did his ancestors who held the office of Tu'i Tonga, traditional head of Tongan society. As he remarked to Magnus Magnusson and myself: 'When you consider the changes that have taken place in Tonga over the last 150 years, they have been very big changes, and yet it hasn't really affected village life all that much, particularly in the smaller more affluent villages.'

It was such a village, Makave on the northern island of Vava'u, which we visited at the King's suggestion. On our arrival we were at once greeted by the chief, the Honourable Tu'i'afitu, one of the hereditary nobles of Tonga, and conducted to the village hall for a ceremony of welcome. This is the ceremony of the *kava*, a drink made from the *kava* root, and its interest is great, since nothing shows more clearly the formalism of traditional Tongan society. Webber has left a beautiful engraving of a *kava* ceremony two centuries ago, which incidentally illustrates well the sophistication of Tongan building using wood and matting. Today, just as two centuries ago (and no doubt for centuries before that), the chief sits cross-legged flanked on each side by his retainers and guests.

In front there is an open space, and opposite is the man who will make the *kava* drink, seated behind a three-legged wooden bowl. On the Chief's right and left are his two *matapules* – 'talking chiefs' or heralds: the herald of the right and the herald of the left. The chief himself says nothing throughout, and it is his *matapule* who pronounces the instructions to grind the root and put it in the bowl, to pour in water, to remove the root after soaking, and then to serve the drink (in a coconut cup) to each of those present, in an order as strictly prescribed by etiquette as the seating of a banquet in Buckingham Palace.

209

*Plate 3.* The Honourable Tuʻiʻafitu at the *kava* ceremony in the village of Makave on Vavaʻu.

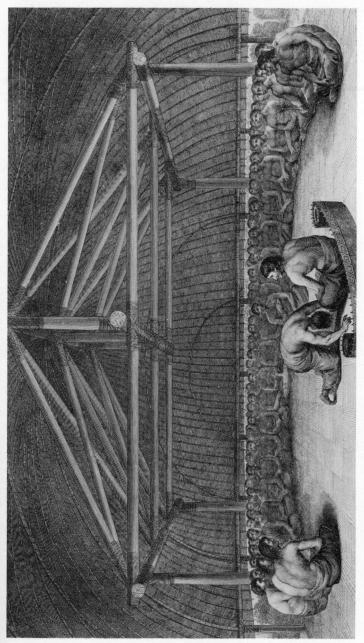

*Plate* 4. The Tongan *kava* ceremony (engraving after Webber).

*Plate* 5. The *inasi* ceremony at Mu'a, with a burial mound (*langi*) behind (engraving after Webber).

I found participation in this ceremony an altogether remarkable experience. Not only was it a great honour to be the guest of the Honourable Tu'i'afitu on such an occasion, but as an archaeologist I could not help remarking on how little of all that went on would find any direct trace in the archaeological record. The most formal *kava* ceremony held during our stay, which involved the presentation of a pig, was held outdoors on the village green. Apart from the stone used to pound the *kava* root, most of the artefacts used were of perishable materials and would not survive in the archaeological record. Even the fine hall depicted in Webber's drawing would leave little for the archaeologist beyond a few post-holes in the earth, very like those which have in fact been found at the henge monument at Durrington Walls in Wiltshire. But above all, the traditional formality and strictness of etiquette was impressive. As Cook put it: 'There is a decorum observed in the presence of their great men that is truly admirable. Whenever he sits down, all those with him seat themselves at the same time in a semi-circle before him, leaving always an open convenient space between him and them.' No one who has participated in such a ceremony could doubt the powers of organisation or the social complexity of a society which, if technology were the only criterion, might have to be regarded as composed of 'mere barbarians.'

The ceremony of the presentation of the pig was interesting in many ways. Once again it was conducted with a formulaic elaboration, according to precise rules. It was presented to the chief, the Honourable Tu'i'afitu, and he, in accordance with convention, in turn sent it on to be presented to the man senior to him in the hierarchy, the Governor of Vava'u. Here in fact is a last vestige of the traditional system of redistribution, a feature of most chiefdom societies.

Redistribution, or at least one component of it, was most strikingly seen by Captain Cook in Tonga at the great *inasi* ceremony, the ceremony of the first fruits, usually held in October. It took place at Mu'a on Tongatapu, the main island of the Tonga group. Mu'a was the traditional home and centre of the Tu'i Tonga, the head of Tongan society, as well as the burial place of his ancestors. Their great burial mounds or *langi* are seen in the background of Webber's drawing. At the ceremony it was usual for the chiefs and population of the area to bring their first fruits and offer them to the Tu'i Tonga. Much of the ceremonial was complicated, and little understood by Cook, who was only allowed to be present on condition that he removed his shirt and loosed his hair. One of his

*Plate 6.* Burial mound or *langi* of the Tu'i Tonga at Mu'a, Tongatapu.

officers wrote:

> We who were on the outside were not a little surprised at seeing
> Captain Cook in the procession of the Chiefs with his hair
> hanging loose and his body naked down to the waist, no person
> being admitted covered above the waist or with his hair tied. I
> do not pretend to dispute the propriety of Captain Cook's
> conduct, but I cannot help thinking he rather let himself down.

Today the verdict is reversed and nothing could more effectively
document the value of Cook as an observer than his respect for the
community which he was visiting.

Such ceremonies in many societies have a religious as well as a
social significance, indeed the two cannot be distinguished, and
Cook's colleague Anderson rightly observed: 'This ceremony which
is call'd Natche has so much mystery running through the whole that
it is hard to tell whether it is most of the religious or political kind.'

There is much more about Tongan society today which recalls
that of two centuries ago – the yam plantations, the manufacture of
bark cloth, the language itself are little changed. And there is much
in both which is perplexing and thought-provoking to an archaeologist asking himself how many of the activities of a sophisticated
and complex society, where many of the artefacts are of wood, will
be preserved in the archaeological record. But let us leave Tonga
with the words of Cook himself:

> I must notwithstanding conclude by observing that the natives
> of Tonga and the isles around it are upon the whole arrived at
> as much perfection in their manual works, as much regularity in
> their government, at as high a pitch in the agriculture and some
> other things as any nation whatever under the same circum-
> stances: and that exclusive of the helps obtained from learning
> the use of metals and communication with nations who have
> these advantages, they are in every respect almost as perfectly
> civilis'd as it is possible for mankind to be. They seem to have
> been long at their ultimum, and at least by what we may judge
> from the general description of them given by Tasman they
> have been so for above these hundred and thirty years, and had
> they not been visited by Europeans would probably ever have
> remained the same.

### The Easter Island Monuments

In the previous section I have not attempted to draw many conclusions from those observations on traditional Tongan society. But
they are already of great value when we come to Easter Island, at the

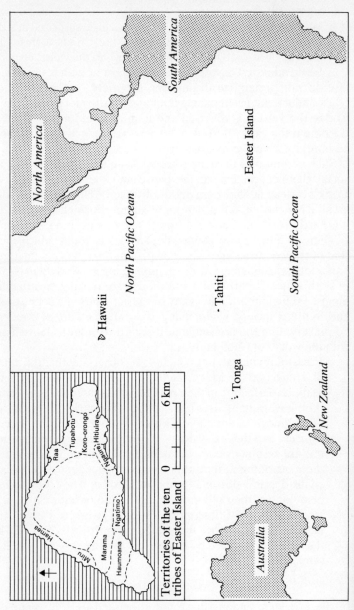

*Figure* 2. Map of Pacific with inset of Easter Island, showing tribal divisions.

extreme eastern end of Polynesia, for the society there was in effect destroyed by the terrible Peruvian slave raid of 1862. It was only after that time that the remarkable wooden inscriptions in the *rongo rongo* script came to light. We have little first-hand knowledge about this Easter Island writing, or about the use of the great monuments, the *ahu*, surmounted by those extraordinary statues.

*Plate* 7. Easter Island *rongo rongo* tablet.

Indeed, it is not surprising that some writers should speak of a 'mystery' of Easter Island. For there is no doubt that one of the most remarkable sights in the world is at the volcanic crater of Rano Raraku, where the statues were quarried. Evidently they were carved before being transported, with only the fine details incomplete, and for reasons which may never be clear, a great many statues were hewn from the rock, presumably well in advance of requirements. There they still stand in their dozens and hundreds, gazing enigmatically across the Pacific.

At the same time the element of mystery should not be exaggerated. The language of Easter Island survives today and it is a Polynesian language. Archaeology has helped to clarify the prehistory of the area, and Easter Island was probably settled by Polynesians coming from the west (perhaps from the Marquesas Islands) around the time of Christ. There seems no need for the theories of Thor Heyerdahl, proposing contact with South America. The custom of building ceremonial monuments is quite common elsewhere in Polynesia, for instance in Tahiti, and statues not unlike those of Easter Island (although smaller in size) are also known.

What is special about Easter Island is the intensity of the *ahu*-building activity. They are dotted along the coast, imposing platforms with one or several statues looking inland, dominating the plaza behind the *ahu*. Their significance was appreciated by Cook

*Plate* 8. Easter Island statues at Ahu Akivi.

and his colleagues, who visited Easter Island in 1774 (although on account of illness Cook did not himself go ashore):

> Stone images whose names we got from the natives, and by what I could understand from them they were erected to the memory of their chiefs, for they all had different names and they always called them *ariki* which I understand to be the king or chief, and they do not appear to pay the respect to them that I should think they would to a deity.

It seems fairly clear that Easter Island at this time was divided into territories, and that each territory was the home of a tribe or lineage (see figure 2). The approximate territorial division was recorded in 1914 and it may be reasonable to regard each of the main image *ahu* as the focal centre for the lineage territory. Easter Island society does not seem to have been welded into a single coherent polity with a single political leader, as Tonga was. So there is no single political centre to compare with the seat of the Tu'i Tonga at Mu'a, with its great series of burial monuments. Certainly Easter Island did have a ritual centre at Orongo, but through much of its history there may have been an element of competition among the various lineages, which is perhaps reflected in the grandiloquent monumentality of their focal *ahu*.

With some knowledge of Polynesian social organisation, it is possible to see how the society of Easter Island, despite its special features, does not stand apart. The *ahu* of Easter Island may be compared with the *langi* of Tonga or with the *marae* of Tahiti. Perhaps their very isolation led to the great florescence in the statue building which accompanied them.

Even the *rongo rongo* tablets can begin to fall into position when we recall that they were apparently used exclusively in conjunction with religious chants. They may have acted as mnemonic devices, like the string figures traditionally made on some other Polynesian islands. Indeed for me the most exciting experience on Easter Island was to meet Amalia Tepano, an old lady who remembers not only how to make some of the traditional string figures but also some of the chants that go with them. I think there is little doubt that some of these are real *rongo rongo* chants, which the wise men of Easter Island society used to sing using not string figures but *rongo rongo* tablets as their *aide mémoire*. Listening to the chant of Amalia Tepano is as close as we shall ever get to the lost secret of the *rongo rongo* writing.

*Plate* 9. Amalia Tepano with one of the traditional string figures of Easter Island.

## Stonehenge Revisited

I have deliberately avoided referring to Stonehenge directly in the two preceding sections. But anyone who has really puzzled over the problem of our neolithic monuments in south Britain will already see something of what I am getting at. It is my belief that the major henge monuments of Britain – great sites such as Durrington Walls, or Avebury or Stonehenge itself – could only have been built by some centralised and coordinated society, of the kind which we can today call a chiefdom society (see chapter 8).

Clearly a degree of mobilisation was needed to provide the manpower for these great works, and the economic device which made all of this possible must have been redistribution. It is likely, although not certain, that this was still a kin-based society – there is no need to suggest the clear-cut division into separate social classes characteristic of state societies. It is likely that there was indeed a

*Plate* 10. (*above*) Stonehenge trilithon; (*below*)
Tonga trilithon, the Ha'amonga a Maui on Tongatapu.

221

paramount chief behind the construction of Stonehenge and Silbury Hill. Yet I believe that in the Salisbury Plain it is possible to distinguish traces of the same kind of territorial division suggested for Easter Island. In the early neolithic period long barrows are seen, burial mounds which may have been the focal points for very small communities. But soon larger and more widely-spaced focal points emerge – the causewayed camps. In the late neolithic period these are superseded by the major henges, which in territorial terms may be regarded as the equivalent of the great image *ahu* of the ten tribal territories of Easter Island. That is to say, they may have been the focal point of the tribal territory, the main home of the tribal chief, and the site of both social and religious ceremonies; as Cook's colleague observed, the religious and the political cannot always be separated. Then at the end of the period, neolithic monument-building in Britain culminates in the erection of Stonehenge and Silbury Hill.

Of course there can be no doubt that Stonehenge represents also a close experience and interest in astronomy: Stonehenge was a solar observatory. Yet here again Polynesia can offer us parallels – although they need be no more than that. The present King of Tonga has claimed that the remarkable trilithon, the Ha'amonga a Maui was used for solar observations, and there can be no doubt that the economic system there allowed for much craft special-isation. There is no reason why the society of Stonehenge should not have allowed for men as erudite as the *rongo rongo* chanters of Easter Island, as steeped in traditional lore as the *matapule* of Tonga, and as skilled in astronomical observation as we know were the Polynesian navigators.

There is no need then to argue that the builders of Stonehenge must have been possessed of some special skills derived from the Near East. Nor do I see much virtue in recent attempts that have been made to suggest that this must have been a state society of the kind represented by the Ancient Maya of Mesoamerica. The Poly-nesian experience does not tell us what happened in England around 2000 BC, but it does show us the potential of chiefdom societies, with a low level of technology and the complete absence of urban centres, in achieving remarkable works of communal endeavour and traditional specialised skill.

Let me stress again, therefore, that my argument here does not depend upon any supposed one-to-one correspondence between traditional Polynesian society and British society of four thousand years ago. There is no cause for the traditional pedantic complaints

*Plate* 11. Magnus Magnusson and Colin Renfrew with
H M the King of Tonga at Nuku'alofa.

about the dangers of 'ethnographic analogy', with which academics like to restrict the range of discussion. My claim is that both the Salisbury Plain of 4000 years ago and Tonga of two centuries ago may be seen as examples, different examples, of a recurrent social form, namely chiefdom society. Many of the resemblances which occur are structural resemblances arising from this underlying regularity: others come from ecological constraints such as the use of wood for domestic architecture.

In conclusion I shall quote once again Cook's colleague Anderson who knew and understood traditional Tongan society as well as any modern anthropologist has done. His remarks apply to many chiefdom societies, and *for this reason* and not through any superficial similarity between two cases, they are relevant to prehistoric Britain:

> In several respects the Government resembles the old feudal states of Europe, where though all acknowledge the Sovereignty of the Prince there are many who seem to exercise their authority with no less restraint in their several provinces, and are in some respects wholly independent unless in the single circumstance of paying homage due to the Lord of all. The island is divided into many districts, each of which has a chief who may be considered as Lords or Barons. . . . The immediate

223

dependents of these Chiefs who are very numerous assume the names of their masters (besides their own proper name) and use it as was customary amongst the Scottish clans.

Each of these no doubt decides differences and distributes justice in their several districts. . . . Whether it be from that mode of government or some other policy to which we are strangers, it does not appear that any civilis'd nations have as yet exceeded them in the great order they observe on all occasions and ready compliance with the commands of their chiefs, nor in the harmony that subsists throughout all ranks and unites them as if one man inform'd with and directed by the same principle.

This, then, is the essential clue to the understanding of chiefdom society and through it to an explanation of the early monuments of Britain. Human originality, and the creative capacity of human societies, albeit with a simple technology, should never be under-rated, whether they border the Atlantic or lie in the Pacific. [1978]

## Acknowledgements

My experience of modern Polynesian society is based on a voyage made in the agreeable company of Messrs David Collison, Roy Henman, Magnus Magnusson, David South and John Tellick, which also owed much to the encouragement of the late Paul Johnstone. In Tonga we were aided by the personal interest of HM King Taufa'ahau Tupou IV, and in Makave I am much indebted to the hospitality and friendship of the Hon. Tu'i'afitu, his wife Luisa and son Niulala and to the help of Mr Epeli Kauvaka. I should like to acknowledge the assistance and advice on Easter Island of Mr Sergio Rapu and Professor and Mrs William Ayres.

# 8

## MONUMENTS, MOBILISATION AND SOCIAL ORGANISATION IN NEOLITHIC WESSEX

*

THE STRUCTURE OF Neolithic societies in Western Europe
may have been a great deal less egalitarian than the lack of
differentiation in their artifacts might lead us to believe.

(R. J. C. Atkinson 1961, 299)

The principal recorded sites of the neolithic period of south Britain
are monumental: either funeral mounds sometimes more than 300
ft long, or circular enclosures, with a bank and internal ditch,
frequently more than 100 ft in diameter. We know much less of
settlement sites, or of more modest burial conventions. Yet the
artefacts found are unimpressive: simple pottery, bone and stone
tools, and some handsome axes, often of imported stone (Piggott
1954). Explanations are needed for the monuments of prehistoric
Britain, and indeed many writers have stressed that both the 'causewayed camps' of the early neolithic, and the 'henges' of the later
neolithic are almost uniquely British features. They can be discussed most profitably in local terms.

The changes for which some explanation is here desired are those
seen in the neolithic of south Britain, and specifically in Wessex
(Wiltshire and Dorset) which resulted in the construction of these
monuments. In the first place there are the long burial mounds or
'barrows', generally earthen, of the early neolithic period. At the
same time as those, probably before 4000 BC in calendar years,
causewayed enclosures were constructed. Then, possibly later in
the earlier neolithic period, there are the remarkable 'cursus'
monuments – earthen banks sometimes running for several miles,
and bounded by parallel ditches about 300 ft apart.

Later in the neolithic, in the third millennium BC (in calendar
years), very large henge monuments were constructed, of which

225

Avebury is the most famous. Around the end of the later neolithic there were two prodigious building feats in this region – the construction in earth and chalk of the huge conical mound, Silbury Hill, which was at least three times the volume of the fluted 'pyramid' of the Olmecs at La Venta (cf. Heizer and Drucker 1968, 52), and, a little later, the erection of the great sarsen structure at Stonehenge.

The difficult general question as to what constitutes an adequate 'explanation' for such changes and achievements will not be touched on here. It will be considered sufficient if the explanation or hypothesis:

i) offers a framework in which the changes seem more intelligible

ii) gives rise to logical consequences which can be tested in subsequent work.

## Chiefdoms in neolithic Wessex

The explanatory model used here is a social one. It unites previous suggestions as to the function of some of the monuments and the organization of their construction. But as we shall see it goes further in relating their distribution to these other ideas, as well as to observed specialization in trade and religious practice.

Already six years ago, Isobel Smith (1965, 19) rejected some earlier views about the 'causewayed camps', and elaborated a suggestion first made by Stuart Piggott (1954, 29) and Richard Atkinson (cf. 1962, 215), that 'the enclosure may have served as a centre or rallying-point for the population of a fairly wide area'.

Such rallying points play an essential role in the lives of some contemporary communities living in a comparable stage of economic and technological development. Assembly of the scattered families or tribal units takes place at one or more intervals during the year, at the slack periods in the agricultural and/or stock-tending cycle, and affords opportunities for the transaction of the necessary business of tribal life. In addition to those matters which may come within the political field in its broader sense, such other matters can be attended to as the holding of initiation ceremonies, matchmaking and weddings, the exchange of stock and seed-corn and perhaps of more durable goods. Rites and ceremonies are performed to ensure the fertility of the flocks and herds and the growing of the corn, and finally to celebrate the harvest. Communal feasts are an inevitable accompaniment of such occasions, and some industrial activities may be undertaken, either because they are less tedious when performed to the accompaniment of a lively

226

exchange of news and gossip, or because there is insufficient time at other seasons.

Miss Smith's further suggestion (1966, 474) that there was a connection and a similarity in function between the early neolithic causewayed enclosures and the later neolithic henges has been discussed by Geoffrey Wainwright in the light of his recent discovery of wooden buildings in some of the larger henges. He compared these to the council houses of the Creek and Cherokee indians of the south-eastern United States and concluded that their function was communal rather than domestic (Wainwright 1970, 38).

This useful discussion of the function of such monuments is supplemented by Atkinson's stimulating reflections on the social organization which produced Stonehenge (1960, 166):

> The building of Stonehenge is . . . unlikely to have been the expression of the common will, but rather the fulfilment of a purpose imposed from above. Now in the rich and martially furnished Wessex graves we can admittedly see evidence of chieftainship, and the grouping of the graves in cemeteries may imply whole dynasties of chiefs. Yet the pattern of society which they represent is surely that of so many other heroic societies, in which clan wars with clan, and rival dynasties carry on a perpetual struggle for power. Under such conditions, can the construction of Stonehenge, involving the displacement of so many hundreds of men from their homes for so long, have been attempted, still less achieved? Surely not; for such great works can only be encompassed by a society at peace within itself. And in such a society of conflicting factions, how is peace imposed except from above?
>
> I believe, therefore, that Stonehenge itself is evidence for the concentration of political power, for a time at least, in the hands of a single man, who alone could create and maintain the conditions necessary for this great undertaking.

It is not necessary to agree with all of this to see that it does pose questions which in general have been much neglected. One point at present in doubt is whether the final structure of Stonehenge was in fact constructed during the rich Wessex early bronze age, of which Atkinson writes, or in an earlier period, as Christopher Hawkes has recently suggested. Nor is Atkinson's notion of chiefly society very much like the one to be presented here. It is, rather, his realization of the social organisation involved in the investment of so much labour which is relevant. The same applies now to Silbury Hill, which a recent radiocarbon date would place as the contemporary or immediate senior of the pyramids of Egypt, just before 2500 BC in calendar years.

It is proposed here that the developments in neolithic Wessex be explained in terms of a developed social stratification in the society, resulting in the formation in or before the late neolithic period of what a number of American anthropologists have recently termed 'chiefdoms'. I am aware that this is now a fashionable concept, of limited meaning when used loosely, and yet have found it particularly apposite in the early bronze age Aegean (Renfrew 1972, chapter 18), a society paradoxically different, in many ways, from neolithic Britain.

Yet the old tripartite social classification of band/savagery, tribe/ barbarism and state/civilization is no longer adequate to our needs. Between the relatively egalitarian tribal society which we may imagine for some early neolithic cultures of Europe – Starčevo perhaps, or Danubian I – and the civilizations of Crete, Mycenae, Classical Greece or Rome, there lies a considerable gap. In this same gap fall the stratified societies of Polynesia – which in Easter Island, Hawaii, Tonga, the Marquesas and elsewhere, likewise produced very impressive and large-scale monuments, illustrated in chapter 7 – and some of the tribes of the south-eastern United States, as well as many others.

This concept of chiefdom arose partly from Paul Kirchoff's notion of 'conical clan', and Raymond Firth's analysis of the 'ramages' of Polynesia. As Morton Fried put it (1957, 1): 'One of the classic tasks in the quest for regularity is an attempt to derive the correlations of specific social institutions with other aspects of culture . . . The main concern is with the relations of social structure and economy'. The term has been well discussed by Elman R. Service (1962, 142–77) and Marshall D. Sahlins (1968). A chiefdom is a ranked society, hierarchically arranged, sometimes in the form of a conical clan where the eldest descendant in the male line from the clan founder ranks highest, and the cadet branches are ranked in seniority after the main line (see p.204).

> Chiefdoms are particularly distinguished from tribes by the presence of centres which coordinate economic, social and religious activities . . . The great change at chiefdom level is that specialization and redistribution are no longer merely adjunctive to a few particular endeavours, but continuously characterize a large part of the activity of the society. Chiefdoms are *redistributional societies* with a permanent centra

228

agency of coordination. Thus the central agency comes to have not only an economic role – however basic this factor in the origin of this type of society – but also serves additional functions which are social, political and religious. Once it is in existence, it can in other words, act to foster and preserve the integration of the society for the sake of integration alone. (Service 1962, 143)

The proposal, then is that this affords an appropriate model for the late neolithic of Wessex. The following are brought out by Service and Sahlins as frequent features of chiefdoms, in addition to the defining ones of 1) a ranked society and 2) the redistribution of produce organized by the chief:

3) greater population density

4) increase in the total number in the society

5) increase in the size of individual residence groups

6) greater productivity

7) more clearly defined territorial boundaries or borders

8) a more integrated society with a greater number of sociocentric statuses

9) centres which coordinate social and religious as well as economic activity

10) frequent ceremonies and rituals serving wide social purposes

11) rise of priesthood

12) relation to a total environmental situation favouring specialization in production (and hence redistribution) – i.e. to some ecological diversity

13) specialization, not only regional or ecological but also through the pooling of individual skills in large co-operative endeavours

14) organization and deployment of public labour, sometimes for agricultural work (e.g. irrigation) and/or for building temples, temple mounds or pyramids

15) improvement in craft specialization

16) potential for territorial expansion – associated with the 'rise and fall' of chiefdoms

17) reduction of internal strife

18) pervasive inequality of persons or groups in the society associated with permanent leadership, effective in fields other than the economic

19) distinctive dress or ornament for those of high status

20) no true government to back up decisions by legalized force.

The strength of the model is that it implies the conjoint occurrence of many of these features. We shall see that many are well documented in neolithic south Britain, while some others are conspicuously lacking.

*Figure* 1. The principal groups of neolithic long barrows in Dorset and Wiltshire, as listed by Ashbee (1970).

## Long Barrows and Territories of Individual Settlements

There are some 120 long barrows known from Wiltshire and Dorset (listed by Ashbee 1970). Most of them are of earth or chalk, sometimes covering the traces of a wooden 'mortuary house'. While in some cases this may have been accessible after the construction of the mound, it will not have stood for more than a couple of decades. After this the barrow was effectively 'unchambered'. There are in this area a number of barrows containing a stone chamber, which certainly was accessible for much longer, and may have been more expensive of labour to construct. For convenience they are included here with the more numerous 'unchambered' barrows.

Grinsell (1958, maps I to V) and others have emphasized how the prehistoric remains of Wessex cluster on the chalklands – the Marlborough Downs, the Salisbury Plain, Cranborne Chase and the Dorset Downs (figure 1). Ashbee has divided the Wessex barrows into five groups, corresponding to these topographic divisions, with separate groups for the east and west Salisbury plain. This is supported by an elementary isarithmic approach, and doubtless could be substantiated by other means, although the east and west Salisbury Plain groups are not well separated.

It has long been recognized that the long barrows sometimes occur in groups of two or three. There is a noted concentration in the region near Stonehenge (which was not itself begun, however, until later), and some lineation along chalk uplands in Cranborne Chase. But in the west Salisbury Plain at least, the spacing is such as to suggest that each barrow (or pair) may have been located in its own individual territory. Even accepting that some barrows have been destroyed, this is made plausible by the simple construction of Thiessen polygons (figure 2; cf. p.183).

An important underlying assumption here is that all the barrows must have been functioning in some sense, although not necessarily for burial, at the same time – no doubt at the end of the early neolithic period – for such a conclusion to be valid. Atkinson has, by implication, suggested the contrary (Atkinson 1968), and his argument must be considered. He points out that on average six bodies only have been found within long barrows, and assumes that long barrows were being built over a period of ten centuries. His conclusion was that if the entire population was buried in such barrows, each barrow could have served a family of about six for about 25 years. On this model the population would be very small, and families would be moving from place to place, so that the ultimate

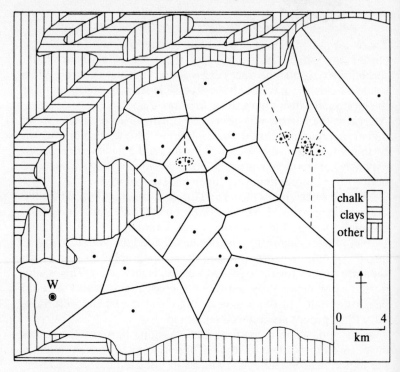

*Figure* 2. Locations of neolithic long barrows (indicated by dots) on the chalklands of the west Salisbury Plain, south Britain. By drawing unweighted Thiessen polygons the chalkland has been divided into 'territories', each with one barrow. (W indicates the enclosure at Whitesheet Hill.) Data from Grinsell (1958) and Ashbee (1970).

distribution of barrows would reflect their wanderings, and in no sense the situation at any point in time. The notion of barrows reflecting territories would be inadmissible.

However it is possible to counter that this argument sets the population impossibly low. A single family of six and their descendants, assuming the population did not increase, would, in 1,000 years, given 25 years per generation, produce 240 dead, requiring (at 6 per barrow) 40 barrows. The barrows of Wessex would thus be the result of three families over this period. A mean population for early neolithic Wessex of 18 persons in more than 3,000 km$^2$ seems, however, too small – less than 0.01 per km$^2$.

The inescapable alternative is that only some of the dead were buried in long barrows, and the others were disposed of by means which have left no trace, as is common in many communities. Indeed the practice of excarnation by exposure may well have operated for those whose bones were later interred in the barrows, since the remains were often altogether disarticulated. The barrow was used only for a few decades and then closed. But it would still have been an impressive monument subsequently, and a possible focus for the religious life of the community.

It is possible that agriculture at this time was on a system of shifting cultivation. Soudsky (1968) has described such a system in the loess lands of Czechoslovakia, where a community of about 125 persons occupied a total area of 2 km$^2$, shifting the location of the village every 15 years to one of four or five sites, and returning after 60 years or so at the beginning of a new cycle. Something of the same, initially in forest clearings, may be envisaged in Wessex, although the groups may have been smaller – from 20 to 100 persons. The territories of roughly 10 km$^2$ seen in figure 2, giving (on this hypothetical assumption) a total land area of 10 to 50 hectares per person should certainly have been adequate. The long barrow would be a permanent feature of the territory.

Ashbee has calculated that the Fussell's Lodge long barrow required 5,000 man hours in its construction, or 500 man days. This is not a large figure and implies no supra-territorial organisation. No doubt the lineage in one territory might aid its neighbour in return for a good feast – and feasting was certainly part of the funeral ritual (Piggott 1954, 60). Such limited cooperation is known from many parts of the world in essentially egalitarian societies – 'family-oriented cooperative projects which are paid for in food given to the workers' (Heizer 1966, 828). It is not clear why only a favoured few should be buried in such a way, yet if the territorial argument is accepted, there were factors favouring the construction of a single barrow in each territory. In other words the existence of a barrow may have been a requirement of the community for social or religious reasons, rather than primarily a means of disposal of the dead. I am not aware of ethnographic parallels for the construction of such a monument soon after the colonization of new land, but perhaps they exist. Certainly the land surface beneath the South Street long barrow (Fowler and Evans 1967), as well as showing unexpected signs of ploughing, suggested only two clearances, separated by at least ten years, prior to its construction.

233

## Larger Monuments and Chieftain Territories

The different classes of neolithic monument in Wessex may be said to form a kind of hierarchy in terms of the manpower involved in their construction. It runs as follows.

i) 10,000 man hours or less. Early neolithic unchambered long barrows. Barrows with stone chambers might take more than 5,000 hours, but could still be of this order.

ii) About 100,000 man hours. Early neolithic causewayed enclosures. I estimate, using the formula proposed by Atkinson (1961, 295), that the ditches and banks at Windmill Hill represent about 120,000 hours.

iii) About 1 million man hours. The major henge monuments, of diameter greater than 600 ft, of which five are known in Wessex (Wainwright 1969; Burl 1969), Wainwright (1970, 30) estimates 1.5 million man hours for Avebury and 0.9 million for Durrington Walls.

iv) Over 10 million man hours. Silbury Hill and the completed cursus monuments (Dorset and Stonehenge cursus). Atkinson estimates a volume of 6.5 million ft$^3$ of earth for the Dorset cursus (1955, 9) which might suggest 9 million man-hours for its construction. He kindly indicates (personal communication) that he would tentatively estimate the minimum labour input for Silbury Hill at about 18 million man-hours. He makes also the important observation that, once begun, the process of construction was continuous, even though there were changes of plan.

v) Over 30 million man-hours. Possibly Stonehenge III. Atkinson has estimated that the transport of the 81 sarsen stones for the final structure of Stonehenge, over a distance of 24 miles, would have taken 30 million man hours. The labour of dressing the stones is assessed at a further 500,000 hours, to which must be added the considerable effort of erecting the stones. If the recent suggestion be followed, however, that the stones of Stonehenge were transported to the Salisbury Plain by glacial action, the labour requirement for transport might be considerably reduced, and the labour involved in Stonehenge III might be no more, or indeed less, than that required for Silbury Hill.

This hierarchy of effort for the causewayed enclosures and long barrows is matched by one of distribution. Each of the areas of long barrows already distinguished has a single causeway camp (although the Marlborough Downs for some reason have three; figure 3.)

*Figure* 3. The neolithic causewayed enclosures of Dorset and Wiltshire in relation to the long barrows. Note that each of Ashbee's barrow groups is served by an enclosure.

| Region | Total no. of long barrows (*stonebuilt barrows in brackets*) | | Causewayed enclosures |
|---|---|---|---|
| Dorset Downs | 20 | (4) | Maiden Castle |
| Cranborne Chase | 35 | (0) | Hambledon Hill |
| West Salisbury Plain | 27 | (0) | Whitesheet |
| East Salisbury Plain | 29 | (0) | Robin Hood's Ball |
| Marlborough Downs | 21 | (16) | Windmill Hill |
| | | | Rybury |
| | | | ?Knap Hill |

If we accept that stone-built barrows involved more labour than earthen ones, the long barrow/camp ratio on the Marlborough Downs is partly explained. Two camps (Hambledon Hill and Whitesheet) lie at the western extreme of their chalkland, but they may well have included within their territory some of the clay and oolite lands to the west.

It is particularly interesting that this territorial division seems to persist into the later neolithic period, although the building of long barrows and the construction of causewayed camps had by then ceased. There are ten henge monuments in Britain with a diameter greater than 600 ft. Five of them are in Wessex. They related closely to the previous territories, and to the causewayed camps (cf. Smith 1971; figure 4).

| Region | Henge | Diameter of henge (feet) | Former causewayed enclosure | Max. diam. c causewayed enclosure (ft |
|---|---|---|---|---|
| Dorset Downs | Mount Pleasant | 1200 | Maiden Castle | 1200 |
| Cranborne Chase | Knowlton South | 750 | Hambledon Hill | 1050 |
| Salisbury Plain | Durrington Walls | 1720 | Robin Hood's Ball/ Whitesheet | 750/640 |
| Vale of Pewsey | Marden | 1700 | Knap Hill/Rybury | 650/520 |
| Marlborough Downs | Avebury | 1390 | Windmill Hill | 1270 |

The causewayed camp at Knap Hill, already noted as anomalous, does not find a corresponding major henge. Nor does Whitesheet, its territory apparently uniting with the east Salisbury Plain. The land which it may have served to the west could conceivably have come within the sphere of the four henges at Priddy, each of c. 500 ft diameter.

There are of course other henges in Wessex, but they are all much smaller, less than 300 ft in diameter except for the second henge at Knowlton and Stonehenge itself. There is no reason to suppose that all henges had the same function, and the special astronomical

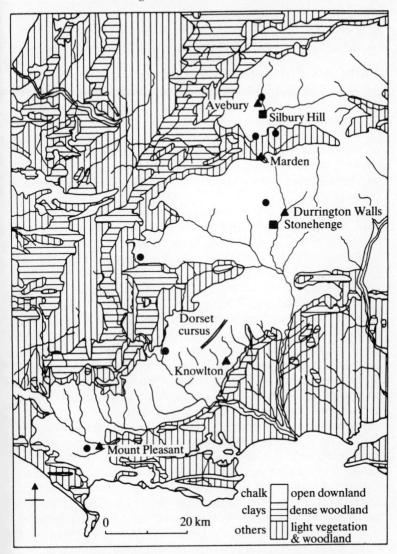

*Figure* 4. The major henge monuments of Dorset and Wiltshire (shown by triangles) in relation to the earlier neolithic enclosures (shown by circles). The large monuments at Stonehenge and Silbury Hill are also shown. Note that each area formerly served by a causewayed enclosure now has a major henge, except the west part of the Salisbury Plain, which is now apparently united with the eastern part.

significance of Stonehenge is well known, so that we may reasonably distinguish these from the major henges.

## The Model Applied

On the basis of the proposed model (itself admittedly hypothetical) we can assert that each early neolithic region served by a causewayed camp was the home of an emerging chiefdom. Each had on the average 20 long barrows, which might suggest a population of between 400 and 2,000 persons. If we assume that one fifth of the population could be mobilised for public works for three months of the year, we have a potential annual work output of between 80,000 and 400,000 man hours. So a causewayed camp could be built in a single year.

It is just possible that the cursus at Dorchester in Oxfordshire was built during the early neolithic period (Atkinson, Piggott and Sandars 1951, 63) and it would certainly present a problem if the same were true of the Dorset and Stonehenge cursus. For the Dorset cursus would then reflect at least 25 years work. But in fact we know that the Dorset cursus was built in at least two, and perhaps in several stages. Moreover Leach (1959, 13) has rightly stressed that what seem today impressive and coherent achievements, reflecting perhaps the concept of a single mind, were often the result of accretions over many centuries. The same is true of Mediaeval cathedrals, and is of course now well documented for Stonehenge, although Silbury Hill was the result of a continuous process of construction. The early neolithic construction of cursus monuments would be more intelligible in these terms.

Turning now to the late neolithic period, we are perhaps entitled to think in terms of an increased population and a more developed social hierarchy. For certainly the carrying capacity of the land should have been greater than the population estimated so far. If we were to take a figure of 10 per $km^2$, and 1,000, 1,400 and 1,000 $km^2$ respectively for the Marlborough Downs, the Salisbury Plain and the Dorset chalklands, this would give us a total Wessex population of 34,000 persons. Each major henge would serve a population of about 5,000 persons, affording a possible annual mobilization of 1 million man hours. This was certainly sufficient to construct the henges. This was, of course, approximately the time of the supposed arrival of the 'Beaker Folk'. But until we know more of their settlement pattern and economy, it is preferable to think of their participating in the emerging social organization, rather than determining it.

For Silbury Hill, on the other hand, and especially Stonehenge III – for which the sarsen stones probably came from the Marlborough Downs anyway – we might well think in terms of further co-operation between the different regions, a 'confederation' like that of the Creek Indians in the eighteenth century. Or better, we might envisage the five Wessex chiefdoms coalescing into one greater chiefdom with five constituent tribes.

This would give a theoretical annual mobilization potential of 7 million man hours. But the concomitant redistribution to support the large work force would imply the transport of produce from south Dorset and the north Marlborough plains to the site of operations. Wheeled vehicles were not, it is thought, available, although river transport should not be ruled out since it was perhaps used for the Stonehenge bluestones (Atkinson 1960, 107). An increase in the size of the social unit, beyond a certain point and without corresponding technological advance, does not necessarily promote greater productivity.

Something of the same territorial pattern seems to have persisted into the early bronze age when Stonehenge III was probably built, although the major henges were perhaps no longer used. The evidence then is from burials, single graves under round barrows, some of them exceedingly rich (Piggott 1938). Fleming (1971) has recently studied the distribution of these barrows and established four particularly dense concentrations of them, with densities well above 6 per $km^2$, in regions which may be related to the four invariant traditions already recognized (figure 5): Maiden Castle/ Mount Pleasant; Hambledon Hill/Knowlton; Robin Hood's Ball/ Durrington Walls; and Windmill Hill/Avebury (figure 4). There is a lesser concentration some way east of Marden, and another near Whitesheet. But what emerges above all is the great concentration in the Stonehenge area and this was clearly the most important burial region. The force of Fleming's elegant analysis is incontrovertible, but it is unnecessary to draw on the hypothesis of a predominantly pastoral economy. The old regional patterns are still visible, and the Wessex early bronze age population preferred to give influential people burial near the centre of tribal areas, in the same way as they used to meet there at causewayed camps or henges. The special importance given to the Stonehenge area would support the tentative suggestion that the Salisbury Plain chief had by now become the paramount of a wider unit at the end of the neolithic.

On the basis of the field monuments of the successive phases in

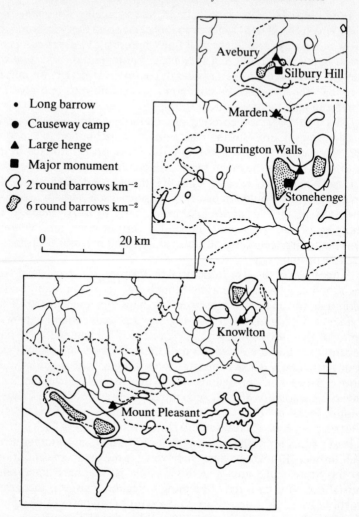

*Figure* 5. Distribution of the early bronze age round barrows on the chalklands of Dorset and Wiltshire (after Fleming 1971) in relation to the principal monuments of the late neolithic. The four main clusters suggest the persistence of regional divisions seen in figures 2 to 4.

Wessex, a hypothetical picture has thus been constructed of emerging chiefdoms in the early neolithic, developing to full scale chiefdoms at the time of the henges, and possibly to a single unified chiefdom with four or five sub-regions at the time of Silbury Hill or

Stonehenge III. This territorial pattern is still seen in the Wessex early bronze age (which may have been the period when Stonehenge III was constructed), but disappears from view in the later bronze age. (A surprisingly similar configuration re-emerges in the iron age, where it is documented by the hill forts. But occupation is by then no longer concentrated so exclusively upon the chalklands, so that a detailed comparison is not quite so striking.) It remains now to consider the relevance of the chiefdom model for features other than the distribution and scale of the monuments.

## Specialization in the Neolithic

Several of the salient features of chiefdoms listed earlier are implied in the preceding discussion, and indeed implicit in the monuments themselves. The organization of public labour (14) on such a scale necessitated some measure of redistribution (2) of food, and some central, organized control (9), at least during construction, presumably vested in an individual (1).

In addition, the very great number of early bronze age barrows compared with those of the neolithic is at least suggestive of an increased population density (3), although not an incontrovertible proof. We should expect this on *a priori* grounds anyway, following the introduction of a farming economy at the beginning of the neolithic (cf. Atkinson 1968, 87). This, and the formation of larger territories documents an increase in the total numbers in the society (4). An increase in the size of individual residence groups (5) cannot yet be documented, although the central monuments increase in size.

One very important feature of the society not yet touched on is the existence of flint mines (Piggott 1954, 19 and 36f.) some of which lie inside our area. With their deep shafts they do imply some specialization, although not necessarily full-time. A radiocarbon date from the Easton Down mines puts their use back into the earlier neolithic period, and there are very early dates from Cissbury in Sussex.

Craft specialization (15) is implied here, sustained perhaps by the central organization, for the large scale of the operation makes freelance activity unlikely. Similar specialization outside our area is indicated by the very wide distribution of axes of igneous stones (Piggott 1954, 287f.) originating in axe-factories in western Britain. Pottery was also traded over great distances (Peacock 1969), as no doubt were the flint axes themselves (Sieveking *et al.* 1970).

In the case of the flint mines, which are inside the chiefdom territory, it may be appropriate to speak of regional specialization within it, associated with redistribution (12). The mechanism for the movement or 'trade' of axes across territorial boundaries is less clear. Clark (1965) has suggested an inter-personal gift exchange, and this no doubt did occur. It would be possible also to suggest some additional and more highly organized mechanism for tribal exchange, using also the redistribution network already established within the territories by the chief for other produce.

The most obvious specialization, however, is in the use of some of the monuments themselves. Wainwright has written of the wooden rotundas in several of the larger henges (Wainwright 1970, cf. Piggott 1940) and very plausibly compared them with the council houses of the Creek and Cherokee Indians which are structurally very similar (giving a wooden prototype for the stone rotunds at Stonehenge). It is not stretching the limits of proper ethnographic comparison too far to suggest that their function may likewise have been as 'centres which coordinate social and religious as well as economic activity' (9). Religious specialization is now hardly to be doubted at the stone circles of Stonehenge and Avebury, and Alexander Thom (1967) has shown how the observations of the sun and moon at such sites was part of a calendrical interest seen (perhaps later) over much of Britain, especially in the highland zone. Even if the megalithic unit of measure was related to the pace or span rather than to a fixed universal standard (Hammerton 1971), there can be no doubting the precision and geometrical skill with which they were laid out. Nor do we need to see an analogue computer in the Aubrey Holes to accept the long and careful observation needed to set up the Station Stones and the Heel Stone at Stonehenge. Specialist observers or 'seers', in effect a priesthood (11), were a feature of this society, as in many others which were not yet civilization-states. Obviously periodic ceremonies and rituals took place (10), perhaps associated, as in Polynesia (Sahlins 1958) with periodic distributions of produce (see pp.212–13).

Parallels for the pre-civilization monuments of neolithic Wessex are not hard to find in several parts of the world. The impressive earthworks of the Ohio/Hopewell culture and of the succeeding Temple Mound period offer a number of resemblances. And, as we have seen, the large chiefdoms of their Creek and Cherokee successors constructed council houses closely analogous to the wooden henge rotundas of Wessex.

Neolithic Wessex society indeed displays many of the features seen in chiefdoms elsewhere, and as Kaplan has stressed (1963,

242

403): 'Just as we often underestimate the ability of many stateless societies to engage in large-scale communal production, so we often under-estimate the high degree to which they are able to specialize their labour on a part-time basis'. There is no need to insist on full-time professionals for any of these enterprises, despite the skill displayed. All of them were probably farmers as well, and there is no reason to suppose that anyone lived entirely from full-scale commercial enterprise or the 'profits' of trade in Wessex chiefdom society, which was still, at base, tribal.

## Conclusions

It has been proposed that chiefdoms developed in Wessex during neolithic times. Using this notion, the size and distribution of the observed field monuments become intelligible, and they are seen as the natural counterpart of other features of the society.

The suggestion at once indicates some further approaches which, in a sense, could serve to 'test' the hypothesis. The first is the greater productivity (6) which is theoretically expected. If more settlements can be recognized and excavated, something further will be learned of farming methods. It may also be possible to follow up the intriguing suggestion of ploughing at this early time offered by the excavations at the South Street long barrow.

Secondly the predicted 'more clearly defined territorial boundaries or borders' (7) could be expected to have an influence both on artefact types and distributions. The recovery of more adequate pottery samples, again preferably by settlement excavation, and a systematic analysis, would be relevant here.

It should at once be admitted, however, that two important features of chiefdoms in some other areas are at present lacking. In the first place there is little evidence for ecological diversity (12). It may be that we should not regard the chiefdom territories as limited to the chalklands, although that is where their monuments lie, but imagine them as exploiting the heathlands on the sandy soils to the south and east, and the woodlands on the clays and oolitic soils to the west. If this could be demonstrated it would strengthen the application of the model.

Secondly, we have almost no direct evidence among the artefacts found (cf. Piggott 1954, *passim*) for personal ranking, as indicated by distinctive dress, ornament or possessions (18, 19). Only the beautifully worked jade axes and stone mace-heads, occasionally found, might indicate this. Dr Isobel Smith (personal communication) kindly points out that two of the three jade axes found in any sort of context in south-west Britain were from causeway enclo-sures. Both were surface finds: one inside the enclosure on Hamble-don Hill, the other from High Peak, Devon. One possibility is that such material signs as existed were of perishable materials. We could then argue that the finery of the Wessex early bronze age, seen in the rich burials, does not reflect a new attitude to personal ownership and display, but merely the greater opportunity for its expression offered by the development of metallurgy.

That would not be entirely convincing. It is wiser to admit that there may be different types of chiefdom society than to try to fit them all into the same mould. Otherwise the concept of chiefdom may become 'the ill-defined catchall' that Steward (1955, 53) de-rides in the notion of 'tribal society'. To use the model of chiefdom for societies such as neolithic Wessex will be useful only so long as it establishes meaningful relationships between hitherto unrelated features of them, and suggests a search for new regularities in the material. Once it has done so, like the 'three age system' for the classification of artefacts, it will have to make way for, or be refined to yield, subtler and less inclusive concepts. [1973]

## Acknowledgements

I am grateful to Professor R.J.C. Atkinson and Dr Isobel Smith for helpful criticisms of this paper.

## Bibliography

Ashbee, P. (1970) *The Earthen Long Barrow in Britain*, London, Dent.
Atkinson, R.J.C. (1955) The Dorset Cursus, *Antiquity*, 29, 4–9.
— (1960) *Stonehenge*, London, Penguin.
— (1961) Neolithic engineering, *Antiquity*, 35, 292–9.
— (1967) Silbury Hill, *Antiquity*, 41, 259–62.
— (1968) Old Mortality: some aspects of burial and population in neolithic England, in J.M. Coles and D.D.A. Simpson, eds., *Studies in Ancient Europe, Essays Presented to Stuart Piggott*, Leicester, University Press, 83–94.
Atkinson, R.J.C., C.M. Piggott and N.K. Sanders (1951) *Excavations at Dorchester, Oxon.*, Oxford, Ashmolean Museum.
Burl, H.A.W. (1969) Henges: internal features and regional groups, *Archaeological Journal*, 126, 1–28.
Case, H. (1962) Long barrows, chronology and causewayed camps, *Antiquity*, 36, 212–6.
Clark, J.G.D. (1965) Traffic in stone axe and adze blades, *Economic History Review*, 18, 1–28.
Fleming, A. (1971) Territorial patterns in bronze age Wessex, *Proceedings of the Prehistoric Society*, 37, 138–66.
Fowler, P.J. and J.G. Evans (1967) Plough-marks, lynchets and

early fields, *Antiquity*, 41, 289–301.
Fried, M. H. (1957) The classification of corporate unilineal descent groups, *Journal of the Royal Anthropological Institute*, 87, 1–29.
Grinsell, L. V. (1958) *The Archaeology of Wessex*, London, Methuen.
Hammerton, M. (1971) The megalithic fathom: a suggestion, *Antiquity*, 45, 302.
Heizer, R. F. (1966) Ancient heavy transport, methods and achievements, *Science*, 153, 821–30.
Heizer, R. F. and P. Drucker (1968) The La Venta fluted pyramid, *Antiquity*, 42, 52–6.
Kaplan, D. (1963) Men, monuments and political systems, *Southwestern Journal of Anthropology*, 19, 397–410.
Leach, E. R. (1951) Hydraulic society in Ceylon, *Past and Present*, 15, 2–26.
Peacock, D. P. S. (1969) Neolithic pottery production in Cornwall, *Antiquity*, 43, 145–9.
Piggott, S. (1938) The early bronze age in Wessex, *Proceedings of the Prehistoric Society*, 4, 52–106.
— (1940) Timber circles, a re-examination, *Archaeological Journal*, 106, 193–222.
— (1954) *The Neolithic Cultures of the British Isles*, Cambridge, University Press.
Renfrew, C. (1970) The tree-ring calibration of radiocarbon: an archaeological evaluation, *Proceedings of the Prehistoric Society*, 36, 280–311.
— (1972) *The Emergence of Civilization, the Cyclades and the Aegean in the Third Millennium B. C.*, London, Methuen.
Sahlins, M. D. (1958) *Social Stratification in Polynesia*, Seattle, University of Washington.
— (1968) *Tribesmen*, Englewood Cliffs, Prentice-Hall.
Service, E. R. (1962) *Primitive Social Organization*, New York, Random House.
Sieveking, G. de G., P. T. Craddock, M. J. Hughes, P. Bush and J. Ferguson (1970) Characterization of prehistoric flint mine products, *Nature*, 228, 251–4.
Smith, I. F. (1965) *Windmill Hill and Avebury, Excavations by Alexander Keiller 1925–1939*, Oxford, Clarendon.
— (1966) Windmill Hill and its implications, *Palaeohistoria*, 12, 469–82.
— (1971) Causewayed enclosures, in D. D. A. Simpson, ed., *Economy and Settlement in Neolithic and Early Bronze Age Britain and Europe*, Leicester, University Press.
Soudský, B. (1968) Criteria to distinguish cultural phases. Paper presented to the Research Seminar on Archaeology and Related Subjects. London, October 1968.
Steward, J. H. (1955) *Theory of Cultural Change*, Urbana, University of Illinois.
Thom, A. (1967) *Megalithic Sites in Britain*, Oxford, Clarendon.
Wainwright, G. J. (1969) A review of henge monuments in the light of recent research, *Proceedings of the Prehistoric Society*, 35, 112–33.
— (1970) Woodhenges, *Scientific American*, 223, 30–7.

# IV

## SYSTEMS THINKING: THE EXPLANATION OF CONTINUOUS CHANGE

*

The task of analysing change, and if possible of explaining it, has always presented formidable problems to the historian. Most explanations seek to identify a principal causal factor, whose influence can be shown, ultimately, as of determining significance. The nature of the explanation offered thus depends upon the kind of causal agency which the analyst ultimately chooses to recognise as important. One school of workers will see environmental factors as of overwhelming importance, and lay stress on changes in climate. Another may see population as a crucial variable. A third will emphasise developing technology.

A multivariate procedure, where the interactions of a number of factors taken in conjunction are considered, can overcome the partiality of the 'significant factor' analysis, but it risks taking on an unmanageable complexity. The systems approach reduces to some kind of comprehensible order the multiple causal influences of interacting variables.

As is argued in chapter 12, the outlook advocated here does not amount to a closely integrated body of theoretical propositions which could reasonably be designated 'systems theory'. No such store of theoretical wisdom exists. Rather than 'systems theory', the approach presented here may properly be termed *systems thinking*. It is a method of analysis: a way of analysing a complex of interactions, in such a manner that its behaviour, which is often counter to one's expectations, and in that sense 'counterintuitive' (Forrester 1973), may be better understood. There is nothing particularly difficult about the approach – indeed one of the best introductions to it is found in C. H. Waddington's delightfully accessible *Tools for Thought* (Waddington 1977). His title is an apposite one. At the same time, however, the approach is sufficiently explicit that it can form a basis for quantitative formulations, such as that found in chapter 11.

Systems thinking, by introducing the notion of *trajectory*, the path through time of the society or other entity whose change is under study, takes a considerable step towards a clear view, where the course of change may be conceived graphically. If we can describe the society at any given time by a large series of observations or measurements, then the observables to be measured are the *parameters* of the system. The changing values of those system variables effectively describe for us the successive *system states* through time. The working of the system can generally be broken down by the analyst into a number of *subsystems*. In each case a change in the *input* to a subsystem will produce a change in *output*. In most complex systems a change in the output results in a subsequent change in the input and there is *feedback*. If the system is self-regulating, it will act to oppose change: in such a case there is *negative feedback*. If the negative feedback is effective the system may achieve a kind of stability or equilibrium in face of small external changes, termed *homeostasis*. These various ideas, and a few more like them, offer a framework of analysis by which the very complex interactions in any living system can be broken down into a much more manageable series of individual actions and interactions, each of which we can consider in turn. We can do so without losing sight of the overall structure, within which each of these various interactions plays a significant but not necessarily determining role.

To my mind some analysis of this kind is absolutely indispensable if we are to focus our attention upon the various components or subsystems in turn. As discussed in chapter 9, the subsystems which one wishes to define for most societies will probably approximate more or less closely to the following:

1) subsistence
2) technological
3) social
4) cognitive/projective
5) external exchange
6) population (although this may be regarded not as a subsystem but as a parameter of scale).

It is instructive to compare this subdivision with the general analysis of society offered by Karl Marx, and most concisely set out in the Preface to *A Contribution to the Critique of Political Economy* (Marx 1859). This was a pioneering attempt to break down the complex whole into a number of intelligible components. It can be summarised in the following diagram, taken from Friedman (1974, 445):

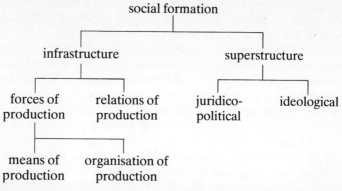

Here the Marxist 'relations of production' correspond approximately with the social subsystem of the systems approach. The 'forces of production' correspond approximately to the subsistence and technological subsystems. The 'superstructure' corresponds approximately to the cognitive subsystem. It should be noted that the Marxist analysis does not put much weight upon external exchange, nor is population included as a parameter of scale as in the systemic approach set out in chapter 9.

When compared in this rather bald way, the two approaches have many similarities, although it has generally been held that Marx assigned a determining role to the economy – to the infrastructure. As Engels (1894) put it:

> What we understand by the economic relations, which we regard as the determining basis of the history of society, is the manner and method by which men in a given society produce their means of subsistence, and exchange the products among themselves (in so far as division of labour exists) . . . It is not that the economic situation is cause, solely active, while everything else is only passive effect. There is, rather, interaction on the basis of economic necessity, which *ultimately* always asserts itself. No. Men make their history themselves, only they do so in a given environment which conditions it, and on the basis of actual relations already existing, among which the economic relations, however much they may be influenced by the other – the political and ideological relations, are still ultimately the decisive ones, forming the keynote which runs through them and alone leads to understanding.

It seems clear from this and other passages that Marx and Engels were reaching out towards a crucial concept which was not in fact to be formulated clearly for another half century: the notion of *feedback*. Marx in several places, and Engels in the passage quoted, were at pains to stress the complexity of the interactions. Indeed it is fair to say that in some respects they anticipated a systems model. Certainly the whole rather fruitless argument among subsequent Marxists as to whether the 'infrastructure' does indeed hold the dominant role over the 'superstructure' is greatly clarified by a systems analysis in which the simultaneous interactions of the various subsystems can be viewed together. There is no need to label any one of them as 'dominant'. Some Marxist writers have indeed adopted the language of systems thinking to a large extent (Friedman 1974), speaking of the 'trajectory' of the system, and drawing diagrams of change which derive from the perspective of the systems analyst. Despite these borrowings they have hitherto tended to denigrate the systems approach as 'vulgar materialism'.

The central weakness of the Marxist analysis is not so much the description of the interacting components of society at a given point in time, but the failure to achieve a satisfying general description of their dynamic interactions. In saying this it is not my intention to belittle the contribution of Marx, for his analysis in terms of 'contradictions' was well ahead of his time and foreshadows in some ways the later systemic approach. But the concept has the overwhelming weakness that Marxist analysts have no criteria to offer by which these supposed 'contradictions' may be recognised other than by their *consequences*. In other words, in order to explain the state of the system at time *t*, we need not only to analyse the system at earlier points in its trajectory, but to have a knowledge of some future states of the system also. Such a framework of analysis dooms the Marxist historian to an unbreakable dependence upon hindsight. (The same difficulty, in effect, faces evolutionary theorists who place overmuch weight during their analysis upon the concept of 'adaptation'. For they rarely suggest how, at a given time, an organism may be judged to be well-adapted or ill-adapted to its specific environment, other than by evaluating whether it did or did not subsequently survive. The explanation offered for the present state of the system thus depends upon an evaluation of future states of the system.)

The systems approach, despite the rather rudimentary state of the art, certainly escapes from these very damaging limitations inherent in the key Marxist concept of 'contradictions' which by making the present explanation dependent upon future states of the system, invites all the criticisms of teleological explanation which the advocates of historical inevitability have justly had directed at them.

It is important to stress, also, that despite the misapprehensions of some of its critics (and indeed some of its advocates also), the systems approach does not imply that the ultimate source of change necessarily lies outside the system. The system is not just a passive punch-bag, responding homeostatically to the buffets of environmental misfortune. This mistake has been made by such enthusiasts as Hill (1977) and Saxe (1977), who see the development in cultural systems as very much a pattern of environmental challenge and systemic response (to use in part the language favoured by Arnold Toynbee). But systemic change can involve the *internal* growth of complexity. A number of authors, notably Johnson (1982), have shown how simple increase in size can favour the development of such complex features as hierarchical structure, although simply to demonstrate which structures would promote an increase in efficiency and of visibility does not in itself explain how they arose.

That point, of course, approaches another criticism, directed at systems thinking, of what is often termed a 'functionalist' viewpoint, that is to say that the presence of various aspects of the archaeological record is explained by stating the function of each in the system as a whole (Giddens 1981, 16; Salmon 1982, 84 and 90). Others dismiss it as based upon an organic analogy, and hence subject to the limitations arising when any analogy is used beyond its proper scope of application.

Both these criticisms, however, seem to me somewhat misguided. It is, of course, perfectly true that all living beings and all communities of animals or plants, can usefully be looked at in systems terms. Notions such as homeostasis and morphogenesis are very relevant to their understanding. It is true also that organic analogies can be very misleading: to talk, for instance of the birth and death of civilisations or institutions is to imply that they behave in the same way as living things, with a definite and predictable life cycle. This is not necessarily true, and the point at which Greek civilisation, for instance, 'passed away' is purely a matter of definition. While in political terms it was certainly eclipsed by the expanding Roman empire, in other ways it did not terminate and it is perfectly possible to see the modern Western world as part of a coherent process of development which can be traced back to that time. To speak of the birth and death of cultures, then, is to use a rather arbitrary model. Indeed the use of this unsatisfactory analogy as an integral part of the structure of his work is, I believe, the main reason for the failure of Arnold Toynbee's *A Study of History* (Toynbee 1946) to make any very significant contribution to his chosen subject. But while the organic analogy – like any analogy – can be misleading, it is important to stress that a systems model is not really an analogy at all. That is to say it does not imply an equivalence or resemblance with any specific existing entity. Instead it sets out to postulate a series of explicit relationships. These may or may not be suitable for the explanation of the chosen case, but there is nothing analogical about them. If systems defined in this way show properties which can be seen also in living systems, this must be because the mechanisms suggested actually produce the behaviour seen in those systems. To the extent that there seems to be an analogy, the systems model is to be respected for generating the appropriate behaviour, or to be rejected if its behaviour does not in fact resemble that of the human group or whatever which one is seeking to understand.

I believe that Salmon is in error when she implies that systems explanations are inherently functionalist. They simply define processes and relationships which can be shown to generate a range of behaviour. The present state of the system can in this way be shown to be the natural outcome of past states of the system and of the various forces acting upon it. Certainly many systems act homeostatically: that is to say that they act in such a way as to keep various variables of the system within certain limits. But the systems analysis often has the object of investigating the various processes which work together with this end result. The aim is often to show how such apparently goal-seeking or equilibrium-maintaining behaviour is the predictable product of definable processes which in themselves are neither goal-seeking nor equilibrium-maintaining. A systems approach, far from being inherently 'functionalist', in this sense actually removes the obligation to think in terms of functions or goals. Instead the analysis seeks to show, by making explicit the workings of the system, how such properties are a natural and predictable result of its constituent relationships and processes.

The systems approach was first introduced to archaeology, in a very general way, by Lewis Binford (1965). It was, however, David Clarke who first employed the wider range of vocabulary then familiar from the field of cybernetics (Clarke 1968, 101), and who offered a concise outline of the analysis of systemic change which remains in many ways the best introduction. Kent Flannery (1968) took a specific instance, the origins of agriculture in Mesoamerica, and showed how the perspective could clarify the interactions of some of the processes at work. In 1972 in my book *The Emergence of Civilisation* I set out to apply the approach for the first time to the origins of complex society, taking a specific case – the bronze age Aegean – and giving a detailed consideration of the archaeological evidence for each subsystem. The introductory and concluding chapters of that analysis (with several omissions) are given below. The book's greater contribution, however, was to take each of the subsystems in turn, and to discuss the available data in some detail from the perspective of each. This systemic treatment of an individual complex society has not yet been followed up in a comprehensive way by detailed application to another comparable instance.

The two chapters which follow thus formed part of a sustained attempt to describe the development of one particular complex society, that of the early Aegean, in terms of processes which were both intelligible and locally operating. As I have emphasised throughout this book, and as others have recently stressed (e.g. Binford 1983, 392), it is appropriate to look at each attempt at archaeological explanation in terms of the context of its time. When these chapters were written, it was widely assumed that complex society in the Aegean could satisfactorily be explained simply by means of detailing its relationships with its contemporaries and predecessors in Western Asia. One main aim of the exercise was thus to show that a coherent, alternative explanation, without unduly emphasising that aspect, was indeed possible. At the time, to do that seemed an important task, and I believe that it was a necessary enterprise. That having been accomplished, a fresh attempt today would set more emphasis upon social and political factors, especially in Crete. It might well emphasise the crucial nature of the transition there to the first palaces in what was probably a rather short space of time. And it would need to acknowledge what now seems to have been the initiatory role of north-west Anatolia in metallurgical developments in the Aegean towards the end of the third millennium BC. There is, of course, a very long way to go before one could feel that the explanation would be a very satisfying one for Aegean civilisation. But part of the interest, I hope, of these papers is that they offer an exemplification of what is in some respects a general model for the development of complex society. What in some ways it lacks is *specificity*: a convincing identification of precisely those factors which were of dominant importance in the Aegean case. On the other hand it does make reference to the very wide range of factors which will to some extent be relevant to every case of the early development of complex society. And it does go on to open the way to more explicit, and quantitative, modelling procedures.

The two alternative scenarios offered in 'The Multiplier Effect in Action' (chapter 10) have sometimes been seen, perhaps by readers wearied by the preceding 470 pages, as once again offering two favoured explanations where the crucial variables are once again singled out. But the real point of the chapter is to show how the different elements can be brought together and expressed simultaneously in the form of a matrix.

At that time I did not have the familiarity with the world of computing to produce an algorithm by which the proposed matrix could be operationalised. My collaboration with the mathematician Kenneth Cooke, and the helpful advice of Robert Rosen, allowed us to experiment with the operation of such a matrix by means of a computer simulation (chapter 11).

It must at once be admitted that the attempt at simulation set out in chapter 11 is so simple, and in that sense so crude, that it could never satisfactorily model the complexities of any specific case. It is not illuminating for the Aegean as such because it has not had built into it to a sufficient degree the various particularities of that specific example. But by its simplicity it does bring out some of the features – and the difficulties – inherent in any modelling exercise of this kind.

At a certain level this experiment of computer simulation was nonetheless extremely rewarding: it was fascinating to see on the display screen the successive steps plotted out for the state variables relevant to each of the subsystems as the system simulation proceeded through time. This is, of course, the general approach employed by the System Dynamics modelling group at MIT inspired by the work of Forrester (1969). In both cases the system proceeds through successive states, the values at one time determining those at the next time point. Similar models underlie most of the economic forecasting procedures currently employed. Gerardin (1979) for example, has used his experience of this kind of modelling to discuss the problems of simulating the trajectories of past societies. Zubrow has gone so far as to take one of the Forrester urban models and apply it directly to ancient Rome (Zubrow 1981). But although the simulation approach can very effectively model the developments within the system in response both to external change and to internal growth, and in doing so produce some interesting and sometimes counter-intuitive behaviour, this does not allow for the internal re-structurings and the various innovations of a social as well as a technical nature, which lie at the root of long-term change in any society.

The problem of modelling long-term change is discussed in 'The simulator as demiurge' (chapter 12), where I speculate about the much more ambitious models which would be necessary before such innovative behaviour could be incorporated into the simulation. This is, however, a problem which is very widely felt in the wider field of simulation and computer studies at present. Artists are devising programmes which allow drawings to be produced by the computer in what are, in effect, simulations (Cohen 1983), and the question of creativity can be seriously discussed in this context (Boden 1983). There is a general analogy here between creativity in this sense (and artificial intelligence also) and the innovative development of new forms, whether in biological evolution or in social development, which one might hope one day to simulate.

Nor is it inevitable that the systems approach be an altogether impersonal one. Admittedly the existing analyses in the field of archaeology have tended to operate at the scale of the society as a whole, and so to lose sight of the individual actor. But it would be perfectly possible to construct models in which the reactions of individuals and of groups of individuals were taken into account at each point. Indeed Doran (1982) has already taken some first steps in that direction. But at the same time it is important not to overlook the overall effects of a great complexity of interactions, which often have outcomes altogether unexpected to the actors, and indeed can be 'counterintuitive.'

The systems approach is still relatively new to archaeology. As I have tried to show, it now offers us the opportunity of clarifying aspects of our thought, without any necessary consideration of quantification. Its great promise for the future, however, is that systems thinking is indeed the logical first step towards computerised modelling, for only the computer has the vast capacity necessary to model the numerous complexities of human society. The instrument is there. It is up to us as archaeologists to develop theories and models which escape some of the naivetés and imperfections of the existing attempts at simulation, and to use the computer informatively. The hardware offers the opportunities, but it cannot provide the answers. Only the archaeologist can do that.

### Bibliography

Binford, L. R. (1965) Archaeological systematics and the study of culture process, *American Antiquity*, 31, 203–210.

— (1983) *Working at Archaeology*, New York, Academic Press.

Boden, M. A. (1983) Creativity and computers, in the exhibition catalogue *Harold Cohen*, London, Tate Gallery, 12–18.

Clarke, D. L. (1968) *Analytical Archaeology*, London, Methuen.

Cohen, H. (1983) Introduction, to the exhibition catalogue *Harold Cohen*, London, Tate Gallery, 7–11.

Doran, J. (1982) A computational model of sociocultural systems and their dynamics, in C. Renfrew, M. J. Rowlands and B. A. Segraves, eds., *Theory and Explanation in Archaeology: the Southampton Conference*, New York, Academic Press, 375–88.

Engels, F. (1894) Letter to W. Borgius, in *Karl Marx and Frederick Engels, Selected Works*, London, Lawrence and Wishart (1968), 693.

Flannery, K. V. (1968) Archaeological systems theory and early Mesoamerica, in B. J. Meggers, ed., *Anthropological Archaeology in the Americas*, Washington D. C., Anthropological Society of Washington, 67–87.

Forrester, J. W. (1969) *Urban Dynamics*, Cambridge, Mass., MIT Press.

— (1973) Understanding the counterintuitive behaviour of social systems, in D. L. and D. H. Meadows, eds., *Towards Global Equilibrium: Collected Papers*, Cambridge, Mass., Wright-Allen.

Friedman, J. (1974) Marxism, structuralism and vulgar materialism, *Man*, 9, 444–69.

Gerardin, L. A. (1979) A structural model of industrialised societies, in C. Renfrew and K. L. Cooke, eds., *Transformations: Mathematical Approaches to Culture Change*, New York, Academic Press, 295–326.

Giddens, A. (1981) *A Contemporary Critique of Historical Materialism*, London, Macmillan.

Hill, J. N. (1977) Systems theory and the explanation of change, in J. N. Hill, ed., *Explanation of Prehistoric Change*, Albuquerque, University of New Mexico Press, 59–104.

Johnson, G. A. (1982) Organisational structure and scalar stress, in C. Renfrew, M. J. Rowlands and B. A. Segraves, eds., *Theory and Explanation in Archaeology: the Southampton Conference*, New York, Academic Press, 389–421.

Marx, K. (1859) Preface to *A Contribution to the Critique of Political Economy*, reprinted in *Karl Marx and Frederick Engels, Selected Works*, London, Lawrence and Wishart (1968), 180–4.

Renfrew, C. (1972) *The Emergence of Civilisation*, London, Methuen.

Salmon, M. H. (1982) *Philosophy and Archaeology*, New York, Academic Press.

Saxe, A. A. (1977) On the origin of evolutionary processes: state formation in the Sandwich Islands, in J. N. Hill, ed., *Explanation of Prehistoric Change*, Albuquerque, University of New Mexico Press, 105–52.

Toynbee, A. J. (1946) *A Study of History*, Oxford, University Press.

Waddington, C. H. (1977) *Tools for Thought*, Frogmore, Paladin.

Zubrow, E. B. W. (1981) *Simulations in Archaeology*, Albuquerque, University of New Mexico Press, 143–88.

257

# 9

## CULTURE SYSTEMS AND
## THE MULTIPLIER EFFECT

*

IT IS VAIN to hope for the discovery of the first domestic corn cob, the first pottery vessel, the first hieroglyphic, or the first site where some other major breakthrough occurred. Such deviations from the pre-existing pattern almost certainly took place in such a minor accidental way that these traces are not recoverable. More worthwhile would be an investigation of the mutual causal processes that amplify these tiny deviations into major changes in prehistoric culture.

Kent Flannery (1968, 85)

AN EFFORT IS made here, however, to treat changes in the rate of growth as determined by the workings of the fundamental variables in the system, rather than as the consequence of exogenous forces.

Walt W. Rostow (1953, 17)

THE SECRET OF the growth of the city is in the process of deviation-amplifying mutual positive feedback networks rather than in the initial condition or in the initial kick. This process, rather than the initial condition, has generated the complexly structured city. It is in this sense that the deviation-amplifying mutual causal process is called 'morphogenesis'.

Magoroh Maruyama (1963, 166)

### Cultures as Systems

Operationally defined, a culture is a constantly recurring assemblage of artefacts. To represent the culture as a system or as part of a system, it is useful to consider not only the preserved artefacts, but the members of the society that produced them, the natural environment they inhabited and the other artefacts (including the non-material ones such as language and projective systems) which they made or used. Obviously we cannot have detailed knowledge of all these for prehistoric societies, but is proposed that we assume

258

they existed. The artefacts available today, which we will take to be of known provenance and approximately known date, are the material remnant of this system.

The components of the system are not only the members of the society but the artefacts which they have made or which they used (including the non-material ones) and all objects in nature with which they come into contact. 'Anything that consists of parts connected together will be called a system' (Beer 1959, 8). What connects the components of this particular (and very large) system are the actions between these three classes of individual: man, artefact, natural object. As Katz and Kahn (1966, 94) have written:

> The problem of structure, or the relatedness of parts, can be observed directly in some physical arrangement of things where the larger unit is physically bounded and its sub-parts are also bounded within the larger structures. But how do we deal with social structures where physical boundaries in this sense do not exist? . . . The structure is to be found in an interrelated set of events. It is events rather than things which are structured, so that social structure is a dynamic rather than a static concept.

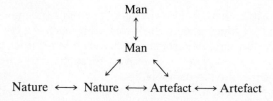

*Figure* 1. Six kinds of interaction, five of them within the culture system, and one (Nature–Nature) outside it.

The dichotomy here established between man and nature does not support in any sense the view that man is not just an integral part of the natural world, inextricably bound with it. Indeed the whole purpose of utilising the systems approach is to emphasise man–environment interrelations, while at the same time admitting that many fundamental changes in man's environment are produced by man himself. They emerge, that is to say, from technological and social changes rather than simply from ecological ones.

Artefact–artefact interactions can come about without the direct presence of man: when the new wine cracks the old bottle, or when the domesticated cow eats the domesticated wheat. Nature–nature relationships (referring to natural phenomena) are relevant too:

259

the cow needs grass, the fisherman fish and both the grass and the fish may be beyond the field of man and his artefacts. The overall system which we have to consider, therefore, is larger than man's culture, in that it includes both his environment and man himself.

It is important to realise that the choice of elements which constitute the system is ours. We are free to define the interacting elements which constitute the system. When there are other elements not defined as part of a system, which interact with it, then the system can be said to have input and output: it is an open system.

There are two important points to consider: the boundaries of the system, and the nature of the connections within the system. First, it should be noted, a system can be simplified and portrayed in a new form when its states are compounded suitably:

> Were the engineer to treat bridge-building by consideration of every atom, he would find the task impossible by its very size. He therefore ignores the fact that his girders and blocks are really composite, made of atoms, and treats them as his units. . . . It will be seen, therefore, that the method of studying very large systems by studying only carefully selected aspects of them is simply what is always done in practice. (Ashby 1956, 107)

It would be possible, therefore, to consider the atomic and molecular structure of the objects and artefacts, regarding each as a system in itself. Equally the humans participating can each be regarded as a system. For the present purpose, however, these natural objects, artefacts and people are our components.

Just as it is convenient to ignore individual atoms and generalise on a higher level, so it can be convenient to lump together these components, and speak of larger units. When these larger units themselves are structured we may designate them as subsystems.

In order to establish the nature of the boundary of the culture, the man–environment system of the given culture can be described in terms of the individual settlement units as distributed in space. No settlement in the Old World is completely isolated from any other: we can imagine the situation, say 5,000 years ago, when each village had at least some contact with its immediate neighbours, they with their neighbours, and so on, creating a great lattice across the whole of Europe and indeed Asia, and only stopping perhaps at the Pacific and Atlantic Oceans. 'No man is an island unto himself, each is a peninsula, a part of the Main.'

In deciding on the spatial boundaries of our system we are thus making a somewhat arbitrary decision – as we are entitled to do. As archaeologists we follow the record of the artefacts. The archaeologist considers the distribution of artefact types, and sets the boundaries of the archaeological culture according to convenient criteria. We follow these, and indeed assume that the uniformity within the culture area is due to the contacts and inter-connections described. The greater difference with the outside region is generally assumed to be due to diminished contacts and interrelations.

For different purposes we shall draw the boundaries differently: at one moment for example we may wish to consider the Minoan civilisation, perhaps in the seventeeth century BC, and will draw the boundaries accordingly, at the next we may refer to the Minoan-Mycenaean civilisation (say, of the fourteenth century BC). Criteria of different degrees of uniformity will lead to the definition of larger or smaller units.

We should note too that with the passage of time the elements of the system are changed: people die and are born, artefacts made and discarded. As von Bertalanffy says of organic systems (1950, 155):

It is the basic characteristic of every organic system that it maintains itself in a state of perpetual change of its components. This we find at all levels of biological organisation. In the cell there is a perpetual destruction of its building materials through which it endures as a whole. . . . In the multicellular organism, cells are dying and are replaced by new ones, but it maintains itself as a whole. In the biocoenosis and the species, individuals die and others are born. Thus, every organic system appears stationary if considered from a certain point of view. But what seems to be a persistent entity on a certain level is maintained, in fact, by a perpetual change, building up and breaking down of systems of the next lower order: of chemical compounds in the cell, of cells in the multicellular organism, of individuals in ecological systems.

No one is saying here, of course, that a cultural system can be equated with an organic system: but it does share certain properties with them, and with Heraclitus's river: 'A man never bathes in the same river twice.'

Our culture system is also of great complexity because of the nature of its interconnections. Already in talking, say, of trading connections alone, it can be broken down into subsystems. Each single settlement unit can itself be regarded as a subsidiary trading subsystem, and they articulate together to form the overall trading subsystem. The division into subsidiary subsystems here is a spatial one, and can be represented in the dimensions of space.

But the elements of our system are not only linked by connections between localities, such as those of trade. The man–artefact–natural-object connections provide food and shelter for men, the man–artefact connections involve the manufacture and use of all manner of things, the man–man connections involve kin relationships, and other social relationships and conventions. This is the consequence of the multi-dimensionality of man's environment.

We can regard the people in society as nodes in a lattice connected in numerous different ways, each way corresponding to one of the various dimensions of the environment.

In defining subsystems in the culture corresponding to each of these types of connections (and to each of these dimensions) we are not dividing the society spatially but simply following different kinds of networks:

> It must be noted that in a real system the 'diagram of internal connections' is not unique. The radio set, for instance, has one diagram of connections if considered electrically, and another if considered mechanically. An insulator, in fact, is just such a component as will give firm mechanical connection while giving no electrical connection. Which pattern of connections will be found depends on which set of inputs and outputs is used. (Ashby 1956, 92)

In the same way we may picture the incredible complexity of a cultural system, acting in several dimensions and with several different kinds of connections between its components which are itself of several different kinds. In the culture system we are free to define the subsystems. As Wolf has written (1967, 449):

> We may regard civilisations as social sets, in which the elements are linked together in a large variety of ways and with different degrees of cohesion. Methodologically this means that we do not have to account for all the elements – only for those which we hold to be significant. When considering civilisation the possible choice is almost infinite.

For our purposes the following subsytems may be distinguished:
*The subsistence subsystem.* The interactions that define this system are actions relating to the distribution of food resources. Man and the food resources and the food units themselves are components of the subsystem which are interrelated by these specifically subsistence-oriented activities.
*The technological subsystem.* This subsystem is defined by the activities of man which result in the production of material artefacts.

The components are the men, the material resources, and the finished artefacts.

*The social subsystem.* This is a system of behaviour patterns, where the defining activities are those which take place between men. It is not possible to distinguish clearly all the activities of the subsistence and technological subsystems from those of the social subsystem, but the essential point in the latter is that we are no longer looking at activities under their aspect of food production, or of craft production, but looking at them as patterned inter-personal behaviour. It would be possible here to distinguish an economic subsystem from the social subsystem, but it is probably simpler in a non-market society to look at the accumulation of wealth as a social phenomenon at least as much as it is an economic one.

*The projective or symbolic subsystem.* Here, we are speaking of all those activities, notably religion, art, language and science, by which man expresses his knowledge, feelings, or beliefs about his relationship with the world. The social systems may involve activities that are expressive of relationships in this way, that are symbolic of relationships between human beings. Making obeisance before the throne of the ruler would be one of these. But we are defining such expression between men as belonging within the sphere of the social subsystem. The projective systems, in other words, are those in which man gives formal expression to his understanding of and reactions to the world. His thoughts and feelings are expressed, that is to say projected, and given symbolic form, whether in language or in worship, in the production of written records or of works of art, including music, dance and other abstract forms amongst those of more explicit meaning.

*The trade and communication subsystem.* This is defined by all those activities by which information or material goods are transferred between human settlements or over considerable distances. The activities here are all those which involve travel, for any of the components of the system whether men or artefacts.

The boundaries between these systems are extremely difficult to define, since a given human action can exist in several dimensions at once. The construction of a temple, for instance, an action of considerable complexity, lies in the first place, in its conception, in the field of the projective systems. It will also involve economic activities. The builders will have to be fed, which belongs in the field of subsistence, and, of course, they will be organised in a manner governed by the social subsystem. This is inevitable since many human actions have a meaning at several levels, with undertones and overtones. And, as we shall see it is the complex interconnectedness of the subsystems which gives human culture its unique potential for growth.

These are the subsystems whose functioning must be isolated if we are to reach an understanding of growth and change in the culture. The growth and development of metallurgy is also given special consideration in the next chapter since it was obviously of central importance in the third millennium Aegean, although in more general terms metallurgy is simply one aspect of craft technology. Population is a basic parameter of society rather than one of its subsystems. Population increase in most early civilisations, was one of the most significant and relevant developments.

### Feedback

In a culture which is not changing, the various subsystems are in a state of equilibrium (or, in more specialised jargon, of quasi-stationary equilibrium). There is continuous activity: food is grown and eaten, buildings collapse and are repaired, imports and exports are produced and consumed, social relationships are observed, religious services are held. This year, next year, the 'same' things happen: people are born, married, die but nothing is new. This is the working of habit and convention. Hawkes (1954, 155) has emphasised this consistency in the norms of human behaviour:

> The human activity which (archaeology) can apprehend conforms to a series of norms, which can be aggregated under the name of culture. . . . The notion of norms in man's activity . . . is an anthropological generalisation based on the extensive degree of conservatism shown by primitive man in his technological traditions. . . . Without this the whole subject would crumple up.

We are all creatures of habit, otherwise we could not face the alarming multiplicity of 'new' problems which would arise. As Samuel Beckett has said, 'L'habitude est une grande sourdine.'

But, of course, the system is not so stable as this: fluctuations in the natural environment alter the equilibrium. Fishing is poor and there are less fish to eat: there are more births than usual and more mouths to feed: it is a wet summer and the roofs leak: an eclipse of the sun is seen as a dread portent. And then there may be 'input' from right outside the system: military attack from another culture, for instance. Or innovations within it: a new tool is invented, or there is dissatisfaction with the conduct of the chief. The remarkable thing is that in every case each subsystem acts homeostatically.

264

to counteract the disturbance. In the subsistence system the level of food is stabilised either by greater investment in fishing, or by switching to other foods. In the utility subsystem roofs are repaired. In the religious system appropriate steps are taken to counteract the alarming disturbance. Military attack is opposed, the new tool replaces the old, the chief takes measures to enhance his authority. Each of the subsystems of the culture is acting like a stabilised or regulated system, in the cybernetic sense. Their variables (food level in the subsistence system, population in the demographic situation, integrity in the defence system, social behaviour in the social system, belief behaviour in the religious system) are kept within assigned limits, as is necessary for survival (Ashby 1956, 197). The behaviour of the culture (and doubtless the artefacts which the archaeologists will recover from it) is essentially unchanged. Various interesting consequences flow from this, for example the need for variety in the culture to oppose undesirable variety outside it (Ashby 1956, 206f.).

Indeed each subsystem can be so regarded as self-regulating. And the different dimensions of life can be considered independently. But at the same time we must remember that in the culture system the component subsystems do not vary independently, they are coupled. This is, of course, simply a statement of anthropological functionalism, that different aspects of a culture are all interrelated. It does not mean, however, that changes in one subsystem *must* necessarily produce changes in all the others.

The equilibrium in a subsystem of the culture is achieved by automatic regulation which acts, like Le Châtelier's principle: 'If a system is in stable equilibrium and one of the conditions is changed, the equilibrium shifts in such a way as to restore the original conditions.' It operates by means of negative feedback: the ability to meet an effect by operating in such a way as to oppose it and thus minimise change. If the food resources of the society suffer a setback (a poor harvest for instance), the society acts in such a way as to restore the level of food supply, for example by trade, and thus to minimise the disturbance. The system acts to counter the disturbing force, so that the feedback is negative.

All this, then, gives us some understanding of the essential coherence and conservatism of all cultures: the behaviour patterns in one generation are communicated to the next generation: the society's 'adjustment' or 'adaptation' to its natural environment is maintained: difficulties and hardships are overcome. Minor changes may be brought about through ineffectiveness in this communi-

265

cation: the pottery decoration of a daughter may differ a little from that of her mother. But this is merely a 'random drift' which does not in itself have a significant effect on the life of the society. Only if the outside disturbance is so great that the homeostatic controls cannot overcome it, is the life pattern disrupted. 'When a system's negative feedback discontinues, its steady state vanishes, and at the same time its boundary disappears, and the system terminates' (Miller, quoted Katz and Kahn 1966, 96).

Thus, a military attack will be resisted by the society. But if it cannot be overcome, it may well produce a disturbance beyond the limits of tolerance of the system: the system breaks down. Or natural environmental forces may produce a serious disturbance: the increasing salinity of the soil of Mesopotamia was a disturbance which the inhabitants of the Sumerian heartland strove to overcome (Jacobsen and Adams 1958). A similar theory, involving progressive flooding and silting, has been used to account for the decline of the Indus civilisation (Raikes 1965). And the eruption of the volcanic island of Thera certainly brought a total end to the human system occupying that island just as that of Vesuvius to Pompeii. It has even been suggested that the disturbance produced by this eruption was so strong as to exceed the homeostatic controls of the entire Minoan system in Crete and to bring about its disintegration.

In all this the culture system is acting negatively, passively almost, simply acting to regulate outside events. While the negative feedback picture is effective, then, in illuminating the stability and conservatism of the society, it does not explain how society will ever change, except through an outside challenge. It is limited to the Toynbee concept of cultural response to natural environmental challenge.

The systems approach does offer also a convenient model for growth, for change occurring *within* a society. Negative feedback itself is never a sufficient explanation for cultural development, for how culture came into being, but merely for how an existing order was modified through external change. Change, progressive change, can however be considered in terms of deviation *amplifying* mutual causal systems.

Such systems are ubiquitous: accumulations of capital in industry, the evolution of living organisms, the rise of culture of various types, the inter-personal processes which produce mental illness, international conflicts, and the processes which are loosely termed 'vicious circles' and 'compound interest', in short of all processes of mutual causal relationship that amplify an insignificant or accidental kick, build up deviation and diverge from an initial condition. (Maruyama 1963, 164)

Kent Flannery (1968, 80) has described such a *positive feedback* system which operated in the system of wild grain procurement in early Mesoamerica and resulted both in the selection for genotypes of the domesticated maize and in the development of food production. As he well says:

> The use of a cybernetics model to explain prehistoric cultural change, while terminologically cumbersome, has certain advantages. For one thing it does not attribute cultural evolution to 'discrepancies', 'inventions', 'experiments' or 'genius', but instead enables us to treat prehistoric cultures as systems. It stimulates enquiry into the mechanisms that counteract change or amplify it, which ultimately tells us something about the nature of adaptation. Most importantly, it allows us to view change not as something arising *de novo*, but in terms of quite minor deviations in one overall part of a previously existing system, that once set in motion can expand greatly because of positive feedback.

A culture, as we have seen, may be considered as composed of coupled systems, and the nature of their coupling is very relevant here and has to be considered. Its stability and growth is determined by the behaviour of these systems – in which human beings participate, of course, and human ideas, so that the growth is not 'determined' in a materialist sense. As Maruyama has written (1963, 178):

> Sometimes one may wonder how a culture, which is quite different from its neighbouring cultures, has ever developed on a geographical background which does not seem to be in any degree different from the geographical conditions of its neighbours. Most likely such a culture had developed first by a deviation-amplifying mutual causal process, and has later attained its own equilbrium when the deviation-counteracting components have become predominant, and is currently maintaining its uniqueness in spite of the similarity of its geographical conditions to those of its neighbours.

This, then, is the growth process which we are seeking to analyse and which can be discussed with the minimum of jargon, although terms such as positive feedback and negative feedback are necessary. Next an attempt is made to look more carefully at the precise conditions which may give rise to growth, and not only to growth in size but to fundamental changes in the structure of culture, leading ultimately to the emergence of civilisation.

## Growth and 'Take-off' in an Economic Subsystem

An informative and stimulating approach to economic growth focuses on the problem of the interaction of different factors (Rostow 1953). The analysis is in terms of factors primarily *within* the system. Rostow's own interest again lies in the problems of developing countries, and the circumstances favourable to their economic 'take-off'. Our own lies in the possible analogy which this suggests for the 'take-off' leading to the formation of early civilisations, and on the insight it may give into the way interactions operate between the component subsystems of the culture.

The analogy is not, of course, a complete one, since none of the early civilisations which we have in mind move beyond Rostow's traditional stage. Yet there are interesting and suggestive parallels between the process of growth from traditional to industrial civilisation, and that from subsistence economy to early civilisation, the transformation which we are seeking to explain.

Rostow's approach is basically one of common sense: its originality lies in a willingness to consider a multiplicity of long-term factors, and above all in the attempt 'to treat changes in the rate of growth as determined by the workings of the fundamental variables in the system rather than as the consequence of exogenous forces'. It is this which makes his work relevant to the present problem.

His analysis of the forces governing changes involves three basic statements about the workings of society:

1. The economic output is determined by the size of the working force, the society's stock of capital, and its stock of knowledge. The rate of growth is therefore a function of the rate of change of these factors.

2. The first of these factors is itself governed by five 'economic subvariables': these comprise the rates of birth and death (prior and current), the role of women and children in the working force, and the skill and degree of effort of the working force.

The second factor, the size and productivity of capital, is seen as governed by six subvariables, namely the volume of research in pure and applied science, the proportion accepted of the flow of innovations, the balance between consumption and current investment, and the yield from additions to capital stock.

3. These economic subvariables are themselves seen as dependent upon six further variables or propensities, 'the human deter-

minants of economic action': the propensity:
- to develop fundamental science
- to apply science to economic ends
- to accept innovations
- to seek material advance
- to consume
- to have children.

These 'propensities' are in turn seen as 'a function of the prior long-period operation of economic, social and political forces which determine the current social fabric, institutions and effective political theory of the institution'. Clearly these propositions do not offer an explicit quantitative analysis of the growth which they set out to explain. But they 'are designed to constitute a link between the domain of the conventional economist on the one hand, and the sociologist, anthropologist, psychologist and historian on the other. . . . They also aim to provide a focus for the efforts of non-economic analysis interested in economic phenomena . . .'

Rostow's book goes on to analyse the problems of modern developing societies in these terms. The interest of these ideas here is the explicit realisation 'that actions which result in economic advance need not to be motivated by economic goals'. The analysis of an economic subsystem is dependent on 'propensities' – such as the acceptance of innovation, or consumption, which are only in part economic and are not necessarily governed by economic factors. Indeed of these six propensities only the last two fall directly within the scope of Malinowski's 'primary needs' (Malinowski 1960, 91).

These are variables which, while endogenous to the society in question, may be regarded as exogenous to the economic subsystem. Once again the interrelations between subsystems are seen as crucial. 'Economic action is . . . the outcome of a complex process of balancing material advance against other human objectives . . .'

The developments in the formative period which led to the establishing of one early state society, will be considered below. They may profitably be regarded in this way, taking economic changes not in isolation but within the context of their impact on the society as a whole. For it is this impact, most clearly evident in social terms, which determines the long-term features of the economic progress in question. It is clear that the period in question was one of change. Many innovations were widely accepted at this time and subsequently, when an international spirit, a cosmopolitan feeling, can be detected. The obvious superiority of the metal tools and weapons, for instance, over their stone counterparts may have led to their rapid acceptance. This in turn led to the adoption of other new methods and ideas. This was a time of change, change induced indeed partly by the sudden significance of metal. And in such times of change, as Boserup (1965) hinted, other innovations seem to have found ready acceptance. The propensity to accept innovations does indeed seem a significant factor in considering these developments.

The metallurgical and other technological developments do indeed show a notable dynamism in the development and application of new techniques and processes. The bearing of Rostow's first two propensities is obvious, although in early state societies there was hardly a valid distinction between pure and applied science.

Above all, the propensity to seek material advance, and to consume, are factors which are relevant to the origins of most early state societies. They are often overlooked in analyses of culture change, or even dismissed as 'superficial reductionist'. (It must none the less be admitted that the simple naming of 'propensities' is in itself far from an explanation of growth, but merely a first step in that sense.) For instance, the development of metallurgy created new forms of wealth, and indeed new forms of consumption. The propensity to consume was given new scope by its introduction.

Probably, however, in most prehistoric societies the propensity to seek material advance was still limited to a large extent by social factors. A prince, or 'head of state' for instance, might well deliberately accumulate wealth in order to dazzle and influence both his subordinates and his peers by its display. But we may question whether there was any very high degree of social mobility at this time, and whether social advance could effectively be secured by increased work or production.

The analysis does, however, suggest an emphasis on one feature common to all civilisations: a willingness to invest income and hence to accumulate what may be regarded as capital. Both goods and labour were lavishly employed in the construction of significant religious or social centres, often of palaces. At first sight much of this investment was unproductive, contributing solely to the magnificent appointments of the palace or to the rich burial goods which accompanied the prince and his family to the grave. but this is to overlook the socially cohesive effects of such investment. And the production of these increasingly magnificent objects (the increase itself a sign of willingness to accept innovation) was the only possible way of conducting 'research' in the fields of pure or applied science. In prehistoric times most knowledge was practical knowledge – and this does not, of course, exclude religious experience, since religion is itself to be regarded in functional terms as a special technology. Innovations must have arisen most frequently not from deliberate research and its application, but from the 'spin off' consequent upon the developing production processes employed in the palace or temple workshops and beyond.

The palace, or the temple, as the focus of highest population density and the location of the majority of specialist processes (at least in many early state societies), from metallurgy to accounting, constituted – together with its implicit social system – the main capital stock of the community. And 'whether a rate of growth can be sustained depends on whether investment . . . is sustained' (Rostow 1953, 95). The developing social system ensured that both investment and the rate of growth were indeed sustained.

This emphasis upon the propensities to consume and to seek material advance is of course not a new idea, and many economists stress that sustained growth over a considerable period requires modifications of economic and perhaps social organisation. As J. K. Mehta has written (1964, 95), continued growth of real income depends

> on the extended use of the ability to plan and organise human efforts. It is organisation whose elasticity can ensure a sustained rate of growth of national income.
>
> If there is any factor that possesses elasticity in a degree that we need for growth, it is organisation. This factor, which is perhaps capable of stretching itself to any required limit, is behind growth. But circumstances must be favourable to enable it to stretch itself. These circumstances are related in the final analyses to the behaviour of producers (determined partly by their habits and partly by their psychological reaction to consumers' behaviour) and the behaviour of consumers.
>
> For the study of growth it is necessary, therefore, to make some plausible assumptions about the behaviour of buyers of productive services (producers) and those of consumption-goods (consumers).

Of course the language of economics, formulated where a money currency establishes a precise and stable equivalence between different kinds of goods and services, cannot be applied to societies without a formal exchange system. It is absurd to read into early societies the economic concepts of modern marketing and currency. Such statements as these cannot be directly applied, but at the level

271

of analogy they are certainly indicative of relevant factors.

At a certain point, indeed, the analogy between economic growth and the growth of a culture or civilisation breaks down. In the first place an important criterion which the economist takes to indicate the transition from a preponderantly agricultural basis to an industrial one is the rate of increase in *per capita* output. In an essentially non-industrial society, even at the peak of its development, the rate of increase, however measured, cannot have been very great. Moreover, such an economic analysis, while refreshingly considering the effect of non-material factors on economic growth, is still restricted in its scope to the growth of the economy, not to the development of the culture as a whole. The analysis does not, therefore, offer full scope for a consideration of the interactions of all the factors relevant to this larger problem, although it works in the same sense. But it is precisely this question, as to how changes in one field of human activity – in one subsystem of society – produce changes in another, which requires further consideration.

## The Multiplier Effect, and the Interaction Between Subsystems

One of the distinguishing features of human societies is the extent to which changes within one subsystem of society bear upon other subsystems. Population does not simply grow, for instance, and then reach a stable level, governed purely by environmental factors, as it might in the case of most animal populations. Instead a dynamic interaction is set up between the population level and the means of food production. There is innovation, and the acceptance of innovation. A new adaptation is seen: a new farming mode, which amounts to a new structure of food-production procedures, a new configuration among human activities. In the terms discussed above, there is very considerable elasticity in organisation.

The growth which we are here considering consists in the establishment (and survival) of new relationships, new patterns of activity. This often implies the desuetude of many of the old relationships and activities, so that the changes which result are often irreversible. The analogy in the organic world of nature is here not with the growth of a single member of a species (the ontogeny), since this implies no real innovations in patterns and relationships already established, and is largely a question of size, of scale. It lies rather with the evolution of a new species (the phylogeny) where real innovatory changes, the result in this case of mutation, lead to new adaptations and the irreversible movement away from old ones.

272

Systems theory has indeed made clear to us the way in which 'regulators' can achieve a dynamic balance in a system. And most branches of human activity are governed in the same way. Human conduct is regulated by all the rules, pressures and incentives of society: there are ways things are usually done, and things which are not done. Indeed it is generally normal in a human culture for things to go on much as they have before.

Here, however, the problem is a different one. The regulatory efficacy of culture is accepted. The question is now the opposite one – how and why does it change or grow?

Growth in numbers or in size is itself inhibited by the regulatory mechanisms. When the birth rate rises very rapidly, for instance, the death rate may also rise, and population growth is limited. These restricting mechanisms can only be overcome by deviation-amplifying mechanisms which actually favour growth of certain kinds. This is the positive feedback also discussed above. In favourable circumstances 'one thing leads to another'. A change, for instance an increase in capital investment, leads to an increase in production. And this outcome works now to amplify the initial change by allowing a further increase in investment. In this way a 'growth cycle' develops, subject to what the economist calls the Law of Diminishing Returns. After a period of sustained change or growth, further change (e.g. further investment increase) no longer has so large an effect as before (e.g. on output). A kind of saturation is reached, and the growth ends. The feedback, in other words, is no longer positive.

Once again there are analogies in chemistry: we have already seen above that when a chemical reaction is reversible, a negative-feedback regulator operates, designated Le Châtelier's Principle. but when the reaction is irreversible this does not hold. In some reactions, which are self-catalysing, the faster a reaction is taking place the faster its rate increases: this is a positive feedback situation. But later, often as the available resources are used up, the reaction rate falls again: by analogy we may say that the law of diminishing returns is operating.

The growth of human societies is not always subject to this law of diminishing returns precisely because the underlying structure is itself changed in the growth process, just as in the economic situation summarised by Mehta above. Innovations arrest or negate the operation of the usual limiting factors. This change of structure is something the cyberneticist can hardly handle yet – the structures of the systems with which he deals do not generally transform themselves into something different.

The key to this process in human cultural development lies in precisely the interconnectedness, identified in the preceding section, among the different activities of the individual in society, the interdependence of the subsystems of society. There is, indeed, a new kind of positive feedback among innovations – an innovation in one subsystem tends to favour innovations (and their acceptance) in another, in a manner quite foreign to the other species of the animal world. (Although there may be a superficial analogy with the working of 'explosive evolution' in organic evolutionary development.)

I propose to term this mutual interaction in different fields of activity, this property of human systems that an innovation (and its acceptance) in one subsystem favours innovation in another, this interdependence among subsystems which alone can sustain prolonged growth, the *multiplier effect*.

This term does not simply imply positive feedback, as in the 'accelerator' and 'multiplier' of the economists. It indicates the process whereby changes in one field of human activity can significantly influence changes of quite a different kind in another field. The following definition of the multiplier effect seeks to emphasise this distinction from the usual working of positive feedback within a single subsystem:

> *Changes or innovations occurring in one field of human activity (in one subsystem of a culture) sometimes act so as to favour changes in other fields (in other subsystems). The multiplier effect is said to operate when these induced changes in one or more subsystems themselves act so as to enhance the original changes in the first subsystem.*

This, then, is a special kind of positive feedback, reaching across between the different fields of human activity. The term multiplier used in this sense implies rather more (although with less precision) than the technical term 'multiplier' in economic theory, as formulated by Kahn and used by Keynes with reference to employment and income (Keynes 1937, 115–16). Already it has been extended beyond this original use by geographers who speak of regional multipliers (cf. Chisholm 1966, 99) to elucidate the way in which industrial expansion, within a specified area, has secondary effects there, arising from the presence of the new population and the need for service industries:

> This analysis stresses the interrelations of sectors *within* a regional economy and the spread of impulses originating in any

one sector to all other sectors either directly or indirectly. Such spreading in essence has a multiplying result. Through the continuous back and forth play of forces (or round-by-round process of interaction), such spreading leads to a series of effects on each sector, including the original one, although these effects need not always be in the same direction, and of significant magnitude. The relevance of multiplier studies for programming regional development is obvious. It neatly points up how growth in one sector induces growth in another. The relevance of such studies for understanding regional cycles is also obvious as soon as we recognise, that some impulses may be positive, others negative; some expansionary, others deflationary. (Isard 1960, 189)

Here, however, we are concerned not solely with different sectors in the economy of a cultural region, but in the different sectors in the culture as a whole, without restricting the discussion to purely material or economic considerations. We are extending the meaning of the term beyond its conventional one as an aid to analysis of feedback effects within the economic system. In discussing the growth and development of culture the independent growth within the component subsystems is naturally itself of interest. But we are now using the term to designate the effect of their mutual interconnectedness, which favours positive feedback between the different components of the culture system as a whole.

Identification of the multiplier effect in the culture system is illuminating not solely because it allows us to visualise, and in this sense understand, the growth of a system in terms of factors endogenous to it. Above all it focuses our attention on their interrelationship. It is a commonplace of 'functional' anthropology that all aspects of a human culture are ultimately interrelated, and that changes in one aspect should affect other aspects of the culture. The definition of the multiplier effect in the field of human culture is an invitation to investigate the mechanisms of this interconnectedness.

## *The Multiplier Effect and the Emergence of Civilisation*

When the multiplier effect comes into operation, and remains in operation, there is sustained and rapid growth, not merely in the scale of the systems of the culture but in their structure. Changes in one area of human experience lead to developments in another. In this way the created environment is enlarged in many dimensions, and itself becomes more complex. This is, as we have seen, something more complicated than the operation of a simple positive feedback, causing growth and amplifying the processes already present: it is a feedback system with coupled subsystems, favouring innovation.

The conditions for the multiplier effect to come into operation in such a way as to result in sustained growth in the different sectors of the culture require close consideration. Some writers have spoken of a threshold or take-off point beyond which striking developments occur. To investigate this threshold is essentially to seek the circumstances which bring the multiplier effect into active operation.

When the emergence of civilisation is considered, it seems that the crucial requirement is that there should exist the possibility for sustained growth (and for positive feedback) in *at least two* of the subsystems of the culture. Clearly, if none of the subsystems were free, through the favourable influence of changes in the society, to grow and develop (e.g. agricultural production to increase through the adoption of more intensive farming procedures), the culture has no potential for growth. And if only one subsystem develops in this way, and the multiplier effect does not operate, the nature of the culture as a whole will not fundamentally be changed.

The 'temple' culture of Malta seems an obvious case where a single subsystem, involving religious activities and the construction of the great temples, clearly underwent dramatic expansive developments. But for whatever reason this does not seem to have produced detectable positive developments in other subsystems (whether technological or economic). Why this should have been so remains to be investigated – perhaps limited agricultural potential, and the lack of raw metals were significant negative factors – but the outcome was not a civilisation, merely a neolithic culture boasting remarkably sophisticated temples.

It seems that no single factor, however striking its growth, can of itself produce changes in the structure of the culture. For a 'take-off' at least two systems must be changing and mutually influencing their changes.

The Sumerian civilisation has at times been attributed primarily to the invention of irrigation, a single factor which supposedly yielded a food surplus, and made possible the Mesopotamian class structure, with its priests and princes, and the growth of the city. This notion of a food 'surplus' as the 'cause' of further growth has been effectively demolished by Harry Pearson (1957, 320) and George Dalton (1960; 1963). It is inevitable, of course, that any society which has non-food-producing specialists of any kind must have a subsistence situation whereby one food-producer can produce more than he eats. But the term 'surplus' in a non-market, non-money economy is without meaning, indeed a contradiction (Dalton 1960, 485): if it refers to an experienced growth of output, it would be better to say so. As Dalton (1963, 389) has forcefully asserted: 'To attribute the existence of non-food producers to a food surplus – in the sense that a growth in food supply actively caused the priests and rulers to arise – is, to put it bluntly, silly.' When French farmers dump their artichokes in the road during a glut, there may well be a surplus, but in what sense is the Sumerian peasant's contribution to the temple 'surplus', or the goods destroyed in a potlatch? To regard all subsistence products not actually eaten by the producer and his family as 'surplus', and to ignore the real significance of activities even so apparently wasteful as a potlatch, is to make so total a distinction between the subsistence economy of the neolithic and the craft economy of early civilisations that the gap cannot be bridged. As Pearson (1957, 339) has said, referring to the many societies where 'potential surpluses' are available (i.e. where an increase in food production would be possible): 'What counts is the institutional means for bringing them to life. And these means for calling forth the special effort, setting aside the extra amount, devising the surplus, are as wide and varied as the organisation of the economic process itself.' Dalton (1963, 392) points out: 'In *some* circumstances a growth in food supply may be a necessary condition for social change to come about: *it is never a sufficient condition.*' This is very relevant to all early civilisations. Indeed he goes on to state: 'In other circumstances, as we are now learning from economic development in primitive areas, just the opposite may be the case: social change may be a necessary condition for allowing an increase in the food supply to take place.'

Since civilisation, with its artificial environment, does imply some specialisation, every civilisation must have an economy which has progressed in some sense *beyond a subsistence economy,* But this does not mean that the growth of civilisation was 'caused' by improved food-production techniques, which may indeed in some cases have long been available. In many cases, I suggest, it did in fact come about through innovations in such techniques *coupled with* social and other developments which at the same time made these subsistence improvments both possible and desirable.

Robert Adams, on the other hand (1966, 12), draws 'the conclusion that the transformation at the core of the Urban Revolution lay in the realm of social organisation.' This view now seems to tend rather towards the other extreme, and recognise as 'cause' what was previously identified as 'effect', and vice versa. One is reminded here of the rather similar divergence in the views of Malthus and Boserup, where the former regarded the food supply as the 'independent variable', and the latter the population density. For indeed, as Adams himself has stressed, the social organisation could not have emerged without the possibility of increased *per capita* food production among the agricultural producers. The two developments are coupled and cannot with profit separately be labelled 'cause' and 'effect'.

The implication of this view, which can indeed be formulated as a testable prediction, is that we shall not expect the archaeological record for the early development of a civilisation to show greatly improved production techniques (e.g. irrigation) and 'surplus' storage facilities arising prior to, or without evidence of social stratification (e.g. palaces) or religious specialisation (e.g. temples). Nor shall we, in the cases where the successful transition to civilisation was later accomplished, expect these social and religious advances to have developed markedly without developments also in food production. On the contrary, the two were linked by the multiplier effect, and it was their coupled expansion which led to rapid changes in the culture in general.

In the same sense, the development and increase of trade, for example in the early Aegean, cannot alone be regarded as the principal factor leading to the development there of civilisation. Without its strong interactions with other sectors of the culture, such as social organisation, the multiplier effect could not effectively have operated.

We may even suggest that social stratification itself is not automatically a necessary contributing element in the growth of civilisation, although the emergence of certain new social structures would indeed seem inevitable. The documented remains of the Indus civilisation, for example, are notably lacking in evidence for great personal wealth, and so far, although public and communal buildings are known, there are no great temples or rich palaces. We can imagine (perhaps a shade frivolously) a socialist state, with communes and with specialists, yet without social stratification in the sense of a hierarchical, rank-order structure in the society. Such a state would have a developed social organisation, of course, but not a pronounced social stratification.

It is, of course, at the level of the individual in society that the multiplier effect actually operates. And it is through the individual that social pressures, for instance, have an economic significance, for the various subsystems of the culture are linked at the level of the individual. It is therefore by a consideration in terms of individuals, on a micro-economic scale, that the precise mode of operation of the multiplier effect must be elucidated.

On a micro-economic scale, then, the farmer in an ideally simplified neolithic society produces enough for the needs of himself and his family. There is little point in producing much more food than they can eat, since there would be nothing for him to do with it. (He thus avoids a surplus, except in occasional years of unexpectedly high crop yields.) His needs are satisfied. His environment is stable.

Various innovations may work to change this situation. The social subsystem may require of him some conspicuous act of generosity or prosperity (such as a potlatch contribution) to maintain or enhance his prestige. Here then is a crucial new concept (although one implied in Rostow's schema) – a derived secondary need in Malinowski's sense.

I find it impossible to envisage an explanation for change and growth in society without some reference to the 'new needs' which the operation of such factors produces, the material demands and obligations arising from social and religious considerations. Man shows great mobility or elasticity in his requirements: workers today will withdraw their labour on the grounds of unsatisfactory conditions, which would have been accepted as generous a century ago. A telephone, a car, a television set are legitimate needs in the city today, while a generation or two ago they belonged to the realm of fantasy. No explanation for culture change which fails to acknowledge the appearance of such new needs can be effective.

Of course there is evidence for competition and display among other animal species (Wynne-Edwards 1962), and it is not their existence, but the way the society is adapted of facilitate them, which is a unique feature of human culture. And the line of argument can become a circular one if we 'explain' a new feature 'because' we believe there to have been a 'need' for it. A more thorough investigation of the nature and working of these 'needs' and 'propensities' is demanded.

Without acknowledging competition as a significant factor there is no way of explaining, for example, the introduction of weapons. And, above all, without acknowledging a desire for prestige, and the principle that prestige frequently relates to wealth, it is difficult to explain social stratification. These propositions do not, however, amount to natural or universal laws for human behaviour – in a monastic order of poverty, for instance, the monk who cannot bring himself to discard earthly riches may be little esteemed.

Most of man's activities exist in many dimensions, as the discussion above sought to show. To draw a further analogy with economics, man's 'currencies' within the different dimensions are to some extent interchangeable. Prestige can be related to economic gain, while religious fulfilment may adequately be substituted for the latter. The notion that 'every man has his price' implies that material goods can be set against a 'currency' in the social dimension, such as honour. Moreover in each dimension man shows considerable income elasticity of demand: 'the more you have, the more you want'. In non-monetary and non-market societies these are not scalar quantities – a man may set life above love, love above honour, and honour above life – and no universal equation is possible. As Rostow implies, it is this interaction between the various dimensions of human existence which, together with man's income elasticity of demand in various fields, makes culture growth possible.

A palace, such as is found in many early civilisations, has functions which far exceed the primary one of providing bodily comfort for a segment of the community. And a temple, whatever its history, is referable also to a quality or propensity in human beings not discernible in other animals. No explanation of civilisation can proceed without recognising this basic difference in potential among species, although we cannot expect to explain these fundamental circumstances – that is the province of psychology, of physiology, of cybernetics perhaps, and of biochemistry. Our explanation must start by assuming that all societies of men share these potentialities, for at present there is no convincing evidence that they do not. Obviously an explanation in terms of group or racial 'superiority' or 'creativity' is to be rejected at once, unless there are striking and conclusive new observations in anthropological science to warrant such a theory. The explanation which we are seeking operates, rather, within the field of man–environment interactions, to trace how innovations and their acceptance produced irreversible changes in certain cultures, leading in some cases to civilisation.

The story of the development of these innate human potentialities during the process whereby *Homo sapiens* emerged from his predecessors belongs largely to the field of physical anthroplogy. But most anthropologists believe that man as born today does not differ significantly from man as born 10,000 years ago. In analysing the genesis of a civilisation we are operating, therefore, in the domain of cultural development and evolution, not of strictly biological evolution.

As this chapter has tried to outline, we have a possible formula for the explanation of culture change. It is accepted that societies and cultures live in a state of equilibrium: the subsystems which operate in the society are regulated so as to minimise the disturbances to the human environment caused by fluctuations in the natural environment, by outside human agencies or by innovations within the society. For any significant change to take place the innovations must be linked in a deviation-amplifying mutual causal system: the innovation produces effects which favour the further development of the innovation. In some cases the innovation arising in one subsystem has marked effects in other subsystems: this is a feature specifically of human societies with their goal mobility, where needs or aims in one dimension are sublimated to other dimensions. In such a case, if positive feedback occurs, the multiplier effect can come into operation: coupled developments occur in both subsystems, and the innovation is favoured. When the structure of the subsystems is such that marked change can occur in them (for instance when a technological threshold such as the invention of metal casting, or the sowing of grain, can be surmounted) a cultural 'take-off' is possible. Most or all of the subsystems of the society will then undergo marked structural change.

The operation of the multiplier effect – of positive feedback situations within *and between* coupled subsystems – produces a 'revolution' in the sense intended by Gordon Childe (1950). This applies equally to the Neolithic, Urban and Industrial Revolutions. Each may take a long time to mature, since these are not sudden quantum shifts, but continuous processes of change. But in each case the rate of innovation and the speed of structural change in the society are much faster over a considerable period, which we regard as the duration of the revolution itself.

Of course these 'subsystems' and the 'positive feedback' between them are theoretical constructs, terms which we have ourselves created in order to talk about such changes. But if they lead us to formulate new hypotheses which can be tested in the archaeological record – to posit, for instance, a correlation between one observable factor and another in a given culture – then they are fruitful constructs. A model such as this offers many features as yet unexplored by archaeologists and anthropologists: it might even be capable of sustaining exact and quantitative formulations, were sufficiently comprehensive archaeological data available.          [1972]

## Bibliography

Adams, R. M. (1966) *The Evolution of Urban Society*.
Ashby, W. R. (1956) *An Introduction to Cybernetics*.
Beer, S. (1959) *Cybernetics and Management*.
Bertalanffy, L. von (1950) An outline of general system theory, *British Journal of the Philosophy of Science*, 1, 134.
Boserup, E. (1965) *The Conditions of Agricultural Growth*.
Childe, V. G. (1950) The urban revolution, *The Town Planning Review*, 21, No. 1, 3.
Chisholm, M. (1966) *Geography and Economics*.
Dalton, G. (1960) A note in clarification of economic surplus, *American Anthropologist*, 62, 483.
— (1963) Economic surplus once again, *American Anthropologist*, 65, 389.
Flannery, K. V. (1968) Archaeological systems theory and early Mesoamerica, in B. J. Meggers, ed., *Anthropological Archaeology in the Americas*.
Hawkes, C. F. C. (1954) Archaeological theory and method: some suggestions from the Old World, *American Anthropologist*, 56, 155.
Isard, W. (1960) *Methods of Regional Analysis, an Introduction to Regional Studies*.
Jacobsen, T. and R. M. Adams (1958) Salt and silt in ancient Mesopotamian agriculture, *Science*, 128, 1251.
Katz, D. and R. L. Kahn (1966) *The Social Psychology of Organisations*.
Keynes, J. M. (1937) *The General Theory of Employment, Interest and Money*.
Malinowski, B. (1960) *The Science of Culture and other Essays*.
Maruyama, M. (1963) The second cybernetics: deviation amplifying mutual causal processes, *American Scientist*, 51, 164–79.
Mehta, J. K. (1964) *Economics of Growth*.
Pearson, H. W. (1957) The economy has no surplus: critique of a theory of development, in K. Polanyi, C. M. Arensberg and H. W. Pearson, eds., *Trade and Market in the Early Empires*, 320.
Raikes, R. L. (1965) The Mohenjo-daro floods, *Antiquity*, 39, 196.
Rostow, W. W. (1953) *The Process of Economic Growth*.
Wolf, E. R. (1967) Understanding civilisations, *Comparative Studies in Society and History*, 9, 446.
Wynne-Edwards, V. C. (1962) *Animal Dispersion in Relation to Social Behaviour*.

# 10

## THE MULTIPLIER EFFECT
## IN ACTION

*

No single cause or factor can furnish a sufficient explanation for growth. Some authors have identified irrigation as the fundamental basis for various early civilisations (e.g. Wittfogel 1957) yet the foregoing discussion suggests that neither this, nor the invention and exploitation of metallury, nor yet the adoption of a redistributive system for agricultural produce can be singled out as the primary determining feature. Nor does population growth in itself explain very much. An adequate explanation can come only from the study of interactions of the various subsystems of the culture. A general model was outlined for this purpose, and a particular kind of interaction, the multiplier effect, identified as of crucial significance.

In this chapter the rise of prehistoric Aegean civilisation is viewed as a specific instance, a rather well-documented example, of a more general process for which the multiplier effect helps to furnish an appropriate model.

Several such models could be constructed for the Aegean culture changes observed. Here two alternative versions of the causal chain explanation are outlined. Both are, I think, plausible, and based upon the evidence now available. Both, as we shall see, have their limitations, and a broader perspective is then offered.

### Subsistence/Redistribution Model

In terms of this model the decisive factor is the development of a redistributive system for subsistence commodities. This emerged as a consequence of the intensive exploitation of a new spectrum of food plants, notably tree crops, yielding a new diversity in produce.

283

## General Statement

Adaptive transformations in human societies may be of three kinds. In the first there is a shift in the spectrum of environmental resources exploited: the exploitation of new resources and the more intensive use of certain traditional ones implies at the same time the reduction or cessation of exploitation of other resources. The most obvious example is the shift from hunting-gathering to food production. Another would be the replacement of stone tools by those of metal. The change in exploitation pattern is often accompanied by a shift in settlement pattern.

A marked increase in the efficiency of exploitation of a given range of resources is a second recurrent cause of societal transformations. In this case traditional resources are not abandoned, nor new ones utilised. The advance is in the field of exploitative efficiency, giving a greater *per capita* yield to the worker. Most subsistence advances are of this kind: irrigation agriculture is perhaps the most striking example.

A third transformation type is the effective enlargement of the range of resources successfully exploited. The traditional resources remain basic, but they are supplemented now by new ones. The first consequence is a new diversity in the range of products. Moreover if the resources in question are not competitors for land or for human labour, an increase in net production is possible. This increased production may permit a rise in population. More significantly the diversity in food products leads both to greater security (in that the failure of one crop need no longer be disastrous) and to some measure of specialisation in production. Some system of exchange is needed to utilise the specialist products. In favourable circumstances – and this depends largely upon the spatial distribution of the various resources – a redistributive system emerges in which the transfer of goods is centrally controlled. This is the locus for an emerging hierarchy of power and of wealth. This third transformation type is relevant to Aegean developments.

## Analogy

An instance of a transformation of this third type is afforded by formative Mesoamerica, where several micro-environments are available (Flannery and Coe 1968). While one response is the intensive exploitation of one micro-environment, another is the exploitation by villages located in each, even in those regions which taken alone could not support a self-sufficient village. Permanent settlement is achieved by means of co-operative specialisation. The social correlates of such an adaptation appear to be a redistributive system, and its control by persons of high status.

## Initial Conditions

By 4000 BC mixed farming was successfully conducted in every major region of the Aegean. The chief product was grain – wheat or barley – and the fertile plains of northern Greece in particular were intensively farmed. The distribution of tell sites emphasises the intensity of exploitation of suitable arable land. Other settlement types naturally used other resources, especially in south Greece – the fishing village of Saliagos is an example – but such settlements were fewer and smaller. Thus while several micro-environments were exploited, fertile arable lands were preferred and most intensively cultivated. There is little evidence for craft specialisation or for a strong hierarchical social structure. Trade was on a limited scale on the basis of reciprocity.

## Causal Factors

1. It is suggested that the domestication of the vine and especially the olive early in the third millennium BC made possible the intensive exploitation of a new micro-environment – the hill slope below 700 m, receiving abundant sun, little rain and no winter frost.

2. The terrain in south Greece is such that a single village can be within reach of both arable land and of hill slopes suitable for olive cultivation and viticulture. The suggested consequence is that a redistributive system emerged *with* the village, favouring the emergence of local chieftains.

A rise in population is expected, since the olive and vine do not compete for land with the cereals, and require labour at periods other than those critical for agriculture.

3. The concentration of commodities for redistribution in the lands of the central 'chief' favours a development at the same spot of specialised services for the community: the smiths and other specialist craftsmen are organised by the chief and live near him. The increased village population reaches the threshold level to support craft specialists. A nucleus of craft specialisation thus occurs at village level in what is still basically a subsistence economy.

## Aegean Development

1. The domestication of the vine was accomplished in the Aegean by the third millennium BC, as the evidence from Sitagroi shows. Finds of olive oil and olive stones from early bronze age Crete and the Cyclades, and the use of oil lamps, document the exploitation of the olive. The adoption of Mediterranean polyculture at this time is strongly suggested by the new distribution of settlements in the southern Aegean, in areas of true Mediterranean climate.

2. Settlement survey indicates a marked rise in population throughout the southern Aegean at this time, while in the north, where olive cultivation is less easy, population apparently increased more slowly.

The use of seals and sealings graphically documents the developing organisation of the redistribution system.

3. Large central buildings and indications of wealth document the emergence of a hierarchical order. Various new products – metal, ivory seals, faience – indicate craft specialisation, documented too by finds of specialised tool kits.

4. The nucleus of craft specialisation at village level, seen clearly at Myrtos, at Lerna and at Chalandriani, is already a palace economy in microcosm. There is little in the palace communities of second millennium Crete and Greece not already foreshadowed in the proto-urban settlements of the third-millennium southern Aegean.

No attempt has been made to frame these observations as 'predictions' arising from the 'hypotheses'. Yet the model does have its prescriptive (and hence predictive) elements. It predicts that in areas of productive diversity (in terms of Mediterranean polyculture: olive and vine as well as cereals) and *only* in such areas will such a redistributive system emerge. It predicts a greater population growth rate in regions of the Aegean with true Mediterranean climate. And it predicts the development of craft specialisation in precisely those areas and not in others. These predictions are not contradicted by our present knowledge of the third millennium Aegean, but the evidence available is not yet sufficient to try them effectively. Further work will test their validity.

## *Craft Specialisation/Wealth Model*

The decisive factor is here viewed as the emergence of a stratified society, where high status correlates with material wealth and military prowess. These features arose largely as a consequence of the development of metallurgy and of maritime trade.

### *General Statement*

A prerequisite for any society with marked internal differentiation (hierarchy, craft specialisation, etc.) is a subsistence system where the food produced will support more than those directly engaged in producing it. Many food-producing communities have a population level lower than full exploitation of their resources would permit. Moreover the *per capita* agricultural production could be increased, were this desirable to the producers, by the greater *per capita* investment of labour. An increase can arise when the agricultural producer, in exchange for his produce, can acquire attractive and desirable goods which will serve to enhance his status, and offer opportunity for the display of wealth. The craft specialist supported in this way supplies goods to an acquisitive society, where social status is closely and competitively linked to the display and consumption of wealth. Hostility and warfare are accompanying features.

*Analogy*

The concept of wealth expressed in goods other than food products is influential in nearly all societies developing beyond the level of a subsistence economy. The precondition for 'take-off' into sustained growth for an industrial society, as described by Rostow (1953) are precisely that production, including agricultural production, be stimulated by a demand for goods, stemming from a propensity to consume them. Although no prehistoric society was an industrial society in this sense, a clearly analogous process may be identified, where the demand for goods must be recognised as a significant factor favouring increase both in craft and subsistence production.

*Initial Conditions*

By 3500 B C essentially self-sufficient villages throughout the Aegean co-existed in relative tranquillity. There is no evidence for high status or pronounced social hierarchy. *Spondylus* bracelets and stone axes are the only prestige objects known. Besides a local reciprocal transfer of such prestige objects, obsidian – a utilitarian material – was collected from the island of Melos and transferred on land on a basis of reciprocity. The smelting of copper was understood, although not intensively practised: the products were awls, pins and small objects, as well as thick flat axes, none of which carried a special prestige significance.

*Causal Factors*

1. It is suggested that the alloying of copper with tin to form bronze allowed in the third millennium, for the first time, the production of a range of weapons able to bestow status and superiority in combat upon their owners. Metallurgical skills produced plate and jewellery of precious metal, incomparably finer as prestige objects than anything formerly available.

2. The geography of the Aegean is such that, given adequate shipping, maritime contact and the search for raw materials rapidly spreads any innovation of form or technique throughout the area. An effective enlargement of the cultural unit from the technological point of view (although not from the political) is the suggested consequence of any major technological discovery.

287

3. The demand for these new commodities favours specialisation in metallurgy and other crafts. The specialists would normally be supported within the original social framework, that is to say at village level. In consequence the status of the village chief, as controlling their production, would be increased, and expressed more conspicuously by fine metal goods and other objects.

4. The covetable nature of the craft products effectively established their position as wealth. Competition for their acquisition can be expected to lead to hostility and warfare, no longer disputing solely territories but also the ownership of goods.

*Aegean Development*

1. An astonishing range of metal types is seen in the Aegean from the Early Bronze 2 period – weapons, tools, plate and adornments. The value to their owners is eloquently indicated by the dagger burials (of the Cyclades for instance) and the great hoards of metalwork at Troy.

2. The distribution of metal types shows how widely and rapidly new forms were imitated. Pottery 'sauceboats', pottery *depas* cups and possibly marble folded-arm figurines, widely found in the Aegean imitate metal types.

3. Smithies and other craft-production areas have been found at Chalandriani, Myrtos, Raphina and other sites. Their control by the chief is hypothetical, but an increasingly pronounced hierarchy of wealth is seen in the graves. Fine daggers (anticipating the ceremonial longsword of Mallia), and silver or gold diadems, express the status of the leader.

4. Stone fortifications are now widely seen in areas where sudden attack from the sea was likely. In such areas there is evidence for a decline (or at least a retardation in growth) of population, and settlements were clearly sited with a view to effective defence.

This model again carries with it implications or associations which may be framed as predictions. For instance, regions rich in copper or tin ores should be outstandingly wealthy – a prediction not testable until a clearer picture is established of the original mineral resources available. Indeed so effectively does the model relate the features observed, which are already based upon substantial evidence, that further predictive tests are not obvious. Predictive power is not the sole criterion, however, for scientific validity: an explanation which simplifies the problem by relating its parameters is not to be dismissed merely as a logical exercise simply because many such relations are *already* documented. For they are not *finally* established: the generalisations and conclusions are always based upon the limited collections of data available at the time in question. They remain corrigible in the light of further research.

Both these models can be more effectively expressed in systems terms as outlined above. There is no prior external variable in either. In the subsistence/redistribution model, the determining event was the domestication of the olive, a plant apparently locally available. In the craft specialisation/wealth model the initial event was the inception of effective bronze metallurgy. Both these initial advances are themselves to be explained within the context of the culture system. The strength of the systems approach is that neither has to be regarded as a prior event, a *fait accompli* initiating the causal chain. Bronze metallurgy undoubtedly came about because of growing interest in the production of the coppersmith; there is a positive feedback relation between supply and demand, between production and the social impact of the product. The same may be true of the domestication of the olive: the olive may have been domesticated, and the vine too, because the juices expressed from the fruit (initially the wild fruit) contributed to the diversity of the subsistence system.

Both models are in large measure substantiated by the data at present available. The predictions of one do not contradict those of the other, although both claim to 'explain' the emergence of a social hierarchy. Yet the two are not simply different expressions of a single theory: they isolate different factors, and proceed to different (although not contradictory) conclusions. They are, to a large extent, complementary, and both could be entirely valid. In effect they are tracing different causal chains among the subsystems of a system where the linkages are exceedingly complex. Many more such models could be created, all equally valid, and all incorporating permutations and combinations of the interactions between the subsystems.

This proliferation of possible models is simply a consequence of the extreme complexity of the system whose growth we are seeking to explain. As indicated above, any human society may be represented as a system: among so many interactions a whole series of feedback loops may be traced, all of them legitimately 'explaining' change in the society.

Such 'explanations' are limited, relating together only some elements of the system, and a 'total' explanation may hardly be possible. None the less a more general treatment can be undertaken in terms of the multiplier effect.

289

## The Multiplier Effect in Action

The conditions favouring growth can be documented much more simply in terms of the multiplier effect, 'this mutual interaction in different fields of activity, this propensity of human systems that an innovation (and its adoption) in one subsystem favour innovation in another, this interdependence among subsystems which alone can sustain prolonged growth' as outlined earlier. The interactions between the subsystems are of crucial importance. They may be expressed as in figure 1, which does not in any way indicate relations between the culture and its environment, since aspects of both are included in each subsystem. It indicates rather the thirty different possible interactions among these subsystems (A → B and B → A are reckoned as separate interactions). Population is not in this sense a subsystem of society but a parameter, whose value is influenced by and influences each of the subsystems defined.

Culture, as we saw earlier, is essentially a homeostatic device, a conservative influence ensuring that change in the system will be minimised. It is a flexible adaptive mechanism which allows the survival of society despite fluctuations in the natural environment. Culture consists, of course, of patterns of learnt activity. These are therefore repetitive patterns: in similar circumstances a given action will normally be performed in the same way as on previous occasions. In each subsystem this determination of activity pattern by learning ensures that innovations are not readily accepted. By definition, what is new cannot have been learned through previous practice, and thus has no place in the existing cultural scheme of things. Wherever possible existing activity patterns will be adjusted to counteract the innovation.

Very few innovations within a functioning subsystem are accepted without strong opposition. The conservatism of non-industrial craft technology is well known: the village blacksmith is only gradually replaced by the engineering workshop. Forms of government, like forms of religion, are rigorously regulated by tradition and precedent. Even in contemporary societies this is a fundamental tenet of the law. Patterns of trade again show a long-term stability, especially when the trade implies social as well as commercial relations. And finally the subsistence basis of a society is not easily changed: pre-industrial man is nowhere more conservative than in his dietary tastes.

Strong social and religious sanctions proscribe most forms of innovation in a society: there is a negative feedback between the other subsystems and the social and the projective systems. Population too is homeostatically regulated in many societies, although the ultimate homeostatic controls of famine (when population taxes the possibilities of the subsistence system) and disease are not often brought into play. Social factors – birth control, abortion, prohibitions on sexual intercourse, even the disposal of unwanted babies – ensure that the population does not normally increase very rapidly.

This conservative nature of culture cannot too strongly be stressed. In terms of our model it is the natural tendency of culture to persist unchanged – apart from a small random drift which arises from the imperfect transmissions of the cultural pattern between generations. It is change, any change, which demands explanation.

This complex of regulatory mechanisms operates so that even when change does occur in one subsystem, the effects upon the others are minimised. An innovation such as the smelting of copper may sometimes indeed be accepted in the craft technology subsystem as an alternative and shorter way of fulfilling an existing requirement, such as the manufacture of beads. On the other hand the production of new kinds of artefacts – new tools or weapons – would require new activities in a different subsystem to permit their use. Such new activities are not usually favoured.

The multiplier effect, where two subsystems enter into a *mutual* deviation amplifying relationship (mutual implies positive feedback), is needed to overcome this innate conservative homeostasis of culture. One or two examples from the early Aegean will illustrate this point.

The domestication of the vine in northern Greece during the fourth millennium BC may be regarded as an innovation solely within the subsistence subsystem. The vine was one of a wide spectrum of plants whose occasional use favoured gradual domestication and improvement, and whose gradual domestication favoured more frequent use. This is positive feedback within the subsystem. In a conservative society the dramatic intoxicating properties of new alcoholic drinks might at first seem socially and religiously undesirable, just as does the use of new stimulants in our own day, although they are prevalent without ill-effects in other societies.

When the subsistence innovation is answered by an innovation in another subsystem, the situation is transformed. If the festive potential of wine leads to the institution of social drinking, as the gold and silver drinking vessels of the Aegean third millennium

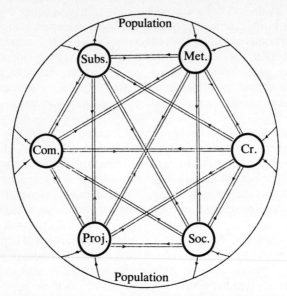

*Figure* 1. Interactions between the subsystems of the culture system. Sustained positive feedback between them – the multiplier effect – results in culture growth and development (see also table 1).

suggest, wine production is favoured. The increase in wine production leads to increased skill in manufacture and greater control over the product, which is thus improved, further favouring its wider adoption. Alternatively the intoxicated ecstasy produced may be recognised as of positive religious benefit; another positive feedback loop between systems is established. In both cases the multiplier effect comes into operation: there is a non-reversible growth both of the social (or religious) subsystem and in range and bulk of production in the subsistence subsystem. The society has grown a little, not merely in size but in complexity.

A small increase in the bulk of objects handled by the trading system, to take another example, may be of little apparent significance. Yet if it is coincidental with a development in craft technology the consequences can be dramatic. The production of the dagger in the third millennium BC gave the trader a new commodity. It coincided too with another development in craft technology, the creation of the longship. These both favoured an increase in trade (as did the need for raw copper). The increase in trade led to increased metallurgical production, to the discovery of new techniques resulting from increased specialisation, and to the acquisition of new ideas and techniques from overseas. Trade and metallurgy grew together as neither could have done without the other.

It is interactions of this kind which make possible the sustained growth and development of new processes within society. The positive coupling of the subsystems overcomes the homeostatic controls which would otherwise stifle new development. Such interactions thus lie at the root of all growth and development within the culture.

The field of possible interactions, in terms of the subsystems which we have defined, as seen in figure 1, is given in table 1. These are the possible interactions which can permit the operation of the multiplier effect, and initiate sustained growth. The growth of any culture or civilisation may be considered and explained in these terms. The figures within the table refer to the specific case in question, the prehistoric Aegean, and are discussed below.

*Table* 1. Interactions between the subsystems of the culture system (and with population).

| $x:$ | Subs. | Met. | Cr. | Soc. | Proj. | Tr. | Pop. |
|------|-------|------|-----|------|-------|-----|------|
| *y:* | | | | | | | |
| Subs. | – | B1 | B5 | B2,B3,B4 | B7 | B6 | B8 |
| Met. | | – | C1 | C2,C3,C4 | | C5 | |
| Cr. | D1 | D4 | – | D2 | D5 | D6 | D3 |
| Soc. | E1 | E2,E3,E4 | E2,E3 | – | E5 | | E6 |
| Proj. | | | F1,F5 | F2,F3 | – | F4 | F6 |
| Tr. | G1 | G2,G3 | G4,G5 | G6 | G7 | – | |
| Pop. | A1 | | A4 | A2,A5 | A3 | | – |

Growth in subsystem *y* favoured by growth in subsystem *x* through the mechanism indicated in the table (cf. list below). The subsystems listed are: subsistence, metallurgy, craft technology, social systems, projective and symbolic systems, trade and communication. Population is also included.

## Factors and Interactions in the Third-Millennium Aegean

The emergence of Aegean civilisation has to be explained in terms of the positive interactions between the various subsystems which can be detected during the third millennium. The following summary lists such principal changes in each subsystem during the third millennium. Changes occurring in other subsystems which may have favoured these are indicated: they are noted in the appropriate space in table 1 above. The list begins with population and settlement which, although not constituting a subsystem of the culture system, are important features of it.

### A. Population and Settlement

a) Population, as estimated on the basis of the number of settlements found, and their size, was increasing throughout the Aegean during the prehistoric period.

b) The growth rate was slow in north Greece, and much more rapid in the south.

c) In the two southern areas which of those surveyed had extensive arable land (Crete and Messenia), the rate of increase from neolithic to late bronze age seems to have been approximately exponential.

d) In the other southern areas surveyed, the initial increase was of the same order, but growth was markedly retarded at the time of the middle bronze age.

e) The size of neolithic village settlements in the Aegean was comparable with that of the smaller Near Eastern settlements. The increase in area from neolithic to early bronze age proto-urban settlement, and from early bronze age to late bronze age settlement was in each case by a factor of about 2. This is much less than in the Near East, where the growth was by a factor of about 10.

f) In neolithic times the settlements were generally not fortified. During the third millennium fortifications of stone are seen in eastern mainland Greece, the Cyclades and western Anatolia. By the late bronze age they are widely found throughout the southern Aegean, with the exception of Crete.

g) During the third millennium in certain maritime areas, notably the Cylades, the number of settlements becomes smaller and the important sites larger in size. They are often located at some distance from the sea, in good defensive positions.

h) A hierarchy of settlements, in terms of size, may be recognised in the later bronze age of Crete, and in certain other regions of the southern Aegean.

i) Specialisation and differentiation of function within the settlements is documented by workshops and by large central buildings, first seen at this time.

*Factors favouring population increase:*

A1. Increased efficiency in food production, and increased diversity in crops grown.

A2. Effective redistribution of foodstuffs within the social unit.

A3. Possible new social and religious beliefs reducing homeo-static control of population level (hypothetical).

A4. Improved medical knowledge, a special aspect of craft tech-nology (hypothetical).

A5. Military security favoured by hierarchical organisation and practical defensive measures.

## B. Subsistence

a) The later neolithic subsistence economy is marked by greater diversity in the range of crops, and greater specialisation, in that much purer crops were produced.

b) These tendencies continued into the early bronze age, when barley was more important than previously, and pulse crops played a major role.

c) Tree crops, notably the olive and the vine, were now domesti-cated. The fig was already exploited in the later neolithic.

d) Industrial products (olive oil and wine) were produced from the third millennium, and stored effectively in large containers.

e) These and other commodities were handled by the redistri-bution system which emerged in the third millennium to form the basis of the later palace economies.

f) The diet was supplemented, but only to a limited extent, by the usual neolithic range of domestic animals, and by fish.

*Factors favouring development in the subsistence subsystem:*

B1. New metal tools increasing agricultural efficiency.

B2. Stimulus on production of the redistribution system, both by the wish to receive redistributed goods, and by sanctions applied if quotas were not met.

B3. Social factors, including the use of prestigious drinking ves-sels, augmenting the demand for wine.

B4. The use of oil lamps augmenting the demand for olive oil (minor factor).

B5. The desire to acquire new craft products in exchange.

B6. The development of overseas trade favouring production increase.

B7. The requirements of subsistence commodities for religious offerings stimulating production (minor factor).

B8. Pressure for increased food production brought about by population increase.

## C. Metallurgy

a) Metallurgical output increased dramatically in the early bronze age, and especially in the Early Bronze 2 period. It followed the limited production of copper and of gold in the final neolithic.

b) The metallurgical skills emerging during the third millennium included:

    i. Alloying of copper with tin or with arsenic to yield bronze.

    ii. Smelting and casting of lead.

    iii. Hammering of gold and silver to produce attractive decorative shapes.

    iv. Raising of sheet metal to produce metal vessels.

    v. Use of rivets.

    vi. Production of wire.

    vii. Ornamentation by granulation.

c) The dagger and spear of bronze both made their appearance. The dagger evolved during the early bronze age to yield the sword.

d) Useful metal tools, including large flat axes and shaft-hole axes were produced.

e) A whole series of smaller craft tools, including awls, borers and gouges was produced.

f) Jewellery and articles of adornment in gold, silver and bronze were now made.

## Factors favouring growth of metallurgy subsystem

C1. Developments in the field of craft technology, notably pyro-technological discoveries of the potter.

C2. The need for weapons arising through the increase in military hostilities.

C3. The desire for objects of display.

C4. The custom of burying valuable metal objects with the dead, which removed them from circulation.

C5. Effective supply of raw materials now available from overseas through trade.

## D. Craft Technology

a) Craft specialisation is implied by some of the products of the time – engraved seals, for instance, or faience – and direct evidence, although rare, yielded by finds from several sites.

b) A new range of tools furthered the traditional crafts like carpentry and masonry.

c) Several crafts, like those of the shipwright and of textile production, were transformed through the creation of new products, through specialisation, and by the availability of new tools.

d) A number of entirely new crafts – the skill of the lapidary, of the faience producer, of the jeweller – came into being.

e) The outcome of these advances in craft technology was a whole new range of craft products, best exemplified in the first palaces with their well-dressed masonry, their rich furnishings, and later their fresco decoration.

*Factors favouring growth of craft subsystem:*

D1. Craft specialisation, made possible by increased agricultural production.

D2. Concentration of resources by redistribution, supporting craft specialisation at the redistribution centre.

D3. Increased population, passing the population threshold for craft specialisation in the village unit.

D4. New metal tools making possible an entire range of new crafts (the stonemason, the sculptor, the shipbuilder, etc.).

D5. Religious representation and the sumptuous decoration of living spaces in the palaces requiring craft specialisation.

D6. The trade in oil, perfume, textiles, etc., favouring specialist craft production.

*E. Social Systems*

a) Objects of value, doubtless implying considerable prestige, are clearly recognisable for the first time in the third millennium. Often they are of metal – weapons of bronze and plate of gold and silver. This is the first clear expression of wealth in the archaeological record.

b) A growing disparity between rich and poor is documented by grave goods from the third millennium onwards.

c) Objects of symbolic importane – diadems and weapons of display – indicate the emergence of a hierarchy in social as well as economic terms. This is supported by the large central buildings at several proto-urban sites.

d) A developing notion of property is indicated by the seals and sealings in the third millennium.

e) The redistribution system developed, anticipating that of the first palaces, in both Crete and southern Greece.

f) Organised warfare, with specialised weapons of offence and stone fortifications for defence, now developed.

g) With war came the emergence of warriors, well documented by graves containing several weapons and heralding those of the late bronze age.

h) Several of these developments make the notion of the rise of chiefdoms at this time an appropriate one.

*Factors favouring the development of the social subsystem:*

E1. Diversity in subsistence production leading to a redistribution system.

E2. New forms of visible and prestigious wealth (the product of metallurgical and other craft production) encouraging the emergence of hierarchical distinctions.

E3. Visible wealth provoking competition and war.

E4. New weapons facilitating war and the emergence of the warrior class.

E5. Writing, aiding redistributive administration.

E6. Increase in population favouring social definition by roles (e.g. craft profession) rather than by kinship.

## F. Projective Systems

a) Concepts of measurement, both of weight and number, were clearly formulated. Standards of measure may already have been set up.

b) Symbolic expression of meaning (on seals) already anticipated the development of hieroglyphic writing in the second millennium.

c) The representation of forms from the world of nature, in painting and sculpture, first animals and then plants, became more accomplished.

d) A more complex religious symbolism emerged.

e) Burial of the dead in built graves, either singly or collectively, became widespread. The dead were accompanied by grave goods.

f) Several musical instruments were now available, for both song and dance.

g) A whole new range of decorative techniques was developed, and coherent styles may be distinguished.

h) New rituals and games are documented at this time.

*Factors favouring development of projective subsystems:*

F1. Craft specialisation necessitating exchange and hence the formation of concepts of equivalence, of weights and measures.

F2. The developing social system favouring new forms of symbolic expression.

F3. The changing social order encouraging corresponding changes in the religious order.

F4. Contact with other lands leading to innovations in artistic expression and religious symbolism.

F5. Improved craft technology offering new means of expression, both in art and in music.

F6. The increasing population promoting new forms of play and ritual, e.g. the bull sport.

## G. Trade and Communication

a) Reciprocity was gradually replaced by redistribution during the third millennium as the principal mechanism for the transfer of goods within the social unit.

b) Reciprocity, doubtless through gift exchange, remained an important mechanism for the transfer of goods between territories.

c) The directional or commercial trade of the later bronze age is heralded, at least in Crete, by the freelance trade which may account for finds of ivory and other materials imported from the Near East and Egypt.

d) Contacts between the Aegean and other Mediterranean areas were few during the third millennium, although communication between Crete and Egypt was established by the end of the final neolithic.

e) Contacts within the Aegean became especially numerous during the Early Bronze 2 period, so that one may speak of an international spirit at this time.

f) The objects most widely distributed in the Aegean were metal weapons, tools and vessels. Pottery forms imitating those of metal are widely found.

g) Transport in the Aegean was always principally by sea, although carts are documented from Crete.

## Factors favouring the growth of the trade and communication subsystems:

G1. The increased diversity in subsistence products.

G2. The wide range of new and desirable products of metal.

G3. The pressing need for raw materials, especially metal.

G4. The emergence of new craft products, especially textiles and olive oil.

G5. Improved ships.

G6. The wealth and high status of chiefs, promoting the exchange of luxury goods.

G7. New forms of expression permitting new modes of communication by artistic and symbolic means.

The developments set out in this list are changes in the culture system, documented or at least suggested by the archaeological record. With them are listed changes elsewhere, in other subsystems, tending to favour the developments taking place.

A number of these contributory factors constitute, along with the change they favour, simple positive feedback loops. For example the production of new commodities, such as metal objects or perfumed oil, tended to increase trade, while increased trade stimulated increased and more efficient craft production. At first sight such statements seem almost tautologous: demand favours production, and production promotes demand. On the contrary, however, they are highly meaningful – increased production does not necessarily promote demand: the converse is often true – and their apparent simplicity should not mask their decisive influence upon growth. Two analogous views to these may be contrasted; food production efficiency determines population density (Malthus), and population density determines food production efficiency (Boserup). In fact when increased food production efficiency favours population growth, and increasing population favours food production efficiency, the positive feedback sets up a sustained growth cycle for just as long as the two propositions remain true. These simple feedback loops are the very basis for culture growth.

These positive interactions are indicated in table 1, and the pattern of their interactions as well as their persistence during change in other aspects of the society, and their strength, determine the growth of the culture. The multiplier effect, the positive interaction between subsystems which comes into play allowing sustained growth, may be said to have brought about the emergence of Aegean civilisation, just as it brought about that of other civilisations. The precise way in which it operates, and the nature of the resultant society which the process creates, are determined by the specific nature of the matrix of interactions. They are themselves, of course, governed both by the natural environment and the initial conditions of the culture whose changes are being studied.

Here, then, is a general model for the growth of culture, sufficiently adaptable to accommodate any initial conditions, whether environmental of social. The matrix of interactions determines the nature and the speed of growth.

Two serious limitations are at once apparent. In the first place, the explanation for growth is descriptive, qualitative, and does not make predictions in precise quantitative terms. This is a regrettable but not insuperable difficulty: economists and geographers increasingly formulate quantitative predictions, and sociologists no doubt will soon follow. A much more serious objection is that we have at present no effective criterion for judging whether or not the postulated interaction is significant at all. A whole range of mechanisms could be postulated to relate any pair of subsystems in a whole variety of different ways. Were this objection to be sustained, the whole explanatory model offered here would indeed be a logical abstraction without any possible practical application.

This apparent weakness is, however, shared by nearly every historical or processual explanation. In outlining a causal chain for the development of a culture or a society, some of the links or steps in the chain inevitably involve human beings, and interaction between them and their environment. Regularities in response are dependent upon regularities in human behaviour. Ultimately an explanation which fails to recognise this will have limitations as serious as an explanation for the behaviour of chemical compounds which refuses to consider the behaviour of the constituent molecules. The multiplier effect model, far from avoiding this difficulty, inherent in any historical or processual explanation, highlights the significance of these human interactions which are at the root of all culture change.

Ultimately the evaluation of the causal links between events raises real philosophical questions. The prehistorian or historian is faced with Russell's paradox of the Two Factory Hooters, sounding simultaneously in two remote cities, A and B, so that workers at A might be said by an external observer to stop work *because* of the hooter at B. When a given consequence in the past *seems* regularly to flow from a specific cause, can we really establish a causal relationship? Indeed we are in greater perplexity, since it is difficult even to establish the true constant conjunction of events in the past. The philosopher's solution is to establish a spatio-temporally continuous chain of events between the occurrences at A and B, 'an intermediate chain of events, some of which are outside the body, some of which are in the ear, some of which are in the auditory nerve, some of which are in the brain' (Braithwaite 1953, 308). When dealing with the growth of human societies, the varieties of human behaviour are an inevitable, if inconvenient, component implicit in all explanations.

That interactions between subsystems, and interactions of eco-

301

nomic, social and spiritual forces operating upon the human individual, are given prominence is thus not necessarily a weakness in the multiplier effect model. These are fields which the archaeologist understandably avoids, since his evidence relating to them is often so inadequate. Yet while the behaviour of the group, of many individual units, may often effectively be described in statistical terms without reference to the single unit, it cannot so easily be *explained* in this way. This is a problem which prehistoric archaeology has yet to resolve: nothing is to be gained by avoiding it.

### The Human Basis for the Multiplier Effect: Interactions among Human Activities

The crucial interactions between the various fields of human activity (the subsystems of the culture system) whose effective operation has been termed the multiplier effect, have been identified as indispensable to sustained growth. Their precise nature and origin must now be considered.

The interactions among the subsystems of the society take place chiefly at the level of the human individual, since the subsystems of a culture are defined ultimately by the activities of individuals. It is the individual who equates wealth with prestige or social rank, for instance, or who forms for himself a projection of the world where social roles and religious concepts both find a place. Here certain essential differences between human and animal behaviour, differences fundamental to the growth of human culture, deserve more comment than they have received from archaeologists.

Recent studies in animal behaviour have indeed revealed a whole range of activities analogous to those which, in humans, are felt to respond to secondary or derived needs rather than to the primary needs of animal existence. Their adaptive significance, like that of many human activities, is not always obvious. A striking instance is display, sometimes competitive display, among members of the same species. Another is the social hierarchy or 'pecking order' established among some social groups of animals. These and other instances of social behaviour, such as territoriality, narrow the gulf which was formerly thought to separate human and animal behaviour. But in other fields this gulf remains a very real one.

The social activities of man are not always expressed in purely social terms. Social hierarchy can indeed be established by personal combat – a purely social form of contact – but more commonly among humans it is determined in other ways. Social actions are effected more often in material terms – by display of material wealth, for instance, or by gifts of valued objects. Out of this equation of material objects and social activities or values, which in cold logic are simply not equivalent, existing as they do in different dimensions, arises the whole complex pattern of interactions among human activities such as those which we have been describing. Such links among the activities in different dimensions of the human individual make possible the links between the subsystems of the culture system which allow the operation of the multiplier effect.

The essential kernel of many of the interactions between activities and between subsystems, interactions which are the mainspring for economic growth, develops from the human inclination to give a social and symbolic significance to material goods. For in this way a whole complex of activities in the material world satisfies aspirations, ambitions and needs which are, at first sight, entirely without adaptive significance in facilitating the continued existence of the individual or the species.

Both the consumption of goods and their storage to ensure later availability are functional activities, in the adaptive sense: they are life preserving. Yet as Veblen (1925) so well expressed,

> It is only when taken in a sense far removed from its naïve meaning that consumption of goods can be said to afford the incentive from which accumulation invariably proceeds. The motive that lies at the root of ownership is emulation; and the same motive of emulation continues active in the further development of the institution to which it has given rise and in the development of all those features of the social structure which this institution of ownership touches. The possession of wealth confers honour; it is an invidious distinction. Nothing equally cogent can be said for the consumption of goods, nor for any other conceivable incentive to acquisition, and especially not for any incentive to the accumulation of wealth.

Keynes made the same distinction in writing of the needs of human beings which

> fall into two classes – those needs which are absolute in the sense that we feel them whatever the situation of our fellow human beings may be, and those which are relative only in that their satisfaction lifts us above, makes us feel superior to our fellows. (Quoted by Galbraith 1969, 145)

This pecuniary emulation is one of the fundamental objectives of the Acquisitive Society, or the Affluent Society. Prestigious goods were evidently valued in the third-millennium Aegean, and while their distribution may have been governed largely by existing con-

303

ventions, their increasing importance cannot be so explained. Factors may already have been operating of a kind which we recognise today:

> Property now becomes the most easily recognised evidence of a reputable degree of success as distinguished from heroic or signal achievement. It therefore becomes the conventional basis of esteem. . . . The possession of wealth, which was at the outset valued simply as an evidence of efficiency, becomes, in popular apprehension, itself a meritorious act. Wealth is now itself intrinsically honourable as it confers honour on its possessor. By a further refinement, wealth acquired passively by transmission from ancestors or other antecedents presently becomes even more honorific than wealth acquired by the possessor's own effort. (Veblen 1925, 28–9)

In the third-millennium Aegean wealth and status were undoubtedly closely related to kinship, as doubtless in neolithic times. Yet the development of new classes of goods, offering new and tempting scope for the acquisition of wealth, was instrumental in the transformation of a self-sufficient peasantry in Aegean society to the acquisitive proto-urban and later urban citizens of civilisation.

Wealth itself became desirable, and pecuniary emulation was the underlying motive for many activities. Another was display, and the conspicuous consumption of this wealth.

> Throughout the entire evolution of conspicuous expenditure, whether of goods or of services or human life, runs the obvious implication that in order to effectually mend the consumer's good fame it must be an expenditure of superfluities. In order to be reputable it must be wasteful. No merit would accrue from the consumption of the bare necessities of life, except by comparison with the abjectly poor who fall short even of the subsistence minimum; and no standard of expenditure could result from such a comparison, except the most prosaic and unattractive level of decency. (*ibid.*, 296–7)

The finery of the Minoan palace, the treasures of the Mycenaean Shaft Graves, the golden drinking cups of Troy, were not conceived solely for the material well-being of those who enjoyed them. They were produced also to signify the wealth of the owner, and to reinforce that impression by extravagance as well as by opulence. Since the owner was the leader, this acted to reinforce his authority and prestige, and hence the effectiveness of his leadership. This conspicuous consumption of wealth is a feature of many agricultural societies, from the potlatch and the gift exchange of barbarism to the wedding or funeral of Western civilisation. The scope for such display and consumption was greatly increased by the creation of new classes of valuable goods – metal objects, for instance, seal-stones, wine, perfumed oil perhaps, cosmetics – in the third-millennium Aegean, and indeed in the formative stages of many civilisations.

Underlying these expressions of social status, these mechanisms for enhancing reputation and self-satisfaction, is a *symbolic equivalence of social and material values*, an equivalence without which the multiplier effect could scarcely operate. The well-being which comes from the satisfaction of primary animal needs is no longer the chief human goal, but rather the satisfaction accruing from prestige, status and good reputation. These too can sometimes be acquired and expressed through material goods. The material world is now the field for a symbolic competition. During the third-millennium Aegean this symbolic equivalence seems to have become far clearer, and the demand for commodities – a demand which is necessary for the promotion of any new production and hence of any growth in the culture – much more pressing. This symbolic equivalence of social and material values became clearer, too, and somehow more explicit through the formulation of a different kind of equivalence, the equivalence of different kinds of commodities. There is nothing to say that so much, by weight, of flour for instance is the equivalent of a given quantity of copper, and reciprocal exchange, the 'total prestation' (Mauss 1954) of gift exchange with its complex social overtones, avoids this considerable conceptual advance. So too, to some extent, does redistributive transfer, and only markets with explicit exchange rates, and ultimately a money economy make the symbolic equivalence explicit, total and fixed. Yet the redistributive system of the Minoan-Mycenaean palaces, with its quotas and its ration allowances, allowed the equivalence to work in practice.

Both these equivalences are symbolic – they are constructs of the human mind. Their adaptive value is enormous, for they alone make possible the interactions between the various activities of a society. In a sense these symbolic equivalences are the means of communication between the subsystems of a culture, which otherwise would function independently.

Alongside these abstract yet fundamental foundations of civilisation – pecuniary emulation, conspicuous consumption, and the symbolic equivalence of commodities – is a fourth, which ensures that a culture continues to grow even when any reasonable absolute demands of its citizens have been met. This is what economists term 'income elasticity of demand' – as the saying goes, 'the more you have, the more you want'. The average citizen in a Western society today has a standard of living and a range of material possessions not merely higher than those of his ancestors of three centuries ago, but higher than any to which his seventeenth-century ancestors could have aspired. Yet he does not feel he has enough, that he can sit back and enjoy these material comforts.

> The urgency of wants does not diminish appreciably as more of them are satisfied. . . . When man has satisfied his physical needs then psychologically grounded desires take over. These can never be satisfied, or in any case no progress can be proved. The concept of satiation has very little standing in economics. (Galbraith 1969, 138).

Once again it was Thorstein Veblen who most clearly expressed an essential principle of wide although not universal validity, that whatever the normal average standards of society, this standard will still seem inadequate and insufficient to those who have attained it.

> As fast as a person makes new acquisitions, and becomes accustomed to the resulting new standards of wealth, the new standard forthwith ceases to afford appreciably greater satisfaction than the earlier standard did. The tendency in any case is constantly to make the present pecuniary standard the point of departure for a fresh increase of wealth: and this in turn gives rise to a new standard of sufficiency and a new pecuniary classification of one's self as compared with one's neighbours. . . . However widely, or equally, or 'fairly', it may be distributed, no general increase to the community's wealth can make any approach to satiating this need (for wealth), the ground of which is the desire of everyone to excel everyone else in the accumulation of goods. If, as is sometimes assumed, the incentive to accumulation were the want of subsistence or of physical comfort, then the aggregate economic wants of a community might conceivably be satisfied at some point in the advance of industrial efficiency; but since the struggle is substantially a race for reputability on the basis of an invidious comparison, no approach to a definitive attainment is possible. . . . The strain is not lightened as industrial efficiency increases and makes a lighter strain possible, but the increment of output is turned to use to meet this want, which is indefinitely expansible, after the manner commonly imputed in economic theory to higher or spiritual wants. It is owing chiefly to the presence of this element in the standard of living that J. S. Mill was able

to say that 'Hitherto it is questionable if all the mechanical inventions yet made have lightened the day's toil of any human being'. (1925, 31–2, 111)

Here is one of the ultimate and hidden sources of change and progress in society, an unremitting influence favouring sustained and increasing growth in human culture. Of course social emulation and the conspicuous consumption of wealth are not the only aspects of behaviour which lead to this crucial, symbolic equivalence of social and material values. Other societies have different sets of personal values, other goals and motivations, and those discussed here perhaps seem to us appropriate precisely because they are very much those of our own acquisitive, consumer society. The desire for status or prestige may be a common feature of most societies, but in many it is rather modesty, and parismony in the acquisition or consumption of material goods which are likely to enhance them. Yet it does seem that, for the multiplier effect to operate, the 'currencies' in the different systems of society must come into some kind of equivalence in this way. Aegean civilisation came about, as doubtless did most early civilisations, as the social and material equivalences just described were established. It was these equivalences which enabled the activities of one subsystem to be relevant to those of other subsystems. Interactions were established which permitted, in a variety of ways, the operation of the multiplier effect. The related developments and innovations in the coupled subsystems, in the several yet now related fields of action, were able to overcome the conservative and homeostatic effects of culture and to sustain a growth not simply in size or scale but in diversity and complexity. The working of the multiplier effect is dependent entirely upon the development of such interation between the subsystems of a culture, and these interactions become possible only through the formulation of symbolic equations like those mentioned. Population increase, another supposed prime mover for culture growth, does not so readily bring about changes of structure: civilisation is not merely the product of population increase. Civilisation comes about through social change coupled with material advance: neither can long be sustained without the other.

[1972]

## Bibliography

Braithwaite, R. B. (1953) *Scientific Explanation*.

Flannery, K. V. and M. D. Coe (1968) Social and economic systems in formative Mesoamerica, in L. R. and S. R. Binford, eds., *New Perspectives in Archaeology*, 267.

*Systems Thinking: the Explanation of Continuous Change*

Galbraith, J. K. (1969) *The Affluent Society*.
Mauss, M. (1954) *The Gift*.
Rostow, W. W. (1953) *The Process of Economic Growth*.
Veblen, T. (1925) *The Theory of the Leisure Class*.
Wittfogel, K. A. (1957) *Oriental Despotism, a Study of Total Power*.

# 11

## AN EXPERIMENT
## ON THE SIMULATION OF
## CULTURE CHANGES

( WITH KENNETH L. COOKE )

*

The problem of the long-term analysis of culture change for specific cultures has long been discussed by philosophers of history such as Spengler (1918) and Toynbee (1947), although the resulting insights have usually been expressed as a series of rather vague generalisations.

The development of systems theory has for some years suggested the possibility that the simulation of the historical trajectories of culture systems might be undertaken using a quantitative approach, although the complexity of any real culture system is clearly very great.

This chapter describes a preliminary and largely unsuccessful attempt to apply this approach. We believe, however, that the attempt is an interesting one, illustrating as it does a simple interaction model, and the various practical decisions which have to be made in applying it. The outcome was not a successful, even if crude and oversimplified, representation of change of a prehistoric culture. Instead we were able to recognise, and then analyse, the manner in which the form of the model, whatever the nature of the actual data used as input, came to determine the 'predicted' behaviour of the system. Comparison with the well-known 'world model' used for the study *The Limits to Growth* (Meadows *et al.* 1972) led in an illuminating way to an analogous conclusion: that at this stage criticism of its assumptions about the present state of the world (i.e., about input data) are largely irrelevant. The nature of the output of that model, like our own, is best appreciated after critical examination of its structure, and of the range of outputs of which it is in fact capable.

The object of this chapter is therefore to describe an experiment in systems modelling during which we gained some valuable experience of the real problems involved. The work arose out of discussions at the Center for the Study of Democratic Institutions, Santa Barbara, California, in which a number of approaches to the use of mathematical modelling, systems theory, and simulation in tracing culture trajectories were discussed by various participants including Wilkinson and co-workers (1973), Rosen (1973), and the authors of the present chapter (cf. Cooke 1973).

## *The Interaction Model*

The problem for which this model was formulated is the explanation of the emergence of complex societies in the Aegean in the third and second millennia BC (Renfrew 1972). The approach is one of very general application, however, and with just a few modifications can be applied to the early development of any complex society.

The fundamental theoretical proposition sustaining the model – with which few will disagree – is that the changes and developments in the cultures in question (in this case the Aegean) were brought about by complex interactions of components in the society. As it stands this asserts no more than the rejection of very simple migrationist or diffusionist views, and naturally leaves room for the assessment of the effects within the society of contacts with other areas.

In the language of systems theory, the society is a system, its components being the members of the society, all the artefacts they made or used (including nonmaterial ones), and all objects in nature with which they came in contact. In this view, there is an essential coherence or conservatism of cultures due to negative feedback. That is, the system acts to counter disturbances. Innovations in society, on the other hand, are due to 'deviation-amplifying mutual causal processes', that is, positive feedback.

In order to use these concepts, it is necessary to decompose the society or system as a whole into a number of subsystems, and then to analyse in detail the interactions among these subsystems. A large part of the work cited (Renfrew 1972) is devoted to this identification of subsystems and their interactions. The subsystems are briefly defined as follows (see chapter 9):

1. Subsistence subsystem. The interactions that define this system are actions relating to the exploitation of food resources. Man, the food resources, and the food units themselves are components of the subsystem.

2. Metallurgical technology.

3. Craft technology. The metallurgical and craft subsystems are

310

defined by the activities of man which result in the production of material artefacts. The components are the men, the material resources, and the finished artefacts.

4. The social subsystem. This is a system of behaviour patterns, where the defining activities are those which take place between men.

5. The projective or symbolic subsystem. Here we are speaking of all those activities, notably religion, art, language, and science, by which man expresses his knowledge, feelings, or beliefs about his relationship with the world.

6. The external trade and communications subsystem. This is defined by all those activities by which information or material goods are transferred across the boundary of the system between human settlements or over considerable distances.

Population does not strictly rank as a subsystem within the framework described here, not representing a class of activity, but a parameter relevant to the description of the system.

This brief description does not begin to describe adequately the analysis of the system into its component subsystems. Nor is it claimed that the subsystems defined represent the only or the best such breakdown. For most cultures, for instance, it would not be desirable to distinguish the metallurgical and craft technology subsystems. What is essential to this approach, however, is some such analysis into subsystems, and an evaluation of the extent to which they interact, so that growth and development in one favours or inhibits development in another to an extent which can be made explicit. Such interactions have been considered in some detail for the Aegean (summarised in chapter 10, above). The matrix of interactions (table 1, p.293) is thus of particular importance. The projection and quantification of such a matrix is a necessary step in an analysis of this kind (cf. Plog 1974, tables 6.1 and 13.1).

Any causal chain, using this framework of analysis, can be illustrated diagramatically as a number of feedback loops, where the subsystems which interact strongly are seen as linked (with a sign to indicate whether feedback is positive or negative). The values (or functions) in the matrix indicate the strength (or the variation) in the feedback for each pair of subsystems. Likewise any matrix of interactions can be represented diagrammatically: When weak or zero linkages are omitted from the diagram the complex web of interactions is more easily seen as a series of feedback loops.

## The Simulation: Objectives and Technique

In all simulations, one wishes to gain insight into the structure of the system by tracing out its performance under a variety of suppositions concerning that structure and under a variety of conditions. Thus, in these experiments, we are interested in the evolution of culture when the subsystems interact as in table 1 (p.293), as well as when alternative interaction matrices are assumed.

Methods for bringing this system within the compass of concrete mathematics technique have been suggested by Cooke (1973) and Rosen (1972, 1973). Here we shall report on experiments with a version of Rosen's method. As in most systems analysis, we must first identify the variables. For us, the variables are in six subsystems listed earlier plus population. Of course, it would be possible to break each subsystem down into smaller parts, for purposes of greater detail, but in this formative stage it has seemed preferable to use a simple, highly aggregated model.

Some comment on 'population' as a variable is required. We mean to measure here the actual size of the population and to ignore all other demographic factors. It could well be argued that population density, age distribution, genetic factors, and so on, are of importance. However, it is convenient for the present discussion to restrict our application to Crete during the Early Bronze Age. Since the land area is thus fixed, there is no need to distinguish between population and population density. Moreover, there is no persuasive evidence of significant racial or genetic change during this period. Also, the available data could be interpreted to indicate an overall regularity of population growth, making it unnecessary to postulate important fluctuations in age distribution, and so on. Thus, population is the chosen variable. Incidentally, we make the usual convenient assumption in deterministic mathematical models that population can be treated as a real variable in the mathematical sense, rather than as an integer variable.

It is now necessary to decide what values the other variables shall be allowed to take. Although there is a possibility of using discrete or qualitative values, we have here elected to allow each variable to take real values.

Finding an appropriate real variable as an indicator for a concept is an important and difficult task. In our case, we seek a variable descriptive of the state of each of the subsystems. One of the ways in which this can be done is to regard each variable as an *index* of the level of sophistication of the subsystem it measures. We have adopted this approach here. It should of course be noted that for the purposes of analysis the state of each subsystem is here regarded as adequately described by a single index. Thus we define $x_i$ to be a numerical variable whose values represent a scale for this variable. In our case, we let $x_i(t)$ be the measure of the $i$th subsystem at time $t$, where the subsystems corresponding to $i = 1, 2, 3, 4, 5, 6$, are those indicated earlier, in the order given. We also let $Cx_7$ be the number of persons in the population, where $C$ is a scaling constant to be chosen for convenience.

In archaeological terms the precise choice of the measure used to give a value for each of the variables is of course a crucial one, and in practice the behaviour of the system will be in part determined by the measure chosen. In each case several approaches are possible. The following formulations are set out simply to show that the problems, although of major theoretical significance to archaeology, do not prevent the selection of indices whose values can in principle be estimated from the archaeological record. For example, we may define the indices as follows:

$x_1$ (subsistence). The number of persons fed by the food-gathering-food-producing activities of one person.

$x_2$ (metallurgy). The number of metal artefacts produced within the territory of the society per head of population per year.

$x_3$ (craft). The range of specialist products in the society, measured in terms of artefact types.

$x_4$ (social). The number of well-defined roles distinguished in the society.

$x_5$ (projective). *Either* the number of abstract concepts in use in the society relating to measure (including units and numerals) *or* the number of man-hours per head per year spent in religious observances or in facilitating them (e.g., by building temples).

$x_6$ (external trade). Proportion of the GNP exported beyond the confines of the system.

Because of the mathematical formalism to be adopted here, it is necessary to *normalise* each variable so that its value lies between 0 and 1. This can be done in various ways. As an example, suppose that $x_1$ is defined as just suggested, and suppose that it is estimated that $x_1$ takes values between 1.05 and 1.8 for the class of cultures under study. Then if we let $\bar{x}_1 = x_1/3$, the values of $\bar{x}_1$ lie between 0.35 and 0.6. These values are certainly between 0 and 1, and values near 1 represent a better developed subsistence system than values near 0. The population variable is normalised by choice of the constant $C$. For example, we might estimate that the population of

Crete was 12,600 in the Middle Neolithic period. If we choose $C = 630,000$, then $x_7 = 0.02$ at this time. Subsequent population increases correspond to increasing values of $x_7$.

We shall henceforth assume that all variables have been normalised, and that measures have been selected for the variables in such a way that the expert in cultures is able to correlate these numerical values with his qualitative perceptions.

A second alternative interpretation of the variable has been suggested by Rosen (1973). Roughly speaking, $x_1(t)$ is regarded as a measure of the percentage of time spent by all members in the population on subsistence-related activities, $x_2(t)$ is a measure for metallurgy-related activities, and so on. (Consequently, the sum of $x_1 - x_6$ must equal 1 at all times.) This interpretation has not been adopted here, for reasons explained at the end of this section.

The next stage in the simulation is to adopt a procedure for changing the values of the variables. The key to this is the matrix of interactions, which is reproduced in table 1 (p.293).

The matrix is to be interpreted in the following way. Growth in a subsystem $y$ in the left column is favoured by growth in a subsystem $x$ in the top row through the mechanism indicated in the matrix. The key to the mechanisms A1, A2, . . ., G7 may be found in chapter 10. As suggested by Rosen, we replace this matrix by the matrix of *signatures*, as follows. Wherever no interaction is indicated, we place a 0. Wherever a favouring mechanism appears, we place $+1$. Wherever an inhibiting mechanism appears, we place $-1$. Thus, we obtain a matrix, which we name $A$, as follows:

$$A = \begin{bmatrix} 0 & 1 & 1 & 1 & 1 & 1 & 1 \\ 0 & 0 & 1 & 1 & 0 & 1 & 0 \\ 1 & 1 & 0 & 1 & 1 & 1 & 1 \\ 1 & 1 & 1 & 0 & 1 & 0 & 1 \\ 0 & 0 & 1 & 1 & 0 & 1 & 1 \\ 1 & 1 & 1 & 1 & 1 & 0 & 0 \\ 1 & 0 & 1 & 1 & 1 & 0 & 0 \end{bmatrix}$$

Later, we shall discuss possible changes in the matrix $A$.

The procedure we have adopted for using the signature matrix has been suggested by Kane (1972) and Kane *et al.* (1972, 1973). First, a choice of the *initial state* of the system is made. That is, values are assigned to the variables at time $t = 0$, corresponding to an estimate of the stage of development of the subsystems. Next, a sequence of subsequent states (i.e., values of the variables) is calculated by mathematical iteration. Consider a system with any number $m$ of variables. (In the application previously described, $m = 7$.) If $h$ denotes one unit of time, the values are determined from the equation

$$x_i(t + h) = x_i(t)^{p_i} \qquad (i = 1, 2, \ldots, m) \tag{1}$$

where $t$ is given the successive values $t = 0, h, 2h, \ldots$, and where the $p_i$ are exponents calculated as follows:

$$p_i = \frac{q_i}{r_i} \tag{2}$$

$$q_i = 1 + \tfrac{1}{2}h\sum_{k=1}^{m}(|a_{ik}| - a_{ik})x_k(t) \tag{3}$$

$$r_i = 1 + \tfrac{1}{2}h\sum_{k=1}^{m}(|a_{ik}| + a_{ik})x_k(t) \tag{4}$$

If we let

$$a^-_{ik} = \begin{cases} |a_{ik}| & \text{if } a_{ik} < 0 \\ 0 & \text{if } a_{ik} \geq 0 \end{cases} \tag{5}$$

$$a^+_{ik} = \begin{cases} 0 & \text{if } a_{ik} \leq 0 \\ a_{ik} & \text{if } a_{ik} > 0 \end{cases} \tag{6}$$

then

$$q_i = 1 + h\sum_{k=1}^{m} a^-_{ik}x_k(t) \tag{7}$$

$$r_i = 1 + h\sum_{k=1}^{m} a^+_{ik}x_k(t) \tag{8}$$

If $A^+$ denotes the matrix with entries $a^+_{ik}$, $A^-$ denotes the matrix with entries $a^-_{ik}$, and $x$ denotes the vector with entries $x_i$, then we may write

$$q_i = 1 + h(A^-x)_i \qquad r_i = 1 + h(A^+x)_i \tag{9}$$

where $(\ \ )_i$ denotes the $i$th component of a vector.

From equations (1) we can generate values of the variables $x_i$ at successive time points $t = 0, h, 2h, \ldots$. The equations are nonlinear, but have certain useful features. First, if $0 \leq x_i(t) \leq 1$ for all values of $i$, then $q_i$ and $r_i$ are both positive, as can be seen from (7) and (8) or (9). Consequently, $p_i$ is positive and therefore $0 \leq x_i(t+h) \leq 1$.

315

That is, the region $0 \le x_i \le 1$ ($i = 1, 2, \ldots, m$) is invariant (variables automatically remain in the prescribed domain). Thus, the equations are suitable for use with variables scaled to lie between 0 and 1. We note also that if $x_i(t) = 0$ or 1 for some value of $i$, then $x_i(t + h) = 0$ or 1. The exponent $p_i$ incorporates the time step $h$ in order to adjust the time scale. Another important property of these equations is that positive feedbacks ($a_{ik} > 0$) increase the number $r_i$ but do not contribute to $q_i$, and negative feedbacks ($a_{ik} < 0$) increase the number $q_i$ but do not contribute to $r_i$. It follows that positive feedback tends to make $p_i$ small and negative feedback tends to make $p_i$ large. If $0 < x_i(t) < 1$, we see from (1) that $x_i(t + h) > x_i(t)$ when $p_i < 1$ and $x_i(t + h) < x_i(t)$ when $p_i > 1$. Thus, a preponderance of positive feedback will result in increasing values of $x_i$ and a preponderance of negative feedback will result in decreasing values. More precisely, if

$$\sum_{k=1}^{m} a^+_{ik} x_k(t) > \sum_{k=1}^{m} a^-_{ik} x_k(t) \tag{10}$$

then $p_i < 1$ and $x_i(t + h) > x_i(t)$ [unless $x_i(t) = 0$ or 1]. Additional discussion of the mathematical properties of (1) is given later.

Underlying this procedure is the assumption that a complex interacting system can be adequately described by a set of binary interactions between pairs of variables – that is, that the influence of $x_k$ on $x_i$ is independent of the values of all variables other than $x_k$. This assumption is frequently made in modelling schemes based on the concept of feedback loops.

It will now be explained why it is not convenient to interpret $x_i(t)$ as a measure of the percentage of time spent by all members of the population on activities related to the $i$th subsystem. To be more precise, Rosen suggested that for each subsystem $i$, and for each person $p$ in the population, we let $f_i(p)$ denote the proportion of time or degree of involvement of $p$ with activity $i$; thus $0 \le f_i(p) \le 1$ and $\sum_{i=1}^{m} f_i(p) = 1$. Then, summing for all the persons $p$ in the population, we let

$$u_i = \sum_{p=1}^{m} f_i(p)$$

Finally, define $x_i = u_i / N$, where $N$ is the total number of persons in the population, so that $0 \le x_i \le 1$. Now clearly we have

$$\sum_{i=1}^{m} x_i = \frac{1}{N} \sum_{i=1}^{m} u_i = \frac{1}{N} \sum_{i=1}^{m} \sum_{p=1}^{N} f_i(p) = \frac{1}{N} \sum_{p=1}^{N} \sum_{i=1}^{m} f_i(p) = \frac{1}{N} \sum_{p=1}^{N} 1 = 1$$

316

## An Experiment on the Simulation of Culture Changes

That is, the normalised variables $x_i$ must sum to 1. However, if we start with variables $x_i$ at time $t = 0$ which sum to 1 and apply equation (1), the new values $x_i$ [i.e., $x_i(h)$] will not, in general, sum to 1. Thus, the use of equation (1) is incompatible with this interpretation of the variables $x_i$.

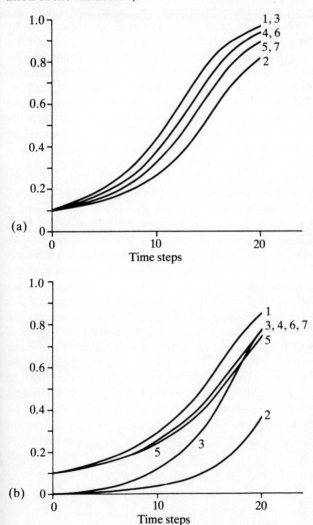

*Figure* 1. Growth pattern of the variables using signature matrix $A$. Initial values: (a) all at 0.1 (b) variables 2 and 3 at 0.01, remainder 0.1.

317

*Initial Trial Runs*

A number of trials were first made to test the behaviour of our system. Simulations were carried out on the computer at Claremont using a program in APL. Visual interactive facilities were used, allowing progressive experimentation with input parameters. All the figures have been re-drawn from Polaroid photographs of the screen display. Figures 1a and b show the growth pattern of the variables when the signature matrix *A* given in the preceding section is used, with two different choices of the initial conditions. In the first case, all variables are started with initial values of 0.1. In the second, variables 2 and 3 (metallurgy and craft technology) are started with values of 0.01. Figure 2 shows the growth when the initial values are all 0.1 but the signature matrix is changed by arbitrarily placing zeros in all entries in the fourth column to simulate the hypothesis that there is no positive feedback from the social subsystem to other subsystems.

Examination of these graphs shows that in all cases, the variables follow an S-shaped growth curve. That is, there is slow growth at first, then approximately exponential growth, and then levelling off toward the maximum possible level. Certain curves tend to lie above the others, notably the graph of $x_i$ (subsistence). However, little can be inferred from this at this time, since no *calibration* of the numerical scales has been adopted.

An implicit assumption in the use of signature matrices of this kind is that the feedbacks are all of equal strength. Whatever the significance of the numerical values, whatever their scalings, this seems unlikely to be true. In fact, there is no reason to restrict the entries to being 1, 0, or $-1$. The mathematical formulas allow any real numbers. By calling on panels of experts, one can assign different weights to different influences. The following matrix was suggested, as a guess at appropriate weightings of influences, by E. Elster and S. LeBlanc:

$$B = \begin{bmatrix} 0 & 0.50 & 0.50 & 1.00 & 0.25 & 0.75 & 0.75 \\ 0 & 0 & 0.75 & 2.00 & 0 & 1.00 & 0 \\ 0.50 & 0.75 & 0 & 0.50 & 0.50 & 0.25 & 0.25 \\ 0.25 & 0.75 & 0.50 & 0 & 0.10 & 0 & 0.50 \\ 0 & 0 & 0.25 & 0.75 & 0 & 0.25 & 0.50 \\ 0.25 & 1.00 & 0.75 & 0.35 & 0.10 & 0 & 0 \\ 0.75 & 0 & 0.1 & 0.85 & 0.10 & 0 & 0 \end{bmatrix}$$

The program was run with initial values 0.3, 0.01, 0.1, 0.1, 0.1, 0.2,

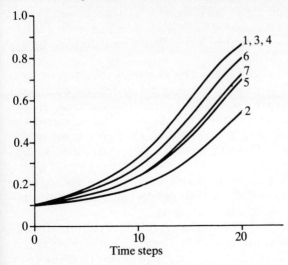

*Figure* 2. Growth pattern of the variables using matrix *A* with zero for all entries in the fourth column.

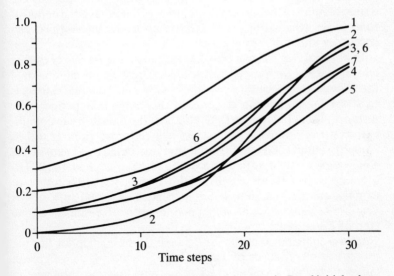

*Figure* 3. Growth pattern of variables using matrix *B* and initial values between 0 and 0.3.

0.1, and the results are shown in figure 3. The chosen initial values reflect an assumption that subsistence and trade were at a higher level than the other subsystems at the beginning of the Early Bronze Age.

The choice of a weighting matrix $B$ such as the one given here again raises questions about the scaling. For example, if we consider any row of the matrix, the sum of its entries in some sense indicates the total influence of all variables on the subsystem associated with that row. The row sums for the $B$ matrix are as follows: subsistence 3.75, metallurgy 3.75, craft 2.75, social 2.1, projective 1.75, trade 2.45, population 1.8.

It will be noted from figure 3 that a large row sum tends to make the corresponding variable increase rapidly but, because of secondary effects, the relationship is not strict.

Each column in $B$ represents the total effect of one subsystem on all others. For the matrix given here, these column sums are 1.75, 3, 2.85, 5.45, 1.05, 2.25, 2. This gives the impression that the influence of the social subsystem is being weighted far more heavily than the influence of any other subsystem.

A problem that arises in interpreting these simulations is the determination of the scale of the time variable. What is the period of time to be assigned to the arbitrary step $h$, the interval between successive states of the iteration?

In any real case some approximate estimate for the rate of change can be reached for most of the variables, and from this the length of the time step may be established. To take one example, estimates exist for the population of Crete at successive time periods. For instance, it has been suggested, although the figures are hypothetical, that the estimated population of Crete rose from 12,600 to 75,000 in about 1500 years. Therefore $x_7$ increased by a factor of 6 in 1500 years. Consulting figure 1a we see that $x_7$ increased from 0.1 to 0.6, that is, by a factor of 6, in about 14.4 time steps. Therefore we can assume that one time step represents about 1500/14.4, or 104 years. The same calculation applied to figure 1b results in a time step of $h = 86$ years, and figure 2 in 84 years. Of course it must be emphasised that this calculation depends on the assumption that the growth curve produced by the model represents the actual growth curve to within acceptable accuracy, and that the estimates in question make a suitable basis for calculation. Any other variable could be used in a similar manner.

As we have observed, all the results so far show steady growth of all subsystems. In fact, in all the experiments described so far, all

320

entries in the matrix are positive. Therefore, (10) holds and all variables must increase at every time step. When all feedbacks are positive, we have a pure growth model. When all feedbacks are negative, we have a pure decay model. Moreover, in the pure growth model, since each variable is increasing, and yet cannot exceed 1, it must level off either at 1 or possibly at some value less than 1. In the following section, we show that only in exceptional cases can the variables approach equilibrium values less than 1. Consequently the expected behaviour is for all variables to follow an S-shaped growth levelling off at 1.

It is clear that no culture system behaves in such a way that all variables increase to some high notional value, and remain indefinitely at this high level. Indeed, as used up to this point, the model, although adequately simulating growth, fails to reflect adequately the property that is most characteristic of all successful culture systems: homeostasis.

A preliminary experiment was to insert some negative values for the indices in one subsystem. Here 'piracy' was imagined as operating negatively on a number of subsystems. (The projective system was omitted in this instance.) The Matrix $C$ is as follows:

|       | Subs. | Met. | Cr.  | Soc. | Tr.  | Pop. | Pir.  |
|-------|-------|------|------|------|------|------|-------|
| Subs. | 0     | 0.50 | 0.50 | 1.00 | 0.75 | 0.75 | −2.00 |
| Met.  | 0     | 0    | 0.75 | 1.00 | 1.00 | 0    | −0.2  |
| Cr.   | 0.50  | 0.75 | 0    | 0.50 | 0.25 | 0.25 | 0.3   |
| Soc.  | 0.25  | 0.75 | 0.50 | 0    | 0    | 0.50 | 0.50  |
| Tr.   | 0.25  | 1.00 | 0.75 | 0.35 | 0    | 0    | −2.0  |
| Pop.  | 0.75  | 0    | 0.10 | 0.85 | 0    | 0    | −0.5  |
| Pir.  | 0.5   | 0.75 | 0.75 | 0.50 | 1.00 | 0.50 | 0     |

All variables were given initial values of 0.3, and the results are shown in figure 4. The negative interactions in this case slow down growth of some variables but do not cause a collapse of the system.

## Range of Behaviour of the Iterates

After a number of trial runs such as the foregoing, it became apparent that a more thorough examination of the properties of the system was required. What behaviour, other than steady growth and steady decay, is possible for the mathematical iteration given by equations (1)–(9)? In attempting to answer this question, we have proceeded in two ways. On the one hand, we have used theoretical

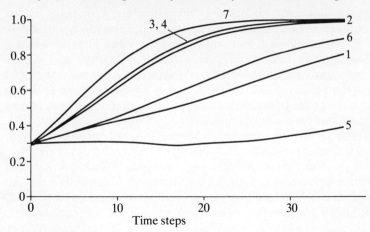

*Figure* 4. Growth pattern of the variables with some negative values for the indices (matrix $C$). All variables have initial value 0.3.

means to locate all possible equilibrium points of the iteration. On the other hand, we have used computer experiments to demonstrate that sustained periodic oscillations can occur.

We begin by describing our results concerning equilibrium states. We let $x$ denote the column vector with components $x_i$, and write $p_i(x, h)$ instead of $p_i$ to emphasise the dependence on $x$ and $h$. Let

$$f_i(x, h) = x_i^{p_i(x, h)} = \begin{cases} \exp[p_i(x, h) \log x_i] & \text{if } x_i > 0 \\ 0 & \text{if } x_i = 0 \end{cases} \tag{11}$$

and let $f(x, h)$ be the vector with components $f_i(x, h)$. Then the iteration (1) has the form

$$x(t + h) = f(x(t), h) \qquad (t = 0, h, \ldots) \tag{12}$$

Suppose that $x(t)$ tends to a constant vector $\hat{x}$ as $t \to \infty$. Then from (2)–(4) we see that $p_i(x(t), h)$ tends to $p_i(\hat{x}, h)$. If $\hat{x}_i > 0$, we also have $\log x_i(t) \to \log \hat{x}_i$ and therefore $f_i(x(t), h)$ tends to $f_i(\hat{x}, h)$. If $x_i(t) > 0$ and $x_i(t)$ tends to $0 = \hat{x}_i$, then $p_i(x(t), h)$ tends to a positive constant and $f_i(x(t), h)$ tends to zero. Therefore, from (11), (12) we deduce that

$$\hat{x} = f(\hat{x}, h) \tag{13}$$

in either case. That is, $\hat{x}$ is a *fixed point* of the iteration defined by (12). The following theorem shows how to find all such fixed points.

*Theorem 1.* Consider the iteration defined by (1)–(4):

(a) if $x(t)$ has all components $x_i(t) \geq 0$ and if $x(t)$ tends to a constant vector $\hat{x}$ as $t \rightarrow \infty$, then (13) is satisfied.

(b) If $\hat{x}$ has all components $\hat{x}_i \geq 0$ and if $\hat{x}$ satisfies (13), then

$$\sum_{j=1}^{m} a_{ij}\hat{x}_j = 0 \qquad \text{for all } i \text{ for which } \hat{x}_i \neq 0 \text{ or } 1 \qquad (14)$$

Conversely, if $\hat{x}$ is a vector for which $\hat{x} \geq 0$ and for which (14) holds for every $i$ for which $\hat{x}_i$ is neither 0 nor 1, then $\hat{x}$ satisfies (13).

*Proof.* Part (a) has already been proved and we turn to part (b). Assume that $\hat{x}_i \geq 0$ and $\hat{x}$ satisfies (13). If $\hat{x}_i \neq 0$, $\hat{x}_i \neq 1$, then from (13) and the definition of $f$, we deduce $p(\hat{x}, h) = 1$. Hence $q = r_i$ and

$$\sum_{k=1}^{m} a^-{}_{ik}\hat{x}_k = \sum_{k=1}^{m} a^+{}_{ik}\hat{x}_k \qquad (15)$$

From this equation, (14) follows. Conversely, let $\hat{x}$ be a vector with $\hat{x} \geq 0$ for which (14) holds. For any $i$ for which $\hat{x} \neq 0$ or 1, we have (15). Therefore, $p_i(\hat{x}, h) = 1$ and $f_i(\hat{x}, h) = \hat{x}_i$. For any $i$ for which $\hat{x}_i = 0$ or 1, we have $f_i(\hat{x}, h) = 0$ or 1 by definition, and again $f_i(\hat{x}, h) = \hat{x}_i$. Thus, (13) holds. This completes the proof.

An important conclusion to be drawn from Theorem 1 is that every equilibrium state (fixed point) of the iteration must have all its components equal to 0 or 1, unless the matrix $A$ satisfies certain linear relations (14). In particular, if $\hat{x}$ is a fixed point with $0 < \hat{x}_i < 1$ for every $i$, then (14) must be satisfied for every $i$. This is equivalent to $A\hat{x} = 0$. Such an $\hat{x}$ therefore exists if and only if $A$ is a singular matrix. This proves the following corollary.

*Corollary.* The iteration has a fixed point $\hat{x}$ with $0 < \hat{x}_i < 1$ for every $i$ if and only if $\det A = 0$.

In general, we expect that the matrix $A$ will be nonsingular, since the set of singular matrices is of 'low dimensionality' or 'probability' among the set of all matrices. Consequently, we can interpret the result as stating that the only equilibrium states $\hat{x}$ possible for the model are those in which at least one component $\hat{x}_i$ equals 0 or 1. That is, some subsystem variable must tend to its minimum or maximum allowable value. The fact that it is impossible to have an equilibrium of the system with all limits $\hat{x}_i$ strictly between 0 and 1 (unless $A$ is singular) seems to indicate that these equations, in their present form, are inappropriate for models in whch equilibrium state are expected. In the following section suggestions are made for extensions that may be more useful in simulation of behaviour over a long time span.

It is possible to analyse the local stability (local attractivity) of the fixed points. However, we omit this discussion here.

We shall now describe a numerical experiment which seems to reveal the presence of periodic behaviour of the iteration. For this purpose it was thought best to simplify by reducing the number of variables. Initially a system was formulated with only three variables (conceived as population, subsistence, and craft technology) controlled by the matrix

$$D = \begin{bmatrix} 0 & 0.5 & -0.9 \\ 0.4 & 0 & 0.2 \\ 0.5 & -0.1 & 0 \end{bmatrix}$$

Figure 5 shows two runs, each made with a time step $h = 0.2$, and with respective initial values (a) 0.23, 0.95, 0.52; and (b) 0.1, 0.1, 0.1. For this matrix there is an equilibrium state with $\hat{x}_1 = {}^2/_5$, $\hat{x}_2 = 1$, $\hat{x}_3 = {}^5/_9$. In both runs, $x_2(t)$ quickly tends to 1, and $x_1(t)$ and $x_3(t)$ oscillate around the values ${}^2/_5$ and ${}^5/_9$, with apparently increasing amplitude.

Figure 6 shows runs made with the slightly altered matrix

$$E = \begin{bmatrix} -0.1 & 0.5 & -0.9 \\ 0.4 & 0 & 0.2 \\ 0.50 & -0.10 & -0.01 \end{bmatrix}$$

There is an equilibrium state $\hat{x}_1 = 1900/9002$, $\hat{x}_2 = 1$, $\hat{x}_3 = 4980/9002$. The runs were made with respective initial values (a) $0.05 + 1900/9002$, 1, 4980/9002; (b) 0.01, 0.5, 0.01; and (c) 0.98, 0.98, 0.05. In all three runs, $x_2(t)$ tends to 1. In (b), $x_1(t)$ and $x_3(t)$ appear to approach periodicity, and in (c) they seem to fall to zero. In the event, fairly complex oscillatory behaviour seems to be possible for iterations of the form under consideration, presumably due to the nonlinearity of the governing equations.

### Extensions and Alterations of the Model

A number of extensions of the model may be considered.

### Interaction Coefficients Varying with Value of Variable

As described earlier each entry $a_{ij}$ in the matrix $A$ is fixed once and for all during an experiment. Although this assumption may be reasonable during the first simple stage of model building, it is clearly inappropriate in any real case in which long-term behaviour

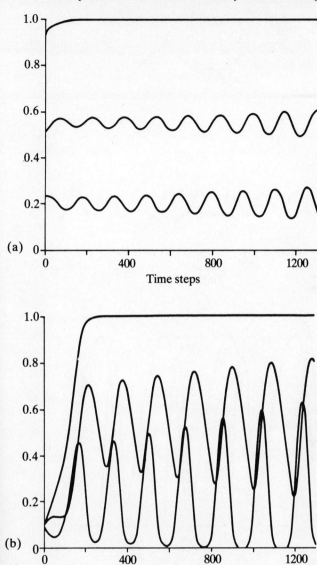

*Figure* 5. Growth pattern of the variables, using three variables with interactions indicated in matrix *D* and initial values (a) 0.23, 0.95, 0.52 and (b) 0.1, 0.1, 0.1.

325

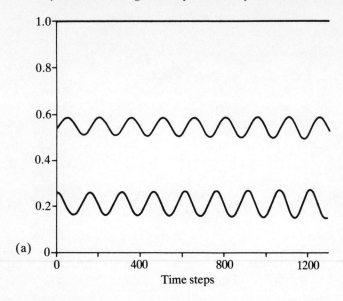

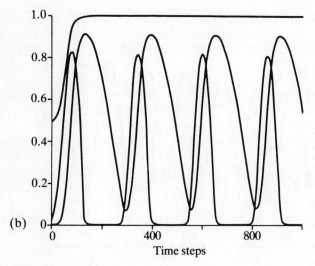

*Figure* 6. Growth behaviour pattern of the variables, with interactions indicated in matrix *E* and with initial values (a) 0.05 + 1900/9002, 1, 4980/9002 (b) 0.01, 0.5, 0.01 (c) 0.98, 0.98, 0.05.

326

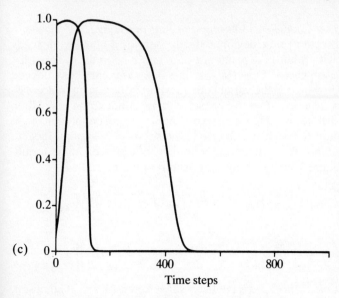

(c)

Time steps

is considered. It may often be the case that an influence is present for small values of a variable but absent for larger values. In some cases the influence could become negative for large values, suggesting some kind of negative feedback. In general, then, the numbers $a_{ij}$ should be allowed to be *state dependent* (i.e., functions of the values of some or all of the variables). In other words, the linear forms in equations (7) and (8) should be replaced by

$$q_i = 1 + h\sum_{k=1}^{m} a^-_{ik}(x)$$

$$r_i = 1 + h\sum_{k=1}^{m} a^+_{ik}(x)$$

where $a_{ik}(x) \equiv a_{ik}(x_1, x_2, \ldots, x_m)$ is an arbitrary function of the variables $x_1, x_2, \ldots, x_m$, and where $a^+_{ik}(x) = a_{ik}(x)$ for $a_{ik}(x) > 0$ and $a^-_{ik}(x) = |a_{ik}(x)|$ for $a_{ik}(x) < 0$. In practice, one might begin by taking $a_{ik}(x)$ to be a quadratic function of $x_k$ only, for example,

$$a_{ik} = (1 - c_{ik}x_k)x_k$$

No investigation of such models has been undertaken so far by us, although one can readily visualise that, with suitably formulated relationships, the stability of the system could be attained.

327

*Interaction Coefficients Varying with Rate of Change of Variables*
The difficulties in achieving a steady rate, or a number of steady
states, with a linear dependence of $q_i$ and $r_i$ upon the value of the
variable suggested the idea that in some cases they may depend
rather on whether the variable in question is increasing or decreasing. For instance, if we are considering the influence of population
on subsistence production, a stable, nonchanging population might
be thought to induce no change in the subsistence system. Indeed,
when we are trying to set up a homeostatic system, some formulation of the following form may be appropriate:

$$q_i = 1 + \tfrac{1}{2}h\sum_{k=1}^{m} \left\{ \left| a_{ik} + \frac{b_{ik}}{x_k}\frac{dx_k}{dt} \right| - \left( a_{ik} + \frac{b_{ik}}{x_k}\frac{dx_k}{dt} \right) \right\} x_k$$

$$r_i = 1 + \tfrac{1}{2}h\sum_{k=1}^{m} \left\{ \left| a_{ik} + \frac{b_{ik}}{x_k}\frac{dx_k}{dt} \right| + \left( a_{ik} + \frac{b_{ik}}{x_k}\frac{dx_k}{dt} \right) \right\} x_k$$

Equations of this kind have been suggested by Kane, Thompson,
and Vertinsky. We have not yet investigated such models. In a
discrete time simulation, the derivatives $dx_k/dt$ can be approxi-
mated by finite differences. A listing of a large FORTRAN program
for systems of this type has been published by Thompson, Vertinsky
and Kane (1974).
*Time Lags.* In many systems, changes in the present are determined
not by the current values of variables but by their values some time
in the past. This can easily be built into the model by allowing $q_i$ and
$r_i$ to depend not only on $x_k(t)$ but also on $x_k$ a given number of time
steps earlier.
*Alternative Forms of Equation (1).* Although the iteration equations
(1)–(4) have certain convenient features, a number of other formulations in terms of differential and difference equations are possible.
Some of these may be more useful by allowing 'physical' interpretation of the parameters and by allowing the insertion of equations
which reflect the supposed interactions more realistically and in
more detail. A number of different mathematical formulations
should be tried and compared.
*Sensitivity Analysis.* In evaluating a model such as the one described
here, it is usually important to conduct a sensitivity analysis. That is,
one endeavours to see how great the variation is in various performance measures when the parameters of the model are varied by a
designated amount. We have not carried out such an analysis for the

present model since we feel that the whole structure of the model is still under investigation.

## Further Outlook

In the present early stage of development, the model proposed cannot be regarded as simulating in any meaningful sense the early development of Aegean civilisation. That specific cultural context has simply been used as the starting point for the formulation of a much more general model, and the exploration of some of its properties.

Indeed, the foregoing discussion allows us to consider more clearly what sort of behaviour would be required of such a model in order that we should feel its behaviour modelled satisfactorily some aspects of the behaviour of the real world. At least four may be suggested:

1. The rate of change and behaviour of the variables should be consonant with that of the limits in the range of real behaviour which they represent.

2. The model should display homeostatic behaviour, in the sense not of absolutely stable states, but of periods of very gradual change.

3. The model should display sustained growth under certain circumstances.

4. Ideally it should also display threshold effects – that is, periods of sustained and fairly rapid growth between periods of relative stability.

We suggest that this approach brings out in an informative way a number of the difficulties inherent in models of system dynamics. In particular it suggests that lengthy discussions of input (or output) data can usefully be deferred until the range of behaviour of the model, when subjected to a wide variety of input data, has been examined and found plausible. Already this approach has led us to consider more closely the mechanism of homeostasis within the culture system. And already it has led us to feel more acutely the danger of ascribing to the real world aspects of model behaviour which instead arise from the constraints built into the model. We were particularly struck by the difficulty in simulating homeostatic behaviour with this model when the values of the coefficients were constant. Indeed it occurred to us to wonder whether this is not a limitation which applies also, although for different reasons, to the model, based on the work of Forrester, used for the study *The Limits of Growth* (Meadows *et al.* 1972). It is apparently the case that not one of the variables studied there in a number of different simulations reaches a steady state within the time span considered, until the population is artificially and externally held constant (ibid. 160).

The aim of the present work is indeed to arrive at (approximately) steady states, but these should arise from the interactions of the variables rather than be imposed quite arbitrarily from the outside.

[1979]

## Acknowledgement

We are grateful to Mr Eric V. Level for his assistance with the computer simulations for this project.

## Bibliography

Binford, L. R. and S. R., eds. (1968) *New Perspectives in Archaeology*, Chicago, Aldine.

Clarke, D. L., ed. (1972) *Models in Archaeology*, London, Methuen.

Cooke, K. (1973) A model of urbanization and civilization, University of Southern California, Dept. of Elect. Engr. Tech. Report No. RB 73–34.

Kane, J. (1972) A primer for a new cross-impact language – KSIM, *Technological Forecasting and Social Change*, 4, 129–42.

Kane, J., W. Thompson and I. Vertinsky (1972) Health care delivery: a policy simulator, *Socio-Economic Planning Sciences*, 6, 283–93.

Kane, J., I. Vertinsky and W. Thompson (1973) KSIM: a methodology for interactive resource policy simulation, *Water Resources Research*, 9, 65–79.

Meadows, D. H., D. L. Meadows, J. Randers and W. W. Behrens (1972) *The Limits to Growth*, London, Pan.

Plog, F. T. (1974) *The Study of Prehistoric Change*, New York, Academic Press.

Renfrew, C. (1972) *The Emergence of Civilization*, London, Methuen.

— ed. (1973) *The Explanation of Culture Change: Models in Prehistory*, London, Duckworth.

Rosen, R. (1972) The simplest dynamical models, Occasional paper, Center for the Study of Democratic Institutions, Santa Barbara.

— (1973) A framework for 'retrospective futurology,' Occasional paper, Center for the Study of Democratic Institutions, Santa Barbara, 4 October 1973.

Spengler, O. (1918) *The Decline of the West*.

Thompson, W. A., L. Vertinsky and J. Kane (1974) KSIM – Policy simulation: User's Manual, *International Technical Cooperation Centre Review*, 3, 57–81.

Toynbee, A. J. (1947) *A Study of History*, Oxford, University Press.

Wilkinson, J., R. Bellman and R. Garaudy (1973) The Dynamic Programming of Human Systems, Occasional paper, Center for the Study of Democratic Institutions, Santa Barbara.

# 12

## THE SIMULATOR AS
## DEMIURGE

*

*Demiurge*: (Greek *demios*, for the people, *ergos*, work): 1a,
a Platonic subordinate deity who fashions the sensible world
in the light of eternal ideas; 1b, a Gnostic subordinate deity
who is the creator of the material world; 2, something that is
an autonomous creative force or decisive power.

*Chambers Twentieth Century Dictionary*

Systems thinking has increasingly been regarded as an essential
component of archaeological theory since its introduction to the
subject nearly two decades ago (Binford 1962). Yet despite the
undoubted attractions of simulating the past, usually within some
appropriate systems framework, simulations in this field have so far
been rather few in number (Thomas 1972, Cordell 1975 and Zubrow 1975 being among the first). Only very recently has system
dynamics modelling been applied to past cultural systems (Hosler,
Sabloff and Runge 1977; Shantzis and Behrens 1973).

It is the very essence of simulation modelling that the simulator
creates a device which will produce some representation of reality.
A good simulation mimics reality closely. But a successful simulation is rarely achieved at the first attempt. If at first you don't
succeed you try again, modifying or tuning the device to give a
better – that is, closer to real – output. The simulator proceeds in
some senses very much like an inventor, trying to get his infernal
device to work. The theoretical content of his creation is often not
altogether clear, being sometimes implicit in the structure of his
invention, rather than set out in advance, neatly and explicitly, in
the form of a number of theoretical relationships.

These two aspects – the frequent necessity for successive attempts
before it 'works,' and the deliberate anticipation of 'unexpected'
behaviour – often combine to make systems modelling seem a very

creative process, in which the new creation has behaviour, indeed, almost a life, of its own. It is this aspect, which often makes systems modelling seem such an exciting undertaking, that prompts the title to this chapter.

Some time ago I pointed out that 'the logical structure of a system model . . . differs fundamentally from that of a hypothetico-deductive explanation' (Renfrew 1973, 1929), and, as several commentators have stressed (Flannery 1973, 51; Perlman 1977, 321), it is important not to become caught up too readily in any preconceived notion as to what logical form a scientific explanation *must* take. Recent excessive emphasis on one specific explanatory mode, the Hempel-Oppenheim covering law model, has risked elevating to dogma what should be no more than informative precept. As Binford (1977, 6) states of theory building: 'This is a creative process for which there are no methodological rules to ensure success.'

Bell (1981) has rightly emphasized the importance of being aware of the procedures by which our models may be compared with reality, thus allowing them to be verified or refuted. Such procedures are the hallmark of empirical science, providing the criterion which distinguishes it from mere metaphysical speculation. Yet problems remain here which still await clarification. That is, indeed, one of the fascinations of this field, which is clearly at a very creative stage of development.

## Systems and Systems Thinking

The systemic approach has been widely advocated in archaeology (Wood and Matson 1973; Munton 1973; Hill 1977a), and a number of optimistic claims have been made, many with good justification. But there have been evident confusions so that terms like Systems Theory, General Systems Theory, System Dynamics, and Systems Thinking are employed almost interchangeably. That perhaps in part excuses the almost entirely negative critique, 'What can systems theory do for archaeology?' recently contributed by a philosopher (Salmon 1978), who does not make these relevant distinctions. In discussing the systemic approach to archaeology, it may be useful to try to distinguish between

1) *Systems Thinking:* A general philosophical approach to the subject, an *intuitional framework* within which specific problems may be tackled;

2) *General Systems Theory:* A consideration, initiated by von Bertalanffy, of the various properties and behaviours shared by a wide range of superficially very different systems;

3) *Mathematical Systems Theory:* An explicit body of mathematical theory which (in common with System Dynamics Modelling) may be regarded as a special aspect or branch of the Theory of Dynamics Systems (see 5 below). It entails the mathematical theory of feedback control systems and optimal control, much used by engineers, but so far has little direct relevance to archaeological problems.

4) *System Dynamics Modelling:* The approach pioneered by Forrester and his colleagues of expressing the behaviour of a complex system by a large number of equations of state and of using the computer to calculate the successive values through time of all relevant parameters by means of these equations, hence achieving a simulation; and the

5) *Theory of Dynamical Systems:* The broad undertaking of mathematicians to create a theory for all systems that evolve according to a dynamical law. These are generally described either by differential equations or by difference equations, whose solutions may be studied by qualitative as well as quantitative methods. Although there are as yet no explicit archaeological formulations using this framework, the methods are of such power and relevance that significant progress is to be anticipated.

Let it be at once acknowledged, as Salmon (1978) has rightly stressed, that there is no single body of explicit formulations called Systems Theory which is ready and available for application to elucidate the behaviour of humans or cultures. On the other hand, there is already, at this early stage, a good deal of useful experience available.

*Systems Thinking* constitutes in my view the most important advance in archaeology in recent years. It implies the use of series of concepts that are now becoming familiar and, one may hope, through that familiarity, are emerging as something more than mere jargon expressions. Among these important notions are: closed system, open system, subsystem, input, output, trajectory, negative feedback, positive feedback, homeostasis, stable and unstable equilibrium, steady state, state variable, flow rate, morphogenesis, transformation, exogeneous and endogenous inputs, variety, equifinality, and so forth.

The value of such an approach and such terms is simply that, for the first time, they offer a framework and a language for the analysis of complex entities, such as societies, organizations, or cultures, in a manner that allows a direct and simple treatment without denying the difficulties inherent in such a task.

The underlying ideas are obvious enough, like most good ideas, when one has acquired a familiarity with them. But to measure the gain, it is sufficient to make comparison with the level of explanation which preceded their introduction. In archaeology, this often amounted to little more than a bald narrative of a sequence of events, often given a false coherence in the light of a diffusionist interpretation. If anyone doubts the value of systems thinking, let him make comparison with almost any purported explanations in the archaeological literature offered prior to 1960 (although every archaeologist could compile his own short list of honourable exceptions).

Systemic ideas were introduced to archaeology by Binford (1962) and set out with great coherence by Clarke (1968); they have already inspired a number of studies (Flannery 1968, Renfrew 1972, Plog 1974). No well-organized body of theory is implied, although it is not necessarily excluded. Rather, systems thinking is simply an approach to the world within one intuitional framework, which implies the exclusion of others that are incompatible with it. Such a framework is, of course, implicit within both General Systems Theory and System Dynamics modelling and is common to simulation in general.

*General Systems Theory*, originated by von Bertalanffy (see von Bertalanffy 1950), is concerned with the formal correspondence of general principles in the behaviour of systems, irrespective of the kind of relations or forces between the components. As such, it goes far beyond the scope of the anthropologist or archaeologist, although patterns may indeed be observed in cultural systems which are common to those of other kinds. Exponential growth and logistic growth are well-known examples (Hamblin, Jacobsen, and Miller 1973).

A similar although more restricted intention underlies the work of a number of anthropologists who seek to make general statements about the behaviour of sociocultural systems (see Flannery 1972; Rathje 1975; Gall and Saxe 1977; Athens 1977; Cherry 1978; Renfrew 1979). The concern here is limited, of course, to systems composed of human societies, but with this limitation, the aim is, indeed, very general.

It would be a mistake to claim that very much has yet been achieved along this path but a still graver one to deny the importance of the undertaking, for the aim here is close to that to which Binford (1968a, 27) many years ago inspired: 'Our ultimate goal is the formulation of laws of cultural dynamics.' Today this need not be read as implying that the formulation will be in a strictly Hempelian lawlike form, nor indeed in any anatomization of a system into specific subsystems. That the goal is as yet dimly perceived does not make it any the less real. To dismiss General Systems Theory on the grounds that it does not measure up to some *a priori* concept of 'theory' risks discarding the conceptual baby with the philosophical bath water.

*Mathematical Systems Theory* is a well-developed field, where the behaviour of precisely defined control systems is subjected to rigorous analysis. Like System Dynamics modelling, it may be seen as a special branch of the Theory of Dynamical Systems. Here the consideration centres on the input and output of a conversional device which lies between them – often a control mechanism. The distinction between Mathematical Systems Theory and the Theory of Dynamical Systems is lucidly expressed by Berlinski (1976, 110) in writing of the former:

> The fundamental systems here are much like dynamical systems. The method by which engineering objects are classified, moreover, mirrors the organization of the theory of differential equations. But it would be a mistake to dismiss the differences between engineering and dynamical systems: engineering is preeminently a concern for the relationship between inputs and outputs, while the mathematical focus of the theory of dynamical systems is on the equations themselves and the models in which they are satisfied.

Usually feedback control is employed, and often optimization procedures to minimize total expenditure or energy, or to operate in least time. Such work can trace its origin back to the same interest in cybernetics (Wiener 1948, Ashby 1956) which is ancestral to much current systems thinking. But it appears to have little to offer archaeology at present, its explicitly formulated problems are not our problems, and few of ours can ever hope to be given definitive formal solutions in this way.

A comparable formulation has nonetheless been attempted in the study of political science by Easton (1965), and the same schema of the archaeologist's culture systems as a 'black box' was set out by Leach (1973, 66). The archaeological or anthropological cases are much less rigorously defined, however, than those of the control engineer, and for this reason are more profitably discussed within the more general framework of the Theory of Dynamical Systems.

*Systems Dynamics Modelling* involves a particular approach to the problems of dynamical systems devised by Forrester (1961,

1969, 1971). Dynamic behaviour simply means behaviour analysed with time as an important variable. There can be many kinds of dynamical systems models, all of them giving explicit formulations for the behaviour of a system through time. System Dynamics models represent a subset of this general field of dynamical systems models, whereby a real and rather complex system is modelled by a complicated structure rich in feedback loops. The components are accumulations or reservoirs, measured by a level (state) variable, between which there is activity measured by a rate (flow) variable. An equation is written for each component of the system stating (predicting) its level or rate at the next point in time in terms of the present levels or rates of all the other components. The computer uses these numerous equations to calculate the values for all these state and flow variables at the next point in time, given the initial values. Then it proceeds to do the same again for the next time point, and so, by a series of iterations, the values of all the variables of the system are simulated.

The model discussed by Zubrow (1981) is a good example, displaying the rather complicated 'spaghetti-and-meatballs' network of flows and interrelations common to such constructions. Despite their apparent complexity, they certainly produce clear results.

The construction of such a model does not necessarily imply any remarkably original theoretical insights. It can be simply a systematic and painstakingly explicit analysis of a familiar if rather complicated situation. But Forrester (1973) has effectively made the point that the behaviour of such complex systems is often counter-intuitive. The whole is greater than its parts. The value of the technique as a research tool lies precisely in this counter-intuitive behaviour.

*The Theory of Dynamical Systems* is a general approach to the problem of change that, in a sense, subsumes the more specific concerns of Mathematical Systems Theory and System Dynamics modelling as defined above but is not limited by the specific assumptions and concerns which serve to define them more closely. It entails the attempt, by specifying the influences causing short-term changes, to derive the long-term behaviour of the system, and involves the use of difference equations or differential equations.

The state of the system is the smallest collection of numbers that must be specified in order to predict uniquely the system's behaviour: the variables in question are related by means of a set of differential equations. The solutions of the equations allow, or would allow, the prediction of the future behaviour of the system.

336

But the solutions of many sets of differential equations cannot be found quantitively, and it is the *qualitative* study of the differential solutions and their properties, interpreted geometrically, which often proves enlightening.

The approach, and its archaeological potential, has been lucidly set out by Cooke (1979), and considered by Berlinski (1976, 47–51), as a preliminary to his critique of System Dynamics modelling undertaken by Forrester and Meadows. The mathematical literature, which extends back a century to the pioneering work of Poincaré, is extensive (see Chillingworth 1976). Yet despite its technical difficulty for the nonmathematician, some aspects of this approach are accessible to archaeologists: the use of phase portraits to illustrate the geometrical properties of trajectories is clear and illuminating at a general level. In this way, one is brought to grips with such fundamental notions as equilibrium, stability, periodic and recurrent motions, attractors, bifurcation, and other important ideas to which the mathematics naturally gives rise.

Living systems, including culture systems, exhibit such modes of behaviour and properties as these, and the opportunities offered by Dynamical Systems Theory to examine such behaviour in the most abstract way possible is valuable. It leads naturally to the preoccupations of mathematical biologists such as Rosen (1979) or Waddington (1977), with which archaeologists are discovering much in common. Catastrophe theory, for example, may be regarded as a branch of the Theory of Dynamic Systems. Important concepts arising from this approach, such as the notion of the chreod and of the epigenetic landscape (Waddington 1977, 103–14), will be found highly relevant to the long-term behaviour of human societies.

Archaeological applications have hardly yet been developed, but in the adjacent field of ecology, the elegant investigation of the predator-prey relationship through the Volterra-Lotka equations (Maynard-Smith 1974, 19–27) suggests how fruitful this general approach can be in practical cases. Equations of comparable form are now being used as models of interaction between two human groups rather than between two species (Cooke and Freedman n.d.), and other explorations using similar approaches are sure to follow.

It seems noteworthy that the pessimism of Berlinski (1976) concerning existing systems analysis in the social, political, and biological sciences does not appear to be directed either toward Dynamical Systems Theory or its application in ecology. My own optimism is based, on the one hand, on the appropriateness of systems thinking for the expression of archaeological problems and, on the other, on the apparent suitability of Dynamical Systems Theory for investigating relationships expressed in systems terms. Nonetheless a gap remains to be bridged: either archaeologists must learn more mathematics (and the right kind of mathematics) or mathematicians must prove willing to immerse themselves in the theoretical preoccupations of modern archaeology.

From the above, it will be seen that the 'systemic approach' can mean a number of different things, and that these should be carefully distinguished. Of course, the term 'system' can be defined in a multitude of different ways, but its chief value in archaeology is in its applicability to the very elaborate complex of interactions which any sociocultural entity represents, which can always be subdivided into a number of subsystems, each meriting analysis in its own right. It is this very complexity which makes the systems approach, with its own flexibility and ability to cope with elaboration, so useful.

This may not be the occasion on which to take issue in detail with what I feel are the problems arising from Salmon's treatment of this general topic. One feature is the apparent equation of mathematical models in general with systems theory in particular. Mathematical Systems Theory is one very specific and perhaps rather minor branch of mathematics. To say of the whole general class of mathematical models used to describe the real world, as exemplified by the simple Gas Law $PV = RT$, 'the classification of such models is thus an important part of Mathematical Systems Theory' (Salmon 1978, 179), may introduce a confusion. The treatment of mathematical models in general is certainly provocative. 'Mathematical models, even when they fit, do not in and of themselves constitute satisfactory explanations' (1978, 182). My main objection to such a statement is not so much that it is questionable (as I believe) but that it has little specific bearing upon the role of systems theory as such in archaeology.

## The Nature of Simulation

Simulations differ in procedure and purpose. Only a few of them fall within the class of System Dynamics models, including the example set out by Zubrow (1981) and the instance presented by Sabloff (Hosler, Sabloff and Runge 1977). Many simulations – particularly those of high complexity – are nonetheless approached within the intuitional framework of systems thinking, but this is certainly not a precondition for a simulation study.

The whole field of simulation, in archaeology and beyond had been thoroughly reviewed by Aldenderfer (1981a), the first such comprehensive survey, and only a few comments are required here.

First, it may be useful to distinguish between two classes of simulation, although many examples fall within both. In the first class, the *output* alone represents the simulation, while the procedures used to obtain it do not set out to mimic those of the real world. The output is thus a *simulacrum*, a representation of reality produced by the simulation. Interest focuses upon the relationship, the goodness of fit, between the simulacrum and the real data set which is being simulated.

An example of such a simulation is the XTENT model (chapter 3, above), by which the computer draws a political map, for instance of modern Europe, plotting in the notional boundaries, given only the location and size of the major cities, without information as to their territorial affiliation. The output is a map, the simulacrum which is to be compared with the real map (or, in archaeological cases, to be used as an approximation to a political map). But the procedures used to reach the conclusion do not follow the real course of events in time; this is not a dynamical model.

In the second class of model, it is not the final state, the terminal output at the last time point, which particularly interests us, but the sequence of events in time. The successive sequence of events experienced by the model is supposed to mirror those experienced in the real world: the real trajectory is *mimicked* by that of the model. Moreover the very computations undertaken in the course of the simulation correspond, at least notionally, to real activities. As Bell has said: 'Every transformation in the computer is also going on out there in the world.' Such is certainly the case for all System Dynamics models, including Zubrow's and Aldenderfer's ABSIM simulation (1981b).

It is arguable, therefore, that any simulation, to qualify as such, must produce as output a pattern representing the real world at a given point in time (that is, a simulacrum). Otherwise it must mimic the world by undergoing a series of operations, each of which has a real-world analog and by producing a series of values representing the trajectory through time of one or more state variables of the system.

Procedures which do not show one or the other (or both) of these features may well require a great elaboration of calculations to reach a final output value, but they are computations, not simulations.

During the discussion of Cordell's Wetherill Mesa analysis (Cordell 1975, 1981), the interesting methodological question was introduced as to whether the procedure used is, in the strict sense, a simulation. Low (1981) raised the point, suggesting that it might rather be seen as a procedure for *calculating* abandonments. The input is a time series, employing the dendroclimatic data of Fritts and others, and Cordell formulated rules by which the suitability for settlement of different areas of land in the study region could be assessed given the varying climatic data, hence allowing quantitative data for abandonment to be predicted. Sabloff, replying to Low, argued on the other hand that this should be regarded as simulation, since a real process is being replicated.

The discussion proved illuminating, focusing on the presence or absence of feedback within the model, feedback being seen by some as an essential ingredient of a simulation model. It was pointed out that if the past system-state has any bearing on the present system-state, then feedback is operating. Models which are completely input-driven need not have any feedback component. But a continuous trajectory – a feature of all living systems – is not possible without feedback.

The other notable feature of the Wetherhill Mesa case is its extraordinary success rate. The predictions for inhabited sites with consecutive occupations, for successive phase transitions, compared with those observed in the field, were respectively 98.6, 96.6, 90.0 and 100.0 per cent. In this sense, it must surely be one of the most successful predictive models in the history of archaeology.

The same question of status, with respect to simulation, was raised in relation to some of Day's economic analyses (1981). In some cases, although successive system states could be completed graphically by iteration, the terminal state of the system was directly predicted by the analysis as much as by the iteration procedure. The question is perhaps ultimately a verbal one, and interest focused on the power of this approach to clarify issues and make predictions in a manner which raised no objections from the 'substantivist' anthropologists present.

In common with recent work by Reidhead (1976) and Keene (1979), Day's work appears to transcend the rather arid debate between 'formalist' and 'substantivist' economic anthropologists and may prove the forerunner to the general (and long overdue) application of formal economic models to early societies. The application advocated by Day of recursive programming – that is to say, successive optimization procedures employing feedback – offers a

340

very appropriate model both for the process of human learning and development at the individual level, and of the developing adjustment of a culture system to its environment. Recursive programming could clearly be used to simulate the developing subsistence and economic strategies of the community or culture against a background of environmental change, both directional and stochastic. Moreover, with its emphasis on cognitive aspects, on the process of 'learning' which a system undergoes as it adapts, the approach goes beyond rigidly deterministic models.

Three very different objectives were evident among the simulations discussed. The first, exemplified by Cordell's work, was the desire to obtain output data that would closely match the data collected in the field for the real case. The object of the simulation here is to offer a test to the underlying assumptions and theory, from which the algorithm for the simulation has been derived. As K.L. Cooke (1981) has concisely pointed out, the sequence of operation in such cases is always concept→theory→algorithm→simulation run→output→test.

It should be stressed that many simulations involve the use of a stochastic process. In this way, a rather elaborate body of data can be generated, using very simple underlying rules together with the stochastic input. This was not a feature of Cordell's model as expounded, but the procedure is seen in most models where spatial pattern is generated. At the end of the simulation, the output is usually compared with the real data.

Aldenderfer's Aboriginal Simulation (ABSIM) model (1981b) avowedly had a different objective. His ultimate aim was to generate data which could then be used to test taxonomic methods upon which he was working. Here is an unusual case where the output is to be used, in its own right, for further procedures, rather than to be tested against real data, as is more often the case.

For us, however, the ABSIM model had a different interest, and the taxonomic procedures for the investigation of which it was originally designed were neither presented nor discussed. Instead, interest focused upon a third use of simulation studies: simulation as a heuristic exercise. Here the desire to simulate the processes of lithic assemblage formation led to a very careful formal analysis of the factors involved, in a manner more explicit and precise than had hitherto been undertaken. There is no doubt that the discipline imposed by constructing a simulation procedure, such as can form the basis for a satisfactory algorithm, brings to light interesting hidden problems which remain hidden in less painstaking investigations. As an aid to clear thought about processes – whether formation processes or culture processes of other kinds – the construction of a simulation has considerable heuristic value.

The fourth function of a simulation, discussed in the next section, is more open-ended than these, which are concerned chiefly (a) with testing the further implications of a number of initial assumptions; (b) with investigating these assumptions more deeply; or simply (c) with generating data for other purposes. The framework can, however, be considerably broader.

### The Simulator as Demiurge

PRODUCER: And where's the script?

FATHER: It is in us, sir. *(The actors laugh.)* The drama is in us. We are the drama and we are impatient to act it – so fiercely does our inner passion urge us on.

Once the characters are alive . . . Once they are standing truly alive before their author . . . He does nothing but allow the words and gestures they suggest to him . . . And he must want them to be what they want themselves to be. When a character is born he immediately acquires such an independence . . . Even of his own author . . . That everyone can imagine him a whole host of situations in which his author never thought of placing him . . . They can even imagine his acquiring, sometimes, a significance that the author never thought of giving him.

Luigi Pirandello
*Six Characters in Search of an Author* (1954, 11, 58)

It is one thing to make certain assumptions, posit certain relationships, and construct a device that will follow these and explore their implications. That, as discussed in the preceding section, implies working within a well-defined frame of reference. It is quite another undertaking to seize upon certain ideas as component parts, to fit them together without any clear notion of exactly where they may lead, and to use the simulation as a means of exploration toward lands as yet uncharted. In this sense, the simulator is like an inventor, creating a device about whose behaviour and properties he is far from certain. He does not know where his brainchild may lead him: possibly in directions remote from his expectation.

Perhaps the most exciting moment in simulation modelling is when the machine is ready for lift-off. As the system proceeds through its dynamic trajectory, it can develop modes of behaviour which in Forrester's term are 'counter-intuitive' (Forrester 1973), and wander off, like the utensils bewitched by the Sorcerer's Apprentice or like Count Frankenstein's monster, into unexpected system states.

Zubrow's interesting work (1981) catches something of this spirit. He has employed Forrester's *Urban Dynamics* model without any very thoroughgoing scrutiny of the underlying theory or assumptions. Instead, he has taken considerable care that the equations for each component should be modified so as to be as appropriate as possible to ancient Rome, and he has gone to some trouble to provide suitable input data. Then it is a case of 'Chocks away, and clear for take-off.'

Zubrow terms his simulation a heuristic device, but I am not sure that this is the correct term. For the task here is not one simply of clarification or illumination or instruction. The exercise is more one of exploration than of elucidation, and the simulator is the inventor of an exploratory mechanism that goes ahead to fashion a simulacrum of the sensible world in the light of his ideas; Zubrow has (like Count Frankenstein) almost the status of demiurge.

The machine which he has created can, indeed, appear to have a life of its own, and thus it is not at all surprising that the simulator should find himself able to fashion and fit together certain components without being able to see where their interactions may lead them. Something of the same feeling of creating the components and then letting them get on with it was expressed by the playwright Pirandello in the construction of his comedy *Six Characters in Search of an Author*. The characters, created by him, had their own logic of behaviour, and the scenario was conceived as the playing out by these characters of their roles, with consequences which, although perhaps in a sense implicit within them, could not be or were not foreseen at the outset.

There is a genuine feeling of creation here. And the nub is this very quality of unexpectedness and unpredictability. For, as in any real and original act of creation, the qualities and potential of the product are not obvious or completely specified at the moment of formation; rather, they remain to be realized during the effective lifespan of the created object.

One point of great interest here is the methodological one. The simulator is not simply testing a hypothesis – in Zubrow's case, he avowedly was not taking explicit theoretical statements as his starting point. On the contrary, the procedure is to construct a system and see what happens. Yet this is not just building a device for its own sake: the exercise remains a simulation in that comparison with the real world is intended. The model becomes a successful one precisely when its behaviour in some respects resembles that of the real world.

In an interesting way, the usual systematic procedures, as set out in standard works on scientific method, are here reversed. In this case, the sequence is not to proceed from theory to deduction, to comparison with real data, to refutation or validation. When the fit between output (simulacrum) and real data is not a good one, the mismatch will not lead to automatic rejection of the generating model but rather to modifications in its structure, to produce a more closely comparable output. (It remains nonetheless true that if, after repeated improvements and modifications, the model is still not able to produce an output adequately resembling reality, it will probably be discarded.)

In many ways, here the activity is more akin to experiment ('Research and Development') than to the testing of pre-existing hypotheses. The model is being used as an exploratory device, and although there must still be underlying equations of state, they need not necessarily be exhaustively considered, nor even explicitly known, before the simulation is undertaken.

This view of the simulator in a creative role, rather than simply as a researcher using simulation in a highly controlled way to test the implications of pre-existing and carefully formulated hypotheses, may seem a shade imaginative. No doubt there is a risk of exaggerating the apparent autonomy in the behaviour of the simulation. The behaviour, it will be argued, is always implicit in the equations of state which govern the behaviour of the system which has been constructed, even if these equations have not been fully analysed at the outset.

Nonetheless, the methodological point made above and at the beginning of this chapter does have a certain validity. System dynamics modelling, and no doubt certain other simulation procedures, do make it possible for the model to be logically (and in reality) prior to the theory.

As an example, I should like to refer to a simulation exercise undertaken some years age by Cooke and myself, with the assistance of Level (Cooke and Renfrew 1979; see chapter 11 above). The starting point was a systemic model concerned with the emergence and development of early Aegean civilization (Renfrew 1972). Subsystem interactions, involving seven subsystems, were summarized in matrix form. When all these interactions were positive, the simulation showed the system as a whole to grow and develop with increasing rapidity. When a number of these interactions were now given negative value (implying both negative feedback and some continuing depletions in the system), the system in some cases, after a period of initial growth, suffered drastic collapse, in the manner to which we have become accustomed from Forrester's *Urban Dynamics* studies, and more particularly from the World Model popularized by the Club of Rome (Meadows *et al.* 1972).

Since the initial values which we were using, as well as most of the matrix coefficients, were highly hypothetical, we did not take this as an unduly adverse judgement on the viability of the Aegean culture system in the past or subsequently. Instead, we reduced the number of subsystems in order to reach some clearer understanding of what was causing the long-term instability of the system. It proved effectively impossible, using the model, to simulate a behaviour for the system which would have long-term stability. Subsequent formal analysis by Cooke showed that there were in fact only a very few equilibrium states for the system, other than those where the coefficients were either zero or infinitely large. In practice these were unstable states, since any small perturbation – which is inevitable as a result of 'noise' in a simulation procedure – results in a departure from the equilibrium and either a collapse or an 'explosion' (move toward infinite values) for the system. Oscillatory behaviour, however, is possible.

Here, then, is a case where behaviour unexpected by us emerged from the simulation. Further analysis was able to give explicit theoretical understanding of that behaviour.

Two further points of interest emerged here. In the first place, the experience led us to ask to what extent the unstable behaviour of the *Limits to Growth* model (Meadows *et al.* 1972) is a behaviour mode specific to that particular model – quite independent of the specific initial values used as input. If it should prove to have the inherently unstable behaviour shown analytically by Cooke to be a property of our own model, much of the discussion surrounding it, and certainly all the effort which has gone into the appropriate estimation of suitable initial values for the state variables, could be seen to be misplaced. The world may indeed be doomed to end, but the matter is not further illuminated by choosing for the world a model whose only terminal state is collapse. It follows that with any model it is important to test the full range of its behaviour modes, with a wide range of different estimates for the parameters involved, before imagining that it is simulating anything but its own behaviour.

The second point arises from this. At what stage is it appropriate to imagine such a model as simulating more than its own behaviour? The simulator is, of course, quite at liberty to give names to certain

345

variables in his equation: 'Let $x_1$ indicate population density, $x_2$ the rate of inflow of labour to the city', and so forth. But at precisely what point should these instructions be regarded as reasonable, and when should it be felt plausible that the model is making statements about the real world, or bearing on the real world? Zubrow has tellingly spoken of 'the willing suspension of disbelief.' When the model can produce so great a richness of behaviour that it is, in many ways, an effective simulation of the real world, there are now philosophical/methodological problems to be considered, indeed perhaps a new chapter to be written in the philosophy of science. The theatrical metaphor is not inappropriate, and there is an uncomfortable analogy between the simulator-demiurge and the dramaturge.

### Long-Term Change: Evolutionary Machines?

The archaeologist has the opportunity to concern himself with long-term change, and hence with problems that only rarely confront many of those undertaking simulation in other disciplines. The consideration of long-term change, indeed, soon highlights the shortcomings of any explanatory model where the range of behaviour is in some ways predetermined at the outset. I have recently made this point elsewhere (Renfrew 1979, 37), and reproduce a table (table 1) intended to show that working *within* such a model is not enough; a way must be found to generate changes in structure. This would appear to be one of the current limitations of most dynamical systems modelling.

*Table* 1. The difficulty of modelling long-term change.

| Approach | Short-term change | Long-term growth: Morphogenesis |
|---|---|---|
| Game theory | Different actual moves, different constraints | Different strategies, different utilities, different rules |
| System dynamics | Changes in value for flow and state variables, and for constraints in model equations of state | Changes in components of system, new feedback loops, new equations of state |
| Directed graphs | Transition to successive states | Radical changes in transition probabilities/times/costs. Possible addition of new states |
| Interaction matrix | Changing strengths of interactions between variables | Introduction of new variables |

It is, however, a point addressed by Day in his discussion of meta-adaptation 'in which rules of behaviour or the population of agents, or both, are variables' (Day 1981). The problem is to explain structural changes taking place within the system that result in patterns of growth which are more than simply change in scale. Ideally we should like to see the model itself *generate* precisely these changes in its own structure. It is not enough simply to state thresholds beyond which different behaviour modes will take place, for it is inherent in the process of evolution, whether in the sphere of natural organisms or of human societies, that new, emergent properties are seen, that epigenesis (Waddington 1977, 110) takes place in the course of the unfolding through time, and that thresholds are defined, not externally, but by the developing system itself.

At this point, it is necessary to correct a serious misconception that substantially mars a previous Advanced Seminar volume (Hill 1977a). There, it is repeatedly asserted that the origin of changes must be sought *outside* the system in question. Thus Hill (1976b, 76) states:

> No system can change in itself, change can only be instigated by outside sources. If a system is in equilibrium it will remain so unless inputs (or lack of inputs) from outside the system disturb the equilibrium. Of course, the individuals in a social system may consciously realize that change is necessary; but the reason the change is necessary lies in the relationship of the system with its environment.
>
> Otherwise, why would change occur at all? In Buckley's approach, why would not the negotiation process eventually lead to stable equilibrium? Why do further 'tensions' arise? Where do they come from? Buckley claims that they are inherent in the system – but this is no answer; it begs the question.

The same point is made with great emphasis by Saxe (1977, 116): 'The processes that result in systemic change for all systems are and must be initiated by extra-systemic variables.'

Of course Hill and Saxe are correct that changes external to the system – and Saxe emphasizes rightly the effect of the arrival of Europeans on eighteenth- and nineteenth-century Hawaii – can be of determining significance, an important trigger to the developments which subsequently take place. But it cannot be too firmly stressed that change within a system can only be understood in terms of the internal structure of that system. Sometimes an exogenously determined alteration in certain variables may be seen as the 'cause' without which change would not have occurred. But in other cases, no such striking environmental alteration is necessary.

Hill's discussion of 'equilibrium' here may be misleading. It is a matter for discussion whether any human cultural system is ever, from the standpoint of the long-term, in equilibrium; long-term processes of change are probably always taking place, whether or not they are of great significance for the future trajectory of the system. And the significance of such changes, often small in themselves, may not be easy to assess. Sanders, during discussion in this same volume, pointed out that population growth can be seen in some cases as a source of change internal to the system, but Saxe (1977, 289), in a reply which is incomprehensible to me, pronounced it external. A rather different view is presented by Perlman (1977) later in that volume, but nowhere is this unfortunate conclusion explicitly rebutted.

Archaeology has already faced this problem in recent years with the rejection of diffusionist explanations (Renfrew 1973; Binford 1968b). To define the system so that the source of change is always external to it is not merely to 'beg the question,' but to reduce all explanation to the status of a will o' the wisp, something which eludes our grasp. It 'has the effect of relegating to the wings all the action of the prehistoric drama' (Childe 1956, 154).

If the source of change is indeed seen as external to the system, it may be necessary to redefine the limits of the system so that the source can be included within it. In practice, however, what is ultimately of significance is not the possible origin of a change in an altered environmental variable, such as decline in rainfall. We seek to understand why and how this particular external change has long-term effects upon the structure (and hence upon the future trajectory) of the system, when other changes do not. Until we see this as the nub of the problem, the question has not been effectively posed at all.

This point has been well made in a recent paper by Bell and Senge (1980): 'A minimum standard for acceptance of many system dynamics models is generating the empirical behaviour of interest with *no exogenous time series inputs*.' Most real cases will indeed have such inputs, but to place the whole weight of the explanation upon them, as those cited above have sought to do, seems to defeat much of the object of the exercise.

The usefulness of systemic simulations for modelling long-term change is likely to depend upon their effectiveness for modelling changes in structure rather than simply changes in rate and level in an existing structure. And here it may be worth speculating whether or not the approach may usefully be linked with others which have been employed in the discussion of morphogenesis. Here I am thinking, for instance, of Catastrophe Theory (Thom 1975: Renfrew 1978), where the focus is upon qualitative change, rather than on precise quantitative modelling.

The Catastrophe Theory approach encourages one to consider the global dynamics of the system and to think of the whole series of stable states which it may occupy. Some insight may thus be gained into its range of possible behaviours, without concerning ourselves at a detailed quantitative level with the values of all the variables in the system. This can bring out in a helpful way that, while the values of variables which we may consider external to the system (which will be numbered among the control variables) are of crucial relevance in determining at just what point certain changes may take place, the nature of those changes is governed by the global topology of the system itself.

Of course, the special strength of system dynamics modelling is that it allows one to work simultaneously at the detailed, quantitative level and to follow the broad, qualitative trends of the developing behaviour as it occurs. In some cases, however, other approaches may help one to see the forest for the trees.

This whole problem of the emergence of form is one which has fascinated mathematical biologists for many decades (Thompson 1942, Thom 1975, Waddington 1977), and I believe that their approach has much to offer us (Rosen 1979). To say that is not to overlook the numerous pitfalls in applying to cultural evolution some of the concepts of Darwinian evolution in a mechanistic way. Burnham (1973) has analysed the circularities that lurk in the application of the concept of 'adaptation' to human societies, and the Darwinian notion of monogenesis, which is of great value to the taxonomic paleontologists, has been positively misleading when applied to archaeology (Renfrew 1979). But there, in the workings of evolution, we can indeed view the genesis of structure, as it unfolds before our eyes. The models now being used to simulate this process will be of great relevance to us.

It is here that simulation may be of special value. If we can adequately simulate the structure and behaviour of an organism or organization, we should be able to see it survive or decline, grow or change along a series of different life histories or trajectories. What will happen if certain changes take place in the structure of the system, changes which we may regard as the analogue of genetic mutations? Under what circumstances along the time trajectory will these minor 'mutations' bring about an evolutionary change of greater significance, a transformation to a new organizational form? In this sense we might be able to view our system simulations as evolutionary machines, plotting out for us different evolutionary paths, and exploring within a relatively short time in the laboratory possibilities which in reality would take centuries or millennia to realize.

In order to reach new structures, however, we must overcome the ultimately deterministic nature of most present system simulations. The system must be enabled to modify itself in ways both initially unforeseen and unpredictable. This implies, referring to table 1, that the system itself must be allowed to generate new feedback loops and new components in a way which is not completely determined at the outset. Perhaps this means introducing a stochastic element, on analogy with mutation. Sometimes that will lead to dysfunction, and the system may not survive. In some cases competition between coexisting systems will lead to some sort of Darwinian 'survival of the fittest,' but in others the system will have no competitor. Unfortunately, we have no obvious way of deciding now which possible 'mutation' is likely to occur and survive.

In some ways, there is little that is new in this notion of human societies and their operation being simulated by evolutionary machines. But in most existing simulations, the level of determinacy is so high that, given comparable initial conditions and similar external conditions along the trajectory, the final states are likely to be much the same. This is not the way to allow interesting new structures to emerge. We may, instead, find it fruitful to create system simulations which have the property of producing the unexpected.

Such a turn of events has intrigued many of those who have written of automata, from Mary Shelley to Arthur Clarke, and, in a different field, has disquieted those who are alert to the potentialities of recombinant DNA. It is perhaps time that, within the framework of our simulations, we should attempt to harness the unexpected in order to generate truly emergent properties. We are, however, dealing with human, not molecular, interactions, and the analogy with DNA must not be stretched too far.

These problems are usefully discussed within a rather different framework by Day (1981) under the heading 'Meta-adaptation.' In the discussion following the presentation of his paper, we began to consider some of the devices by which human societies have successfully countered disequilibrium. These are innovations, such as the introduction of coinage, for instance, or of the limited liability company, or of currencies of account, which result in the long run in major changes in society which we can regard as structural changes.

One of the most promising features of the adaptive economics framework which Day proposes is the manner in which the development of 'disequilibrium mechanisms' may be approached. For it is very clear that what may originate as a mechanism simply to restore equilibrium may develop until it represents a significant structural change in the system, a major innovation in the unfolding development and growth process. This, then, is an aspect of the adaptive economics approach which will repay further exploration. Nor need the use of the term *economics* here inhibit the application of comparable ideas to other aspects of the culture system such as social structure. The underlying notion is a perfectly general one.

Some evolutionary changes in human societies, just as in living organisms, may be regarded as an increasingly effective *mapping* of the environment. Thus the development of the eye can, with the wisdom of hindsight, be seen as a positive adaptive response – a successful innovation in the mapping of an environment rich in electro-magnetic radiation of the appropriate wavelengths. An analogous case in human culture might be the tapping of atomic energy, or within the archaeological time range the 'invention' of metallurgy. Such inventions, which simply imply the new exploitation of a pre-existing (although not hitherto perceived) environment, may be regarded as an improvement in the mapping effected by the human society. It may be that, in cases where we as simulators already possess the relevant 'map,' an effective simulation of the mapping activity of past societies could be possible. (If we do not possess the relevant map – as in the case of controlled thermonuclear reactions – the simulation will not be so easy.)

These, however, are cases where the developments are ultimately determined by the structure of the environment, although in a different and perhaps more subtle sense than that of Hill and Saxe. More problematical, and, at the present stage in our understanding of human societies, more interesting, are the evolutionary changes within the structure of society, where the society is adjusting to essentially human problems. Many human social institutions are of this kind – all of the wide range of hierarchical structures, the various devices for controlling and processing information, the different types of exchange and the devices for facilitating it. When we have constructed simulations which can begin to come up with new structures of this kind – although not necessarily with just those

351

devices which societies known to us have produced, then we shall be at a new and more productive stage of modelling.

There are mere speculations at the moment. Yet many of the necessary ingredients are already available. It is an impressive experience to see how a skilled systems analyst can break a given problem down and express it in system dynamics terms. Low (1981) undertook this task for Cordell's Wetherill Mesa case, setting out in a logical analysis the loops and flows required to express fully the proposed insights into the causes of settlement abandonment. The next stage, which he could clearly have accomplished without difficulty, would be to write the necessary equations and proceed to a full simulation in the Forrester manner.

Already, then, it is possible to give an analytical account of the detailed behaviour of specified aspects of a culture system, which will include predictions about its future behaviour, at least over the short term. Such predictions are possible because we have an explicit understanding of the structure of the system, whose behaviour is thus, in a sense, determined, although it may not be known to us until the implications of the structure are explored by simulation.

The next stage must be to explore the future behaviour and the future structural evolution of systems whose evolution is not uniquely determined by their present form, but which have themselves the potential for generating emergent properties.　　[1981]

## Note

I should like to express my thanks for useful critical comment on an earlier draft of this chapter from R. H. Day and for some important and helpful suggestions from K. L. Cooke.

## Bibliography

Aldenderfer, M. S. (1981a) Computer Simulation for Archaeology: an Introductory Essay, in *Simulations in Archaeology*, ed. J. A. Sabloff, Albuquerque, University of New Mexico Press.

— (1981b) Creating Assemblages by Computer Simulation: the development and uses of ABSIM, in *Simulations in Archaeology*, ed. J. A. Sabloff, Albuquerque, University of New Mexico Press.

Ashby, W. R. (1956) *An Introduction to Cybernetics*, London, Methuen.

Athens, J. S. (1977) Theory Building and the Study of Evolutionary Process in Complex Societies, in *For Theory Building in Archaeology*, ed. L. R. Binford, New York, Academic Press.

Bell, J. A. (1981) Scientific Method and the Formulation of Testable Computer Simulation Models, in *Simulations in Archaeology*, ed. J. A. Sabloff, Albuquerque, University of New Mexico Press.

Bell, J. A. and P. M. Senge (1980) Methods for Enhancing Object-
  ivity in System Dynamics Models, in *System Dynamics* (Studies
  in the Management Sciences 14) eds A. Augusto, A. Legasto,
  J. W. Forrester and J. M. Lyneis, North Holland, 61–73.
Berlinsky, D. (1976) *On Systems Analysis*, Cambridge, MIT
  Press.
Bertalanffy, L. von (1950) An Outline of General System Theory,
  *British Journal of the Philosophy of Science*, 1, 134–65.
Binford, L. R. (1962) Archaeology as Anthropology, *American
  Antiquity*, 28, 217–25.
— (1968a) Archaeological Perspectives, in *New Perspectives in
  Archaeology*, eds. S. R. and L. R. Binford, Chicago, Aldine.
— (1968b) Some Comments on Historical Versus Processual
  Archaeology, *Southwestern Journal of Anthropology*, 24,
  267–76.
— (1977) General Introduction, in *For Theory Building
  Archaeology*, ed. L. R. Binford, New York, Academic Press.
Burnham, P. (1973) The Explanatory Value of the Concept of
  Adaptation in Studies of Culture Change, in *The Explanation of
  Culture Change*, ed. C. Renfrew, London, Duckworth.
Cherry, J. (1978) Generalisation and the Archaeology of the State,
  in *Social Organisation and Settlement*, eds. D. Green,
  D. Heselgrove and M. Spriggs (British Archaeological Reports
  International Series vol. 47, pt. 2).
Childe, V. G. (1956) *Piecing Together the Past*, London, Routledge
  and Kegan Paul.
Chillingworth, D. R. J. (1976) *Differential Topology with a View to
  Applications*, London, Pitman Publishing.
Clarke, D. L. (1968) *Analytical Archaeology*, London, Methuen.
Cooke, K. L. (1979) Mathematical Approaches to Culture Change,
  in *Transformations: Mathematical Approaches to Culture
  Change*, eds. C. Renfrew and K. L. Cooke, New York,
  Academic Press.
— (1981) On the Construction and Evaluation of Mathematical
  Models, in *Simulations in Archaeology*, ed. J. A. Sabloff,
  Albuquerque, University of New Mexico Press.
Cooke, K. L. and H. I. Freedman (n.d.) A Model for the Adoption
  of a Technological Innovation, Unpublished paper.
Cooke, K. L. and C. Renfrew (1979) An Experiment on the
  Simulation of Culture Change, in *Transformations:
  Mathematical Approaches to Culture Change*, eds. C. Renfrew
  and K. L. Cooke, New York, Academic Press.
Cordell, L. S. (1975) Predicting Site Abandonment at Wetherill
  Mesa, *The Kiva*, 40, 189–201.
— (1981) The Wetherill Mesa Simulation: a Retrospective, in
  *Simulations in Archaeology*, ed. J. A. Sabloff, Albuquerque,
  University of New Mexico Press.
Day, R. H. (1981) Dynamic Systems and Epochal Change, in
  *Simulations in Archaeology*, ed. J. A. Sabloff, Albuquerque,
  University of New Mexico Press.
Easton, D. (1965) *A Systems Analysis of Political Life*, New York,
  John Wiley.

Flannery, K. V. (1968) The Olmec and the Valley of the Oaxaca, in *Dumbarton Oaks Conference on the Olmec*, ed. E. P. Benson, Washington D.C., Dumbarton Oaks.

Flannery, K. V. (1972) The Cultural Evolution of Civilisations, *Annual Review of Ecology and Systematics*, 3, 399–425.

— (1973) Archaeology with a Capital S, in *Research and Theory in Current Archaeology*, ed. C. L. Redman, New York, John Wiley.

Forrester, J. W. (1961) *Industrial Dynamics*, Cambridge, MIT Press.

— (1969) *Urban Dynamics*, Cambridge, MIT Press.

— (1971) *World Dynamics*, Cambridge, MIT Press.

— (1973) Understanding the Counterintuitive Behaviour of Social Systems, in *Towards Global Equilibrium: Collected Papers*, eds. D. L. and D. H. Meadows, Cambridge, Wright-Allen.

Gall, P. L. and A. A. Saxe (1977) The Ecological Evolution of Culture: The State as Predator in Succession Theory, in *Exchange Systems in Prehistory*, eds. T. K. Earle and J. Ericson, New York, Academic Press.

Hamblin, R. L., R. B. Jacobsen and J. L. L. Miller (1973) A Mathematical Theory of Social Change, New York, John Wiley.

Hill, J. N. (1977a) Discussion, in *Explanation of Prehistoric Change*, ed. J. N. Hill, Albuquerque, University of New Mexico Press, School of American Research Advanced Seminar Series.

— (1977b) Systems Theory and the Explanation of Change, in *Explanation of Prehistoric Change*, ed. J. N. Hill, Albuquerque, University of New Mexico Press, School of American Research Advanced Seminar Series.

Hosler, D. H., J. A. Sabloff and D. Runge (1977) Simulation Model Development: A Case Study of the Classic Maya Collapse, in *Social Process in Maya Prehistory*, ed. N. Hammond, London, Academic Press.

Keene, A. S. (1979) Economic Optimisation Models and the Study of Hunter-Gatherer Subsistence-Settlement Systems, in *Transformations: Mathematical to Culture Change*, eds. C. Renfrew and K. L. Cooke, New York, Academic Press.

Leach, E. R. (1973) Concluding Address, in *The Explanation of Culture Change: Models in Prehistory*, ed. C. Renfrew, London, Duckworth.

Low, G. W. (1981) Using System Dynamics to Simulate the Past, in *Simulations in Archaeology*, ed. J. A. Sabloff, Albuquerque, University of New Mexico Press.

Maynard-Smith, J. (1974) *Models in Ecology*, Cambridge, Cambridge University Press.

Meadows, D. H., D. Meadows, J. Randers and W. Behrens III (1972) *The Limits to Growth, A Report from the Club of Rome's Project on the Predicament of Mankind*, New York, Universe Books.

Munton, R. J. C. (1973) Systems Analysis: À Comment, in *The Explanation of Culture Change*, ed. C. Renfrew, London, Duckworth.

Perlman, M. L. (1977) Comments on Explanation and on Stability and Change, in *Explanation of Prehistoric Change*, ed. J. N. Hill,

Albuquerque, University of New Mexico Press, School of American Research Advanced Seminar Series.

Pirandello, L. (1954) *Six Characters in Search of an Author*, trans. F. May, original Italian in 1921, London, Heinemann.

Plog, F. (1974) *The Study of Prehistoric Change*, New York, Academic Press.

Rathje, W. (1975) The Last Tango in Mayapan: A Tentative Trajectory of Production-Distribution Systems, in *Ancient Civilization and Trade*, eds. J. A. Sabloff and C. C. Lamberg-Karlovsky, Albuquerque, University of New Mexico Press, School of American Research Advanced Seminar Series.

Reidhead, V. A. (1976) Optimization and Food Procurement at the Prehistoric Leonard Haag Site, Southwest Indiana: A Linear Programming Approach, Ph.D. dissertation, Indiana University.

Renfrew, C. (1972) *The Emergence of Civilization: The Cyclades and the Aegean in the Third Millennium B. C.*, London, Methuen.

— (1973) Review of *Explanation in Archaeology*: An Explicit Scientific Approach, by P. J. Watson, S. A. LeBlanc and C. L. Redman, *American Anthropologist*, 75, 1928–30.

— (1978) Trajectory Discontinuity and Morphogenesis: The Implications of Catastrophe Theory for Archaeology, *American Antiquity*, 43, 203–44.

— (1979) Transformations, in *Transformations: Mathematical Approaches to Culture Change*, eds. C. Renfrew and K. L. Cooke, New York, Academic Press.

Renfrew, C. and E. Level (1979) Exploring Dominance: Predicting Polities from Centres, in *Transformations: Mathematical Approaches to Culture Change*, eds. C. Renfrew and K. L. Cooke, New York, Academic Press.

Rosen, R. (1979) Morphogenesis in Biological and Social Systems, in *Transformations: Mathematical Approaches to Culture Change*, eds. C. Renfrew and K. L. Cooke, New York, Academic Press.

Salmon, M. H. (1978) What Can Systems Theory Do for Archaeology? *American Antiquity*, 43, 174–83.

Saxe, A. A. (1977) On the Origin of Evolutionary Processes: State Formation in the Sandwich Islands, in *Explanation of Prehistoric Change*, ed. J. N. Hill, Albuquerque, University of New Mexico Press, School of American Research Advanced Seminar Series.

Shantzis, S. B. and W. W. Behrens (1973) Population Control Mechanisms in a Primitive Agricultural Society, in *Toward Global Equilibrium*, eds. D. L. and D. H. Meadows, Cambridge, MIT Press.

Thom, R. (1975) *Structural Stability and Morphogenesis*, Reading, Benjamin.

Thomas, D. H. (1972) A Computer Simulation Model of Great Basin Shoshonean Settlement Patterns, in *Models in Archaeology*, ed. D. Clarke, London, Methuen.

Thompson, D'A. W. (1942) *On Growth and Form*, 2nd ed., Cambridge, Cambridge University Press.

Waddington, C. H. (1977) *Tools for Thought*, St Albans, Paladin.

Wiener, N. (1948) *Cybernetics*, Cambridge, MIT Press.

Wood, J.J. and R.G. Watson (1973) Two Models of Sociocultural Systems and Their Implications for the Archaeological Study of Change, in *The Explanation of Culture Change*, ed. C. Renfrew, London, Duckworth.
Zubrow, E.B.W. (1975) *Prehistoric Carrying Capacity: A Model*, Menlo Park, Cummings.
— (1981) Simulation as a Heuristic Device in Archaeology, in *Simulations in Archaeology*, ed. J.A. Sabloff, Albuquerque, University of New Mexico Press.

# V

DISCONTINUITY
AND LONG-TERM
CHANGE

*

One of the apparent limitations of the systems approach, indeed of many analyses of change, is that it is altogether *gradualist* in nature. It leads one to see how, by a long series of steps, changes can be reinforced by a process of positive feedback, so that in the outcome marked and irreversible change ensues.

The archaeological record, on the other hand, often shows relatively sudden changes which cannot at first sight be explained in these gradualist terms. A decade ago, when diffusionist or indeed migrationist thinking was still widely prevalent (see Adams *et al.* 1978), the temptation to explain sudden change in essentially migrationist terms was still a strong one, even though a processual approach was more readily accepted for changes which took place in a more gradual way. Indeed the distinction between sudden and gradual was linked, in the minds of some, with that between historical and processual explanation. Historical explanations, it was felt, were appropriate to the understanding of events, while processual explanations, perhaps in systems terms, were conceivably acceptable for more gradual, long-term changes. This was to some extent the view of Sabloff and Willey (1967), which was called into question by Binford in his 'Some comments on historical versus processual archaeology' (Binford 1968).

The difficulty of relating sudden change to more gradual processes is one that underlies much historical discussion, and it has been treated with clarity by Braudel. 'Events are the ephemera of history'; (Braudel 1973, 900) they are to be contrasted with 'persistent structures' and 'the slow progress of evolution'.

It was the purpose of the two papers which follow to show that sudden change need be no less 'processual' than gradual variation through time. That is to say that sudden change, which would certainly be perceived by participants as a significant event or series of events, can be the direct and intelligible result of the operation of more gradual factors which we can describe in a perfectly straightforward way, whether or not in the language of systems thinking.

358

This I regard as a major methodological point and – speaking for myself – a lesson which once learnt in one context may equally be applicable in another.

The body of theory which for me solved this problem in an elegant and persuasive way was Catastrophe Theory, as developed by the French mathematician René Thom, whose book *Structural Stability and Morphogenesis* (Thom 1975) carries many overtones of interest for history (and archaeology) as well as biology. Christopher Zeeman has applied these principles in a number of interesting specific cases: his treatment of stock exchange collapse (Zeeman 1974) is one of the most suggestive to the archaeologist. The application of similar reasoning to the phenomenon which I have called systems collapse, and in particular to the sudden demise of various early state societies allows the discontinuous (the event) to be explained coherently in terms of the continuous (the process).

At this point a word of caution is in order. For, as many critics have pointed out (e.g. Zahler and Sussman 1977) Catastrophe Theory can readily be misunderstood, and be thought to be explaining rather more than is in fact the case. What it does do, very effectively, is show how the change in question may be expected in some cases to be sudden. In the cases I am dealing with it is the *suddenness* of the change which is being explained by these means. The question of why the change should occur at all (be it sudden or gradual) is an altogether different one, and one which it is up to the archaeologist to elucidate in the cases presented here. Catastrophe Theory is not some all-purpose explanatory device, able to bring instant enlightenment in all fields of endeavour. Indeed it is appropriate to note the words of the mathematician Stephen Smale in the context of his critical review (Smale 1978, 1365) of Zeeman's volume on the application of Catastrophe Theory (Zeeman 1977):

> Good mathematical models don't start with the mathematics, but with a deep study of certain natural phenomena. Mathematical awareness or even sophistication is useful when working to model economic phenomena, for example, but a successful model depends much more on a penetrating study and understanding of the economics.

What applies to economics applies with equal force, of course, to archaeology. The quality of the application is dependent entirely upon the appropriateness of the model utilised. In several cases, however, the possibility of an analysis in terms of Catastrophe Theory has stimulated the more careful formulation of the underlying problem, with potentially useful consequences (e.g. Renfrew and Poston 1979).

In the way in which I have sought to employ it (Renfrew 1978) it has two uses. The first, as I have described, is to help us to see why certain changes – which in themselves it is our job as archaeologists to explain – come about with discontinuous suddenness rather than more gradually. The second use, to which I will return below, is to help us understand the emergence of completely new forms: the phenomenon known to the biologist as morphogenesis.

In the papers which follow, once that simple but crucially important point has been accepted and assimilated, the detailed discussion in terms of the cusp catastrophe has not much further contribution to make (and I have shortened the mathematical formulation in chapter 13 for this reason). But I believe that the argument is nonetheless a very important one. For it solves very elegantly the problem of discontinuity, and in terms of the archaeological debates of a decade ago, it removes one of the last arguments for a migrationist approach. In saying this, of course, I am not trying to assert that migrations of people never occurred, nor that it is in any way inappropriate to seek archaeological evidence for them. The point, which is scarcely a new one now but was undoubtedly relevant in the '70s, is that evidence of discontinuity in the archaeological record is no longer in itself an argument for sudden causal factors such as perhaps the migration of groups of people.

These two papers, then, set out to explain the suddenness of two important kinds of changes which have, in the past, very widely been interpreted on the basis of their sudden nature, as the result of sudden causal factors of this kind. What comes out of both of them is something more than this however. The consideration of systems collapse led me to develop a general formulation of the phenomenon, set out at the beginning of the chapter, which turns out to be of relevance in quite a wide range of cases, and in a rather well-defined way. Rahtz (1982), for instance, has used this formulation in his consideration of Dark Age England, and the application seems to him a relevant one. In Chapter 13, the approach is presented in relation to the Mycenaean and Maya cases. The Maya collapse in particular has been the subject of a number of explicit formulations (e.g. Hosler *et al.*, 1977; Hamblin and Pilcher 1980; Doran 1981), which have much common ground between them. None, perhaps, elucidates so effectively the suddenness of the collapse.

The whole question of suddenness and discontinuity has recently been a matter of discussion and debate among evolutionary biologists considering the gradual or alternatively the sudden emergence of new species. The concept of 'punctuated equilibria' has enjoyed a considerable vogue (Eldredge and Gould 1972; Gould and Eldredge 1977; Gould 1980). The underlying idea is of course a very similar one. Indeed, when one is familiar with the basic ideas of Catastrophe Theory, the notion that species should emerge suddenly rather than gradually, if they are going to emerge at all, is altogether unsurprising, and has already been coherently expounded (Dodson 1976; Zeeman 1982). When these ideas have been fully worked out, we shall perhaps be able to lay to rest the misconception shared by Darwin (Maynard Smith 1982, 125) that 'gradual = natural; sudden = miraculous', and one of the obstacles to coherent thought in archaeology as in biology will have been removed.

The second issue which is raised here, at least by implication, is the phenomenon of long-term change. It is of course a fundamental point that sustained growth and significant change involve not simply alterations in scale but transformations involving fundamental restructuring (Renfrew 1979). This is precisely what the biologists term *morphogenesis*, the emergence of form, and the term is a useful one for the social scientist and the archaeologist also (Rosen 1979, 1982; Renfrew 1982). One important notion here is that of positive feedback, discussed in the last section (see Maruyama 1963) but the concept of growth, entailing significant changes in structure, implies something more.

I have the hunch that the various mathematical ideas in this general area, relating to the qualitative behaviour of dynamical systems, have much promise for those researchers, including archaeologists, who are concerned to study the emergence of structure. There are, of course, other approaches than Catastrophe Theory (e.g. Allen 1982), although this was my own personal introduction to the field. It is naturally important for the non-mathematician to avoid being seduced by the mystification which readily surrounds imperfectly understood mathematical formulations (Smale 1978, 1366). That, of course, is where one needs to draw upon the expertise of the relevant specialist (e.g. Pattee 1973; Poston 1979; Rosen 1982). Already, however, it is clear that informative new ways of looking at social change are possible (e.g. Waddington 1977; van der Leeuw 1981).

The cases chosen for discussion here appear to be among those where it is possible, and perhaps useful, to generalise, and to do so in a manner which applies to a whole range of contexts different in place and time. Despite the frequent claims among processual archaeologists that such generalisation is their goal, they have, with a few honourable exceptions, conspicuously failed to employ wide ranging comparisons. Indeed one of the most conspicuous short-comings of the New Archaeology in the United States is that much of it began in the American Southwest and never managed to move out of it.

Of course Julian Steward, one of the most influential of the precursors of the New Archaeology, attempted trial formulations of a very wide-ranging character (Steward 1949), and several other scholars have deliberately worked with more than one area and time period in mind (e.g. Flannery 1972; Athens 1977; Gall and Saxe 1977; Cherry 1978). But, as I suggested at the beginning of this volume, the problem of successful generalisation remains a pressing one.

But there inevitably comes a point, in any given case, when a certain level of detail is sought, and when the general framework can no longer serve as an adequate guide. General formulations always risk failing to satisfy in those instances when unique aspects of the individual case are under consideration: they only operate at a general level. Often, however, it is at that level that we can most effectively work. It is pertinent to quote once again the words of Braudel (1973, 1244):

> In historical analysis, as I see it, rightly or wrongly, the long run always wins in the end. Annihilating innumerable events – all those which cannot be accommodated in the main ongoing current and which are therefore ruthlessly swept to one side – it indubitably limits both the freedom of the individual and even the role of chance.

The consideration of discontinuity and of morphogenesis thus leads on to wider issues of great interest. But neither of these papers sets out to explain a particular event, or even to show in full and convincing detail how a particular case falls within the scope of some more general regularity. To do that in a satisfying way it is necessary to work also at a more concrete level, and to consider how specific and contingent features of the society in question were able to determine or at least to condition its future behaviour. Broad generalisation alone is not enough. I am very much aware that a satisfying explanation of the particular case will not only show how it is a specific instance of processes more discernible, but at the same time show how local particularities helped to determine its own characteristic pattern of growth and development.

## Bibliography

Adams, W. Y., D. P. van Gerven and R. S. Levy (1978) The retreat from migrationism, *Annual Review of Anthropology*, 7, 483–532.

Allen, P. M. (1982) The genesis of structure in social systems: the paradigm of self-organisation, in C. Renfrew, M. J. Rowlands and B. A. Segraves, eds., *Theory and Explanation in Archaeology: the Southampton Conference*, New York, Academic Press, 347–74.

Athens, J. S. (1977) Theory building and the study of evolutionary process in complex societies, in L. R. Binford, ed., *For Theory Building in Archaeology*, New York, Academic Press, 353–84.

Binford, L. R. (1968) Some comments on historical versus processual archaeology, *Southwestern Journal of Anthropology*, 24, 267–75.

Braudel, F. (1973) *The Mediterranean and the Mediterranean World in the Age of Philip II*, vol. 2, London, Collins.

Cherry, J. F. (1978) Generalisation and the archaeology of the state, in D. R. Green, C. C. Haselgrove and M. J. T. Spriggs, *Social Organisation and Settlement* (BAR Supplementary Series 47), Oxford, British Archaeological Reports, 411–38.

Dodson, M. M. (1976) Darwin's law of natural selection and Thom's theory of catastrophes, *Mathematical Bioscience*, 28, 243–74.

Doran, J. (1981) Multi-actor systems and the Maya collapse, in G. L. Cowgill, R. Whallon and B. S. Ottaway, eds., *Coloquio: Manejo de Datos y Metodos Matematicos de Arqueologia* (Tenth International Congress, UISPP), Mexico City, UISPP, 191–200.

Eldredge, N. and S. J. Gould (1972) Punctuated equilibria: an alternative to phyletic gradualism, in T. J. M. Schopf, ed., *Models in Palaeobiology*, San Francisco, Freeman Cooper, 82–115.

Flannery, K. V. (1972) The cultural evolution of civilisations, *Annual Review of Ecology and Systematics*, 399–426.

Gall, P. L. and A. A. Saxe (1977) The ecological evolution of culture: the state as predator in succession theory, in T. K. Earle and J. E. Ericson, eds., *Exchange Systems in Prehistory*, New York, Academic Press, 255–68.

Gould, S. J. (1980) Is a new and general theory of evolution emerging?, *Palaeobiology*, 6, 119–80.

Gould, S. J. and N. Eldredge (1977) Punctuated equilibria: the tempo and mode of evolution reconsidered, *Palaeobiology*, 3, 115–51.

Hamblin, R. L. and B. L. Pilcher (1980) The Classic Maya collapse: testing class conflict hypotheses, *American Antiquity*, 45, 246–67.

Hosler, D. H., J. A. Sabloff and D. Runge (1977) Simulation model development: a case study of the Classic Maya collapse, in N. Hammond, ed., *Social Processes in Maya Prehistory*, London, Academic Press, 553–90.

Leeuw, S. E. van der (1981) Information flows, flow structures and the explanation of change in human institutions, in S. E. van der Leeuw, ed., *Archaeological Approaches to the Study of Complexity* (Cingula VI), Amsterdam, Van Giffen Instituut, 230–312.

Maruyama, M. (1963) The second cybernetics: deviation-amplifying mutual causal processes, *American Scientist*, 51, 164–79.

Maynard Smith, J. ed. (1982) *Evolution Now, a Century After Darwin*, London, Nature.

Pattee, H. H. (1973) *Hierarchy Theory: the Challenge of Complex Systems*, New York, Brazilier.

Poston, T. (1979) The elements of Catastrophe Theory or the honing of Occam's Razor, in C. Renfrew and K. L. Cooke, eds., *Transformations, Mathematical Approach to Culture Change*, New York, Academic Press, 425–36.

Rahtz, P. (1982) Celtic society in Somerset A. D. 400–700, *Bulletin of the Board of Celtic Studies*, Oxford, 30, 176–200.

Renfrew, C. (1978) Trajectory discontinuity and morphogenesis, the implications of catastrophe theory for archaeology, *American Antiquity*, 43, 203–44.

— (1979) Transformations, in C. Renfrew and K. L. Cooke, eds., *Transformations, Mathematical Approaches to Culture Change*, New York, Academic Press, 3–44.

— (1982) Comment: the emergence of structure, in C. Renfrew, M. J. Rowlands and B. A. Segraves, eds., *Theory and Explanation in Archaeology, the Southampton Conference*, New York, Academic Press, 459–64.

Renfrew, C. and T. Poston (1979) Discontinuities in the endogenous change of settlement pattern, in C. Renfrew and K. L. Cooke, eds., *Transformations, Mathematical Approaches to Culture Change*, New York, Academic Press, 437–61.

Rosen, R. (1979) Morphogenesis in biological and social systems, in C. Renfrew and K. L. Cooke, eds., *Transformations, Mathematical Approaches to Culture Change*, New York, Academic Press, 91–111.

— (1982) On a theory of transformations for cultural systems, in C. Renfrew, M. J. Rowlands and B. A. Segraves, eds., *Theory and Explanation in Archaeology: the Southampton Conference*, New York, Academic Press, 301–13.

Sabloff, J. A. and G. R. Willey (1967) The collapse of Maya civilisation in the southern lowlands: a consideration of history and process, *Southwestern Journal of Anthropology*, 23, 311–36.

Smale, S. (1978) Review of E. C. Zeeman, Catastrophe Theory: Selected Papers 1972–7, in *Bulletin of the American Mathematical Society*, 84, 1360–8.

Steward, J. H. (1949) Development of complex societies: cultural causality and law: a trial formulation of the development of early civilisations, *American Anthropologist*, 51, reprinted in J. H. Steward, 1955, *Theory of Culture Change*, Urbana, University of Illinois Press, 178–209.

Thom, R. (1975) *Structural Stability and Morphogenesis*, Reading, Mass., W. A. Benjamin.

Waddington, C. H. (1977) *Tools for Thought*, Frogmore, Paladin.

Zahler, R. S. and H. J. Sussmann (1977) Claims and accomplishments of applied Catastrophe Theory, *Nature*, 269, 759–63.

Zeeman, E. C. (1974) On the unstable behaviour of stock exchanges, *Journal of Mathematical Economics*, 1, 39–49.

Zeeman, E.C. (1977) *Catastrophe Theory, Selected Papers 1972–7*, Reading, Mass., Addison Wesley.
– (1982) Decision making and evolution, in C. Renfrew, M.J. Rowlands and B.A. Segraves, eds., *Theory and Explanation in Archaeology: the Southampton Conference*, New York, Academic Press, 315–46.

# 13

## SYSTEMS COLLAPSE AS
## SOCIAL TRANSFORMATION

*

THE MYCENAEAN POLITY never really recovered from the
onslaughts made on it at the end of the thirteenth century.
The elaborate administration that had maintained its power
disintegrated, its trade which was its life blood was disrupted
and the fabric of its society decayed to an inglorious end. We
are on the threshold of the Dark Ages.

Lord William Taylour (1964, 178)

### Introduction

Many writers in different areas have described, quite independently, the archaeological evidence in their region which clearly
documents the sudden collapse of an early state society. Suddenly,
and without any very obvious cause, a brilliant and flourishing
society with a highly structured, central administrative organisation
disappears from the archaeological record. The immediate aftermath is always less clearly understood, because the range of archaeological evidence is much less adequate. Sometimes literacy is lost:
always written records (if any) are notably fewer. The early state
society fragments into a whole number of smaller units which (if
they can be defined at all) are at a much lower level of sociopolitical
integration. There is a decline in many activities, including craft-
specialist production and trade, and often of population.

The overwhelming impression is one of discontinuity, and it is
natural that in every case archaeologists have sought the cause of
the collapse in some overwhelming cataclysm, either a natural
disaster or a destruction through invasion. Yet, except in rare cases
where a sudden natural cataclysm such as a volcanic eruption is
evidently the cause, the precise explanation of the collapse remains
elusive.

Further research generally shows that although the organisation-

366

al structure did indeed disappear, there are elements of continuity with the succeeding period, the 'dark age.' Almost invariably the progress of research makes that Dark Age less dark, and reveals a pattern of less highly structured societies showing some of the organisational features recognised in the early developmental phases of the state society many centuries (or even millennia) earlier. Often the first, obvious explanation for the collapse, that it was brought about by the irruption of invaders or destroyers, proved difficult to substantiate. Frequently other monocausal explanations show themselves equally inadequate.

In each case the society has 'relaxed' or 'relapsed' organisationally with striking discontinuity, although continuity of certain other elements persists (usually, for example, there is no immediate language change). The collapse of central power is followed by competition among various small power groups inside the former territory and on its borders. The new central organisation which in many cases develops in the same area often after a few centuries traces its origins back to one of these small groups. Indeed the new administration may seek to legitimatise its authority either by claiming direct lineal descent from the previous state, or alternatively by claiming to have overthrown it by heroic force of arms, a claim often all too readily accepted by later historians.

This scenario has deliberately been expressed in very general terms, and I think it will be recognised by archaeologists in many parts of the world. It seems to represent a rather general pattern, a type of change widely distributed in space and time among early state societies. It is this kind of diachronic pattern which I have sought to characterise (Renfrew 1979, 16) as an allactic form.

Before giving specific examples, it may be worth setting down more precisely some of the very general characteristics that specific instances of this allactic form often display. It then becomes pertinent to seek an underlying explanation for these repeated patterns, and here catastrophe theory can help form our thinking. The following section owes much to a discussion by Adams (1973, 22) of the Classic Maya collapse, and rather more to descriptions of the Mycenaean Dark Ages (e.g., Snodgrass 1971, Desborough 1975), like that which is quoted at the beginning of this chapter.

### General Features of System Collapse

*Collapse*
1. Collapse of central administrative organisation of the early state:
    a) Disappearance or reduction in number of levels of central

place hierarchy

  b) Complete fragmentation or disappearance of military organis-
     ation into (at most) small, independent units
  c) Abandonment of palaces and central storage facilities
  d) Eclipse of temples as major religious centres (often with their
     survival, modified, as local shrines)
  e) Effective loss of literacy for secular and religious purposes
  f) Abandonment of public building works
2. Disappearance of the traditional elite class:
  a) Cessation of rich, traditional burials (although different forms
     of rich burial frequently emerge after a couple of centuries)
  b) Abandonment of rich residences, or their re-use in impover-
     ished style by 'squatters'
  c) Cessation in the use of costly assemblages of luxury goods,
     although individual items may survive
3. Collapse of centralised economy:
  a) Cessation of large-scale redistribution or market exchange
  b) Coinage (where applicable) no longer issued or exchanged
     commercially, although individual pieces survive as valuables
  c) External trade very markedly reduced, and traditional trade
     routes disappear
  d) Volume of internal exchange markedly reduced
  e) Cessation of craft-specialist manufacture
  f) Cessation of specialised or organised agricultural production,
     with agriculture instead on a local 'homestead' basis with
     diversified crop spectrum and mixed farming
4. Settlement shift and population decline:
  a) Abandoment of many settlements
  b) Shift to dispersed pattern of smaller settlements
  c) Frequent subsequent choice of defensible locations – the
     'flight to the hills'
  d) Marked reduction in population density

*Aftermath*
5. Transition to lower (cf. 'earlier') level of sociopolitical integration:
  a) Emergence of segmentary societies showing analogies with
     those seen centuries or millennia earlier in the 'formative'
     level in the same area (only later do these reach a chiefdom or
     'florescent' level of development)
  b) Fission of realm to smaller territories, whose boundaries may
     relate to those of earlier polities

c) Possible peripheral survival of some highly organised communities still retaining several organisational features of the collapsed state
d) Survival of religious elements as 'folk' cults and beliefs
e) Craft production at local level with 'peasant' imitations of former specialist products (e.g., in pottery)
f) Local movements of small population groups resulting from the breakdown in order at the collapse of the central administration (either with or without some language change), leading to destruction of many settlements
g) Rapid subsequent regeneration of chiefdom or even state society, partly influenced by the remains of its predecessor
6. Development of romantic Dark Age myth:
a) Attempt by new power groups to establish legitimacy in historical terms with the creation of genealogies either (i) seeking to find a link with the 'autochthonous' former state or (ii) relating the deeds by which the 'invaders' achieved power by force of arms
b) Tendency among early chroniclers to personalise historical explanation, so that change is assigned to individual deeds battles, and invasions, and often to attribute the decline to hostile powers outside the state territories (cf.5f)
c) Some confusion in legend and story between the Golden Age of the early vanished civilisation and the Heroic Age of its immediate aftermath
d) Paucity of archaeological evidence after collapse compared with that for preceding period (arising from loss of literacy and abandonment or diminution of urban centres)
e) Tendency among historians to accept as evidence traditional narratives first set down in writing some centuries after the collapse
f) Slow development of Dark Age archaeology, hampered both by the preceding item and by focus on the larger and more obvious central place sites of the vanished state

*Diachronic Aspects*
7. The collapse may take around 100 years for completion (although in the provinces of an empire, the withdrawal of central imperial authority can have more rapid effects).
8. Dislocations are evident in the earlier part of that period, the underlying factors finding expression in human conflicts – wars, destructions, and so on.

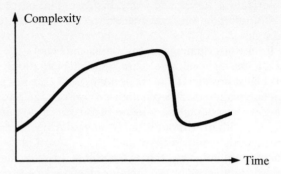

*Figure* 1. System collapse: the sudden decline observed in several early state societies.

9. Boundary maintenance may show signs of weakness during this time, so that outside pressures leave traces in the historical record.

10. The growth curve for many variables in the system (including population, exchange, agricultural activity) may take the truncated sigmoid form seen in figure 1.

11. Absence of single, obvious 'cause' for the collapse.

These criteria seem sufficient to document a social allactic form in much the same way as, for example, astronomers recognise that different stars in the sky are, on the basis of their short-term behaviour, to be classed as supernovas. Likewise, vulcanologists classify volcanic eruptions on the basis of behaviour through time as well as their geochemistry, into eruptive types, of which Plinian eruption is familiar to archaeologists for its destructive effects upon human settlement. It is claimed here that early state collapse ranks with supernova formation and Plinian eruption as an allactic form – all three classes of allactic form sharing a behaviour of sudden change after a much longer period of quiescence.

It is interesting to speculate whether early state collapse may in some cases be cyclic in nature – as Plinian eruption is – while supernova formation is not.

Space does not allow different specific cases to be presented in detail. I hope to present elsewhere a consideration of the end of Mycenaean civilisation in these terms. One feature that does emerge from such a comparison, however, is the remarkable extent to which not only the symptons of the collapse are often comparable, but also the *explanations* which have been offered for them

370

by scholars working quite independently in different areas (compare Sabloff 1973, 36 with Rhys Carpenter 1966).

Among specific cases that I would claim as instances of the more general allactic form whose characteristics have just been outlined are the following:

*The Mycenaean civilisation.* A paradigm case for a 'Dark Age' in the Old World (see Desborough 1975, 663, Snodgrass 1971, Ålin 1962).

*The Minoan palaces.* Around 1450 BC, towards the end of the Late Minoan Ib period, nearly all major administrative sites in Crete, whether palaces or villas, were destroyed (Hood 1973, Marinatos 1939, Page 1970). Sometimes an explanation for this decline has been sought in the volcanic eruption of the nearby island of Santorini (cf. Ninkovich and Heezen 1965), but this simple explanation may not be sufficient. Invasion by mainland Mycenaeans is another recognised possibility, but there is at present little evidence to suggest whether this was immediately prior to or after the destruction of the Minoan palaces. Curiously the demise of Minoan civilisation at this time, some three centuries before the Mycenaean quietus, has not often been treated together with the latter as an instance of systems collapse.

*The Indus Valley civilisation.* The great cities of the Indus Valley civilisation, notably Mohenjo-daro and Harappa, flourishing round 2000 BC, were destroyed some time around 1800 BC (Piggott 1950, Wheeler 1968, Allchin and Allchin 1968). The explanations offered focus either on some specific and radical environmental change or on the supposed invasion of Aryans from the north and west.

*The Hittites.* The Hittite empire of central Anatolia ended around 1200 BC. The great Hittite capital of Bogazköy was destroyed, other important sites such as Alaca and Alishar were likewise destroyed by fire, and in the central area of the empire, literacy ended (Akurgal 1962, 75). This pattern is conventionally accounted for the activities of Phrygian barbarians who 'overthrew' the Hittite empire but whose military success diminished further south.

*Egypt: First Intermediate period.* At the end of the Sixth Dynasty of Egypt, 'the central power was too weak and divided to hold back the surging tide of anarchy, and the civilisation of the Old Kingdom was swept away with the political system which had created it' (Aldred 1961, 100). Literacy was, however, uninterrupted, and the continuity of Egyptian culture was not totally ruptured. This may therefore be a doubtful case of systems collapse, but the period is certainly seen as a Dark Age by Bell (1971).

*The Classic Maya.* The paradigm case for early state collapse in the

371

New World. The whole subject has been reviewed in *The Classic Maya Collapse*, edited by Culbert (1973).

*Tiahuanaco*. There is evidence that the state organisation centred on Tiahuanaco in the Titicaca area of southern Peru underwent a striking and perhaps sudden decline in the twelfth century A D. The Wari empire of the Southern Highlands collapsed at about the same time, and pan-Andean unity dissolved into a series of regional traditions (Lumbreras 1974, 159; cf. Sanders and Marino 1970, 80). This may provisionally be considered a possible case of early state collapse.

*Other cases*. Collapse has been claimed for China in the 'Warring States' period, and no doubt other cases can be documented. A rather different phenomenon, certainly related to system collapse as defined here, is the withdrawal of central, imperial power from a province of empire formerly held under strong military rule. Britain at the end of the fourth century A D offers a well-known example, and the 'Dark Ages' of Britain conform in most respects to the description given earlier, although it is difficult to regard the collapse in Britain as entirely endogenous.

The discussion here focuses on the collapse of early states, where the similar trajectories followed constitute the allactic form which we have sought to define. But it is relevant to note that relatively sudden collapse seems to be a feature of other societies with a degree of centralised organisation. One of the best documented and most interesting cases is the sudden decline of the Anasazi town sites in the southwestern United States in the thirteenth century A D (cf. Vivian 1970). Various cataclysmic explanations have been offered (Martin, Quimby and Collier 1947, 146), including 'a great epidemic of some virulent but unknown disease.' A multicausal explanation of the kind offered here for early state collapse may prove more satisfactory.

## Stability and the Growth of Systems

Before turning, in the following section, to catastrophe theory, I would like to focus here on two very simple insights relating to complex societies. The first relates to hyperdevelopment, and the second to stability and growth.

### Before the Crash: The Options Narrow

To adapt too well, too fully, and too effectively to present conditions may be to restrict the flexibility of response available to cope with a future change in those conditions. This is a truism of evolutionary biology, where high specialisation can prove highly adaptive for a species in the short term but fatal in the long. Perhaps too it holds for many cases of system collapse.

In many early state societies there was a high degree of specialisation among craftsmen and even among agriculturalists, co-ordinated by a central bureaucracy. Efficiency of production *per capita* was greatly increased by this specialisation but the price was a very high measure of interdependence. A craftsman (e.g., a potter) working full time could produce far more of his product and of far better quality than could five farmers each devoting one-fifth of his time to making the same product. In favourable conditions, then, it is very sound strategy for a society to maximise specialisation through the agency of a central redistributive organisation. In this way it is possible, through economies of scale, to support a very much larger population than would be the case if each individual family or village had to be largely self-supporting, producing all the commodities which it used.

The danger may come, however, if the external circumstances become less advantageous, so that it becomes difficult to support the existing population. The option of becoming less specialised is not open to the society or to its decision-making agency at the centre. For although this would meet the change in external circumstances, it would mean a decrease in productive capacity, at least temporarily, and hence starvation for some of the community, which might in turn endanger the stability of the whole.

The only alternative is to increase productive efficiency by further increasing specialisation. To specialise in this way, instead of to diversify, seems a natural homeostatic adjustment. If, however, external circumstances worsen, the situation may cross the homeostatic limits of tolerance of the system which simply cannot manage any longer and breaks down. That is to say that even further specialisation and an increased work load cannot prevent a fall in production, with consequent starvation and perhaps unrest which will endanger the survival of the central bureaucracy.

Systems of this kind which, by virtue of their high specialisation, depend heavily on the central bureaucracy to distribute the necessities of life, are highly vulnerable. For if the central bureaucracy is disrupted and the distribution of products ceases, there is a sudden drop in efficiency and those specialists who are not actually producing food risk starvation. One imagines very much of this situation for the palace-centred polities of Mycenaean Greece, whose administrative archives have been preserved at Pylos and in part at other centres. The collapse of a central polity there might well prove irreversible, and there are special factors, such as the very long time needed to cultivate young olive trees before achieving effective production should the olive groves be destroyed, which reinforce this effect.

This phenomenon is what Rappaport (1978) has termed 'over-segregation' or overcentralisation, and is related to Flannery's (1972) 'hyper-coherence' or 'hyperintegration'. The system has adapted to existing diversity in the environment by specialising and centralising: This makes it very effective for limited changes, but in the face of sustained change it may simply collapse.

Betancourt (1976) has written illuminatingly in similar terms about the Mycenaeans, and Willey and Shimkin (1973, 490) analyse the Maya collapse as follows:

> The success of the system produced growths of population and of competing centres which led to increasing rigidity in the system as it was subjected to internal stresses and external pressures. The system failed through inadequate recognition of these stresses and pressures and through inappropriate responses to them. The economic and demographic bases of the society were weakened; the consequences were the collapse of the system, the decimation of the population, and a retrogression to a simpler level of sociopolitical integration.

It is worth noting that several 'crash' phenomena in human society are of this general kind, where the only available response to a severe deficiency of strategy is to work more intensively at the same strategy. A sure way for a gambler to avoid loss may be to keep betting on the same number, doubling the stake at each throw. But if he is unlucky assets will run out before his number comes up. Stock exchange crashes are sometimes caused by an analogous 'overheating' effect. The attraction to speculators of a rising index favours speculative buying, thus pushing share prices still higher. Profits can be realised only by selling: The price falls and the crash comes. The crisis of confidence which results in bankruptcy can arise when a financial organisation becomes 'overstretched' in a similar manner.

### The Dangers of Zero Growth

For some human societies, stability (in the sense of peace and prosperity) is assured only by continued growth. Zero growth does not for them represent a stable state, and negative growth can accelerate to disintegration.

It is generally argued that stability and long-term survival in a system are assured through homeostasis. There is some resistance to any innovation, and such change as comes about is regarded as a response to outside stimuli, by way of a minimal adjustment to them. But when we are talking of culture change we are concerned with sustained growth, which somehow overcomes the negative feedbacks of the homeostatic controls. Sustained growth comes about through positive feedback effects, not only within individual subsystems but between subsystems – the multiplier effect (Renfrew 1972; chapters 9 and 10 above).

It is possible, therefore, to model growth by constructing a system with strong positive feedback loops which can outweigh in their effect the homeostatic, negative feedback loops (Cooke and Renfrew, chapter 11 above). Yet if there is an external factor tending to reduce growth or even induce negative growth, the rate of growth of the system may ultimately become zero. And a system with strong positive feedback loops and zero growth will usually be in an unstable or metastable situation, for a small negative growth will be reinforced during the growth phase and magnified, giving an increased rate of decline. A crash can easily be modelled in this way (see Hosler, Sabloff and Runge, 1977).

There are, moreover, indications that some subsystems of society can become adjusted to a steady positive rate of growth in such a way that this same rate can be peacefully sustained over a longer period, whereas a reduction to a smaller (but still positive) rate will have disruptive effects. In many modern Western economies, for instance, a positive rate of growth is considered the norm, and if wage rates do not increase, in real terms, by a positive amount each year, there is dissatisfaction.

If a society is to adjust to zero growth after a prolonged period of positive growth, it must disconnect the positive feedback loops which made that growth possible. Such an adjustment may not be easy, and if it is not brought about, the multiplier effect may produce collapse. Bryan Feuer (1974) has fruitfully applied this model to the collapse of Mycenaean civilisation.

## The Cusp Catastrophe

A general description of the process of early state collapse can by given using the cusp catastrophe (Amson 1974, Poston 1979, Thom 1975, Zeeman 1977). Limitations of space prevent a full discussion of the model employed, which has been concisely set out elsewhere (Renfrew 1978), but the outline is given here to sustain the new ideas in the two succeeding sections.

The sociopolitical system under consideration, the early state, can be described by a number of variables whose values represent the circumstances, the states, of its various subsystems. We shall choose a single variable, which could be one of these subsystem variables or some function of them, to represent in outline the general behaviour of the system as a whole. Its value will change suddenly, for instance, when the system collapses.

For our model of early centralised society, we shall define this behaviour variable, *degree of centrality D,* which is represented as a coordinate $x$ in the behaviour space $X$. This is some measure of actual control of territory by a central authority through a pronounced hierarchical structure. High values will be reflected archaeologically by a hierarchy of central places, by insignia of kingship, by the maintenance of bureaucratic records, and by the other epiphenomena of state society. But degree of centrality refers as much to the software, the social reality, as to the hardware, the stock of palaces and temples. It can change rapidly, indeed in a time no longer than it takes to cut a few throats. Indeed it should be thought of as some measure of the information-carrying capacity and effectiveness of the administration.

We visualise also a control space $C$, or parameter space, as a horizontal plane of points $c$ with coordinates $a$ and $b$. The choice of control variables is crucial to the model, as is a decision as to the number of control variables necessary. At first, to present the simplest possible example, the case with two control variables is chosen. Later four control variables can be considered. The proposed control variables are $I$, accumulated investment in charismatic authority, and $N$, net rural marginality.

Charismatic authority refers to the structured organisation in society which results in adherence to the polity which the centre symbolises. It is not a measure of popularity or belief but of the energy assigned to cultural devices used to promote adherence to the central authority. The second control variable, net rural marginality, relates to the economic balance for the rural population. On the income side of the account are the fruits of their agricultural or craft endeavour. On the debit side are the material contributions, in goods or labour, required of them by the central state authority as the price of citizenship and to escape punishment.

The idea of marginality is designed to give simultaneous consideration to productivity on the one hand, and the level of taxation or levy on the other. A given level of taxation may be entirely acceptable at one stage, but if productivity *per capita* decreases (perhaps through increase in population) the same burden is heavier to bear and marginality is high.

The notion of a model, of any explanation, implies that there is a relationship between the state and control variables, although we do not always need to know precisely what it is. We suppose that the evolution (the dynamics) of the system is governed by a family of functions $f_c$, which we may think of as generalised potential functions. The stable states of the system under consideration are represented by maxima or minima of this function. In this case we may think of $f_c$ as representing a measure of the viability or stability of the culture system. Another way of looking at this is to think of $f_c$ as representing the 'attractiveness' of the system for the given value of $x$. The main hypothesis required for a catastrophe theory treatment is that the system in general acts so as locally to maximise $f_c$ (when the function represents viability or attractiveness or benefit, or alternatively to mimimize $f_c$ when this is a potential function). The other important hypothesis is that of structural stability (genericity), discussed in detail by Thom (1975, ch. 3).

Thom's theorem, crudely paraphrased and assuming structural stability, states that if the number of control variables is no more than five any singularity (or specially twisted region of the map which underlies the discontinuities in observed behaviour) is equivalent to one of a finite number of types called elementary catastrophes (Thom 1975, 9; Poston 1979). In particular when there are only two control variables the only singularities of $M$, the graph of maxima and minima, are fold curves and cusp points.

The cusp catastrophe has the form seen in figure 2. A discussion of its properties is given by Zeeman (1977) and Amson (1974), and is not repeated here (see also Renfrew 1978).

We can now use the properties of the cusp surface $M$, and in particular those of discontinuity and divergence, to help us grasp the anatomy of system collapse. For instance, if we start with high values of $a$ and $b$ (in control space $C$), the corresponding point in state space $X$ is on the upper sheet of the cusp surface $M$. $x$ has a high value. But if the value of $a$ steadily diminishes, while $b$ holds steady with a high value, the movement of the control point $c$ in $C$ brings the point $(c, x)$ along this upper surface toward the edge of the fold. When $c$ enters the area of $C$ enclosed by the bifurcation curve $B$, there are two values of $x$ for each pair of values $(a, b)$ corresponding, respectively, to the upper and lower sheets of $M$. If the system *locally* maximises $f_c$, it will stay as long as possible without sudden change (following the delay rule), that is, until $c$ reaches the other side of the region of bimodal behaviour, enclosed by the bifurcation set $B$. At this point there is suddenly only a single maximum of $f_c$, on the lower sheet of $M$, and $x$ will undergo a sudden change of value. As $a$ continues to decrease (if it does), change in $x$ will now be smooth and steady again. It is this sudden change in $x$, corresponding to a discontinuous crash in the system, which represents for us the system collapse.

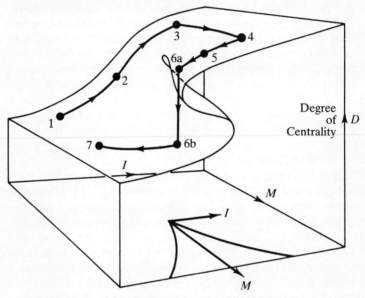

*Figure* 2. System collapse modelled by the cusp catastrophe.

We therefore postulate a function $f_{I,M}(D)$ that expresses in some appropriate form the stability and viability of the system, reflected in the well-being of the rural population. The rural population, indeed the system at large, acts in such a way as locally to maximise the viability $f$, taking into account the various constraints implied by $I$ and $M$. $D$, the degree of centralisation, is here seen as reflecting the success or failure of the central authority in commanding or attracting the adherence of the rural population to the central system and hence ensuring its viability and survival.

Let us now follow a typical systems collapse time trajectory, as it might be for the Maya or Mycenaean civilisation. The story starts at point one representing $t_1$. Marginality is low, and so is investment in charismatic authority. The degree of centrality is low. This is a prosperous non-centred society, which may well be egalitarian. *I* increases, through points $t_2$ and $t_3$, so that *D* increases: the state develops. But marginality is now increasing: it is no longer easy for the rural population to increase the *per capita* yield further in order to make the required contributions to the central administration. As population increases, or fertility decreases, or the tax burden is augmented, marginality now increases, with increase in *I* also to point 4.

But now the system is under stress, with high *M*, and *I* decreases slightly to point 5. There is now also a low value of *D* (on the lower sheet with the same values of *I* and *M*) for which efficiency is also a maximum. But the delay rule (representing the inertia of the system through its complex feedbacks) means that not until $t_6$, when the local maximum vanishes altogether, does the value of *D* change suddenly (point 6b on figure 2). This very rapid change, the collapse of central government, will bring in its wake many other changes. In particular, the central personnel, no longer exercising control or imbued with the charisma that accompanies it, can no longer command *I*, the investment in charismatic authority. The instantaneous collapse of *D* (the rupture of centralised control) is followed by the rapid but slower diminution of *I* to point 7. The administrative population, with its specialist officials and craftsmen, either die or emigrate (or return to rural cultivation), and marginality is reduced (point 1).

This formulation, it should be noted, can take account of sudden changes in the external circumstances, caused for instance by a natural cataclysm, which can of course result in sudden changes in the control variables. These in turn may result in the catastrophe collapse of the system.

## Acephalous and Centred Societies: Anastrophe

The cusp catastrophe model described in the preceding section was set up in order to seek some general explanatory formula for the very widespread phenomenon of system collapse. Like all models, however, it brings with it certain further properties and implications which were not envisaged in the initial formulation (Braithwaite 1953). These are themselves very interesting, and underline the fruitfulness of the approach.

## Divergence

An important property of the cusp and higher order elementary

379

catastrophes is bifurcation. If two systems start off at $L$ with identical initial conditions (with identical values for the control variables and for the state variable), they can end up with identical values for the control variables yet in very different final positions $M_1$ and $M_2$ (with different values for the state variable $D$). The final value of $D$ depends not only on the values of the control variables $a$ and $b$ at that point, but on the *past history* of the system, that is, on the trajectory between $L$ and $M$. This is an important property of culture systems.

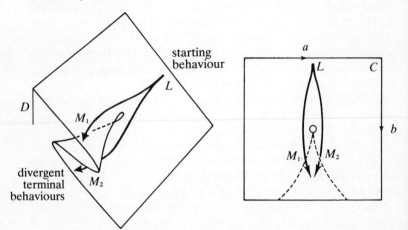

*Figure* 3. Divergence: two societies with analogous social organisations that start off at the same point ($L$) can finish with centralised authority ($M_1$) and acephalous structure ($M_2$) respectively, in the same environmental conditions.

This property is illustrated in figure 3. Two systems start off at point $L$. The first undergoes a slight increase in $a$ (the normal factor) before being subject to substantial increase in $b$ (the splitting factor); the second undergoes slight decrease in $a$ before $b$ increases. After the increase in $b$ the value of $a$ returns for each to the same initial figure. Yet one is now on the upper surface of the cusp surface, with high $D$, and the other on the lower, with low $D$. Of course if $a$ were to decrease markedly, the first would undergo catastrophic decrease in $D$ and both systems would again be in the same state. But there is no reason to expect this to occur. $M_1$ and $M_2$ are both stable states of the system or systems.

If now we consider a whole series of systems, starting off at or near $L$, with comparable initial conditions, as their subsequent

varied histories, we can predict that some will end up on the upper
sheet and some on the lower sheet. At a given time, if $b$ should be
low they may show a fairly continuous distribution in terms of $D$
(figure 4, upper). But if $b$ should be high, the distribution will be a
bimodal one, with many on the upper sheet (high $D$) and many on
the lower sheet (low $D$) and very few with intermediate values of $D$
(figure 4, lower).

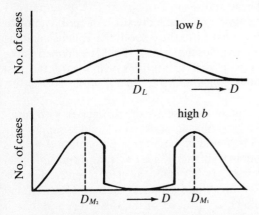

*Figure* 4. Frequency distribution of social forms (variable $D$, degree of
centrality) when splitting factor $b$ is low (*above*) and high (*below*) as
predicted by the cusp catastrophe (see figure 3).

Now returning to the variables used in the preceding section, we
can imagine a number of separate polities in a given region in similar
environmental conditions. Initially the population density is low
and other factors may work to keep marginality low. Some of these
polities will invest in charismatic authority to some extent, others
much less so. As population increases, and perhaps other factors
operate to increase marginality, a situation will develop in which
some societies will show a pronounced degree of centralisation, and
others very little. If marginality is high, there will be few intermediate forms, although with low marginality the spectrum of
centrality will be a continuous one.

It is interesting that this effect is precisely what some observers
have recognised for traditional African societies. To quote Fortes
and Evans-Prichard (1940, 5):

> It will be noted that the political systems described in this book
> fall into two main categories. One group, which we refer to as
> Group A, consists of those societies which have centralised

authority, administrative machinery and judicial institutions – in short a government – and in which cleavages of wealth, privilege, and status correspond to the distribution of power and authority. This group comprises the Zulu, and Ngwato, the Bemba, the Banyankole, and the Kede. The other group, which we refer to as Group B, consists of those societies which lack centralised authority, administrative machinery, and constituted judicial institutions – in short which lack government – and in which there are no sharp divisions of rank, status or wealth. This group comprises the Logoli, the Tallensi, and the Nuer. Those who consider that a state should be defined by the presence of governmental institutions will regard the first groups as primitive states and the second group as stateless societies.

Some writers have sought to correlate the distinction with population density, and the foregoing analysis would tend to support the correlation, although it should be noted that population density is only one component of marginality, since environmental and social factors are also relevant. It has been argued recently that the distinction between group A and group B, between centred and acephalous, is very much an artefact of the observer, and that in reality the distribution is very much a continuous one. Inadequacies of observation or categorisation by the anthropologist are not, however, to be ascribed to the model itself: it simply predicts that, given the underlying assumptions and with a fairly high marginality, there will be a bimodal distribution corresponding to societies of group A and group B.

One of the features of African political organisation, however, which has particularly excited comment (e.g., Richards 1960) is that both centred and acephalous societies appear to exist in the same ecological region, often in close proximity, without apparent good reason to explain their coexistence or determine which form will be stable in a particular case. But this is exactly what our model predicts: that there should be stable states at $M_1$ and $M_2$, with a high and a low value of $D$, respectively, corresponding to centred and acephalous polities (high and low $D$) in precisely the *same* environmental conditions and indeed with certain similarities in their internal functioning (represented by the same values of $a$ and $b$ – in terms of our model of $I$ and $M$).

Clearly this observation merits much closer study, but it is exciting that the model appropriate for the analysis of system collapse should make predictions which go some way toward clarifying what has hitherto seemed a paradox of political organisation.

## State Formation: Anastrophe

After the collapse of an early state, we have predicted that feedback among the variables, and in particular from *X* to *C*, will reduce the marginality fairly quickly. Subsequent further investment in charismatic authority may lead to increase in degree of centrality. Increasing marginality and further changes could then ultimately lead to a further collapse, so that the behaviour might be cyclical (figure 5).

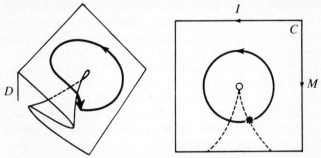

*Figure* 5. Cyclical state formation (gradual) and collapse are possible (*left*) as the control variables change (*right*). Catastrophe.

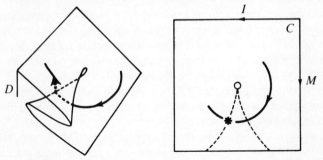

*Figure* 6. Anastrophe: if the control variables follow a path close to the reverse of that seen in figure 5 (*right*), sudden state formation can occur.

Yet there is nothing in the model to suggest that the feedback on the lower sheet necessarily always works to reduce marginality. Instead it is tempting to consider the circumstances in which a system on the lower surface, with low *D*, might undergo a sudden 'upward collapse' onto the upper surface, rapidly becoming a highly centred polity with high *D*. Within the context of the present discussion *I* propose to designate this phenomenon of 'upward collapse' by the term *anastrophe* (figure 6). It is the counterpart, therefore, of the catastrophe of system collapse. From the mathematical standpoint, of course, sudden increase of $D$, like sudden decrease, is simply a discontinuous change of the state variable: Both are catastrophes (in the sense of Thom) with only the relatively trivial matter of a change of sign to distinguish between them. While recognising this, however, the distinction in the applied case does not appear trivial at all. So anastrophe will here refer to the discontinuous increase in the state variable $D$ (which represents degree of centrality), and catastrophe to discontinuous decrease.

Continuous decrease of the normal variable $a$ (in this case investment in charismatic authority), when the splitting variable $b$ (in this case marginality) is held at a constant high value, produces a catastrophic decrease in $D$ (degree of centrality). As we have seen, the system acts so as locally to maximize $f_c$ with the operation of the delay rule, and the switch to the lower sheet is deferred until the last possible moment. The model predicts that for an acephalous society, when marginality is high, steady increase in investment in charismatic authority will produce an anastrophe, a discontinuous rise in $D$. The model is here predicting for us another allactic form, the rapid formation of this state. If we define $D$ by the size of territory or population, the anastrophe will entail the fusion of a number of acephalous polities to yield a single centred society (state formation by amalgamation). Alternatively, if $D$ is defined in terms of levels of hierarchical organisation without reference to scale, the anastrophe entails the sudden emergence of new structures of authority and administration by the insertion of a new hierarchical level, without any necessary change of scale (state formation by intensification). In practice sudden state formation will usually involve both these processes.

It is important to recognise that the model in itself, as formulated, tells us nothing of the nature of state organisation, and a fuller analysis would undoubtedly require a deeper insight into the hierarchical structure and communication network implied by high centrality. Nor does it tell us that state formation implies any discontinuity. When marginality is low, investment in charismatic authority and degree of centrality can increase smoothly together, just as has been envisaged in figure 5. What the model does do is to suggest that in certain conditions the state formation will be sudden, and to offer some suggestion as to what those conditions may be.

I suggest that the formation of the Zulu state may have been of this kind (see Gluckman 1960), and likewise the emergence of a centralised Saxon kingdom with a state organisation in Britain in the ninth century A D.

The model itself does not indicate whether the anastrophe comes about as the result of war or by peaceful means. When an acephalous society is threatened by attack from outside, one response may well be to increase investment in charismatic authority, in the form of war leadership. But the change can also be a peaceful one: the formation of the Iroquois confederacy may be a change with elements of both.

The model here harmonises with, and I think helps to sharpen, the insights of Robert Netting writing of political adaptation in Africa (1972, 332 ff):

> Let me suggest that political development in many cases takes place internally and voluntarily rather than by imposition or wholesale borrowing from neighbouring groups, and that the main lines of development and channels for change are prefigured in existing institutions and patterns of behaviour.

In his discussion (1972, 233) he stresses the role of charismatic leadership in the genesis of state organisation:

> I would claim that on the road to statehood, society must first seek the spiritual kingdom, the essentially religious modes of focusing power are often primary in overcoming the critical structural weakness of the state. . . . The overwhelming need is not to expand existing political mechanisms (they are in certain respects radically inelastic) but literally to transcend them.

The model propounded here suggests that increasing marginality, whether arising from increased population, circumscription or whatever, may be one of the preconditions for the sudden anastrophic formation of a state society. Intriguingly it is likewise a necessary condition for the catastrophic collapse of the highly centred political system. I find it illuminating that a model conceived to describe the latter process should also prove relevant to the former.

## Transformations

What started as an analysis of systems collapse has taken us far further, toward an analysis, or at least a description, of the transformations by which polities change their nature. At the outset the notion of allactic form was put forward, of which systems collapse is one of the most clearly recognisable.

Yet one of the first lessons which the discussion underlines is that the sudden collapse of an early state society is simply one of a number of possibly rapid changes of state of relatively simple agrarian societies. The most obviously discontinuous, or at least very rapid, changes in the archaeological record are collapses, catastrophes to use Thom's term. But the discussion reminds us that sudden formations, sudden increases in organisational complexity and centrality, here termed anastrophes, can also occur.

There is little doubt, also, that the analysis holds several more insights which I have not spelt out, or which I have not seen. For instance, it would seem to be true that the well-known cases of systems collapse entail a catastrophic switch from early state society to segmentary society without stopping at the intermediate level of centrality, the chiefdom, on the way. Why is this? Is it that the level of marginality has to be so high before collapse ensues that it has already exceeded the limits of tolerance of a chiefdom society?

The property of divergence allows us to see how it is that discrete social forms may be observed, without intervening variants, rather than a complete spectrum of societies. This is indeed one of the most interesting aspects of catastrophe theory, that it generates thresholds and hence different forms. Further applications are likely to cast some light upon similar sociopolitical dichotomies, among which the Highland Burmese distinction between *gumsa* (ruled by chiefs) and *gumlao* (repudiating hereditary class difference) is particularly well known (Leach 1964, chapter VI).

In this chapter I have tried to bring out the features which arise from the mathematics of catastrophe theory and those which arise from my own specific formulation. Undoubtedly the problems raised here could be formulated differently, although the use of a different vocabulary sometimes masks the reality that same distinctions are in fact being drawn. This is to some extent true, I feel, of Friedman's recent repudiation (Friedman 1974) of a systems terminology in favour of a neo-Marxian one. But without arguing that issue it is pertinent to remark that the notion of 'trajectory' is very much at home within the context used here, and that transformations between different system states or social formations in the sense of radical, possibly discontinuous changes are not only permitted but required by catastrophe theory. Indeed the terms transformation and catastrophe (or anastrophe) are in most cases interchangeable. It is not of course surprising that the study of structural stability and morphogenesis should illuminate 'structuralist' argumentation, but the underlying explanation or description of the transformations observed rests, in the case of catastrophe theory, on a much surer basis than an appeal to the altogether nebulous concept of 'contradictions' (Friedman 1974, 465). The approach outlined here could, I feel, be translated into Marxist-structuralist thought (and language) to the benefit of the latter.

It must be admitted that many of the observations here do not derive directly from catastrophe theory: I do not claim to have 'proved' anything in the mathematical sense. Yet the theory has worked as a valuable heuristic tool. For archaeologists badly need a framework of thought that will allow changes to be studied and compared. The classification of elementary catastrophes encourages the hope that allactic forms may indeed be recognised so that the analysis of cross-cultural regularities can be set on a more sound and formal basis, without encountering the objections which many anthropologists seem to hold for ethnographic analogies. Naturally each culture at a particular time is unique, and the sequence of events will from one perspective be unique also. A model of this kind can describe only those features with which its limited level of complexity allows it to deal. My argument here is that there are certain underlying regularities which it is useful to discern and to analyse. Such a procedure can in itself allow us to define more closely the special or unique features of the individual process, but it will never predict the infinite complexity and variety of each individual case. In the words of René Thom (1975, 320):

> It is tempting to see the history of nations as a sequence of catastrophes between the metabolic forms; what better example is there of a generalised catastrophe than the disintegration of a great empire like Alexander's! But in a subject like mankind itself, one can see only the surface of things. Heraclitus said, 'You could not discover the limits of the soul, even if you travelled every road to do so: such is the depth of its form'.                                                  [1979]

## Bibliography

Ålin, P. (1962) *Das Ende der mykenischen Fundstätten auf dem griechischen Festland*, Lund (Studies in Mediterranean Archaeology I).

Adams, R. E. W. (1973) The collapse of Maya civilisation: a review of previous theories, in T. P. Culbert, ed., *The Classic Maya Collapse*, Albuquerque, University of New Mexico Press, 21–34.

Akurgal, E. (1962) *The Art of the Hittites*, London, Thames and Hudson.

Aldred, C. (1961) *The Egyptians*, London, Thames and Hudson.

Allchin, B. and R. Allchin (1968) *The Birth of Indian Civilisation*, Harmondsworth, Penguin.

Amson, J.C. (1974) Equilibrium and catastrophic models of urban growth, in E.L. Cripps, ed., *Space Time Concepts in Urban and Regional Models* (London Papers in Regional Science 4), Pion, London, 108–28.

Bell, B. (1971) The Dark Ages in ancient history: 1. The first Dark Age in Egypt, *American Journal of Archaeology*, 75, 1–26.

Betancourt, P.P. (1976) The end of the Greek bronze age, *Antiquity*, 50, 40–47.

Braithwaite, R.B. (1953) *Scientific Explanation*, Cambridge, University Press.

Carpenter, R. (1966) *Discontinuities in Greek Civilisation*, Cambridge, University Press.

Culbert, T.P., ed. (1973) *The Classic Maya Collapse*, Albuquerque, University of New Mexico Press.

Desborough, V.R. (1975) The end of Mycenaean civilisation and the Dark Age, the archaeological background, in I.E.S. Edwards, C.J. Gadd, N.G.L. Hammond and E. Sollberger, eds., *Cambridge Ancient History*, (3rd edn.), II, ch. 36, 658–77.

Feuer, B. (1974) An explanatory model for the collapse of the Mycenaean civilisation, unpublished seminar paper, California State University, Long Beach.

Flannery, K.V. (1972) The cultural evolution of civilisations, *Annual Review of Ecology and Systematics*, 3, 399–426.

Fortes, M. and E. Evans-Pritchard (1940) *African Political Systems*, Oxford, University Press.

Friedman, J. (1974) Marxism, structuralism and vulgar materialism, *Man* 9, 444–69.

Gluckman, M. (1960) The rise of a Zulu empire, *Scientific American* 202, (April), 157.

Hood, M.S.F. (1973) *The Minoans*, London, Thames and Hudson.

Hosler, D.H., J.A. Sabloff and D. Runge (1977) Simulation model development: a case study of the Classic Maya collapse, in N. Hammond, ed., *Social Processes in Maya Prehistory*, London, Academic Press, 553–90.

Isnard, C.A. and E.C. Zeeman (1976) Some models from catastrophe theory in the social sciences, in L. Collins, ed., *The Use of Models in the Social Sciences*, Tavistock Press, London, 40–100.

Leach, E.R. (1964) *Political Systems of Highland Burma*, London, Athlone Press (London School of Economics Monographs on Social Anthropology no. 44).

Lumbreras, S. (1974) *The Peoples and Cultures of Ancient Peru*, Washington, Smithsonian Institution Press.

Marinatos, S. (1939) The volcanic destruction of Minoan Crete, *Antiquity*, 13, 425–39.

Martin, P.S., G.I. Quimby and D. Collier (1947) *Indians before Columbus*, Chicago, University Press.

Netting, R.M. (1972) Sacred power and centralization aspects of political adaptation in Africa, in B. Spooner, ed., *Population Growth, Anthropological Implications*, Cambridge, Mass., MIT Press, 219–44.

Ninkovich, D. and B. Heezen (1965) Santorini tephra, *Colston Papers*, 17, London, Butterworth, 413–53.

Piggott, S. (1950) *Ancient India*, Harmondsworth, Penguin.

Poston, T. (1979) The elements of Catastrophe Theory, or the honing of Occam's Razor, in C. Renfrew and K. L. Cooke, eds., *Transformations, Mathematical Approaches to Culture Change*, New York, Academic Press, 425–36.

Poston, T. and I. N. Stewart (1976) *Taylor Expansions and Catastrophes*, (Research Notes in Mathematics 7), London, Pitman.

Rappaport, R. A. (1978) Maladaptation in social systems, in J. Friedman and M. J. Rowlands, eds., *The Evolution of Social Systems*, London, Duckworth, 49–72.

Renfrew, C. (1972) *The Emergence of Civilisation, the Cyclades and the Aegean in the Third Millennium B. C.*, London, Methuen.

— (1976) Megaliths, territories and populations, in S. J. De Laet, ed., *Acculturation and Continuity in Atlantic Europe*, (Dissertationes Archaeologicae Gandenses 16) Brugge, De Tempel, 198–220.

— (1978) Trajectory discontinuity and morphogenesis, the implications of Catastrophe Theory for archaeology, *American Antiquity*, 43, 203–44.

— (1979) Transformations, in C. Renfrew and K. L. Cooke, eds., *Transformations, Mathematical Approaches to Culture Change*, New York, Academic Press, 3–44.

Richards, A. I. (1960) Social mechanisms for the transfer of political rights in some African tribes, *Journal of the Royal Anthropological Institute*, 90, 175–90.

Sabloff, J. A. (1973) Major themes in the past hypotheses of the Maya collapse, in T. P. Culbert, ed., *The Classic Maya Collapse*, Albuquerque, University of New Mexico Press, 35–42.

Sanders, W. T. and J. Marino (1970) *New World Prehistory*, Englewood Cliffs, Prentice-Hall.

Snodgrass, A. M. (1971) *The Dark Age of Greece*, Edinburgh, University Press.

Taylour, W. (1964) *The Mycenaeans*, London, Thames and Hudson.

Thom, R. (1975) *Structural Stability and Morphogenesis*, Reading, Mass., W. A. Benjamin.

Vivian, R. G. (1970) An inquiry into prehistoric social organisation in Chaco Canyon, New Mexico, in W. A. Longacre, ed., *Reconstructing Prehistoric Paeblo Societies*, Albuquerque, University of New Mexico Press, 59–83.

Wheeler, R. E. M. (1968) *The Indus Civilisation*, Cambridge, University Press, 3rd edn.

Willey, G. R. and D. B. Shimkin (1973) The Maya collapse, a summary view, in T. P. Culbert, ed., *The Classic Maya Collapse*, Albuquerque, University of New Mexico Press, 457–502.

Zeeman, E. C. (1977) Catastrophe theory, in *Catastrophe Theory, Selected Papers 1972–1977*, Reading, Mass., Addison-Wesley, 1–64.

# 14

## THE ANATOMY OF
## INNOVATION

*

How do major technological changes occur in human societies? In what circumstances are existing products and practices set aside in favour or radically new ones? Just what is it that makes a particular new fashion at a specific time displace an old one?

Innovation, the development or introduction of what is new, is evidently a process whose understanding is fundamental to the study of society and especially of change. It is one which archaeology has yet to deal with successfully. The purpose of this paper is twofold. First to argue that the recent popularity of 'diffusionist' explanations in archaeology, and the undoubted success of modern geographers in studying innovation diffusion as a spatial process, have obscured an important central point: that in many cases a spatial framework is not the most appropriate for the study of innovation. Secondly, to offer an alternative model where the crucial mechanism is human choice – the conscious decision by the individual to adopt one mode of undertaking a particular activity rather than another. In many cases human choice is bimodal – a yes/no decision between two alternatives. Catastrophe theory may be used to investigate the properties of discontinuity, hysteresis and divergence which accompany bimodal change. The rapid and widespread appearance of an innovation in the archaeological record need not indicate the operation of some external agency upon the culture system.

These problems of invention and adoption are inextricably linked in much archaeological literature on the subject, yet I believe that they can profitably be separated, since in some cases very different processes are at work. A good example is offered by copper metallurgy, first seen in the Old World at a very early date in the Near East. Yet a productive copper technology with a large output developed only millennia later in that area, by which time indications of the necessary technical skill to smelt and cast copper are evident in south-east Europe and perhaps in Iberia. That this circumstance should not automatically be seen as the working of 'diffusion' has been argued in a number of places (Renfrew 1969, Tringham 1971, 198) and refuted in others (Wertime 1964, 1257). Some rather more careful analysis is desirable.

## Change in Society

Innovation is to be distinguished from invention. Invention is the discovery or achievement by an individual of a new process or form, whether deliberately or by chance. Innovation as it will be understood here implies the widespread *adoption* of a new process or form, and clearly it must be preceded by the relevant inventions whether by a short or by a long period. 'In the usual terminology the inventions, small and large, needed for progress become "innovations" when entrepreneurs adopt them in industry. The innovational process requires of course not only the production but the distribution of additional knowledge, and it requires entrepreneurial decisions' (Felliner 1971, 2). Whether we are speaking of industrial or domestic activity it is essential to distinguish between *invention* and *adoption*.

The initial knowledge required to carry out the process in question may have been gained locally by invention or may have been introduced into the area in question as a result of contacts with another area where the invention was earlier made. This process is frequently termed 'diffusion' by archaeologists although the mechanism of transmission of the knowledge is often not defined. Sometimes the knowledge transmitted may be only partial: contact may impart some general knowledge of the outlines of a process or form without its precise details, which are re-invented anew under the stimulus of the contact. This is what Kroeber (1940) calls 'stimulus diffusion', and he gives as examples the development of fine ceramics in western Europe under the influence of Chinese porcelain, and the invention of a written syllabary for the Cherokee language after contact with the European writing system. But Kroeber does not make the distinction emphasised here: only the first of his examples ranks as an innovation. The second is merely an invention, since the Cherokee writing devised by Sequoya did not become widely used.

In the same way the circumstances favourable to the adoption of a new process may develop entirely locally, or they may come about through continuing contacts with another society, whether or not the initial invention was learnt from that source. Childe's model for the development of bronze age society in central Europe under the influence of a developing trade with the Mycenaean world (Childe 1958) is an example of the latter kind. Analogous mechanisms are implied in Fried's distinction between 'pristine' and 'secondary' civilisations (Fried 1967), the essential innovations of the latter being assumed to derive from the former.

Archaeologists in recent years have rightly stressed the importance of the adoption process, and the circumstances in the social context which favour it. As Flannery (1968, 80) puts it,

> The use of a cybernetics model to explain prehistoric cultural change, while terminologically cumbersome, has certain advantages. For one thing it does not attribute cultural evolution to 'discrepancies', 'inventions', 'experiments' or 'genius', but instead enables us to treat prehistoric cultures as systems . . . it allows us to view change not as something arising *de novo*, but in terms of quite minor deviations in one overall part of a previously existing system, that once set in motion can expand greatly because of positive feedback.

The systems approach does indeed offer a framework whereby the adoption of an invention can be examined. Positive feedbacks linked to give a 'multiplier effect' (Renfrew 1972, 27–44; chapter 9 above) may be used to explain gradual changes. But they do not so readily explain the sudden innovation, the rapid adoption, which is often taken as an indication of external intervention, and that is where catastrophe theory can help.

## Diffusion as a Spatial Process

Radical changes in the productive technology and the organisation of human society are often described and investigated in terms of 'diffusion' – that is to say within an explanatory framework where spatial co-ordinates have a special significance. It is important to realise, however, that the underlying assumptions, rarely stated by archaeologists, do not always hold. Moreover there are arguments for suggesting that these assumptions are valid less often for prehistoric times than for the twentieth century AD.

It should be noted also that the term 'diffusion' is used in some contexts in the sense of 'migration'. Chemists speak of diffusion of molecules across a membrane, for instance. And some geographical analyses have found that similar models are effective whether one is speaking of the introducion of a new population into an empty area

or the spread of an invention in an already existing human population. By diffusion we mean a process in which very few human
individuals are displaced by more than a few kilometres.

One of the most successful diffusion models for the mechanism of
culture change is the 'infectious' or 'genetic' explanation. Here the
progressive adoption of a new process in a human community is
analysed spatially. The underlying postulate or assumption is that
the new process can only spread by contact with a carrier – someone
himself already 'infected' with the innovation, someone already
carrying the crucial gene. The law of transference by personal
contact usually brings as a consequence a spatial continuity in the
dispersal of the observed innovation (unless an infected individual
travels rapidly to a new location and starts fermenting infection
there). The basic mechanism of the culture process is infection
through contact (although it need not be assumed that 100 per cent
of those exposed to infection in fact catch the innovation). The role
of the receiving individual (or culture) is entirely passive–he may
have a high or low resistance to infection, be an 'early adoptor' or a
'late acceptor' – but his personal contribution is about as significant
as that of a guinea pig exposed to a virus.

In geography the simulations of Hägerstrand and his colleagues
have indeed illuminated significantly the processes of spatial diffusion of technological improvements in recent Europe as well as
the movements of settlement. Hägerstrand's *Innovation Diffusion
as a Spatial Process* (1967) is one of the most important works of the
past decade, for the archaeologist as well as the geographer, and
introduces several refinements in terms of differing receptiveness
and effectiveness of communication which make it strikingly apposite for the cases studied.

It is not my purpose to doubt the value of such models here, but
simply to present an alternative perspective which may, in certain
cases, be preferable. It should be stressed, moreover, that these
models are formalisations of a general outlook which has been
widespread and too little questioned within archaeology for more
than a century.

Most diffusion models carry with them, or rather with their
application, two fundamental assumptions which, if applied very
generally, would between them exclude most of the fundamental
workings of culture process:

1) Change is exogenous to the location in question.

2) Widespread adoption of a new process follows rapidly in a
regular manner after exposure to 'infection' (i.e. knowledge of the

invention), allowing for different degrees of receptiveness among those infected, and for various delays related to efficiency of communication.

The first assumption if applied over very wide areas carried with it the logic of Childe's splendidly 'useful heuristic hypothesis that each innovation has been made but once.' (Childe 1956, 154). The view that the fundamental inventions only occur once in human history is a basic tenet of doctrine among some students of the history of technology, for instance among many metallurgists:

> One must doubt that the tangled web of discovery, comprehending the art of reducing oxide and the sulfide ores, the recognition of silver, lead, iron, tin and possibly arsenic and antimony as distinctive new metallic substances, and the technique of alloying tin with copper to make bronze, could have been spun twice in human history. (Wertime 1964, 1257)

The second assumption fails to take into account that the basic technology required for the adoption of many new processes is often available, whether through local development or as a result of contact with neighbouring societies, decades or centuries before it is in fact utilised on a large scale.

These comments are not intended as adverse criticism of Hägerstrand's work, and I do not suppose that he would disagree with them. In his discussion of the characteristics of innovation diffusion (1967, 133–4) he notes what can be regarded as spatial regularities of the cases under study:

Stage 1. Local concentrations of initial acceptancy;

Stage 2. Radial dissemination outward from the initial agglomerations, while those original centres simultaneously continue to condense;

Stage 3. The growth ceases. He explicitly states that 'the model population is imagined to be in the process of adopting a cultural innovation of exogenous origin.' (*ibid.*, 138).

In the first of his proposed models, which does not prove effective, it is assumed (a) from the beginning the entire population is informed about the new process, and (b) acceptances occur independently of one another in random order of precedence. In his second model (a) in the beginning only one person in the population is informed about the new process and (b) acceptance occurs immediately upon the receipt of information. In his third model: (a) only one person in the population has accepted the fictional new process from the beginning, and (b) acceptance does not occur until resistance (according to the given scale) has been overcome through repeated receipt of private information from persons who previously adopted the invention. In the second and third models, therefore, which are those which Hägerstrand develops, the crucial process is that of exposure to information about the new process.

The two basic assumptions indicated above do in fact hold for some important cases, and their success with these has obscured their unsuitability in others. In the first place they are highly relevant when one is dealing with an introduced species new to the area. You cannot have cereal farming without cereals, or silk without silkworms, any more than bubonic plague without a bacillus. Until genetic engineering develops further, assumption (1) is in fact true for all areas but the homeland of the exotic species in question. Assumption (2) may well hold also where the new species or variety fits easily into the existing agricultural system. (The model of Ammerman and Cavalli-Sforza (1973), although based on ideas of epidemiology, works because of the increase in population density which they see as associated with the inception of agriculture, and it does not rest on assumption (2).)

The assumptions are appropriate also for certain technological advances in the modern world, such as those which Hägerstrand discusses, where the positive benefits of the innovation are unquestionably very substantial. The case is not considered (except briefly, in a regional context) that the invention may be of benefit to some individuals but not to others according to circumstance, nor that the benefits themselves may vary through time.

Prior to the Industrial Revolution, invention did not take place primarily in Research Institutes or in Research and Development Laboratories within a framework of pure science, but rather was the result of practical men discovering improvements in the course of their craft activities. Discovery and invention were the work of craft specialists rather than pure scientists. The opportunity for invention was thus present wherever specialist crafts were practised: there were more potential primary centres. It may be reasonable for Hägerstrand (1967) to assume that tuberculin testing was exogenous to rural Sweden, but the principle of exogenous origin cannot be readily assumed by prehistorians.

I would argue moreover that many early inventions or discoveries, for example the exploitations of domesticable plants or the widespread manufacture of copper tools, only became profitable and hence viable as innovations with gradual change in a number of circumstances. Assumption (2), appropriate enough as used by Hägerstrand, cannot reasonably be accepted prior to the Industrial

Revolution, except for a limited number of inventions. Indeed it applies directly only to those inventions which allow an existing process to be carried out more cheaply and efficiently without any compensating disadvantages, and without substantial capital cost.

In order to construct a clear, alternative model, let us reverse these two diffusionist assumptions, replacing them by two others:

(i) Any functional invention or innovation in human technology or culture will ultimately occur again, and recurrently, irrespective of time, space or ethnic group, given the appropriate conditions.

(ii) Widespread adoption of a new process does not follow automatically upon the inception (whether locally or by outside contact) of the new process or form but depends in a complicated way upon individual choice governed by social and other factors. Availability of the technical means is a necessary but not a sufficient condition for the adoption of new inventions or discoveries.

It will be argued below that the early origin of copper metallurgy in Europe offers an excellent example for the development of these alternative assumptions. The technical processes of smelting and casting of copper are crucially dependent on the local availability of raw material and fuel, and the pyrotechnical skills to handle these materials. Both these conditions were fulfilled in the Balkans at the inception of the Copper Age and in the Iberian peninsula at the onset of the Chalcolithic, copper technology following in both cases upon ceramic technology. We see, therefore, the early handling of copper and other metals, in several areas with a settled, farming population and developed ceramic technology. Sometimes, as in the fourth millennium in the Aegean area, the technical skills were available for up to a millennium before the invented process was widely adopted, with a developed metal age as consequence.

It is necessary therefore to contrast the rather naive (although often strikingly effective) simplicity of the 'infection' model (figure 1) with the more careful consideration of the 'innovation choice' model (figure 2).

| Contact by receptor with invention | $\longrightarrow$ | Adoption of invention by receptor |
|---|---|---|

*Figure* 1. Innovation by infection / diffusion.

Under different conditions each will be appropriate, and it is not my purpose to question the usefulness of the former, simply its universality. It is in fact a special case of the latter. The focus of our

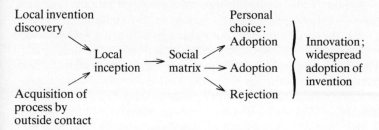

*Figure* 2. Innovation through contextual choice.

interest will more often be upon the mechanisms governing *choice* in the society, and not upon those of spatial contact.

## Catastrophe Theory and Bimodal Choice

Change in human society often occurs suddenly. Settlement patterns alter rapidly, centralised organisations undergo rapid collapse, and new processes are widely adopted within a short space of time. In these circumstances, not surprisingly, the archaeologist and the historian have frequently sought some equally striking cause – something new and influential to explain the rapid change, sometimes seen as an apparent discontinuity in the archaeological record. The obvious first choice as an explanation for the observed discontinuity has often been a discontinuity in the circumstances resulting from an invasion or migration. In the absence of evidence for these, the obvious second choice has been decisive influence from outside the society in question to account for the radical change.

One of the insights offered by catastrophe theory is that striking discontinuities in the behaviour of systems are to be expected, under certain circumstances, from the smooth and perfectly continuous change in the conditions which govern behaviour. Thus the collapse of early state societies, and in some circumstances their sudden formation, can be described without the intervention of exogenous forces. Sudden shift in settlement pattern is to be predicted, given certain gradual changes operating entirely within the culture system. As we shall see, innovation, the widespread acceptance of a new process in society can take place quite suddenly, through the local operation of relevant factors, changing quite smoothly. Whether the technical process underlying the innovation was ultimately of local or outside inception can be quite immaterial to the analysis.

397

Although the argument here was prompted by recent applications of catastrophe theory in various fields (Thom 1975, Zeeman 1976), the discussion does not require us to use any very advanced mathematics. Moreover the cusp catastrophe, the only one of Thom's 'magnificent seven' elementary catastrophes with which we have to deal, has already been described in chapter 13 and a number of accessible papers (Amson 1975, Isnard and Zeeman 1976, Renfrew 1978, Wagstaff 1976) and the description here can be brief.

We imagine a system whose behaviour may be described by a single variable, which we shall call the behaviour or state variable $x$. In the case we are to discuss, bimodal choice, $x$ represents the behaviour of the individual who is doing the choosing. He is choosing between two options, one represented by positive values of $x$, the other by negative values. This is not, however, simply a yes/no decision but a strategy mix – for instance the percentage of two crops grown, or the householder wishing to decide how many gas and how many electrical appliances to use in his house, or the traveller deciding how many miles to travel by bus and how many by rail.

The behaviour is influenced by variation in two control variables, $a$ and $b$. For instance $a$ could represent relative speed of travel, and $b$ comfort of the bus versus rail example – or in crossing the Atlantic by ship or aircraft; or $a$ could represent the crop yield of a particular mix of crops, and $b$ the labour input required to cultivate that mix.

We further imagine a potential function or utility function $f(a, b, x)$ whose value $\phi$ represents the perceived overall benefits or attractiveness of the strategy $x$ for different values of $a$ and $b$.

$$\phi = f(a, b, x)$$

We assume that the individual acts in such a way as to choose the value of $x$ that is locally optimal (in terms of perceived benefits or attractiveness). Then for given values of $a$ and $b$ the possible equilibrium values of $x$ are the maxima of $\phi$, and hence will be solutions of

$$\frac{\partial \phi}{\partial x} = 0$$

As the control variables $a$ and $b$ vary, the values of $x$ which are the maxima of the above equation determine a surface in the space $(a, b, x)$. In most cases such surfaces are single sheets, there being a single maximum (optimum) values of $x$ for each point $(a, b)$ in the control space defined by the control variables. But there may also

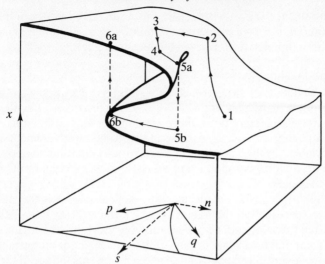

*Figure* 3. The cusp catastrophe, illustrating bimodal choice.

be values of ($a$, $b$) for which there exists more than one maximum of $x$, in which case the surface is folded. When there is more than one maximum value of $x$, the state variable, for given values of $a$ and $b$, the control variables, a sudden change of state of the system may occur as $x$ moves discontinuously from one maximum to the other. Such a sudden change is termed by Thom (1975) a 'catastrophe'. Thom's Theorem of Elementary Catastrophes, crudely para-phrased, assuming structural stability, states that if the number of control variables of such a system is not more than 5, any singularity (or specially twisted region of the map which underlies the discontinuities in observed behaviour) is equivalent to one of a finite number of types called elementary catastrophes, seven in number. When there are only two control variables the singularities can be of only two specific kinds, which Thom calls the *fold catastrophe* and the *cusp catastrophe*.

The cusp catastrophe is illustrated in figure 3. It represents the most complicated local behaviour possible when we have two control variables, and at the same time the simplest when we know that there is indeed a discontinuity which we wish to examine in which the state variable suddenly changes from one value to another.

The surface is given by the equation:

$$x^3 + ax + b = 0$$

399

On this surface the values of *x*, *a* and *b* are such that the utility function $f(a, b, x)$ is a maximum (or minimum, saddlepoint, etc.). The utility function itself is given by the equation:

$$f(a, b, x) = \tfrac{1}{4}x^4 + \tfrac{1}{2}ax^2 + bx$$

Yet the beauty of the approach is that this form need not in fact be known for a particular application. Thom's theorem states that, given his initial assumptions, there are only a few ways that discontinuous change can occur, corresponding to his seven elementary catastrophes. In this case with two control variables there are only two. The cusp catastrophe is appropriate for the consideration of bimodal choice.

Let us now consider a specific hypothetical case. *x* is the state variable representing the extent to which the strategy mix of the individual traveller under consideration favours rail rather than car travel (running for instance from $-50\%$ to $+50\%$ for all car to all rail respectively). The control variable *p* represents the speed for a given journey for rail as opposed to car, and *q* the cost for a given journey for rail as opposed to car.

The overall benefits $\phi$ of a given strategy mix *x* are seen in figure 4 for different values of *p* and *q*.

Figure 4a indicates the situation when *p*, the relative speed of rail travel, is high, and *q*, its relative cost, is low. The benefits are greatest (optimal) for a high value of *x*. A high percentage of the total miles travelled by the individual will be by rail (although not, of course, all, since not all his itinerary will be served by railways).

Figure 4b shows the case where the relative speed of rail to car *p* is low and the relative cost *q* is high. The benefits are greatest for low *x*, with most of the travel by car.

Figure 4c shows the case when both *p* and *q* are intermediate – costs of both rail and car are about the same, and so is speed. In such a case the optimum of *x* will take an intermediate value representing a balanced strategy between car and rail.

Figure 4d shows the case when *p* and *q* are both high. There are now two optimum values for *x* – one high (representing the rapidity of rail travel, despite its greater cost) and one low (representing the relative cheapness of car travel, despite the greater time required).

At this point we can appeal to Thom's theorem and state that if there are singularities, and given certain further assumptions of a mathematical nature, then the most complicated form the configuration can take is that of the cusp catastrophe (figure 3).

We are now in a position to grasp the complete anatomy of the

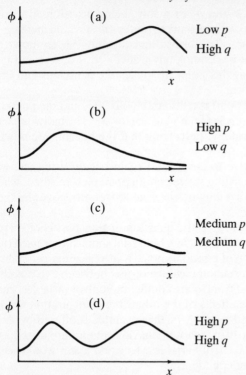

*Figure* 4. The value of the utility function $\phi$ against the measure for strategy choice $x$ for different fixed values of the control factors $(p, q)$.

situation. The surface seen in figure 3 represents the values of $x$ for which the function $\phi$ is a maximum – it shows the value of $x$ (for the given values of $p$ and $q$) representing an optimising strategy in terms of both the variables. It therefore represents the values of $x$ for which the system is in equilibrium. So as $p$ and $q$ change (for instance along the trajectory times $t_1$ to $t_3$ represented by points 1 to 3) so does the optimal value of $x$ and hence the behaviour of the individual concerned.

If, for example, $q$ is initially high and $p$ low, car travel being cheaper and faster than rail, then the individual will wherever possible travel by car, and $x$ is low (point 1). If petrol costs rise, reducing $q$, he may balance his strategy (point 2). But then rail travel is improved and becomes faster (point 3). At $t_4$, however, the cost of rail travel is increased and the surface is two-valued in $x$ for the given values of $p$ and $q$. Probably, being accustomed to rail travel, our individual will continue to prefer this, until an increase in car speeds (decrease of $p$) brings him to point 5a. By now the attractiveness of rail has completely waned – it is dearer and it is now no faster – so at this point he makes the conscious and firm decision to travel by car.

The switch at this point is a discontinuous one, and the point on the surface moves from 5a (high $x$) to 5b (low $x$). The individual has now switched his strategy, perceiving that the benefits are now in favour of car travel.

If rail speed relative to car should again rise ($p$ rising) he will tend to stick to his existing strategy until point 6a is reached, when the proposition of travelling by car is no longer attractive: he then switches to rail (6b).

We shall return below to the question of transport choice (see also Ferguson 1976; Wilson 1976), but first it should be stressed that the above description of bimodal choice is of very great generality. In general, if $x$ represents the choice or mix between two possible courses of action, and $p$ and $q$ are conflicting control variables, each acting to counter the effects of the other, the configuration will be precisely as described here. A further example is offered by Zeeman's dog (Zeeman 1976) whose behaviour modes are attack and flight, although the control variables, fear and anger would seem difficult to observe independently.

It should be noted that the two control variables should be independent, in order to produce the cusp. If one variable simply represented costs of alternative A and the other costs of alternative B, that would amount to a single control variable, for instance $(A-B)$ or $A/B$, and one could simply state that $x$ varies proportionately with $(A-B)$, or for complete bimodality that $x=1$ when $A>B$, and $x=-1$ when $A<B$, yielding a step function.

An alternative way of defining the control variables is to define a *normal* factor ($n$ on figure 3) and a *splitting factor* ($s$ on figure 3) which in this case could be regarded as equivalent to the vector sums $(q-p)$ and $(q+p)$ respectively. In general the normal factor represents the forces tending to push the state variable to one extreme or the other, while the *splitting factor* determines whether the change is smooth, on the single sheeted part of the surface (low $s$) or discontinuous, on the double sheeted part of the surface (high $s$).

A good example of a cusp surface representing bimodal behaviour is afforded by Euler buckling (Zeeman 1976), and here the force acting transverse to the beam is the normal factor, tending to make it go either up or down, while the compression on the beam is the splitting factor, enhancing the stability of equilibrium whichever position it is in and resisting change.

We can take a different and informative pair of control variables governing a bimodal choice to illustrate normal and splitting factors rather than conflicting factors. We take $x$ once again as the state variable representing a two-way strategy mix, for instance the number of gas and electrical appliances in use in the house of the individual. Change to a new value of $x$ is induced by change in the normal factor $n$ which measures the economic benefits arising from the innovation. The splitting factor $s$ represents the installation costs of the innovation, or the lack of capital for investment.

The argument follows much as before. If $s$ is low, change in $n$ will be accompanied smoothly by change in $x$, and the householder will shift from electricity to gas and back with no difficulty or delay. But if $s$ is high, representing the high cost for changing the central heating (for example) from gas to electric, or vice versa, then we shall be over the two-sheeted part of the cusp (see Renfrew 1978). As the running costs of electric installation become progressively lower, there will be a sudden discontinuous switch as the individual previously using gas predominantly switches to electricity for all but a very few appliances.

The cusp (figure 3) shows a number of very interesting properties. That of *discontinuity* has already been discussed. Hysteresis (figure 5) is the phenomenon whereby the 'jump' does not take place for the same value of $n$, the normal factor, when the jump is from the upper to the lower sheet of the surface as when it is in the other direction. Following the Perfect Delay Rule (see Amson 1975, 182; Isnard and Zeeman 1976, 49), the system acts so as *locally* to optimise utility: so long as there is a maximum value for $x$, the state will not jump discontinuously. In other words, although there is another, more distant value of $x$ with a maximum which would actually give a greater value of $\phi$, the utility function, no jump will occur until the fold in the sheet is reached, and the total maximum for the present value of $x$ entirely disappears. An alternative behaviour is described as Maxwell's Convention (Amson, *ibid.*; Isnard and Zeeman, *ibid.*), whereby the value of $x$ moves at once to give the global maximum (the dotted line in figure 5) rather than optimising locally until the local maximum disappears. Other features have been well described by Zeeman (1976) and by Amson (1975, fig. 8).

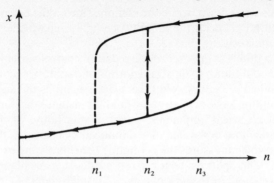

*Figure* 5. The hysteresis effect. Change in the behaviour variable *x* against that of the normal factor *n* (for a constant positive value of the splitting factor *s*). The perfect delay rule gives a hysteresis effect, while Maxwell's convention (represented by the broken line in the centre) does not.

## Bimodal Choice and Group Behaviour

So far we have considered the form which individual choice follows, in the face of two options. It does indeed appear to be the case that individuals generally show hysteresis in the exercise of bimodal choice, sticking to what is known rather than following Maxwell's Convention and moving at once to a new global optimum. One reason, of course, is that the individual can rarely be sure that he has an unobstructed and undistorted view of the competing maxima. In practice embarking on a new course of action (with discontinuous change in *x*, the state variable) may well entail taking risks. I would argue that the notion of 'risk' is equivalent, in the framework of the present model, to 'imperfect view of competing utility maxima'. The longer terminology may not at first sight seem an improvement – but it is because it brings the entire discussion into relation with the unifying concept, the cusp.

A second reason is simply the difficulty of teaching an old dog new tricks. We have spoken of installation costs as a splitting factor, delaying innovation and inducing discontinuous behaviour. There is a direct psychological analogy here, where the time and mental energy involved in mastering a new process is the direct analogue of installation cost. It is easier not to change 'unless you have to' – i.e. to follow a strategy of local optimisation.

It is my contention that most innovations involve, at least initially, little more than new ways of doing old things. Even metallurgy seems to have started in most areas with techniques suited to the working of stone (drilling and cold-working before annealing), and with products (thick copper axes resembling stone ones, and small decorative objects) simply replacing existing goods. The first products of any new material are generally skeumorphs. It follows then that the initial decisions involved in the acceptance of invention were whether or not to carry out a particular process or produce a particular object, in the new way (with new material) or in the old way. All innovation therefore involves bimodal choice in the first instance. Only later do technical developments amplify the existing divergence so that important innovations are seen as new products and new technologies in their own right. Seventy years ago an automobile was simply a 'horseless carriage', and a radio a 'wireless' telegraph; the 'talkie' emerged from the 'movie', and the moving picture from the kinetoscope.

An individual can change behaviour mode either as soon as the new maximum is globally more attractive than the old (Maxwell's Convention), or at the last moment, when the old maximum disappears (Perfect Delay Rule), or somewhere in between (Imperfect Delay). There is no way he can change earlier than the first of these, or later than the second, without failing to maximise utility even locally. The Imperfect Delay convention is discussed by Amson (1975, 197), and several procedures are in fact possible. One is that there should be a certain threshold value, and once the global maximum exceeds the local maximum by more than that value, change will occur even though the local maximum has not yet disappeared.

Now let us consider a group of individuals whose past history has been much the same, and who are stationed at approximately the same point on the cusp surface. For the moment let us imagine them all following the Perfect Delay Rule. First if they are perfectly homogeneous – identical to one another – and subject to the same influences, they will all change at once, even though the behaviour of one does not affect the behaviour of another. Secondly, if there is now some variation in their behaviour, some dispersal in their position, they will not come together to the edge of the fold of the cusp, and they will not all change together. The overall effect will then be a fuzzing out of the discontinuity. But in the third case, if their behaviour is now in some way coupled, with positive feedback between individuals, so that the action of one affects that of others, they may well move together although not themselves perfectly homogeneous.

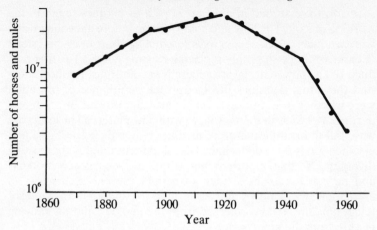

*Figure* 6. Gradual change in traction strategy (number of horses and mules on a logarithmic scale) after Hamblin, Jacobsen and Miller (1973). The curve is essentially a smooth one, artificially and need-lessly represented in straight-line segments.

### Homogeneous Individuals (No Coupling)

An elegant example of such behaviour is afforded by the growth and decline of the railroad system in the United States. It is one of the clearest examples I have found of catastrophic behaviour involving bimodal choice.

In their discussion of exponential growth and exponential decline, Hamblin, Jacobsen and Miller (1973, 92) graphically illustrate the rise and decline in the use of the horse in the US (figure 6). Although they link the points with straight line segments, supposedly describing 'exponential epochs' (since the vertical scale is logarithmic), a smooth curve might do as well. We may imagine this as described by the equation $N = e^{kt}$, where $k$ is also a variable and changes smoothly and gradually from a positive value in 1870 to zero around 1920 to a subsequent negative value.

If we fit this onto our picture of the cusp catastrophe, with the exponent $k$ as the state variable (represented by $x$ in figure 3) then some normal factor is declining while the splitting factor is constant at zero. In effect we are saying that the exponent $k$ is a function of $t$: $k = f(t)$. Indeed approximately $k = l - m.t$ (where $l$ and $m$ are constants not varying with time). So far this has nothing to do with the bimodial behaviour of the cusp catastrophe: it can adequately be shown on the single-sheeted surface of the cusp.

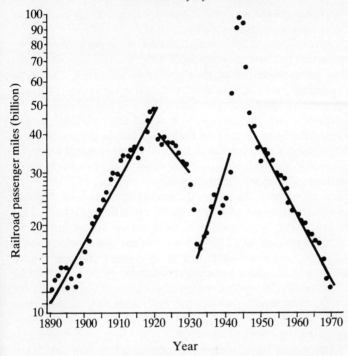

*Figure* 7. Catastrophic jumps in travel strategy, resulting from bimodal choice between road and rail travel under varying conditions of cost and convenience (railroad miles on a logarithmic scale) after Hamblin, Jacobsen and Miller (1973). Sudden changes of slope represent sudden changes of the exponent.

But turning now to figure 7 we see very different behaviour. Hamblin *et al.* (1973, 94) have drawn straight lines as shown, indicating that the exponent $k$, which is equivalent to the slope of the lines, when the ordinate is plotted on a logarithmic scale, is switching from a high positive value (1890–1920) to a high negative value (1920–1932), to a high positive again (1932–1942) further increasing from 1942 to 1947, with a catastrophic switch to a strong negative value from 1947 to the present.

Very reasonably they relate these changes to competition between rail and car:

> The 1917–1925 period also ushered in a new epoch in auto-mobile use, an epoch in which the automobile became the dominant mode of transportation, apparently because of its

improved reliability and lasting qualities and its differential convenience and privacy. (*ibid.*, 95)

Reversal from 1930 to 1942, with increase in railroad miles 'probably occurred because many people simply could not afford the luxury of automobiles during the depression' (*loc. cit.*). That trend was accentuated during World War II, and reversed in 1947, with increase in automobile mileage and decrease in rail mileage.

We can now use the cusp with $k$ as the state variable to give behaviour closely analogous to that described in the last section, and for precisely the same reasons, with the same control variables. Sudden switches in the value of $k$ (the slope of the lines in figure 7) arise with gradual change in the control variables.

We are seeing here, therefore, the operation of bimodal choice *en masse*. The constraints are acting equally upon the great bulk of the population, and are reflected in mass decisions. Many further examples could no doubt be found of such behaviour, not only in the field of transportation choice, but in advertising and commercial marketing, where sudden switches in consumer shopping behaviour can follow relatively modest changes in pricing. It should be noted that in this example only the switch in 1942, soon after the American entry into the War, was subjected to direct external constraint through rationing of petrol and tyres.

We cannot document any prehistoric strategy switches as clearly as this example, but effects of this kind, of purely local origin, may well underlie the sudden expansion of metallurgy in several regions in the early bronze age, or indeed the emergence of farming over a fairly wide area of the Near East after more than a million years of hunting and gathering.

*Inhomogeneous Individuals (No Coupling)*

If we now consider a group of individuals who are not perfectly homogeneous, although they have been subject to the same constraints (the same control variables) each will have his own utility function close but not identical with that seen in figure 3. For a given point $(p, q)$ in the control plane there will be a whole series of values of $x$, perhaps normally distributed with a mean value $x$ on the surface seen in figure 3. We are dealing now with a congeries of surfaces lying close to that seen in figure 3, but not identical to it.

If each individual follows the Perfect Delay convention, he will stay on the upper surface of his particular sheet as the control variables alter in such a way as to bring him to the fold and he will then switch to the lower surface. The effect, I assert, which will be

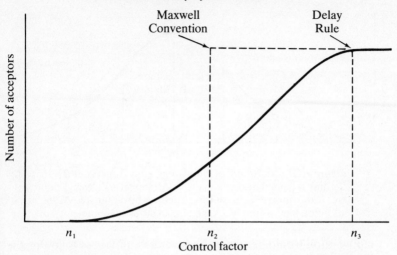

*Figure* 8. The number of acceptors plotted against change in the control factor (usually equivalent to change through time): (a) when individuals are homogeneous *or* if there is strong coupling between them – shown by broken lines for the alternative cases of Maxwell's convention and the perfect delay rule; (b) for inhomogeneous individuals with no coupling – shown by the bold line.

similar to the case where the entire population of points lies on the sheet seen in figure 3, but shows a slight fluctuation in the effective operation upon each of the control variables $(p, q)$, distributed normally about the mean individual with values $(p', q')$. The pattern of change will not then be the sudden switch (seen dotted in figure 8), which a single individual will still show, but a cumulative effect which corresponds closely with the 'adoption curves' shown in works dealing with innovation (Rogers 1962, 109).

If we show this instead, in figure 9, with rate of change on the ordinate, we shall simply obtain an approximation to the normal distribution. This can be arbitrarily divided into the 'innovators', 'early adopters', 'early majority', 'late majority', 'laggards' and 'non-adopters', of the conventional treatises on innovation (Rogers 1962, 110).

We can show, therefore, that such a pattern is predicted on the basis simply of a measure of inhomogeneity in the population. The effect would be accentuated if the inhomogeneity extended to the delay convention followed: in such cases those following Maxwell's

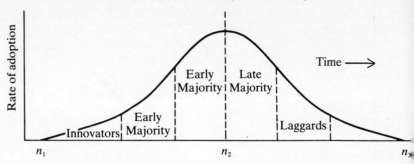

*Figure* 9. The 'diffusion' of innovation, after Rogers (1962). In reality nothing is gained by dividing this into 'innovators', 'early majority', etc. If the number of acceptors in figure 8 be designated $N$, the rate of adoption here is simply $dN/dt$, and no diffusion is implied.

Convention would be termed 'innovators', and those following the Perfect Delay Rule 'laggards'.

It should be noted however, that individuals do not make decisions about innovation in isolation, but are strongly affected by their neighbours and peers, so that there is a measure of coherence. The effect of this is to reduce the spread and promote bunching.

*Coherence: Coupling Between Individuals*
Human organisations – governments, business firms, societies – behave in certain ways like individuals. The analogy can be a misleading one, for instance when talking about the 'birth' and 'death' of a civilisation. Yet as concerns decision-making it has a certain usefulness. For it is (or used to be) the basis of good government, enshrined in the principle of cabinet responsibility, that the pros and cons of a decision are debated at length, after which a decision is taken, often by majority vote. The decision is then adopted as 'policy', and all party or government members, including those who opposed it warmly at a previous stage, are now expected to support it, or at least refrain from opposition. The observed behaviour is thus perfectly bimodal, and the fuzzing seen in the behaviour of inhomogeneous individuals without coupling does not appear. It is the feedbacks within the organisation which give it this property of coherence, of behaving 'as of one voice' like an individual, although in fact composed of many.

The behaviour of such organisations can be modelled by the cusp catastrophe, and indeed more complicated behaviour, including compromise, has been approached by Isnard and Zeeman (1976) in

410

terms of the butterfly catastrophe. The same state variable and control variables, seen in figure 3, are appropriate. The strategy mix implied by $x$ will now represent company policy for the travel of its employees rather than the decision of a single individual.

When we are speaking of innovation, the argument is again much as set out above, with $n$, the normal factor, representing the advantages of change, for instance in reduced running cost, and $s$, the splitting factor, the capital (installation) costs of changeover. The behaviour of large organisations does indeed show discontinuity and hysteresis, as a consideration of the Concorde project will amply document. At the time of writing the British and French governments, following the Perfect Delay rule (local optimisation) must now be approaching the fold of the cusp, at which further production of the unfortunate aircraft will be stopped. Had they followed Maxwell's Convention (global optimisation), the project would have been scrapped as soon as it became clear that it was certain to lose money. In this case we are speaking of a decision or 'innovation' to stop producing a product, but the anatomy of the situation is no different when we are considering a positive decision to shift from hydrocarbon to atomic-powered electricity generation, or to computerise accounting.

Coherent group behaviour is modelled as effectively by the cusp catastrophe as is that of the individual. The analogy is important, yet it is equally important to see that it is simply an analogy. Group behaviour is *not* the same as individual behaviour: by using the same model to describe it we are focusing on those aspects which are analogous. Why the same model is appropriate to each is a more subtle and less obvious problem than it may at first seem.

## An Example: the Inception of Metallurgy in Europe

The foregoing discussion offers us a framework within which to approach several specific and major innovations in the prehistoric period, of which the inception of metallurgy in south-east Europe will be considered here. This has traditionally been advanced as a classic case of the diffusion of culture (Childe 1957). The recognition of a number of relatively complex features including terra-cotta sculptures and copper objects as sites such as Vinča led to comparison with comparably complex traits at sites to the south and east such as Troy. The chronological arguments for believing the Balkan finds, such as those of Vinča, to be independent of the Aegean early bronze age have been advanced elsewhere (Renfrew 1969). So far the discussion has been polarised between those who

411

follow the view of Wertime (1964), quoted above on p.394, that metallurgy was invented only once, and those who argue for a number of independent metallurgical centres, in the Near East, in the Balkans, perhaps in Iberia (Renfrew 1967) and of course in south-east Asia as well as in the Americas. Instead, however, we can begin to discern that it was not the invention of the relevant techniques nor their dissemination in space, but their *adoption* in the cultural context in question which was the fundamental core of the innovation process. Moreover it becomes clear that a relatively sudden adoption is in some circumstances to be expected.

In several areas of the Old World an interesting pattern may be discerned, where many of the essential metallurgical processes were known at an early date, as occasional finds of copper objects testify. Yet the knowledge, the invention, was not widely exploited at this time: in the Balkans, in Anatolia, in Mesopotamia, in Iran and in Egypt we have, at different dates, the same pattern of an early knowledge of copper (the invention) and only later a rather sudden expansion of a metallurgical industry (the adoption).

In the Balkans, for instance, a copper awl 14.3 cm in length and made of native copper has been found at Balomir in Transylvania belonging to the end of the Körös culture and hence earlier than 5000 BC on a calibrated chronology (Bognár-Kutzián 1976). In the succeeding middle neolithic, around 5000 BC, copper beads are found in the Cernica cemetery of the Romanian Boian culture (Cantacuzino and Morintz 1963), and a whole series of beads, awls, chisels and fish-hooks are found in the late neolithic of the Balkans prior to 4500 BC. But it is only with the beginning of the so-called copper age of the Balkans that metal objects appear in great abundance, including solid hammer axes with their cast-in shaft holes (Charles 1967). One of these was found at Chotnitsa in Bulgaria in a Gumelnitsa culture context (Angelov 1958, 403). It is at this time that the Karbuna hoard with its 444 copper objects may be placed (Sergeev 1963). The find of small gold ornaments at Chotnitsa should also be noted. The relative chronology of these finds has been well discussed by Bognár-Kutzián (1972, 210–11).

If the early copper age sees a very marked development in the metallurgical industry, the late copper age, *c.* 4300 to 3700 BC sees its floruit. By this time copper mines were working at Rudna Glava in Jugoslavia (Jovanović 1971) and at Aibunar in Bulgaria. Several hoards of axe-hammers and chisels have been found at Pločnik in Jugoslavia. Most interesting of all are the cemeteries at Devnja, Goljamo Deltchevo and Varna in Bulgaria. At Varna a remarkable series of gold objects has been found (cf. Gimbutas 1977), and the site rivals Troy in importance, the finds being perhaps a millennium earlier than the treasures of Troy II.

The point here, then, is that metallurgy began in a modest way at an early date in the Balkans, with the cold working and later the annealing of native copper. Only something like a millennium later was casting undertaken, but even the invention of casting did not at once produce a great upsurge in metallurgical production. That upsurge came, however, and it was associated both with new forms of useful tools (the hammer-axes and axe-adzes) and with a series of new prestige items. Significantly more than one metal was involved; for gold also played an important part.

All of this suggests that what needs analysing in each area is the *role* which metal objects played in the society before, during and after the phase of widespread adoption. If for heuristic purposes, the cusp catastrophe be selected as a model suitable for cases where bimodal choice may be involved, then the normal factor will be some measure of advantage in the use of metal objects. Advantage here implies efficiency in use, and takes into account both running cost and effectiveness. The splitting factor is some measure of the investment cost involved in producing or using metal objects. The value of the cusp configuration is that it shows us how gradual changes in these factors can bring about a sudden shift in the behaviour $x$ of the individual or the group in relation to the use or non-use of metal objects.

It allows us to focus on adoption, the basic techniques (the invention) being available much earlier without promoting any large-scale industry. The widespread adoption of metalworking was relatively sudden when it came, although figure 9 reminds us that it was not instantaneous. Conceivably it may also have been reversible, like the changes in transport behaviour illustrated above (figure 7), although in most cases, as discussed below, the adoption of metallurgy ranks as an irreversible 'revolutionary' change. But in fact by 3000 BC metallurgy had become very much rarer or even extinct in the Balkans, and did not flourish again until the developed early Bronze Age of the area some centuries later.

No invocation of the cusp catastrophe will, in itself, result in a suitable analysis of the social and economic context of early metal-lurgy, but it does offer a framework. Clearly new inventions can have the effect of reducing the capital costs of existing production, so that in favourable cases newly invented techniques, whether originating inside or outside the society, can have instant effects: it is not necessary to think of the cusp in such cases. But more significant will be changes in 'advantage' in using metal objects. And advantage includes not only practical ergonomic benefits, but any perceived advantage, however non-material. It is here that I feel the social aspects can most clearly be recognised.

In south-east Europe the marked increase in metal production in the copper age, which effectively determined the moment of adoption and hence of significant innovation, coincided with the widespread use of metal objects as remarkable prestige goods. During the neolithic there were already sporadic occurrences of metal objects as chisels, axes etc. – that is as tools of little importance, adding little to the range of functions already offered by stone tools. At the same time we see copper beads in cemeteries like Cernica, but in contexts where shell beads also occur (for instance *Spondylus* at Cernica). It is not until the next phase that gold pendants are seen (for instance at Chotnitsa) and the splendid gold plaques and other objects of the Varna cemetery. At this time also we begin to see the axe-hammers which are in fact the earliest metal shaft-hole tools, and are followed by the large axe-adzes of the later copper age.

I believe that we can begin to discern here the outlines of an explanation for the innovation. To argue it properly would require a careful analysis of the contexts of discovery of all metal objects of the period, and particularly of those contexts, such as burials, where the value or prestige-rating assigned to the objects might be estimated (cf. Shennan 1975). My prediction is that immediately prior to, and during, the real boom period – the catastrophe jump from little use to widespread use – metal objects will have taken on, for the first time, a high prestige value. This will then have shifted the value of the advantage factor sufficiently (and the shift need not have been a very large one) to bring the point on the equilibrium surface to the edge of the cusp.

In the Aegean, to take another region, an equivalent catastrophe jump is seen in the metal industry at the beginning of the Early Bronze 2 period around 2700 BC. Before that time copper was little used, although once again it is sporadically found in very much earlier contexts, (e.g. the copper axes from neolithic Knossos, from Sesklo and from Alepotrypa cave). Rather suddenly the metal industry changes altogether, and this change coincides with the first appearance of metal objects in cemeteries, with the first 'treasures' (at Troy, Poliochni etc.) and with the widespread use of the bronze dagger. The alloying of copper with tin to make bronze may have an important role here, but the boom appears to have happened before alloying became universal, so that the use of tin (or arsenic) may be a consequence rather than a cause of the striking developments of the time. This important question of technological development and improvement is mentioned again in the next section.

The argument developed here, for the Balkans, in the sketchiest outline, may thus have a wider applicability. For, although the specific control factors would differ somewhat in each case, the basic cusp catastrophe configuration, relating to bimodal choice, could still hold. In each case, internal developments within the society would have shifted the 'advantage' factor, and these changes will have been as much social as technical. Similar arguments may apply for the north European bronze age. For there again, in some areas, copper objects had long been known, yet no major development occurred until the moment when metal adopted a striking prestige role, often in a 'Beaker Culture' context. Once again technical development (involving the use of bronze) followed rather than preceded the widespread acceptance of the metallurgy.

A similar sequence of events may have accompanied the widespread use of metallurgy in other parts of the world. Certainly the 'treasure horizon' in the Near East has often been the subject of comment: rich hoards and finds like those of Alaca Hüyük, Horoztepe, Troy, Poliochni and Ur seem surprising to us precisely because they come so early in the development of metallurgy in each area. The find of rich prestige goods at the beginning rather than the climax of the widespread use of metal in a region may be more than fortuitous.

## The Great Revolutions

It was Childe who coined the terms 'Neolithic Revolution' and 'Urban Revolution', no doubt with the Industrial Revolution in mind, and in *The Bronze Age* (1930) gave reasons for thinking that in Europe, at least, the inception of metallurgy was of comparable significance. They were termed 'revolutions' because of the fundamental significance of the changes which took place, and Childe did not claim that they occurred rapidly in the original homeland. But he did stress in each case the rapidity of the adoption of the new process outside the area of its initial inception. In his view, the central organising process of European prehistory was diffusion, 'the irradiation of European barbarism by Oriental civilisation' (1958b, 70). The idea that metallurgy was diffused is still widely accepted, and the same view is widely argued for agriculture (e.g. Ammerman and Cavalli-Sforza 1973). Comparable arguments for

415

the spread of the urban way of life to the Indus and elsewhere were set out a few years ago by Wheeler (1961, 248), and are still accepted by many. I would argue that, in a very general sense, the same underlying pattern of change is operating in each case giving rise to analogies in the explanations offered. Of course each development in each area, to be properly understood, has to be studied in its own terms. But to the extent that the terms 'Metallurgical Revolution' or 'Neolithic Revolution' have any meaning, it may be valid to analyse their superficial similarity. Diffusion need no longer be the result of the analysis.

Barker (1977) has stated the position well:

> The study of early metallurgy is developing along the same lines as the study of early agriculture; a choice between two apparently opposing models, diffusion or independent invention, is now seen to be a hopelessly inadequate theoretical basis for understanding when, how and why early agriculture developed in some parts of the world and not in others, and I would argue that the same is true for early metallurgy.

The key to an effective understanding in each case, I believe, is to separate the invention – the technical discovery, or the availability of a specific plant or animal species – from its widespread adoption. In the case of agriculture, sporadic finds of wheat or barley in upper palaeolithic deposits, not yet very well documented, suggest the possibility that these species may have been exploited in the Near East and perhaps in south-east Europe well before the neolithic period. The significant step would not then be the first use of the potential domesticate, but the shift to a pattern of exploitation with a very high dependence on a narrow range of species and a much less broad spectrum of exploitation in general.

If we now think of figure 3 as relating to the subsistence strategy of hunter-gatherers, with $x$ representing the degree of dependence on cereal foods, then some insight can be obtained. The normal factor $n$ represents the benefits of using cereals intensively, and $s$ the capital costs of altering the subsistence strategy. In certain environmental or demographic circumstances a sudden shift of strategy must occur, and of course much thought has been devoted in recent years to analysing just what those circumstances might be.

There is one further ingredient in this case which makes the switch decisive, and in certain circumstances irreversible. It is that after some years or decades, if the new strategy is maintained, *new technological developments arise.* In the case of the cereal crops one of these is the formation of a tough rachis, which greatly increases the effective crop yield. There are of course further changes associated with 'domestication' which make the domesticate a more satisfactory crop than its wild prototype. Much of the same is true of metallurgy: after a few decades of intensive exploitation (smelting and casting) of oxide ores in favourable areas, the use of alloys is likely to be discovered. Analogous consequences flow from the developments in craft specialisation associated with urban life. These are 'multiplier effect' phenomena (see pp.272–6 above) and in general they are not the product simply of human behaviour but also of the nature of the physical world. Only in such cases where a new strategy has unforeseen consequences of a technical nature do growth and change continue, in this way making the innovation irreversible. It is precisely to these cases that the term 'revolution' is sometimes applied.                                [1978]

## Bibliography

Ammerman, A. J. and L. L. Cavalli-Sforza (1973) A population model for the diffusion of early farming in Europe, in C. Renfrew, ed., *The Explanation of Culture Change*, London, 343–58.

Amson, J. C. (1975) Catastrophe theory: a contribution to the study of urban systems? *Environment and Planning B*, 2, 177–221.

Angelov, N. (1958) Der Sidelungshügel bei Hotnica, in V. Beshevliev and V. L. Georgiev, eds., *Studia in Honorem Acad. D. Decev*, Sofia, Bulgaria Academiya na Naukite, 389–403.

Barker, G. (1977) Early metallurgy in the Troad: the European and Asian context. Unpublished paper presented at the conference on Troy, Sheffield, April, 1977.

Bognár-Kutzián, I. (1972) *The Early Copper Age Tiszapolgar Culture in the Carpathian Basin*, Budapest, Akademiai Kiado.

— (1976) The origins of early copper processing in Europe, in J. V. S. Megaw, ed., *To Illustrate the Monuments: Essays in Honour of Stuart Piggott*, London, 70–6.

Cantacuzino, G. and S. Morintz (1963) Die jungsteinzeitliche Funde in Cernica, *Dacia 7*, 27–89.

Charles, J. A. (1967) Early arsenical bronzes – a metallurgical view, *American Journal of Archaeology*, 71, 21–6.

Childe, V. G. (1930) *The Bronze Age*, Cambridge.

— (1956) *Piecing Together the Past*, London.

— (1957) *The Dawn of European Civilisation* (6th Edn.), London.

— (1958a) *The Prehistory of European Society*, Harmondsworth.

— (1958b) Retrospect, *Antiquity*, 32, 75–9.

Clarke, D. L. (1968) *Analytical Archaeology*, London.

Felliner, W. (1971) *The Economics of Technological Advance*, New York.

Ferguson, J. A. (1976) Investment decisions and sudden changes in transport, *Surveyor*, 9th July, 1976, 10–11.

417

Flannery, K. V. (1968) Archaeological systems theory and early Mesoamerica, in B. J. Meggers, ed., *Anthropological Archaeology in the Americas*, Washington D. C., 67–87.
Fried, M. (1967) *The Evolution of Political Society*, New York.
Gimbutas, M. (1977) Gold Treasure at Varna, *Archaeology*, 30, 44–51.
Hamblin, R. L., B. R. Jacobsen and J. L. L. Miller (1973) *A Mathematical Theory of Social Change*, New York.
Hägerstrand, T. (1967) *Innovation Diffusion as a Spatial Process*, Chicago.
Haggett, P. (1965) *Locational Analysis in Human Geography*, London.
Isnard, C. A. and E. C. Zeeman (1976) Some models from catastrophe theory in the social sciences, in L. Collins, ed., *The Uses of Models in the Social Sciences*, London, 44–100.
Jovanović, B. (1971) *Metalurgija Eneolitskog Perioda Jugoslavje*, Belgrade.
Kroeber, A. L. (1940) Stimulus diffusion, *American Anthropologist*, 42, 1–20.
Renfrew, C. (1967) Colonialism and megalithismus, *Antiquity*, 41, 276–88.
— (1968) The autonomy of the south-east European copper age, *Proceedings of the Prehistoric Society*, 35, 12–47.
— (1972) *The Emergence of Civilisation, the Cyclades and the Aegean in the Third Millennium B. C.*, London.
— (1978) Trajectory discontinuity and morphogenesis, the application of catastrophe theory in archaeology, *American Antiquity*, 43, 203–22.
Rogers, E. M. (1962) *Diffusion of Innovations*, New York.
Sergeev, G. P. (1963) Rannetripolskij klad u s. Karbuna, *Sovietskaya Arkheologiya* 1963 (1), 131–51.
Shennan, S. (1975) Social Organisation at Branc, *Antiquity*, XLIX, 279–88.
Thom, S. (1975) *Structural Stability and Morphogenesis*, Reading, Mass.
Tringham, R. (1971) *Hunters, fishers and farmers of Eastern Europe 6000–3000 B. C.*, London.
Wagstaff, J. M. (1976) Some thoughts about geography and Catastrophe Theory, *Area* 8 (4), 316–20.
Wertime, T. (1964) Man's first encounters with metallurgy, *Science*, 146, 1257.
Wheeler, R. E. M. (1961) The civilization of a sub-continent, in S. Piggott, ed., *The Dawn of Civilization*, London, 243–52.
Wilson, A. G. (1976) Catastrophe theory and urban modelling, an application to modal choice, *Environment and Planning A*, 8, 351–6.
Zeeman, E. C. (1976) Catastrophe theory, *Scientific American*, 234, 65–83.

# INDEX

*

Adams, R. E. W., 367
Adams, R. McC., 72, 266, 267
Adams, W. Y., 5, 358
administration in early societies, 94, 95,
 97, 98-101, 105. *See also* central places;
 Early State Module; trade
Aegean, the, 110, 114, 115, 116, 130;
 Bronze Age, 254-5, 278; tomb dating,
 170
Aegean, prehistoric: craft specialisation,
 286-7, 288, 289, 295-6, 298; craft technology, 296-7; cultural stability and
 conservatism, 291; metallurgy, 288,
 289, 291, 292, 296; mixed farming, 285,
 295; population and settlement patterns, 294-5; productive diversity, 286;
 projective concepts developed in subsystems, 298-9; social subsystems, 297-
 8; subsistence and subsystem development, 295; trade, communication and
 sea transport, 299; vine and olive oil
 production, 285, 291-2; wealth, status
 and kinship, 304-5
Alden, J. R., 27
Aldenderfer, M., 5, 339
Alin, P., 371
Allan, W., 90
Allen, P. M., 362
Ambrose, W. R., 117
Ammerman, A. J., 135, 188, 189, 192,
 395, 416
Amson, J. C., 375, 377, 398, 403, 405
Angelov, N., 412
anthropology, social, 9, 10, 31; analytic,
 based on study of language, 31-2, 38;
 'emic' and 'etic' approaches, 32; and
 study of territoriality, 44; and trade as
 local interaction, 88
archaeological inference, 9; and study of
 spatial patterning, 51, 54
archaeology, 3, 9; based on prehistoric
 data, 31-2; processual, 15, 17; and

questions of analysis, 117; study of
 material culture, 10; and a scientific
 methodology, 16, 17. *See also* New
 Archaeology; Social Archaeology
Arnaud, J. M., 170
artefacts: Aegean, 287, 304-5; cultural
 influences in Europe queried, 81; distribution, 49, 54; documentation and
 analysis of materials, recent, 117; gold
 and copper, European, 412, 413, 414;
 jade and stone, 243-4; as material
 remnants of culture systems, 258-9;
 obsidian and bronze trade, 115-16;
 prestige items brought by external
 trade, 113; provenance, 80; significance of variability, 130
Ashbee, P., 230-5
Ashby, W. R., 260, 262, 265, 335
astronomical observation, 222, 242
Atkinson, R. J. C., 225, 226, 227, 231,
 234, 238, 239, 241, 244
Atlantic Europe, 168-9
authority, the concept of chiefdom,
 12
Avebury, 200, 201, 226, 234, 236
axioms for investigation of socio-political
 organisation, 54-5; and related
 assumptions, 55
Ayres, W. and G., 224

Ball, S. S., 26
Barker, G., 416
Beaker Folk, 238, 415
Beckett, Samuel, 264, 404
Beer, S., 259
Behrens, W. W., 309, 330
Bell, B., 371
Bell, J. A., 332, 339, 348
Bellman, R., 310
Berlinski, D., 335, 337
Berry, B., 26, 55
Betancourt, P. P., 374

419

spatial diffusion, 392-4; and 'stimulus diffusion', 391, 392. *See also* bimodal choice

Chapman, A., 8, 122, 160, 161

Chapman, R., 8

Charles, J. A., 412

Cherry, J. F., 83, 334, 362

Chiefdoms, the concept: emergent in late neolithic Britain, 182; and the exercise of authority, 12; based on meeting places, central and special, 42, 44; and periodic ceremonies, informational, 107; in prehistoric, non-urban societies, 158-9

chiefdoms and neolithic specialisation; craft development of flint mines and axe-factories, 241-2; increased population density, 241; religious and astronomical use of monuments, 242

chiefdom societies: Anderson's observation of Tongan society, 223; characteristics, 205; a confederation of tribes in Wessex, 239, 243; the conical clan, 204, 228; Cook's Polynesian observations, 203-5, 207, 213-14, 215; craft specialisation, 241-2; a model relevant to Wessex, 229-30; in modern Tonga and Easter Island, 205-6; modifications in the Wessex model, 243-4; parallels between Polynesia and America and the building of Stonehenge, 220-3, 242; as redistribution societies, 228-9; Polynesia visits, 209-15, 219; a single political power productive of Stonehenge, 227; social structure and economy, 228

Childe, V. Gordon, 5, 25, 34, 82, 86, 186, 187, 281, 348, 392, 394, 411, 415; culture as an entity, 33; 'barbarism' used as a classification, 41; diffusionist view of trade and civilisation, 113-14; the megalithic idea, 165, 169; *Social Evolution*, 6-7, 8; survey of 'culture sequences in barbarism', 8, 9

Chillingworth, D. R., 337

Chisholm, M., 90, 274

Christaller, W., 27, 30, 55

cities: centres of empty ceremonial, 110-11; endogenous formation from hamlets, 110. *See also* XTENT

civilisation, emergence of: based on social change and material advance, 307; factors in Aegean development,

278; and innate human potentialities, 280, 283; Maltese 'temple' culture, 276; and the multiplier effect, 275, 307; social change and economic growth, 277; and Sumerian irrigation, 176-7. *See also* Aegean, prehistoric; multiplier effect

Civilisations, early: 'civlisation without cities', 110-11; early state modules, 95-104; emergence as social sets, 262; endogenous growth processes, 105-10; exogenous growth by urban imposition, implantation and emulation, 112-13; and external trade, 112-13; Indus Valley untypical, 106; irrespective of personal wealth, 105-6

Claeson, C. F., 136

Clark, J. D. G., 167, 187, 242

Clarke, David, 35, 100, 253, 334

Coe, M. D., 109, 283

Cohen, H., 256

Cohen, S. B., 26

coinage, currency and trade, 129-30

Coleman, J. S., 87

collapse of early societies, *see* societies, collapse of

Collier, D., 372

Collingwood, R. G., 14-15

Collis, J. R., 129

Collinson, David, 224

colonisation, 82, 83; and trade, 112

Colt-Hoare, Sir Richard, 201

communal centres; causewayed camps and henges, 226; council houses, N. American Indian, 227

computer files; location, map outline and population, 61. *See* XTENT

computer simulation of systems thinking, 255

computer simulation, creativity and artificial intelligence, 256

computer simulation, experimental, the results: Cities of Europe, 67-9, 70, 71, 72; Late Uruk Settlement, Warka, Mesopotamia, 72-3, 76; Malta, neolithic temples, 64-7; USSR, Eastern Europe and Transcaucasia, 70, 71. *See also* XTENT

Cook, Capt. James, 31, 206; the Great Circumnavigator, 203; discovery and observation of chiefdom societies, 203-5; visits to Tonga and Easter Island, 203, 206, 207, 213-14, 215, 217, 219

424

# Index

Marcus, J., 7, 24, 26, 49
Martinatos, S., 371
Marino, J., 372
markets, various, periodic, 90, 93, 94
Martin, P. S., 372
Martin, R. D., 194
Maruyama, M., 258, 267, 361
Marx, Karl: analysis of society, 249-50, 251
marxist theory; dominance of natives by colonials and urban capitalists, 82, 83; and status of chief, 159, 160
Matesi, C., 136
Mauss, Marcel, 87, 305
Maya, the 7, 57, 76, 98, 112, 115, 141, 151, 360
Maynard-Smith, J., 189, 190, 337, 361
Meadows, D. H. and D. L., *The Limits to Growth*, 309, 329, 337, 345
megaliths: alternative theories of origins and purpose, 166-8, 174-6, 201-2; concepts of continuity and acculturation, 169, 186; continuous tradition of funerary use, 183; and the demographic stress situation, 194-6; environmental factors, 186; Fleming's 'Tombs for the living', 180-1; Iberian phases dated, 169-70, 171-3, 201; local conditions for an Atlantic distribution 168-9; Montelian view of megalithic burials, 165-6, 169; Orcadian tombs, superceded by henges, 160, 182, 195, 202; radiocarbon calibration of chronology, 167; ritual functions of Irish court-cairns, 181; social hierarchy productive of Stonehenge and Silbury Hill, 182; as symbolic ritual centres, 160, 178-80, 181-2, 195, 196-7; as territorial markers, 160, 176, 178-80, 182; uniformity of scale, 182; West Mediterranean and Aegean, 169-70. *See also* segmentary societies
Mehta, J. R., 271
Mellor, D. H., 18
Mesoamerica, 81, 97, 360, 366, 370
Mesopotamia, 51, 72, 76, 98, 106, 122, 128, 130; salinity of soil, 266
metallurgy: Aegean, 287-8, 414; Balkan, 411-15
methodology, scientific, advocated, 17-18
Miller, J. G., 266
Miller, J. L. L., 334, 406, 407

Minoan Crete, 98, 128, 170
Montelius, O., 165, 166, 169
monuments; collective work of groups, 157; group-orienting or individualising, 161; henges as ritual centres, 161; of Imperial Rome, 48; Maya stelae, 7; as territorial markers, 160, 178-80; as recordings of social structure, 11-12, 45, 156-7; use, religious and astronomical, 242. *See also* megaliths; Wessex
Morintz, S., 412
Morrill, R. L., 140
multiplier effect, 272-5, 281; Aegean civilisation as example, 283; civilisation based on social change and material advance, 307, 417; culture a conservative and stabilising force, 291; cultural growth and validity of interactions, 300-2; goods, the incentive of ownership, 303; human basis for individual and social interaction, 302-3; innovation of wine-drinking, 291-2; metallurgy, trade and longships, 292; production, demand and population, 300; standards of living and man's perpetual wants, 305-6; subsistence/redistribution model, 283-4; subsystem interactions tabulated, 293; symbolic equivalence of social and material values, 305
Munton, R. J. C., 332
Murdock, C. P., 44
Mycenaean Greece, 82, 96, 97, 360, 366, 370

Netting, R., 385
New Archaeology, 3-4, 6, 15, 362
Newton, R. G., 118
Ninkovitch, D., 371
Nissen, H. J., 72

obsidian trade, 121, 124-5, 138, 141, 150, 287
Olsson, G., 136
Oppenheimer, P., 14, 16
Orkney, 160, 175, 182, 183, 186, 195, 202
Orton, C., 37, 65
O'Shea, J., 8

Pattee, H. H., 361
Peacey, J. S., 117
Peacock, D. P. S., 117, 241

425